AF608012

RUIN AND REDEMPTION

The Struggle for a Canadian Bankruptcy Law, 1867–1919

PATRONS OF THE SOCIETY

Blake, Cassels & Graydon LLP

Chernos Flaherty Svonkin LLP

Gowlings

McCarthy Tétrault LLP

Osler, Hoskin & Harcourt LLP

Paliare Roland Rosenberg Rothstein LLP

Torys LLP

WeirFoulds LLP

The Osgoode Society is supported by a grant from The Law Foundation of Ontario.

The Society also thanks The Law Society of Upper Canada for its continuing support.

RUIN AND REDEMPTION

The Struggle for a Canadian Bankruptcy Law, 1867–1919

THOMAS GW TELFER

Published for The Osgoode Society for Canadian Legal History by
University of Toronto Press
Toronto Buffalo London

www.utppublishing.com
www.osgoodesociety.ca

ISBN 978-0-8020-9343-1

Publication cataloguing information is available from Library and Archives Canada.

University of Toronto Press acknowledges the financial assistance to its publishing program of the Canada Council for the Arts and the Ontario Arts Council, an agency of the Government of Ontario.

University of Toronto Press acknowledges the financial support of the Government of Canada through the Canada Book Fund for its publishing activities.

Dedicated to
Patricia, Alexander and Patrick

But while I was dreaming, my ship on the sea
Was tossed in the water's commotion;
Her sails were all set, she was coming to me
Across the great boisterous ocean,
But the storm fiercely beat, and she slowly sank low
To the dirge of the wind's mournful measure,
My dreams have all vanished, I'm bankrupt I know –
No time and no hope and no treasure.

Katherine A. Clarke, "My Ship," in Katherine A. Clarke, *Lyrical Echoes* (Toronto: W. Briggs, 1899) 133

The present Government ... will deserve well of their country for the abolition of the infamous Insolvent Act, of 1875. It was a monstrosity in law, an anomaly of civilization. Under the provisions, every one is benefited, except the unfortunate creditor, or the honest debtor, and the official Assignee most of all. It was the easiest thing in the world to defraud a creditor.

"Nofes From the Capital," *[New Westminster] Mainland Guardian* (28 May 1879)

The payment of debt, like the keeping of a promise, is a moral duty of so sacred a nature, that no human power can liberate anyone from the responsibility ... Therefore an insolvency law is an immoral law, and being such should be objectionable to every right-thinking man.

"Insolvency," *Bobcaygeon Independent,* reprinted in *Toronto World* (29 August 1882) 2

Contents

ILLUSTRATIONS, FIGURES AND TABLES xi

ABBREVIATIONS xiii

FOREWORD xv

PREFACE xvii

1 Ideas, Interests and Institutions 3

Part One: 1867–1880

2 Constitutional and Legislative History 1867–1880 21

3 The Rise and Fall of Bankruptcy Law 1867–1880: The Equitable Distribution of Assets 32

4 The Repeal of Bankruptcy Law 1867–1880: The Discharge 58

5 The Role of Institutions 1867–1880 81

Part Two: 1880–1903

6 Living with Repeal and the Failure of Federal Reform 1880–1903 101

7 The Constitutional Question and the Impact of Federalism 1880–1903 116

8 The Bankruptcy Law Debates 1880–1903 127

Part Three: 1903–1919

9 Reform Achieved: The *Bankruptcy Act of 1919* 145

10 Conclusion 174

NOTES 187

BIBLIOGRAPHY 261

INDEX 289

Illustrations, Figures and Tables

Illustrations

2.1: "The Modern Nero: Fiddling at the Destruction of Canadian Commerce" 24
2.2: "Never before was Canada so prosperous as it is today" 25
2.3: A cartoon from the *Canadian Illustrated News* depicting John Joseph Caldwell Abbott talking to an unidentified individual about shooting a horse carrying a bag named the Insolvency Act 1875, but a third unidentified individual suggests that they try to save the horse 30
5.1: *Insolvent Act* poster setting out terms of sale by an Official Assignee 86
5.2: "Turn about is fair play" 88
5.3: "Othello's occupation gone!" 93

Figures

2.1: Number of Commercial Failures in Canada 1873–85 23
9.1: Number of Commercial Failures in Canada 1902–18 149

Tables

2.1: Percentage of Voluntary Bankruptcy Proceedings under the *Insolvency Act of 1869* by County 29
5.1: 1879, House of Commons, Repeal Bill, 5 May 1879 84

Abbreviations

AO	Archives of Ontario, Toronto
Bankruptcy Act of 1919	*Bankruptcy Act of 1919*, SC 1919, c 36
Bankruptcy and Insolvency Act	*Bankruptcy and Insolvency Act*, RSC 1985, c B-3
BNA Act	*British North America Act, 1867* (UK), 30 & 31 Vict, c 3
Commons Debates	House of Commons Debates
Commons Journals	House of Commons Journals
Insolvent Act of 1869	*Insolvent Act of 1869*, SC 1869, c 16
Insolvent Act of 1875	*Insolvent Act of 1875*, SC 1875, c 16
LAC	Library and Archives Canada, Ottawa
Senate Debates	Debates of the Senate
Trade Review	*Trade Review and Intercolonial Journal of Commerce*

Foreword

THE OSGOODE SOCIETY FOR CANADIAN LEGAL HISTORY

Professor Telfer's deeply researched book shows that between Confederation and 1919, when the federal parliament passed the Bankruptcy Act that remains the basis of the current law, Canadians debated insolvency law with a perhaps surprising amount of passion. The discharge raised deep issues of commercial morality, as many still clung to the idea that paying one's debts was a paramount concern. At the same time, arguments about priorities pitted local against regional and national interests, for a statutory scheme removed the advantages held by those closest to the debtor. Federalism complicated the story, as it often does in Canadian legal history, as the federal parliament, after initially legislating for the new nation, abandoned its jurisdiction over bankruptcy for decades, leaving a patchwork quilt of regulation at the provincial level.

The purpose of the Osgoode Society for Canadian Legal History is to encourage research and writing in the history of Canadian law. The Society, which was incorporated in 1979 and is registered as a charity, was founded at the initiative of the Honourable R. Roy McMurtry and officials of the Law Society of Upper Canada. The Society seeks to stimulate the study of legal history in Canada by supporting researchers, collecting oral histories, and publishing volumes that contribute to legal-historical scholarship in Canada. It has published ninety-six books on the courts, the judiciary, and the legal profession, as well as on the history of crime and punishment, women and law, law and economy, the legal treatment of ethnic minorities, and famous cases and significant trials in all areas of the law.

Current directors of the Osgoode Society for Canadian Legal History are Robert Armstrong, Kenneth Binks, Susan Binnie, David Chernos, J. Douglas Ewart, Violet French, Martin Friedland, Philip Girard, William Kaplan, C. Ian Kyer, Virginia MacLean, Patricia McMahon, Roy McMurtry, Madeleine Meilleur, Janet Minor, Dana Peebles, Paul Perell, Jim Phillips, Paul Reinhardt, William Ross, Paul Schabas, Robert Sharpe, Alex Smith, Lorne Sossin, Mary Stokes, and Michael Tulloch.

The annual report and information about membership may be obtained by writing to the Osgoode Society for Canadian Legal History, Osgoode Hall, 130 Queen Street West, Toronto, Ontario, M5H 2N6. Telephone: 416-947-3321. E-mail: mmacfarl@lsuc.on.ca. Website: www.osgoodesociety.ca.

R. Roy McMurtry
President

Jim Phillips
Editor-in-Chief

Preface

The genesis of the book can be traced to what was to be a short historical introductory chapter for a comparative study of Canadian and US bankruptcy law. However, a review of the parliamentary debates revealed that there was a broader historical story to tell. With the comparative study set aside, I set out to explore why Canada enacted bankruptcy legislation shortly after Confederation and repealed it in 1880. After repeal, why did Parliament take nearly forty years to enact the *Bankruptcy Act of 1919*? It was these central questions that drove the historical study.

I received financial support from a number of sources. A grant from the University of Western Ontario Academic Development Fund enabled me to travel to the Library and Archives Canada in Ottawa, where I examined many government and interest group sources. The grant also allowed me to travel to the Archives of Ontario in Toronto, where I consulted nineteenth-century bankruptcy court files. I am indebted to the many archivists who assisted with my research. The Canadian Bankers' Association permitted me to have access to their archives. I have received funding from fellowships from Borden Ladner Gervais and Cassels Brock LLP. Deans Ian Holloway and W. Iain Scott at the Faculty of Law at Western University also made funding available to hire summer research assistants. I would like to thank research assistants Ruth Trask, Andrea Tratnik, Puneet Grewal, Daniel Stober, Jennifer Mitchell, Jessica Wong and Meaghan Loughry for their efforts on this project.

The project would not have been completed without the input and support from Michael Trebilcock, who provided encouragement from the very start. I have benefited from comments by Daniel Ernst, Emily Kadens and Rande Kostal who read earlier drafts of a published article that in part has been incorporated into this work. A special thank you to Jassmine Girgis, who took the time to read the entire manuscript. Jacob Ziegel supported this undertaking from the outset. Dick Risk provided feedback at the early stages of this project. Jim Phillips also read the entire manuscript and provided invaluable input. My thanks to my administrative assistant Tigger Jourard, who proofread the manuscript and provided editorial suggestions. I also thank the editors at the University of Toronto Press for their helpful assistance. Comments provided by two anonymous referees have improved the manuscript.

I would like to thank the following publishers for their permission to publish: Thomas GW Telfer, "The Canadian Bankruptcy Act of 1919: Public Legislation or Private Interest?" (1994–5) 24 *Canadian Business Law Journal* 357–403 (reprinted by permission of Canadian Business Law Journal Inc., and Canada Law Book, a division of Thomson Reuters Canada Limited); Thomas GW Telfer, "The Evolution of Bankruptcy Exemption Law in Canada 1867–1919: The Triumph of the Provincial Model" [2007] *Annual Review of Insolvency Law* 593–651 (reprinted by permission of Carswell, a division of Thomson Reuters Canada Limited).

Finally, I must dedicate this book to my wife Patricia, and our two sons, Alexander and Patrick. Without their support and patience, this project would not have been completed.

Thomas GW Telfer
Auckland Anniversary Day 2014

RUIN AND REDEMPTION

The Struggle for a Canadian Bankruptcy Law, 1867–1919

1

Ideas, Interests and Institutions

In 1909, James Crowe had no choice but to flee Canada for the United States. He was one of the thousands of Canadian debtors who had been "banished" to the United States. Although Erie, Pennsylvania, was not that far from Canadian soil, James Crowe could not return to his homeland. The repeal of the *Insolvent Act* in 1880 left Canada without any national bankruptcy law and many debtors without hope. In the absence of such a federal statute, creditors could enforce judgments and seize the debtor's assets without the need to worry about a federal bankruptcy law interfering with collection efforts. Further, without a bankruptcy law, there was simply no means for a debtor to obtain a statutory release of debts through a discharge. The United States offered debtors a reprieve from Canadian creditors. Crowe wrote to Prime Minister Laurier claiming, "My own case represents thousands of men obliged to live in another country rather than return to be pinched and harassed by some Loan Co., Bank, or ... Lawyer, for debts and Judgments beyond hope [or] ability to pay." He demanded that Laurier's government enact a new Canadian bankruptcy statute or what Crowe dubbed "an Emancipation Act."[1]

Crowe pleaded with Laurier to provide judges with the power to "give the debtor his freedom when the Court is satisfied that his failure was not fraudulent and that he has been stripped of all he possess[es]." While the "humane" governments of the United States and England had enacted bankruptcy legislation, "[t]he absence of an Insolvency

Act from the Statute books of Canada is far from being creditable to your Government." Pointing to the United States, which had enacted a national bankruptcy law in 1898,[2] Crowe claimed, "Even Uncle Sam strikes off the festers which eat into the life and limb of the same class which your so called Christian Government leaves to rot in Legal Claims which promise no hope ..." Demanding legislation, Crowe appealed to Laurier's sense of humanity: "Is it humane or Christian that men who have lost their all by fire, by endorsing for friends who abused their confidence, by unforeseen landslides in business and otherwise, should have the gates of mercy closed to them forever." Laurier was not moved by Crowe's plea. Laurier's blunt reply to James Crowe symbolized the Prime Minister's consistent policy on bankruptcy: "In answer, I have to inform you that public opinion in this country does not seem to favour such a law as you suggest. The existing legislation in every province seems to be satisfactory."[3]

The exchange of correspondence was emblematic of many of the themes that would dominate the debates about bankruptcy law between 1867 and 1919. First, absconding debtors were a common problem during this era and could be traced back to the pre-Confederation period.[4] Debtors regularly left the country to avoid creditors. Second, bankruptcy and insolvency was a matter of federal responsibility under the Constitution. How was it that Laurier reached the conclusion that provincial legislation provided an appropriate solution for a federal matter? Finally, this was not a debate about the content or substantive provisions of a bankruptcy statute. The exchange of letters represented the more fundamental question of whether there should be a bankruptcy statute in Canada. It would not be until 1919 that Canada finally adopted a permanent bankruptcy statute.

1. Posing the Question: Why No Bankruptcy Law in Canada from 1880 to 1919?

Modern bankruptcy scholarship has long moved past the question of "whether bankruptcy law should exist at all" and has now focused on "how much it should do."[5] But in late nineteenth- and early twentieth-century Canada, the central question was whether there should be a bankruptcy law at all. During this time, Canadian bankruptcy legislation was not widely accepted as a means to distribute assets to creditors or as a way to discharge debts. Both of these central goals of bankruptcy law proved to be controversial. After Confederation, Parliament passed bankruptcy legislation in 1869 and again in 1875.[6] However, opponents of bankruptcy law began to call for repeal shortly after the Act of 1869 came into effect, and between 1869 and 1880 Parliament debated ten separate repeal bills.[7] In 1880, Parliament repealed the *Insolvent Act of 1875* and abandoned its constitutional jurisdiction over bankruptcy and insolvency until 1919.[8] After 1880, the provinces sought to ameliorate the effects of the federal repeal by enacting legislation that provided some means of distributing an insolvent debtor's assets. As provincial law could never provide for a discharge or a uniform solution, Parliament revisited the bankruptcy reform issue on numerous occasions after repeal. All federal bankruptcy bills between 1880 and 1903 failed. By the end of the century, provincial regulation became entrenched, and it was not until after the First World War that bankruptcy again became a national issue.

Why Canada rejected bankruptcy law in 1880 and did not pass a national uniform statute until 1919 is the central question of this study. A more specific question arises when one notes that much of the opposition to bankruptcy legislation in the nineteenth century centred on the discharge of debtors. However, by 1919 many argued that bankruptcy legislation was a commercial necessity. What had been deemed an evil in 1880 became an essential form of business regulation after the war. This study accounts for the nineteenth-century opposition to bankruptcy law, the lack of federal legislation for nearly forty years, and the success of the legislation in 1919.

While the *Bankruptcy Act of 1919* might be perceived as an important "change and innovation," a more important question to ask is "why a legal change did not occur when society changed, or when perceptions about the quality of the law changed. Why, one must always ask, did the legal change not occur before?"[9] In this light, it becomes important not only to understand the introduction of a new Canadian regime in 1919 as a significant innovation, but also to examine why such reforms were delayed for a lengthy period.

The socio-economic history of late nineteenth- and early twentieth-century Canada cannot fully be understood without examining the role of bankruptcy legislation and how it sought to manage the question of debt, debtors and the competing interests of creditors. Specifically, this book addresses the rise of Canadian bankruptcy legislation in the early post-Confederation period, its ultimate repeal in 1880 and the reinstatement of a national law in 1919. The work examines the Canadian historical experience to understand the ideas, interests and institutions that have shaped the evolution of Canadian bankruptcy law. Bankruptcy law represented both a conflict of ideas over the morality of the bankruptcy discharge and a distinct divergence of interests[10] between local and distant creditors over the advantages and disadvantages of an equitable distribution of the debtor's assets. Finally, institutions exerted "an independent influence on what interests and ideas in particular policy domains are given effect to or marginalized" in policy decisions.[11] Institutional factors such as federalism, courts and the emerging regulatory state also played an important role.

2. Fundamental Policies of Bankruptcy Law

Before proceeding, a few preliminary points need to be made on use of the terms *bankruptcy* and *insolvency*.[12] In the modern context, *bankruptcy* refers to the formal legal proceeding whereby an individual debtor's assets are realized and distributed in a *pro rata* fashion. The distribution is normally followed by a discharge. Generally, *insolvency* refers to the debtor's financial status rather than a formal legal proceeding. Thus, a debtor may be insolvent but not yet formally bankrupt.[13]

Canada's first bankruptcy statutes were known as the *Insolvent Acts of 1869* and *1875*. Although they were labelled as insolvent Acts, the courts interpreted them as bankruptcy Acts. Thus, the words *insolvent* and *insolvency* in nineteenth-century Canada were "equivalent to the terms bankrupt and bankruptcy."[14] In 1919, Canada adopted the *Bankruptcy Act of 1919*. This book is a study of the evolution of federal bankruptcy law and uses that term to describe the formal legal process to distribute assets to unsecured creditors and provide a discharge of the individual debtor.

The study of bankruptcies within the specific legislative context enables historians to more accurately describe financial failure. One historian who examined the early bankruptcy statutes of England claimed that the term *bankrupt* was often mentioned by historians but rarely understood. Debtors who encountered financial difficulty were described as bankrupts, without officially becoming a bankrupt under the statute. English bankruptcy statutes from 1571 to 1861 applied only to traders.[15] Similarly, the Canadian *Insolvent Acts of 1869* and *1875* restricted their application to traders. Only debtors who bought and sold were eligible for bankruptcy in nineteenth-century Canada. This had the effect of excluding a large number of debtors, such as farmers or wage earners, from formal bankruptcy proceedings. If historians wish to describe bankruptcy rates or levels of financial failure, this legal distinction must be kept in mind.[16]

However, any explanation of the Canadian story should begin with a consideration of the nature of bankruptcy law. Bankruptcy law is a statutory exception to the common law and interferes with the ordinary relations between debtors and creditors.[17] Two fundamental goals lie at the heart of all bankruptcy statutes.[18] First, bankruptcy legislation provides for an equitable distribution of assets among all unsecured creditors on a *pro rata* basis. The equal treatment of creditors is supported by the statutory prohibition that prevents debtors from making preferential payments to favoured creditors prior to bankruptcy. Second, bankruptcy law entitles an individual debtor to obtain a release of his or her debts through the order of discharge.[19]

3. Factors Influencing the State of the Law: Ideas, Interests and Institutions

The Equitable Distribution of Assets and the Role of Interest Groups

Bankruptcy's first policy, the equitable distribution of assets, fundamentally changed the common law. The common law rewarded the most diligent creditor, meaning that the first to enforce was paid in full, leaving other creditors with little or nothing.[20] In nineteenth-century Canada, in the absence of a bankruptcy statute, the common law created a race to the debtor's assets.[21] Those creditors who obtained the first execution against the debtor were not required to share the benefits of execution with subsequent creditors. This advantaged local creditors, relatives or friendly creditors at the expense of distant creditors. The enactment of the *Insolvent Acts* destroyed the common law race and put all creditors on an equal footing by creating a *pro rata* distribution scheme and by prohibiting preferential payments to local or family creditors. Further, the mandatory and collective nature of the bankruptcy regime prohibited creditors from continuing to pursue the debtor once bankruptcy had begun.[22] A centralized bankruptcy system reduced risks for distant or foreign creditors, and destroyed local creditor advantage.[23] The *Insolvent Acts of 1869* and *1875* marked a fundamental change from the common law. Repeal in 1880 returned Canada to the common law system of "first come, first served." Studying the interests favoured or disadvantaged by repeal contributes to our understanding of why Parliament opted for a return to the common law.

Assessment of lobbying efforts of specific commercial coalitions and interests groups is essential to determine why the law failed or succeeded during a particular time. Under public choice theory,[24] the political process is conceived of as an "implicit market" in which voters, interest groups, politicians, regulators and the media "tend to be motivated by material self-interest."[25] As Dennis Mueller notes, public choice is defined as "the economic study of nonmarket decision making, or simply the application of economics to political science." Under this theory, public decision-makers seek to maximize political support rather than opt for a course of action that would advance the broader public interest.[26] Public choice theory explores "the implications of self interest for the legislative and other institutional decision making." Public choice encompasses interest group theory. Further, as David Skeel notes, "[C]oncentrated interest groups often benefit at the expense of more widely scattered groups, even if the diffuse group has more at stake overall." Legislators tend to rely upon the better informed, more concentrated interest group.[27]

Creditors who traded across regional or provincial boundaries focused on bankruptcy's policy of equal distribution in an effort to prevent repeal during the 1870s. Creditors who traded at a distance favoured a national bankruptcy law and feared the common law race to the debtor's assets, because the race inevitably favoured local creditors who may have been neighbours or family members of the debtor. In the nineteenth century, commercial organizations such as the Montreal and Toronto Boards of Trade as well as a new national organization, the Dominion Board of Trade, represented interests that extended credit over distances. These urban-based Boards of Trade lobbied for the retention of a federal bankruptcy law. However, uniform legislation was not a widely accepted goal and the Dominion Board of Trade was itself divided over the issue. The defeat of national bankruptcy legislation in 1880 suggests that some creditors may have preferred local markets and a return to a system of "grab" or "first come, first served" law.

During the First World War, a new national interest group emerged to advocate for a national Act. The Canadian Credit Men's Trust Association (CCMTA) led the call for national reform. Although debtors may have had a substantial stake in the outcome of bankruptcy reform, they were diffuse and scattered across the country without any informed voice. Parliament relied upon a well-informed and concentrated interest group: the CCMTA.[28] The CCMTA sought to protect the interests of creditors and retained a solicitor to draft a bill that became the basis for the *Bankruptcy Act of 1919*. The advantages of a national bankruptcy law, first debated in the nineteenth century, could no longer be denied.

The Discharge and the Role of Ideas

An assessment of the competing interests favouring the common law race or a bankruptcy regime does not provide the complete picture. While interest groups quite clearly address the distribution question, much of the debate came to be dominated by the contested ideals over the morality of the discharge. Bankruptcy's second policy, the release of debts through the statutory discharge, played a fundamental role in the demise of bankruptcy law in Canada in 1880. Ideology,[29] therefore, represented an independent variable affecting policy choice. Policymakers inevitably "work within a framework of ideas." The ideas "specif[y] not only the goals of policy ... but also the very nature of the problems they are meant to [address]."[30] In nineteenth-century and early twentieth-century Canada *pacta sunt servanda*[31] (contracts must be kept) competed with the notion that an honest but unfortunate debtor deserved a discharge. The discharge became the focus of public discourse in late nineteenth- and early twentieth-century Canada. In the nineteenth century, forgiveness of debt through a statutory discharge was not readily accepted. Repeal in 1880 was in many ways an explicit rejection of the discharge.

By 1919, bankruptcy law became a commercial necessity. Creditors came to realize that a discharge operated in their favour. Without the hope of obtaining a statutory discharge, debtors engaged in misconduct by sequestering assets or by absconding to the United States. Creditors began to learn that it was not in their interests to make debtors responsible for the entire debt in eternity. The discharge provided debtors with an incentive to cooperate and turn over assets for distribution and reduced instances of debtor misconduct. Creditors were willing to turn over the responsibility for releasing debtors to the courts under the *Bankruptcy Act of 1919*. The discharge in 1919 had little to do with notions of debtor rehabilitation. Creditors demanded and obtained a discharge regime that operated in their interests. Indeed advancing the cause of bankruptcy reform in the name of debtor rehabilitation may have been shielding private creditor interests. One must always assess public discourse to determine whether it disguises the "true interests and ideas at play." As Trebilcock and Kelley note, it is "strategic for an interest group to disguise its self-interest under the rubric of a broader normative idea in order to engage the support of other members of the political community who may share the idea but not the interest."[32]

The Role of Institutions

While ideas and interests provide two sources of inquiry, the study of institutions is also important to our understanding of legislative change. Historical institutionalism studies "institutional evolution over time." In other words, "history matters." A historical institutionalist approach begins by "posing a puzzle about why something important happened, or did not happen, or asking why certain structures or patterns take shape in some times and places but not in others."[33] Why did Canada enact two bankruptcy statutes in the nineteenth century, only to repeal the bankruptcy regime in 1880? Why did 1919 mark an important time for Canada to enact a new national bankruptcy law? In part, answers to these questions may be found by examining the role of institutions. Scholars interested in institutions study "how political struggles 'are mediated by the institutional setting in which they take place.'"[34] Political activities are "conditioned by the institutional configurations of governments and political party systems." Therefore, "[c]onstitutions and political institutions, state structures, state interest group relations, and policy networks all structure the political process."[35]

Although in the literature there is a significant debate over what is an institution,[36] this work examines some more traditional institutional structures such as the weakness of the state,[37] party systems, bankruptcy administrative structures, the courts and federalism.[38] These institutions exerted an autonomous influence on policy choice.[39] Public policies are directly related to "historically changing institutional arrangements" of the state and political parties. In the words of Douglass North, "History matters ... because the present and the future are connected to the past by the continuity of a society's institutions."[40]

The weakness of the state inhibited the implementation of stable and lasting bankruptcy legislation. During the 1870s, there was little sense that bankruptcy law was part of a larger regulatory state. Until 1919 Parliament never adopted bankruptcy law as a government reform measure, and there was no specialized government department responsible for the legislation. Governments of the day showed little interest in the legislation, and mismanaged reform. Political parties showed clear signs of internal division over the issue of repeal, with parties dividing on crucial votes. In the nineteenth century neither of the major parties took a lead on bankruptcy reform.

Between 1875 and 1880, the federal government appointed Official Assignees under a patronage system. Yet there was no direct government supervision of Official Assignees. The misconduct and corruption of Official Assignees contributed to the unpopularity of legislation.[41] Nearly forty years later, the passage of the *Bankruptcy Act of 1919* as a government measure coincided with an unprecedented growth of federal regulation during the war. In Parliament, the bill was justified as an important war measure to deal with the economic dislocation following the end of the conflict.

Courts were also an important institutional factor that had an impact on the direction of policy reform.[42] In the nineteenth century, courts did not always apply the legislation strictly. There was a strong anti-debtor element in the debates and the legislation, yet the courts did not always uphold the notion that a debtor had a moral obligation to pay. Although the legislation gave the courts the jurisdiction to grant a "second class" discharge so as to attach an order of bankruptcy stigma against a debtor who had not been entirely honest, few judges made such an order. Finally, county courts tolerated collusion between family creditors and the debtor. Although the *Insolvent Act of 1875* prohibited voluntary proceedings, the courts allowed related or family creditors to petition a debtor into bankruptcy. This form of collusion enabled the debtor to obtain a discharge without having to wait for an arm's length creditor to begin proceedings, meaning that in practice, at least for some proceedings, the *Insolvent Act of 1875* operated as a voluntary scheme.[43]

Federalism affected the timing of the legislation.[44] Provincial jurisdiction over "property and civil rights" provided Parliament with an opportunity to repeal an unpopular bankruptcy law in 1880. The possibility of provincial legislation, which might provide for the equitable distribution of debtors' assets in the form of a *Creditors' Relief Act*,[45] gave Parliament the option to jettison a controversial matter. Ontario passed the *Creditors' Relief Act* in 1880 immediately after the repeal of the federal bankruptcy law. The provincial law provided for an equitable distribution of the debtor's assets but did not provide for a discharge.

The ability of the provinces to regulate voluntary assignments and the administration of debtors' estates constrained reform at the national level after 1880. With the growth of provincial regulation, bankruptcy law became a constitutional issue as litigants challenged the validity of provincial regulation. The decision of the Privy Council in *Attorney General of Ontario v Attorney General for the Dominion of Canada*[46] held that section 9 of the Ontario *Assignments and Preferences Act*[47] was constitutional. In the late nineteenth century, politicians relied upon this ruling to demonstrate that no further federal reforms were required. The ruling contributed to the growth of provincial regulation and removed the immediate need for federal legislation until after the turn of the century. Provincial law became entrenched as the primary means of regulating debtor-creditor matters and became the solution favoured by Prime Minister Laurier. It was not until after the First World War that bankruptcy law again became a national issue. Although it is important to note the role of institutions, historical institutionalists "rarely insist that institutions are the only causal force in politics." Scholars who study institutions also take into account the role of socio-economic development and the role of ideas.[48]

If the discharge and the distribution of assets lay at the core of the public policy debates, corporate rescue did not. Companies played only a minor role in the debate over bankruptcy legislation. Corporate reorganization did not feature as a major issue between 1867 and 1880. While companies existed, many businesses preferred to carry on as partnerships or sole proprietorships. Specific statutes had created many of the pre-Confederation companies, and if a company became insolvent, specific amendments often restructured the particular company outside of the bankruptcy regime.[49] The *Insolvent Act of 1875* applied to individuals as well as companies;[50] however, Parliament adopted the company provisions without debate. The company sections were rarely invoked. Thus, when Parliament and the public debated the merits of the *Insolvent Acts of 1869* and *1875*, its attention was squarely focused on insolvent individual debtors.

Similarly, when Parliament began to debate bankruptcy reform bills between 1880 and 1903, insolvent companies did not feature in the debates. This absence can be explained largely by the emergence of a separate statute to deal with insolvent companies. Once the *Insolvent Act of 1875* was repealed, Parliament realized that there was no general legal mechanism to liquidate insolvent companies, and in 1882 Parliament took steps to enact legislation to deal with insolvent banks, insurance companies, loan companies, building companies and trading companies. The legislation would later become known as the *Winding-Up Act*.[51] The modern dichotomy of consumer and corporate bankruptcy, therefore, did not exist under nineteenth-century Canadian bankruptcy statutes. The bankruptcy law debate focused almost entirely on individual debtors engaged in some form of trade. While companies came within the scope of the *Bankruptcy Act of 1919*, the statute was concerned primarily with liquidation, and twenty-first century conceptions of corporate reorganization were well beyond the vision of Parliament.

4. Research Sources

In order to analyse the evolving attitudes towards the discharge, the clash of local and distant creditors and the relevance of institutions, a number of sources need to be considered. First, as bankruptcy law is a creature of statute,[52] any study of the history of the legislation must examine the parliamentary debates and the legislation itself.[53] However, as this book is also concerned with the failure of federal bankruptcy reform efforts for a period of nearly forty years, unsuccessful federal bankruptcy bills will also be examined.

An evaluation of certain key provisions of the legislation provides a measure of how bankruptcy law evolved. One may compare the scope of the legislation by examining what debtors were eligible for bankruptcy over time and determining whether bankruptcy law operated as a voluntary or involuntary regime. The availability of the discharge and the ease by which it could be obtained also provide important indicators of the character of the legislation. Access to the bankruptcy regime and the discharge itself became more difficult as the 1870s wore on. The *Insolvent Act of 1875* abolished voluntary proceedings, allowing only creditors to initiate the bankruptcy process.

The legislation and parliamentary debates do not provide a complete picture. The courts had a significant role to play in interpreting the legislation, particularly when decisions did not match the expectations of the rigorous statute adopted by Parliament. This book assesses how reported case law itself contributed to the unpopularity of the legislation. In addition, this book examines Ontario County Court bankruptcy records. Such files provide an insight into actual bankruptcy proceedings, often revealing creditor attitudes towards the bankruptcy proceedings. Finally, the effect of federalism on legislative reform is examined by studying the constitutional litigation on the validity of both federal and provincial legislation. While the rulings of the Ontario Court of Appeal and the landmark 1894 ruling of the Privy Council[54] may have been relevant to the ongoing evolution of constitutional doctrine, the political impact of the decisions is more germane to this book.

In order to evaluate the role of interest groups on the Canadian legislative process, a number of sources become relevant. Petitions to Parliament also identify specific groups supporting or asking for repeal of bankruptcy legislation. Private correspondence of Prime Ministers and papers of the Department of Justice are reviewed. Records of proceedings of private interest groups, political parties, newspapers and business periodicals are also examined.[55] These sources indicate prevalent attitudes towards bankruptcy law and debt. How values evolved as the economy shifted from a local to a national economy is an important part of the explanation, and trade journals, law reviews, business newspapers and bankruptcy texts are examined.[56]

This work will fill a significant gap in the literature on the history of Canadian bankruptcy law. Writing in 1917, one author claimed that bankruptcy law scholars considered a historical treatment of the subject as "unnecessary, uninteresting, or impossible."[57] This work will seek to demonstrate that the subject is anything but uninteresting and it will complement the vast literature that has emerged on the history of bankruptcy law in the United States and the United Kingdom. Historical studies of English and American bankruptcy law have flourished. The origins of English bankruptcy law have been well documented. Broader works on both the eighteenth and nineteenth centuries place individual financial failure in both the context of the Industrial Revolution and the regulatory framework. English authors have also examined specific issues such as attitudes toward debt, and bankruptcy law and literature.[58] The most recent book examines the parliamentary history of nineteenth-century legislation and discusses the role of interest groups on the legislative process. The long period of continual revision of nineteenth-century English bankruptcy law culminated in the passage of the landmark reforms of 1883.[59] This English bankruptcy statute of 1883 would ultimately influence the shape of Canadian reforms, but not until 1919.

The history of American bankruptcy law is equally well represented in the literature. Following the formation of the republic, the United States enacted three short-lived national bankruptcy statutes before finally settling on what was to become a more permanent solution in 1898. Charles Warren's Depression-era book traces the political history of the national legislation, while Peter Coleman's study places the national legislation in the context of the various state-level reforms.[60] David Skeel's recent work traces the evolution of bankruptcy law up to the late twentieth century.[61] Other works have focused on the separate

Bankruptcy Acts of 1800, 1841, 1867, and *1898*[62] or on the interface of financial failure and broader cultural trends.[63] American scholars have identified several factors that explain the evolution of US bankruptcy law. For example, some have presented the debate on bankruptcy law as representing ideological division within American society and have linked opposition and support of bankruptcy law to specific political parties.[64] Further, Balleisen has identified a "clash between two competing versions of commercial morality – one premised on special financial obligations to one's closest business associates and another ... of an integrated, national economy that mandated equal treatment to everyone in the marketplace."[65] Other studies have linked economic change to legislative development. Coleman's study suggests that several structural or economic changes made a national bankruptcy law more acceptable. As American life became "inexorably commercialized, depersonalized, and channelled through the corporate, legalistic, and institutionalized structure of commercial finance, the need for bankruptcy systems became imperative."[66] Finally, Skeel's work emphasizes organized creditor groups, "the countervailing influence of populism" and the emergence of the bankruptcy bar.[67] This rich body of literature has allowed American historians to place bankruptcy law developments into the wider history of the regulation of the American economy and provided the prospect for further regional studies and an examination of how bankruptcy affected particular groups in society.[68]

In contrast there is no full-length study of the early *Insolvent Acts of 1869* and *1875* and the establishment of the new *Bankruptcy Act of 1919*. Canadian historians have tended to focus on the financial difficulties of larger enterprises that played a significant role in the business history of the country. Any consideration of business failure in Canada must include a discussion of government intervention to subsidize and salvage failing enterprises.[69] The history of financial failure in Canadian history includes significant involvement of the state in areas of public infrastructure such as the Welland Canal and railways.[70] Companies that were the largest and had the biggest debts "seem, throughout Canadian history, to have been rescued in one form or another."[71] The Canadian statute books are full of specific Acts of Parliament that deal with insolvent banks, insurance companies and railways.[72] However, small and medium-sized businesses were allowed to collapse "with impunity."[73] The success or failure of these enterprises had a significant impact on the survival of many other small firms, sole proprietorships and partnerships. Failure of a small business had dramatic effects upon individuals connected to these firms. Yet little is known about the legislative framework that regulated individual insolvent debtors.[74] Personal debt and its relationship to late nineteenth-century Canadian bankruptcy legislation have been overlooked.[75] The short-lived bankruptcy statutes of 1869 and 1875 have either become historical footnotes[76] or been ignored altogether.[77] Pre-Confederation bankruptcy laws have attracted more attention from Canadian historians.[78]

5. Outline of the Book

The central part of this study is concerned with the period 1867 to 1919. This time frame can be divided into three separate eras, and this book is divided into three parts. Part One consists of chapters 2–5, which will account for the ultimate repeal of bankruptcy legislation in 1880. Whereas chapter 2 provides an overview of the legislative history between 1867 and 1880, chapter 3 examines how the equitable distribution of assets created a tension between local and distant creditors. Chapter 3 also considers how bankruptcy law fundamentally changed the common law and how interests were either favoured or disadvantaged by repeal in 1880. The common law's race to the assets and the ability of the debtor to make preferential payments favoured family or local creditors, suggesting that creditors extending credit across distances would have been disadvantaged by repeal.

Chapter 4 studies the impact of ideas in the divisive discharge debate. The argument that a debtor had a moral obligation to repay all debts competed with the notion that an unfortunate, honest debtor deserved a discharge. However, this was not a purely disinterested competition of ideas. The leaders of one economic interest – the farm lobby – tapped into the rhetoric of moral obligation to advance the cause for repeal. The *Insolvent Acts* applied only to "traders" (i.e. those who bought and sold), thereby excluding professionals, wage earners and farmers. Debtors excluded from the Act were ineligible for a discharge.[79] Invoking the moral obligation to pay, the farming community, in league with compliant Members of Parliament, sought repeal in order to place farmers on an equal footing with commercial interests.

Chapter 5 concludes with a study of institutional factors such as agencies of the state, political parties, bankruptcy administration including the role of Official Assignees, the courts and federalism.[80] Each of these institutions played a part in the ultimate repeal of bankruptcy legislation in 1880.

Part Two consists of chapters 6, 7, and 8. Chapter 6 examines the legislative history of reform efforts at provincial and federal levels for the period 1880–1903. During this time it was not certain whether provincial legislation would adequately fill the gap or whether the federal government would take action to reinstate a uniform law. Previous accounts of the legislative history of Canadian bankruptcy law have ignored the fact that Parliament debated twenty reform bills between 1880 and 1903. All bills failed and only two bore the imprint of government policy. Chapter 6 also considers the important interrelationship between institutions and interest groups. After 1880, the federal government continued to be indifferent towards bankruptcy policy. Parties in power were unwilling to expend political capital on a divisive issue. The continued absence of a strong government department and bureaucracy inhibited the implementation of stable and lasting legislation. Bankruptcy reform had no institutional backing by the governing party. At the government level there was a vacuum of leadership over bankruptcy reform. Private interest groups filled this vacuum.

Chapter 7 examines the role of federalism between 1880 and 1903. In many ways federalism[81] and the possibility of provincial reform ultimately impeded and inhibited efforts to pass a national bankruptcy law.[82] Although the Constitution granted the federal Parliament jurisdiction over the field of "bankruptcy and insolvency," provincial jurisdiction over "property and civil rights" became the more important field to regulate debtor-creditor matters in this era. In 1894, the Privy Council in *Attorney General of Ontario v Attorney General for the Dominion of Canada* upheld the validity of provincial legislation. The decision contributed to the growth of provincial laws and largely ended federal reform efforts.

Chapter 8 examines the essential nature of the bankruptcy law debate for the period 1880–1903. Although forgiveness of debt was an important concept, the more dominant idea, moral obligation to pay debts, triumphed with many reform measures contemplating a bankruptcy law without a discharge. Tension between local and distant creditors also remained an important factor, with interest groups seeking legislation that would provide for an equitable distribution of assets and prohibit preferences. The reluctance of Parliament to commit to a uniform law and the slow response of the provinces to prohibit preferences suggests that local creditors benefited from the absence of federal and provincial legislation.

In Part Three, chapter 9 accounts for the success of the *Bankruptcy Act of 1919* and its important legacy. The chapter discusses the rise of the CCMTA and the important role that it played in lobbying for and shaping the content of the Bankruptcy Act. The chapter studies the transformation of the discharge to one of commercial necessity and considers how creditor interest groups came to see the discharge as operating in their favour. The *Bankruptcy Act of 1919* had little to do with concepts of debtor rehabilitation. Chapter 10 concludes.

PART ONE

1867–1880

2

Constitutional and Legislative History 1867–1880

In all commercial countries one of the most difficult problems to be solved by legislation has been the settlement of the relations between a creditor and his bankrupt debtor, in such a manner as to give the former as much power as possible over the estate of the latter, without unduly harassing the honest debtor. The difficulty of attaining this aim has been felt in Canada as elsewhere.

– Ivan Wotherspoon, *The Insolvent Act of 1875*[1]

The enactment of the *Insolvent Act of 1869* might be seen as watershed in the history of Canadian bankruptcy law. For the first time Canada had embraced a national bankruptcy law. The *Insolvent Act of 1869* repealed any provincial statutes that were inconsistent with the terms of the new bankruptcy statute.[2] However, opponents of bankruptcy law began to call for repeal shortly after the Act of 1869 came into effect. The introduction of a more creditor-friendly *Insolvent Act of 1875* did little to placate demands for repeal. Between 1869 and 1880, the House of Commons debated ten separate repeal bills, with seven of these bills being presented between 1877 and 1880.[3] In 1880, Parliament repealed the *Insolvent Act of 1875* and abandoned its constitutional jurisdiction over bankruptcy and insolvency matters for a period of nearly forty years.[4]

This chapter sets out the constitutional and legislative history of bankruptcy law and follows the rise and fall of Canadian bankruptcy legislation between 1867 and 1880. Why did Parliament enact legislation pursuant to its jurisdiction over bankruptcy and insolvency law, only to abandon an important national power only eleven years later? While answers to this important question are considered in more detail in chapters 3–5, this chapter seeks to provide the background for what follows.

One objective of Confederation was to create a strong central government while permitting the provinces to regulate their local affairs. The long list of federal powers in section 91 of the *British North America Act* (*BNA Act*),[5] which were designed to establish a national economy,[6] included jurisdiction over "bankruptcy and insolvency."[7] Although the framers of the *BNA Act* gave no express reason for the inclusion of bankruptcy and insolvency in section 91, bankruptcy law fitted naturally with the other listed national powers, including "trade and commerce," "navigation and shipping," and "banking." A national bankruptcy and insolvency law instilled confidence in foreign and distant creditors and was more accessible than the possibility of numerous provincial variations. Foreign capital may have been put at risk if provinces were allowed to legislate in distinctive ways to favour local creditors. A federal law applied equally to all creditors and allowed the collection of the debtor's assets wherever they were located.[8]

While the grant of jurisdiction over bankruptcy and insolvency was exclusive, the provinces retained the right to regulate debtor-creditor matters generally. The *BNA Act* gave the provinces the power to legislate in local matters, including "property and civil rights."[9] Thus, the *BNA Act* created the possibility of some overlap in the regulation of debtors. Bankruptcy law therefore could not be separated from constitutional law. Parliament's abandonment of bankruptcy legislation and the provincial legislation that followed suggests that consensus on the need for a national bankruptcy law did not survive long after Confederation. Despite the clear federal power over bankruptcy and insolvency law in the *BNA Act*, federal governments in the nineteenth century did not view bankruptcy law as a fundamentally important economic power.

A brief overview of the legislative history of the *Insolvent Acts of 1869 and 1875* demonstrates that there was little, if any, commitment to retaining bankruptcy and insolvency law as a national power. Although the equitable distribution of assets and the discharge dominated much of the policy debates, throughout the 1870s Parliament became involved in the larger question of whether to have a bankruptcy law at all. And it was not long after the 1869 Act came into force that the need

Figure 2.1: Number of Commercial Failures in Canada 1873–85

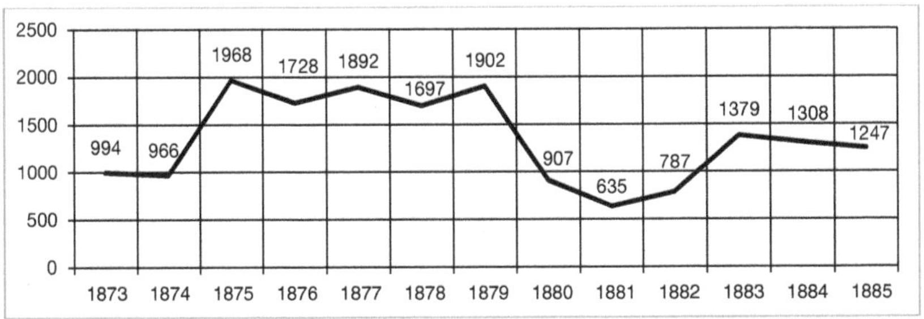

for a uniform national bankruptcy statute began to unravel. Even while the bankruptcy statutes remained in force, it was not feasible to establish complete uniformity, since varying provincial court rules meant that a national standard of bankruptcy law was difficult to achieve.[10] The inconsistent qualifications and practices of Official Assignees, who were to administer the bankrupts' estates, also undermined Parliament's goal of uniformity. More importantly, the repeal of bankruptcy legislation in 1880 and the diverse provincial legislation that followed suggests that a commitment to a national Act as expressed in the 1869 preamble and the Constitution did not survive the decade.

In part, the concern over the role of bankruptcy law was exacerbated by the international financial panic that began in 1873, which precipitated five years of falling prices and financial failure.[11] An examination of the number of commercial failures between 1873 and 1880 illustrates a sense of crisis (see figure 2.1). In 1875, the number of commercial failures doubled from the prior year. Failures continued to increase, peaking in 1879.[12]

In Quebec, between 1872 and 1880, 149 wholesalers and manufacturers "were swept entirely out of existence." During the same period three Canadian banks failed and three others significantly reduced their capital.[13] Some members of the public believed that bankruptcy legislation was the cause of the rising number of failures.[14] The movement for repeal peaked in 1879–80. The economic crisis created an intense debate about debt as political actors and interest groups sought to "provide compelling and convincing diagnoses" for the federal bankruptcy reform question.[15]

Further, American and English developments also created a sense of urgency about repeal north of the border. The United States repealed

Illustration 2.1: "The modern Nero: Fiddling at the destruction of Canadian commerce," *Grip* (24 January 1880). The cartoon depicts the growing number of business failures in 1879. Liberal Leader Alexander Mackenzie is a modern-day Nero fiddling while Canadian commerce burns. He smiles, as his comparative record on the extent of commercial failures is better than that of John A. Macdonald. J.W. Bengough, *A Caricature History of Canadian Politics*, vol 2 (Toronto: Grip, 1886) 107.

Illustration 2.2: "Never before was Canada so prosperous as it is to-day," *Grip* (7 February 1880). Finance Minister Sir Leonard Tilley had earlier stated that Canada was enjoying a prosperous time. Here he is confronted by "Hard Times" and all the evidence of the lingering downturn in the economy. J.W. Bengough, *A Caricature History of Canadian Politics*, vol 2 (Toronto: Grip, 1886) 111.

its bankruptcy statute in 1878[16] at the very time when Parliament was considering whether the Canadian Act should continue. Canadian opponents of bankruptcy law seized upon the growing American repeal movement, hoping that "this example would be followed by the Canadian Parliament."[17] England debated the merits of repeal during the 1870s, and between 1869 and 1879 the English Parliament considered thirteen separate bankruptcy bills before finally producing comprehensive reform in 1883. While suggestions for the abolition of the entire English bankruptcy regime never prevailed, the controversy nevertheless attracted the attention of Canadian Members of Parliament.[18] The English repeal movement was "synchronized ... with the debates in the Canadian House of Commons on the same subject in 1879 and 1880."[19] While the economic crisis and US and English developments had an important influence on the direction of Canadian policy debates, they do not provide the complete picture. What follows below is an overview of the legislative history of Canadian bankruptcy law from 1867 to 1880.

On 10 November 1867, the Canadian federal government appointed a Parliamentary Select Committee to "inquire into and report upon the nature and the operation of the laws of bankruptcy now in force in the several Provinces of the Dominion." In particular the Committee was interested to learn "whether the whole of the operation of the law had been beneficial, or the reverse."[20] In its report issued on 17 April 1868, the Committee noted that the Maritime legislatures never passed any bankruptcy laws, and the only major bankruptcy statutes enacted prior to 1867 were the Lower Canadian Bankruptcy Act of 1839 and the Province of Canada Acts of 1843 and 1864.[21] Indeed the unpopularity of pre-Confederation bankruptcy statutes did not bode well for legislation enacted post-Confederation.[22]

The most significant pre-Confederation Act was the *Insolvent Act of 1864*, which applied to the regions of what are now Ontario and Quebec. The *Insolvent Act of 1864* had not been readily accepted, and in June 1867, the Council of the County of Huron demanded its repeal. The Council took direct aim at the bankruptcy discharge: "It is notorious that numbers, daily increasing, resort to the Act to shirk their just debts, which they might exert themselves to pay, had they not so a facile a method to relieve themselves from their debts." The ease with which debtors could obtain a release of their debts affected the morality of individuals: "We view the act as legalised inducement held out to parties to cheat, and a great means of demoralising numerous people who, otherwise, might be tolerably honest." The Council concluded, "[T]he Act is conducive of much more evil than good, therefore it should be taken off the Statute Books of the Country."[23]

A year later one editorial claimed that the *Insolvent Act of 1864* was an Act to "white-wash debtors and to enable them to slip through its meshes, with as much property out of their hands." An editorial in the *Trade Review* similarly condemned it. There was no "disgrace" in becoming a bankrupt. A bankruptcy "injures a man's credit only in a trifling degree, and ... he comes out before the world with as fine a reputation as ever." The statute enabled the debtor "to whitewash himself and cheat ... his creditors out of their rights."[24]

After the issuance of the Select Committee report, Prime Minister Macdonald entrusted John Abbott to forge a new national bankruptcy statute. Abbott was a renowned commercial lawyer, a Member of Parliament, the Dean of the Faculty of Law at McGill, and the drafter of the *Insolvent Act of 1864*.[25] However, even Abbott's expertise would not be enough to persuade Parliament that there should be a permanent bankruptcy statute. In 1868, Macdonald introduced the first federal bankruptcy bill, but it failed to pass, and Macdonald blamed both opposition parties for taking "every objection" to it.[26] In 1869, Macdonald re-introduced the bill, and in opening the debate in the House of Commons he highlighted the extent of division over whether to adopt such a law, noting that a "strong opinion had arisen that all laws relating to insolvency were inexpedient." In contrast, many argued that a bankruptcy law "was essentially requisite in a commercial community." As Macdonald presented it, "The question was whether they should have an Insolvent Act or not."[27] The *Insolvent Act of 1869*, which received Royal Assent on 22 June 1869,[28] sought to create a uniform system of bankruptcy law. The preamble stated, "WHEREAS it is expedient that the Acts respecting Bankruptcy and Insolvency in the several Provinces ... be amended and consolidated, and the law on those subjects be assimilated in the several Provinces of the Dominion."[29]

The statute marked only a tentative beginning for a bankruptcy regime. First, Parliament designed the law as a temporary four-year measure. However, the law was extended twice, in 1873 and again in 1874.[30] Second, the year during which the Act came into force, Parliament debated its repeal, and two further attempts were made to remove the legislation from the statute books in 1871 and 1872.[31] The government sought to defer second reading of the 1871 bill but the motion to defer was lost by a vote of 79–60. The repeal bill passed on second reading in the House but never became law. In 1872 the repeal movement tried once again. The House of Commons passed a repeal bill, only to have the Senate kill the bill by deferring reading.[32] These repeal efforts, although unsuccessful, were significant, given that the law would have expired on its own terms.[33]

The scope of the law that Parliament was seeking to overturn was not broad, but even a narrowly drafted bankruptcy law proved objectionable. The legislation did not make the discharge available to all debtors. Rather, it applied only to traders who traditionally were defined by the courts as a person "seeking to gain his living by buying or selling."[34] Non-traders such as labourers or farmers were excluded from the scope of the legislation, and debate over whether to broaden the bill's scope to encompass them threatened its very success. Parliament could agree only on a law that retained the trader rule.[35] In addition, the Act did not define "trader," leaving the courts to work their way through the confused state of English jurisprudence.[36]

Debtors, who qualified as traders, gained access to the legislation by one of two means. Creditors could force a debtor into bankruptcy on proof that the debtor had engaged in one of the listed acts of misconduct. Under this regime, debtors who committed one of the thirteen separate acts were deemed to be insolvent and subject to the compulsory liquidation provisions of the legislation.[37] The legislation also permitted debtors to file for bankruptcy. While one author claimed that voluntary bankruptcy law was in accordance with the "spirit of modern legislation,"[38] this proved to be an overly optimistic view. By adopting a voluntary procedure in 1869, Parliament moved beyond what was acceptable to society. Voluntary proceedings proved contentious after 1869 and Parliament abolished this right in 1875.

A survey of select Ontario County Court records reveals that the vast majority of bankrupts had accessed the bankruptcy and discharge regime under the 1869 Act through voluntary proceedings (see table 2.1).[39]

The high rate of voluntary proceedings contributed to the growing sense that bankruptcy law was a pro-debtor measure. Assignments became unpopular as debtors used the ability to threaten assignment "as a lever to secure extension of time." Creditors who sought to collect on debts "were continually met by a threat to assign if they ventured to press their legal remedies."[40] Small traders often made a voluntary assignment in bankruptcy without consulting their creditors.[41]

Table 2.1: Percentage of Voluntary Bankruptcy Proceedings under the *Insolvent Act of 1869* by County

County	%
Huron	75.51
Lambton	78.13
Lanark	88.61
Oxford	95.24
Peel	82.35
Perth	80.00

The *Insolvent Act of 1875* came into force on 1 September 1875[42] and replaced the *Insolvent Act of 1869*.[43] There was a consensus that the Act of 1869 had not gone far enough to protect creditors who required further means of discovering and punishing fraud.[44] The "'poor creditor' proposes now to take his innings, the 'poor debtor' having had ... a good time of it for many years past." Although the 1869 legislation had contained many provisions favourable to creditors, the "object of the [1875] bill was to give the creditors greater control of the estate."[45] Parliament's decision to abolish voluntary assignments was the most significant policy change. Voluntary proceedings under the Act of 1869 had been a central point of opposition. The *Insolvent Act of 1875* allowed only creditors to initiate proceedings.[46] If access to the bankruptcy regime best measured the balance between creditor and debtor interests, voluntary proceedings had tipped the scales too far in favour of the debtor. In 1875, the creation of a single compulsory system represented a sharp return to the creditor-oriented regimes of the past. The abolition of voluntary assignments appeased those who sought repeal of all bankruptcy laws.[47]

After the *Insolvent Act of 1875* came into force, one author optimistically identified a "general feeling amongst the mercantile community ... [that] an Insolvent Act should remain as a permanent Statute Book." He concluded that, in accordance with the wishes of the commercial classes, "an Insolvent Act will henceforth be recognized as a necessity in this country."[48] But these views misread the emerging consensus that repeal was inevitable, and the 1875 amendments did little to quell the opposition to bankruptcy.

Parliament debated further repeal bills in 1877,[49] 1878,[50] 1879[51] and again in 1880.[52] Prime Minister Macdonald, returned to power in 1878,

C-072078

Illustration 2.3: John Joseph Caldwell Abbott talks to an inspector about shooting a horse carrying a bag named the Insolvency Act 1875, but a third individual suggests that they try to save the horse.
John Abbott: "Well, gentlemen, what shall I do with him?"
Inspector: "I think it's high time he were shot."
Alex: "O we will try and patch up the old fellow once more."
Canadian Illustrated News 19:18 (3 May 1879) 273, LAC (reproduction copy no C-072078, control no ICON80986).

was under pressure to allow a repeal bill to pass. One individual wrote to Macdonald, hoping "you will wipe out that accursed insolvent act ... the country will sustain you and call you blessed."[53] No longer committed to retaining the federal law and uncertain how to proceed, the government established a Select Committee in 1879 to study the matter.[54] The 1879 Select Committee was to consider all options, including the "expediency of continuing, amending or repealing such Laws." At the first meeting, the committee found itself "very much divided in sentiment," noting that Parliament and the country were also divided on the wisdom of continuing the *Insolvent Act* or repealing it "pure and simple."[55]

The House of Commons debated a reform bill (Bill 85) at length. However, in the end, the House unexpectedly abandoned the comprehensive reform bill to consider Bill 15, which simply proposed to repeal the *Insolvent Act of 1875*. On 5 May 1879 the House of Commons voted to repeal the Act.[56] When the 1879 repeal bill moved to the Upper Chamber, the Senate voted to delay the bill for six months, which effectively put the bill into abeyance.[57] In 1880, one Member of Parliament considered repeal a forgone conclusion.[58] Momentum and support in favour of repeal could not be stopped, and in 1880 the House of Commons passed a repeal bill with little debate. In the Senate, Macdonald's government finally conceded and decided to allow the *Insolvent Act of 1875* to be repealed. The Senate approved repeal by an almost 3–1 margin on 11 March 1880, and the repeal bill received Royal Assent on 1 April 1880.[59] The idea of bankruptcy and insolvency law as an essential national power had been tested and lost. The rather quick demise of national bankruptcy statutes over the course of just one decade raises important questions of why the legislation did not fit well with late nineteenth-century conceptions of credit and debt.

3

The Rise and Fall of Bankruptcy Law 1867–1880: The Equitable Distribution of Assets

The great objects of bankruptcy are: firstly, To create as great a sensation as possible; and, secondly, To make money. Remember that you must have some assets, but let them be as small as possible. All your household furniture can be made to belong to somebody else. Here, a wife is very useful. There is not the slightest necessity for having a balance at your bankers. Draw the money out by degrees – (not all at once, – that looks suspicious) – and forward it to me.

"Uncle Wordly's Letters To His Nephews," *Grinchuckle* 1:5 (4 November 1869) p. 41

When Smith endorsed a promissory note on behalf of a debtor, he could not have anticipated having to take dramatic and rather drastic steps to collect on the debt when the debtor defaulted. In December 1866, Smith heard that the debtor had absconded or was about to abscond to the United States. Smith believed that the only opportunity to recover the money was to hire an agent to track him down. Smith asked his agent to pursue the debtor across the suspension bridge at Niagara Falls into the United States. The agent located the debtor in a private room in a hotel, where the agent "threatened to institute criminal proceedings" against the debtor and "have him arrested"[1] unless the debtor paid up. The debtor denied having any funds, but when the agent pressed further, the debtor handed over the required sum. The debtor subsequently became a bankrupt. Clearly the payment to Smith prejudiced other creditors, as the payment preferred Smith at the expense of other creditors. The Official Assignee challenged the payment as a preferential payment, which was simply unfair to other creditors and disturbed the equality principle.

However, the court did not uphold the equality principle in this case. Consistent with case law of this era, courts interpreted the preference provisions in a way that favoured the preferred creditor. This not only undermined the equality principle but it also contributed to the unpopularity of the legislation. In *Roe v Smith* the court concluded that the payment was made under duress, and this fit within the common law doctrine of pressure, which validated a transaction. Where pressure had been applied, the transaction was valid, notwithstanding that it violated the equality principle. Here the court concluded that "there was nothing unjust in the defendants having obtained it ... and that neither the policy nor the spirit, nor even the terms of the Insolvency Law were violated by it." The court refused to set aside the payment,[2] as pursuing an absconding debtor into the United States combined with a threat of prosecution was clear evidence of pressure.

However, one of the policies, if not spirit, of the bankruptcy legislation was equality. This chapter not only explores the importance of the equality principle but also considers how the actions of debtors and the courts undermined the principle during the 1870s. Debtors regularly engaged in preferential transactions with related creditors. Courts played an important institutional role by regularly interpreting the preference provisions in a way that favoured the preferred creditors. This chapter considers repeal from the perspective of the equitable distribution of assets.

Two central ideas competed for attention during this era. Bankruptcy law's equal treatment of creditors competed unsuccessfully with the notion that debtors were entitled to arrange their affairs with local or related creditors.[3] Debtors simply ignored the equality principle, and in practice debtors could ensure that favoured creditors would be paid first. This was not too far away from a pure common law regime of "first come, first served," as under that system local creditors benefited from their proximity to debtors. The equality principle benefited creditors who traded across great distances. Bankruptcy law protected the interests of distant creditors by removing the need to monitor distant debtors. Local or related creditors saw no need for an equality principle, since they could largely ignore it. However, when the Official Assignee did intervene and challenged preferential payments, the courts interpreted the legislation in a way that favoured the preferred creditor.

Section 1 of this chapter examines the contrasting position of equality under a bankruptcy regime and the common law's race to the assets. Section 2 examines the idea of equality in a bankruptcy regime and contemporary support for the equality principle. Sections 3 and 4, however, demonstrate that equality had a fragile meaning during the 1870s. These sections illustrate that courts as institutions played an important role in shaping the bankruptcy law debates. Section 3 illustrates how local creditors had a unique advantage in bankruptcy litigation. Section 4 analyses actions to recover preferential payments or transfers and concludes that courts undermined the equality principle by interpreting the *Insolvent Acts* in a manner that favoured the local creditors. Section 5 concludes with an examination of the interest groups that became embroiled in the repeal debates. National or regional creditor interest groups that extended credit over a distance sought to prevent the demise of the *Insolvent Act* throughout the 1870s. However, distant creditors did not prevail in their attempt to retain a national and uniform bankruptcy statute.

1. Equality vs the Common Law

The ultimate repeal of the *Insolvent Act of 1875* can best be understood by comparing the equality principle of the bankruptcy regime with the common law position of "first come, first served." Repeal destroyed bankruptcy law's equality principle, or *pro rata* sharing, among creditors and restored the common law principle of rewarding the first creditor to seize or execute on the debtor's assets.[4] The common law priority rule advantaged local, friendly or even related creditors and disadvantaged creditors who extended credit over distances. In the absence of a bankruptcy statute, the common law provided that a creditor who obtained the first execution against the debtor was not required to share the benefits of execution with other creditors.[5] Pre-Confederation courts recognized the problems inherent with the common law approach. In 1864, Justice Wilson, in *Gottwalls v Mulholland*, noted that the common law was unsatisfactory, as it permitted "the creditor who can first get a judgment and execution to have a preference, by allowing him to have his debt paid in full, with no regard either to the interest of the debtor or the other creditors."[6]

In contrast, the *Insolvent Acts of 1869* and *1875* abolished the common law race to the debtor's assets by providing for a *pro rata* distribution to all unsecured creditors.[7] It was this very feature of the common law that led the English Parliament to enact the first bankruptcy statute in 1543.[8] The common law system encouraged fraud and collusion amongst debtors and creditors as the parties sought to anticipate and outwit each other in the race of diligence.[9] The first section of the English Act provided that the debtor's assets were to be distributed: "to every one of the said creditors, a portion rate and rate alike according to the quantity of their debts."[10] Coke described the policy of the statute in *The Case of the Bankrupts*: "The intent ... was that there should be an equal and rateable proportion observed in the distribution of the bankrupt's goods amongst the creditors, having regard to the quantity of their several debts."[11] While much of the English legislation was intended to assist creditors to "recover their money from those debtors who were attempting to defraud them,"[12] the Act nevertheless established the core principle of equitable distribution. The *pro rata* distribution of the debtor's assets put all creditors, near and far, on an equal footing.

Other aspects of the bankruptcy legislation upheld the equality principle.[13] The *Insolvent Acts* prohibited preferential payments or transfers of property by an insolvent debtor to a creditor in advance of the bankruptcy proceedings. This ensured that a single creditor was not able to disrupt the equitable distribution of assets. In 1858, an *Upper Canada Law Journal* editorial recognized that preferential payments threatened the equality principle: "[A]s the law now stands in Upper Canada ... a debtor, though largely embarrassed, may select any one or more of his creditors to the exclusion of all others, and to the 'select few' pay their demands in full to the impoverishment of all others not so lucky. These few are 'friends' ... Oh, that the bulk of the creditors could get one peep behind the curtains in cases such as this!"[14] Bankruptcy also became a mandatory collective proceeding[15] such that execution creditors could not collect ahead of all other creditors by initiating collection proceedings after the bankruptcy had commenced. The *Insolvent Acts* imposed a stay of proceedings precluding all actions against the bankrupt. This ensured that all claims would be assessed within a single bankruptcy proceeding rather than allow individual creditors to obtain an advantage outside of the bankruptcy.[16] A judgment creditor was therefore to be deprived of any preferred status, "leaving him to come in *pro rata* with the other creditors." The new provisions "remove[d] ... the opportunity for the preferential judgments so usually given by debtors in insolvent circumstances."[17] As section 2 discusses, there was much initial support for the equality principle. A vexing question, however, is why that support eroded by the end of the 1870s.

2. Support for the Equitable Distribution of the Debtor's Assets

John Abbott, who drafted the *Insolvent Act of 1864* and influenced the shape of the *Insolvent Act of 1869*,[18] clearly understood how local and distant creditors fared under a common law system. Where a "creditor at a distance took proceedings for recovery of his debt," the debtor would come up with some sham plea or defence so as to "protract the judgment in favour of the creditor at a distance." In the meantime, "the neighbour, father or brother of the debtor" obtained a consent judgment "so that the neighbour or friend got the whole proceeds, to the exclusion of other creditors."[19] Another author claimed that the common law gave "the power of a bankrupt to give disgraceful preferences by allowing a favoured creditor to get a judgment by default, and secure priority of execution."[20]

In 1877, James Young, "an outspoken backbencher"[21] in the Liberal Government of Alexander Mackenzie, objected to the bankruptcy repeal bill before the House. He clearly understood the competing interests in play: "If the Insolvent Act were repealed and the country fell back on the old system of confession of judgment and preferential assignment, the local creditors would lay hold of the estate and creditors at a distance would be placed at a great disadvantage ... If the measures by which the creditors could at least obtain a share of the debtor's estate in the case of failure were removed, a serious blow would be struck at all credit, and injury would be inflicted on the people of the distant provinces and the commercial community as a whole."[22]

In Parliament there was support for bankruptcy's equality principle on both sides of the House. In 1877, John A. Macdonald asked whether the country was ready to "go back to the law of preference when everyone caused a confession of judgment and obtained an advantage over his neighbour, thus causing universal distrust throughout the whole country." The moment that the bankruptcy law was repealed, "it would be a race on the part of the creditors to the nearest and sharpest law officer they could find." That same year, Edward Blake, the Liberal Minister of Justice, defended bankruptcy law on the basis that it provided for "a speedy means of obtaining ... the property of the debtor ... and its realization and distribution, pro rata among ... creditors." The following year the Conservative Minister of Justice, James McDonald, equally supported the virtues of a bankruptcy law. The debtor's estate "shall be distributed among his creditors in equal proportions; he shall not be allowed to appropriate to one individual what ought in justice be distributed amongst the whole."[23] A Canadian bankruptcy law therefore reduced the risk for distant or foreign creditors and destroyed local advantage.[24]

Support for the equality principle on occasion came from debtors. One debtor, in a letter to a creditor, expressed regret in not being able to uphold creditor equality: "I am sorry to inform you that it is impossible for me to meet my note falling due ... There [are] now five Division Court executions in the hands of the Bailiff ... It is utterly impossible to meet my engagements. I am sorry to be obliged to own up to the fact but it is useless to try to weather the storm any longer and do my creditors equal justice ... But the pressure is [too] great now for me to stand."[25]

In Kent County one debtor sought an extension of time to pay so that he "should be enabled to pay all my creditors." Without such an extension of between six and nine months, the debtor would be forced to "go to the Wall" like many others. Selling existing stock would realize only fifty cents on the dollar.[26]

Many appellate court rulings emphasized the importance of the equality principle.[27] Parliament enacted the bankruptcy statute to provide "for the equal distribution of the insolvent's estate among all his creditors."[28] In *Adams v McCall* the court concluded that if one creditor "obtains payment in full ... while the others get nothing, it is an 'unjust preference' contrary to [the law's] letter and true spirit."[29] *Brown v Wright* summarized the policy of the *Insolvent Act*: "The insolvents were enabled by the statute to make the voluntary assignment to the official assignee, and it becomes the duty of the official assignee named therein to act upon it, in whom all the property of the insolvents is vested for the benefit of all the creditors, and for effecting the object of the Act, viz., an equal distribution of the assets among all the creditors."[30]

McLeod v Wright went further and emphasized that the prohibition against preferential payments supported the equality principle: "The policy of the Insolvent Law is, that a man who knows himself to be in a helpless state of insolvency should not prefer one of his creditors however urgent he may be for payment, but should give up all his property for the general benefit of all his creditors."[31]

The Supreme Court of Canada in *Milloy v Kerr* concluded that the bankruptcy statute required any debtor "not to make any preference" where he had a "reasonable doubt" about his ability to pay all his creditors.[32] Notwithstanding these statements of support for the equality principle, sections 3 and 4 demonstrate that in practice equality had a rather fragile meaning.

3. Local vs Distant Creditors

The nature of the Canadian economy in the period 1867 to 1880 was still primarily rural and agricultural.[33] In 1867, the population of 3.5 million was 80 per cent rural,[34] and by 1880 little had changed.[35] While the American economy came of age in the late nineteenth century, it would take some time before a national Canadian market emerged. Michael Bliss compared the economies of the two countries and concludes, "The age of Carnegie and Rockefeller and J.P. Morgan and young Henry Ford in the United States, from about 1875 to 1910, was in Canada still the age of the general storekeeper on the prairies, sawmills in the Gatineau, shoe factories in Quebec and textile mills and candy factories in New Brunswick." Canadian markets were "scattered over vast distances and were minuscule by American or European standards."[36] The existence of a more locally based rural economy shaped the nature of the debate over whether to repeal the federal bankruptcy law.

The new constitutional framework of the *BNA Act* did not immediately create a national economy. Confederation in 1867 can be viewed as a "means for achieving provincial and particularistic, rather than national, goals." Taylor and Baskerville argue that most visions of Confederation were "firmly rooted in sectoral, regional, and metropolitan contexts."[37] Ben Forster's study of mid- and late-nineteenth-century Ontario found that when manufacturers began to market brand names directly to consumers, there was no immediate shift to a nationally based system of distribution and market. Forster argues that customers continued to prefer to buy from local suppliers and producers, as "[c]redit arrangements could be more flexible, and faulty goods might be more readily repaired."[38]

It is within this context that local creditors had a unique advantage over distant creditors, even within the bankruptcy regime of the 1870s.[39] Creditors by virtue of their locality might obtain a monopolistic position over the debtor's finances. Thus the local creditors of a shoe dealer in Yarmouth, Nova Scotia, were secured "to such an extent that outsiders will not realize over 10c on the dollar." Even where the debtor moved from his original location, the original local debts would follow, and in one case led to a "business casualty" in Stonewall, Manitoba. Wholesale creditors at a distance who made further extensions of credit were at risk of not fully understanding the debtor's financial situation. An 1876 Letter to the Editor of the *Monetary Times* reported that distant creditors had offered an extension of time to a debtor on the basis of the debtor's statement of affairs. According to the letter, the extension of time to pay had the effect of "floating [the debtor] farther into the sea of bankruptcy." Local creditors knew better and cut their losses. The extension of time was "sufficient for sharp local creditors to get from under."[40]

Local creditors might be in a position to prevent an absconding debtor from leaving the country. In 1878, the *Journal of Commerce* reported an incident at the Richmond, Quebec, train station. Fletcher and Baker, who were indebted to several creditors, were about to take the train to flee to the United States. "[L]ocal creditors got wind of their movements at the last moment." The creditors "made instant tracks" for the railway station, where they "lay forcible hands upon the absconding party." They refused to release the debtors "until the debtor paid all claims in full." The local creditors nearly succeeded in making away with the debtor, had it not been for the intervention of the police, who released the "prisoners in time to catch the train that bore them away to pastures new."[41]

Family creditors frequently took advantage of information about the debtor's financial situation. Debtors permitted family members to obtain a default judgment against them to the prejudice of other creditors. In *Re Jones* the debtor allowed his mother to obtain a default judgment against him while he defended other claims. The debtor's actions enabled his mother to enforce her judgment against the debtor, who later became a bankrupt. The debtor "acted so as to prejudice his general creditors ... by procuring" his mother's seizure. The court called into question whether the debt to the mother was actually due and ultimately set aside the execution proceedings in favour of the Official Assignee.[42] Though the family member did not succeed in this particular case, it demonstrates how related creditors sought to obtain an advantage.

In a parallel case Calvin Day, the younger, allowed his father, Calvin Day senior, to obtain default judgment. Here the father succeeded at the expense of at least one other creditor. The son permitted the father to execute on the judgment and recover all of the son's assets; even though the son had one additional creditor, Thomas Parke. The son subsequently made an assignment in bankruptcy and under oath admitted to the Official Assignee that he had no assets "whatever." The son subsequently obtained a discharge. Nine years later Parke contended that the discharge was void on the basis that the default judgment enabled the father to "sweep away all his assets." According to Parke, the entire insolvency proceedings were intended "to benefit the father" to Parke's prejudice. Although a debtor's entry into bankruptcy with no assets was according to the court "a perfect mockery of the Insolvent Act,"[43] it did not provide Parke with grounds to challenge the discharge. Waiting nine years to challenge the discharge without previously launching an appeal was fatal to Parke's case.

The pull of a family relationship often meant that family members were paid ahead of other creditors. William Thompson owed his son $367 for wages. With insufficient funds to pay the balance, Thompson mortgaged "all his remaining Real Estate in favour of his son" to secure the amount owing on the wages. Further, Thompson "secreted a large sum of money." He had given the money to his wife "thinking she had the best right to his." When questioned, Thompson "could not tell what his wife had done with it."[44]

Husbands and wives specifically sought to defeat creditors. A letter to the editor of the *Monetary Times* complained bitterly of the steps a husband had taken to defeat his creditors. The action of a husband paying his wife to shield his assets from creditors was said to "ruin honest tradesman by ... knavery and incapacity ... The very first thing ... which a man does ... is to put another story on his 'wife's' house, buy a carriage and all its belongings, with his 'wife's' money, collect interest on his 'wife's' mortgages, spend the money his 'wife' allows him for pocket money, and then swears he has no income and no funds, not even so much as would pay for a ride on the streetcars."[45] Marital assets were viewed with suspicion. In Kent County, one debtor sought to justify the allocation of his marital property. The debtor told a meeting of creditors that "I got married 6 mos. ago. I took about $800 to furnish my home. The piano belongs to my wife and [was bought] by her own money."[46]

In 1879, the Ontario Court of Appeal considered a husband's attempt to transfer all property into his wife's name with the object of allowing him to continue to carry on business. In *Re Gearing* Mr Gearing carried on a mercantile business until he became bankrupt. While waiting for his discharge, creditors decided that the business assets would be sold to Mrs Gearing for the purchase price of $8000. The Court of Appeal concluded that the entire object of the transaction was to enable Mr Gearing to continue with his business. The shop was reopened, the signage remained the same and "to the ordinary on-looker the business appeared to be carried on precisely as before Gearing's insolvency." Mrs Gearing purchased goods in her name but Mr Gearing always gave the orders to buy. Mr Gearing wrote the correspondence for the business. Moss CJA could not "believe that ... creditors seriously entertained the idea that this lady designed to embark in business on her own account." Notwithstanding the use of Mrs Gearing's name to carry on the business, Mr Gearing eventually obtained his discharge, at which point he began to carry on business in his own name.[47]

Wives of bankrupts also took a more active role in the bankruptcy proceedings. In one Wentworth County bankruptcy proceeding, the wife of the bankrupt sought to interfere with the seizure of assets. When the Official Assignee sought to enforce the Writ of Attachment and seize assets, the wife claimed to own the chattels and household furniture at the residence. She also claimed to be the owner of the building where her husband, the bankrupt, carried on his business. As owner of the building, she sought to distrain a large quantity of chattels for rent owing to her.[48]

Transcripts of the examination of bankrupts also reveal pre-bankruptcy transfers in favour of a related party. In the bankruptcy of Joseph Wilson, the bankrupt admitted to having $174 in cash the evening before the proceedings began. He gave $100 to his wife, as he had no other means to support his family. He had four children and his wife was about to be hospitalized for some time. The bankrupt claimed, "[M]y wife holds the money for family use ... The $100 paid to my wife is all the means of support I have."[49]

Ontario county court records also reveal the existence of a number of female bankrupts.[50] This eligibility for bankruptcy likely arose because of reforms to the property rights of married women in Ontario beginning in 1872. The reforms enabled women to hold their earnings separate from their husbands' and to manage and dispose of their own personal property.[51] Under the new property regime, however, "couples used the new right of the wife to own property as a means of insulating land and chattels from seizure by legitimate creditors; some wives colluded with husbands and were active, dishonest agents in the marketplace."[52] Husbands and wives together ignored the higher obligation to pay debts. Creditors did not refrain from initiating bankruptcy proceedings against female debtors.

Notwithstanding the existence of a mandatory equality distribution scheme found in the bankruptcy statute, local and family creditors ignored this bankruptcy principle to the detriment of other creditors. It undermined confidence in the bankruptcy regime, leading many to take the position that if the system was not working effectively it was better to do away with it rather than amend it. While there was much public support for the equality principle in the House of Commons, in practice debtors overlooked the concept. As section 4 demonstrates, the unique problem of preferential transactions – payments to one creditor at the expense of others – further undermined confidence in the bankruptcy regime.

4. Preferential Transactions

Both of the *Insolvent Acts* prohibited preferential transactions and enabled the Official Assignee to set aside payments to a preferred creditor. However, the provisions did not always favour the Official Assignee. Debtors simply ignored the provisions and selected the creditor who would receive payment ahead of all others. Further, where the Official Assignee challenged the transaction, the courts interpreted the legislation in a way that favoured the preferred creditor. In many cases courts dismissed challenges to preferential transactions. This served to undermine equality.

Preferences and Local Creditors

UNJUST PREFERENCES

Local creditors could benefit if they were able to extract a preferential payment from the debtor prior to bankruptcy. In 1877, the New Brunswick Supreme Court, Equity Appeal Division, in *McLeod v Wright* set out the consequences of a preference: "The giving [of] a preference is the necessary consequence of a payment by a debtor to one of his creditors. The creditor is preferred because he has received his debt and the other creditors have not. The debtor being insolvent has not the means to pay his creditors, and by paying one in full, or transferring all his tangible property to one creditor leaving nothing for the rest, has defrauded others of the just proportion of his estate."[53]

The *Insolvent Acts* prohibited an "unjust preference" where it was made "in contemplation of insolvency."[54] This required proof of a debtor's intention to prefer.[55] A preferential transfer was null and void and could be "recovered back for the benefit of the estate by the Assignee."[56] An additional provision in the *Insolvent Acts* targeted all payments made within thirty days of bankruptcy.[57] Such payments were void and could be recovered by the Assignee for benefit of the bankrupt's estate.[58] The power to set aside unjust preferences and thirty-day payments supported the equality principle. County court files contain numerous references to preferential transactions. Debtors sold their business and transferred their entire stock in trade to one creditor while insolvent, without the consent of all other creditors, and without satisfying their claims. In one court file, the debtor executed a chattel mortgage in favour of a creditor over all his household furniture and personal effects.[59] Although the *Insolvent Acts* prohibited preferences, in practice preferences went unchallenged or courts interpreted the provisions against the interests of the Official Assignee and in favour of the preferred creditor. This contributed to the unpopularity of the legislation, leading some to wonder whether it was worth having bankruptcy legislation at all.

Preferences were so important that, in issuing a final order of discharge, courts would specifically note that the discharge had not been induced by a preferential payment. In a Haldimand County court file, one judge concluded that "no one of the creditors who have signed the said Deed of Composition and Discharge has been induced to do so by any preferential payment promise of payment or advantage whatsoever made secured or promised to him by or on behalf of the said Insolvent." In Wentworth County, a creditor objected to the discharge (obtained with creditor consent) on the basis that the bankrupt was guilty of "fraudulent preferences and evil practices in procuring the consent of the creditors to the execution of the deed of composition and discharge." The allegation in substance meant that the bankrupt had paid creditors to vote in favour of the discharge.[60]

In Kent County, one debtor, sensitive to the suspicion of preferential payments, made it perfectly clear that all transactions were above board: "I have no assets myself ... I never gave my wife a cent since I failed ... All my assets have been given over – my books show all my assets. I have not transferred my goods or any property [in] any way. I have not taken out any cash. My creditors have it all."

Another debtor in Wentworth County more explicitly denied making a preference: "I have not been guilty of any fraud or fraudulent preference within the meaning of the above Acts or of fraud or evil practice in procuring the consent of any of my creditors to my discharge."[61]

Notwithstanding the policy against preferences, debtors regularly ignored the provisions. In 1869, the *Journal of Commerce* demanded amendments to the legislation: "There is surely nothing worse taking place under the Insolvency Act than the preferential assignments which were so common before 1864, and by which a brother, or a cousin, or some favoured creditor, was put in possession of an insolvent's entire estate, and all the other creditors left to whistle to the wind ... [B]ad things are taking place everyday under the operation of the present law."[62]

The goal of equal treatment of creditors was most obviously defeated where a debtor sought to prefer family or local creditors. Creditors, who maintained close connections with debtors, were in a position to demand and sometimes pressure for payment. The examples below, drawn from reported cases and original archival case files, represent a fraction of all preferential transactions involving a bankrupt. Where the debtor absconded or the family member dissipated assets or could not be located, the Official Assignee would have no basis to proceed with a suit to challenge the transaction. In the nineteenth century, with rudimentary means of communication, the Official Assignee had few means by which to trace the favoured creditor and even fewer ways to find an absconding debtor who had no intention of being found. Further, the lack of proper books and records made proof of preferences difficult.

Debtors entered into preferential transactions for many reasons. In part, payments or transfers placated a creditor who threatened to pursue an action on outstanding debts. A payment to a financial institution may have staved off the debtor's "financial embarrassment." A debtor might be "utterly and hopelessly insolvent" and resort to fraud to raise funds.[63] Such funds could then be funnelled to pay off debts with a bank. In other circumstances a debtor might obtain the required level of creditor consent to a discharge by inducing favourable votes or by making preferential payments to some creditors but not others. A contractor who had been retained to build a local school made a preferential payment to a subcontractor for stone and brickwork, to ensure completion of the building.[64]

In some cases the Official Assignee was successful in setting aside preferential payments or transfers. In *Pineo v Gavaza* the bankrupt and his relatives entered into a series of transactions seeking to avoid the reach of the Official Assignee. Prior to the bankruptcy, the debtor sold assets under a bill of sale to an uncle. It was also discovered that the debtor's brother had purchased all of the debtor's real estate for a nominal sum. The Nova Scotia Supreme Court in appeal proceedings held that the bill of sale was an unjust preference made in contemplation of insolvency. The close family connections between the debtor and the creditors influenced the court's reasoning. The court considered "the circumstances attending the insolvency and transfers of property, the close relationship which existed between the insolvent and the persons to whom his property was transferred, and the creditor who instituted the insolvency proceedings immediately after the expiration of thirty days from the date of filing of the bill of sale."[65]

Preferences were granted not only to family creditors. Creditors with knowledge of the debtor's financial difficulty were in a position to take advantage of that information by demanding a preference. In April 1876 Hergert, a London, Ontario, tobacconist, owed Albert Smith $123. Hergert identified Smith as someone who would "be able, from his knowledge of my affairs, pretty much to know how my standing was." Court proceedings describe Smith as a person "who seems to have been on terms of intimacy" with the debtor. Hergert was indebted to other creditors by at least three times the amount owing to Smith, who was well aware of a pending action against Hergert. On 5 April 1876 Hergert executed a chattel mortgage in favour of Smith over all of Hergert's stock and trade. When Smith sought to enforce the mortgage, another creditor initiated bankruptcy proceedings, leading the Official Assignee to challenge the validity of the Smith mortgage. Smith realized that the execution of the mortgage in his favour had detrimental effects on other creditors. Two or three days after the execution of the mortgage, Smith told the creditor who had initiated a lawsuit against Hergert that "he would not get a cent now from Hergert."[66] The Ontario Court of Appeal set aside the mortgage as a preference.

However, as the case law below suggests, the prohibition against preferential payments or transfers of property provided little deterrent. Debtors and family or local creditors arranged their affairs with a direct intent to prejudice creditors. This suggests that the preference provisions did not always operate in favour of the Official Assignee, nor did they in practice uphold the equality principle. Unjust preferences and thirty-day payments were not always set aside, and courts circumvented the equality principle by upholding transfers to creditors.[67] In many cases, courts interpreted the legislation in favour of the preferred creditor. In refusing to set aside an alleged preferential chattel mortgage in favour of a creditor, an Ontario court claimed that the tendency of judges was to avoid the application of "technical rules as a test of fraud, and to assist mercantile convenience as far as possible." That goal could be achieved by allowing an honest man to raise money "on an emergency upon the security of his stock-in-trade."[68] One court concluded that the *Insolvency Act* should be interpreted in favour of the creditor so as "to leave creditors some latitude to exercise vigilance to secure their debts, and debtors hopeful and energetic to work out their salvation."[69]

Courts forgave a preferential payment where the transaction allowed the debtor to carry on business. In *Smith v McLean* the court held that the arrangement with the creditor had the effect of enabling the debtor to carry on business. Here the transaction was intended to assist the debtor in paying off some of his liabilities and was thus not set aside.[70] Therefore where "the sole motive of the debtors" in granting a mortgage "was to obtain the further advance to carry on their business," there was no preference.[71] Similarly courts refused to set aside a transaction "in the ordinary course of business." The Legislature did not intend to "forbid ordinary transactions with an embarrassed trader in the regular course of affairs and *bona fide*."[72] In Wentworth County a debtor sought to avoid bankruptcy in an involuntary proceeding by claiming that he had not made "any sale or disposal ... of my furniture or stock ... except mere sales in the ordinary course of trade."[73]

Further, courts held that the Official Assignee did not establish that the preferential payment was made with the intent to prefer or, in the words of the statute, made in the "contemplation of insolvency."[74] In *McCrae v White* the Supreme Court of Canada recognized that not all debtors in financial difficulty entered into transactions in contemplation of insolvency. Giving credence to the debtor's optimistic disposition, W.J. Ritchie CJ concluded that "the natural inference would be that a man with such a sanguine temperament would easily delude himself with the idea that certain prospects of success were before him." In light of the debtor's sanguine character and the deal he had reached with the creditor, "he was not thinking of insolvency, but was ... looking forward to a career of business success." The Supreme Court refused to set aside the mortgage given in favour of a creditor. The mortgage had not been entered into in contemplation of insolvency, as "many men struggle on in hope of retrieving their affairs and avoiding insolvency long after their affairs become embarrassed, anticipating they may rally and come round."[75] The ruling meant that the debtor's subjective, yet optimistic belief undermined the ability of the Official Assignee to prove "contemplation of insolvency."[76]

Such optimism is evident in county court records. In Wentworth County a debtor professed, "[I]f I am allowed to continue my business I will soon be able to pay all my creditors in full – trade being generally slackest during the winter in my business." Robert Griffith of Wentworth County swore, "[M]y neglect to pay the plaintiff's claim is only caused by a temporary embarrassment which I expect will soon be removed and is not caused by any fraud or fraudulent intent or by any insufficiency of assets to meet my liabilities." Another debtor from the same jurisdiction held the same sentiment. Having sent a request for an extension of time to pay the creditor, he found himself facing an involuntary bankruptcy proceeding. In an affidavit he pleaded, "[T]he stoppage of payment is only temporary and ... it was not caused by any fraud or fraudulent intent ... or by the insufficiency of my assets to meet my liabilities."[77]

THIRTY-DAY PAYMENTS

Section 90 of the *Insolvent Act of 1869* and section 134 of the *Insolvent Act of 1875* provided the Official Assignee with the opportunity to set aside payments made within thirty days of bankruptcy. Under the provision, the Official Assignee had to establish the insolvency of the debtor and that the creditor receiving the payment knew of the debtor's insolvency. However, a number of cases interpreted the thirty-day provision in a way that the creditor could retain payment. In 1874, the Ontario Court of Queen's Bench expressed concern about the broad scope of section 90 of the *Insolvent Act of 1869*. The court concluded that the provision was similar to earlier English and Commonwealth enactments, "which expressly over-reached the transactions of traders which were made within the prohibited period, without regard to the innocence of the parties concerned, because the public interest was supposed to be served by their avoidance."[78]

The concern about the section being too broad and over-reaching translated into an interpretation that favoured the preferred creditor. In 1879, the Ontario Court of Appeal warned against an overly broad interpretation of the thirty-day payment provision. In *Smith v Hutchinson* the Assignee sought a broad interpretation of section 134 of the *Insolvent Act of 1875* and argued every payment made within thirty days was void, even if the payee had no reason to suspect the debtor's insolvent state. According to the Ontario Court of Appeal, the language of section 134 did not require such an interpretation, "[n]or do considerations of public policy demand so harsh a construction of the enactment." The Official Assignee's position in the case, for a broad reading of section 134, "would be so serious to the conduct of mercantile business, that it is satisfactory to feel assured that neither precedent nor principle requires us to lend it the slightest countenance."[79]

In a subsequent Ontario Court of Appeal case, the court further narrowed the scope of section 134. One key element of section 134 was that the creditor receiving payment must have known of the debtor's insolvency. In *Nelles v Paul* the court concluded that mere suspicion of insolvency was not sufficient to establish an impeachable transaction: "No one proves that there was a whisper even among the mercantile community, breathing upon his solvency. Until the last moment he appears to have been able to obtain credit, and so far as we can judge to have worn the garb of prosperity. The grounds of suspicion ... are too hypothetical and shadowy to form the basis of judicial action."[80] Under this test there was no obligation on the creditor to make further inquiries or investigations on a mere suspicion of insolvency. The ruling operated to the advantage of the preferred creditor, while at the same time it created a more difficult burden for the Official Assignee. Thus courts played an important institutional role in interpreting the legislation that favoured the preferred creditor.

The Doctrine of Pressure and the Erosion of the Equality Principle

The traditional English doctrine of pressure further operated to the advantage of local creditors and undermined the equality principle.[81] Since the law had long required proof of an intent to prefer, case law recognized that a payment made under pressure could not be set aside. The law regarded a transfer made at the request of a creditor "as being induced not by a desire to defraud other creditors, but by a desire to satisfy a just demand." By acceding to the creditor's request, the debtor did not intend to prefer but rather sought to avoid the "coercive influence" of the threatened proceedings, "which will injure his business or affect his personal liability."[82] Making a payment to a creditor "under pressure" was simply inconsistent with the notion of paying the creditor voluntarily[83] or through an "exercise of free will."[84] If a creditor "presses and insists upon having a security for his debt, and the debtor yield[s] to that pressure, and give[s] the security," the transaction was "perfectly good and valid," even though the effect of the transaction was to give the particular creditor a preference and defeated and delayed all other creditors.[85] Pressure simply relieved the transaction from "any taint of illegality" and made the transaction valid. At the heart of the doctrine of pressure lay a fundamental, yet doubtful proposition: an active creditor who secured payment at the moment of the debtor's financial difficulty was a "highly meritorious personage." The incessant application of the doctrine of pressure had implications for distant creditors who failed to arrive in time to apply their own pressure. Pressure allowed one creditor to "aggrandize himself at the expense of others."[86]

From the outset, many Canadian courts upheld the doctrine of pressure, holding that the conveyance was not voluntary where the creditor "requested and pressed" the debtor to make the payment.[87] While it was "impossible to declare the minimum of language or of conduct on the part of a creditor"[88] to establish pressure, the case law nevertheless established a minimal threshold. The doctrine did not require a creditor to initiate legal proceedings. In other words, a "mere demand or request, even without suit, would be sufficient to protect the transaction from the stain of a fraudulent preference."[89] Thus a refusal to ship goods might also constitute pressure. Pressure might also arise from the ordinary attempts of the debtor to make payments on an overdue account to a supplier of goods.[90] Where a creditor "incessantly" pressed for an assignment of accounts, the transaction was held to be valid, as the assignment "did not originate with, nor was it voluntary on the part of" the debtor. Here the debtor entered into the assignment only "reluctantly, and only on the solicitation importunity and pressure of" the creditor.[91] Given the wide scope of what constituted pressure, a creditor could "under almost any circumstances obtain, and then uphold, security for his debt."[92] In some instances a creditor went beyond a mere demand. A bank's demand for a chattel mortgage combined with a threat to have the debtor arrested for illegally obtaining money on a bill of exchange was sufficient to establish pressure.[93]

In *Campbell v Barrie*, Barrie, the creditor, lived twenty miles from the debtor, Chalmers. Barrie wrote to Chalmers asking for a meeting: "SIR, As you have not been to Perth for some time, I wish you would call and arrange matters first time you are in." The parties eventually entered into a mortgage transaction in favour of Barrie. When one of Chalmers' other creditors forced Chalmers into bankruptcy, the Official Assignee sought to set aside the mortgage as an unjust preference. The court allowed the mortgage to stand, since it had been entered into under pressure. What mattered for the court was the fact that Barrie "wrote to [Chalmers] to call and arrange matters." As a matter of law, Barrie's request "took away from the debtor his perfect freedom of mind and of action," and thus it was not a voluntary transaction.[94]

Even where a court recognized that the application of pressure resulted in a creditor obtaining a preference over other creditors, it still applied the doctrine, with one judge noting, "I cannot avoid it." In 1876, an Ontario court was of the view that the doctrine was so entrenched that "if deemed unsound, can only be got rid of by a decision of the Ontario Court of Appeal, or Act of the Legislature."[95] In that year, the Upper Canada Court of Error and Appeal court (hearing appeals from Chancery Court) sought to overturn the doctrine of pressure in *Davidson v Ross*.

Davidson was a clear attempt to discredit the doctrine of pressure. Justice Burton concluded that on bankruptcy the property of the bankrupt was for all the creditors. Thus when a debtor is unable to pay all his creditors in full, a payment "in full to one creditor ... is an unjust preference of him over the others."[96] Justice Patterson reasoned that pressure, therefore, was inconsistent with the broader purpose of bankruptcy law: "The policy of the insolvent law, being to secure the just and ratable distribution of the assets among the creditors of the insolvent, is opposed to the doctrine that one creditor, by pressure which may consist of mere importunity or even of a request which does not amount to importunity, can secure to himself an unequal share."[97] The decision was significant in that it shifted the interpretation of the preference provisions to an effect-based regime rather than intention-based test.[98] A payment could be set aside if it had the effect of preferring a creditor regardless of the debtor's intention and irrespective of pressure. It was an unjust preference, whether "it springs from the debtor's mere volition or is procured by importunity of the creditor, if it has the effect of preventing a ratable distribution."[99] The court in *Davidson* concluded that the Canadian regime did not require proof of intent, and all that mattered was whether the creditor in fact received a preference.[100] This interpretation swept "away the notion of fraudulent intent as an ingredient of unjust preference, and with it the whole foundation of the doctrine of pressure."[101]

In a subsequent decision of the Ontario Court of Chancery, Vice Chancellor Blake endorsed *Davidson*. The *Davidson* decision would "close many of the avenues whereby creditors ... escaped with large portions of their debtor's assets which now must be disposed of rat-ably."[102] The *Monetary Times* claimed that those who had relied upon pressure as a settled doctrine "will experience a rude awakening on learning the effect" of *Davidson v Ross*. The paper claimed that the judgment was so clear that "it must be taken to sweep away the last vestige of the old doctrine."[103]

Although *Davidson v Ross* made the task of the Official Assignee much easier, the optimism expressed by Vice Chancellor Blake was misplaced. The Ontario Court of Appeal did not further expand *Davidson v Ross* and continued to issue decisions that upheld preferential transactions.[104] In *Smith v Hutchinson*, the Court of Appeal concluded that the payments in question were not "obnoxious either to the letter or to the spirit of the insolvency law."[105] Notwithstanding *Davidson v Ross*, decisions continued to focus on the intent of the debtor. A number of courts, in upholding payments to creditors, failed to find that the Official Assignee had met the burden of proving that the transaction was made in contemplation of insolvency.[106] A court "endeavoured" to apply *Davidson v Ross* but could not find that the "transactions have been successfully impeached." A case involving a preferential transaction was re-heard on the basis that *Davidson v Ross* might govern the appeal. The court concluded that the arrangement entered into by the debtor and creditor enabled the debtor to carry on business. "As the transaction was a *bona fide* one intended to aid a debtor in discharging his liabilities, and to enable him to carry on his business," the case did not fall within *Davidson v Ross*. One commentator speculated that had the *Insolvent Act* remained in force, *Davidson v Ross* "would, sooner or later, have been overruled."[107] Given the repeal of the *Insolvent Act of 1875*, the courts were not given the opportunity to review the validity of the ruling under that statute. However, with repeal, the principle of *Davidson v Ross* was called into question.

In 1882, within two years of repeal of the *Insolvent Act of 1875*, the Ontario Court of Chancery resurrected the doctrine of pressure as it applied to provincial preference legislation. In interpreting the Ontario provincial preference legislation, the court concluded that the "so-called doctrine of pressure now occupies the same position as it did" before the passing of the *Insolvent Act of 1875*. That same year, the

Ontario Court of Appeal conceded that a transaction might be taken outside the scope of the Act "in consequence of *bona fide* pressure on the part of the creditor."[108] By 1883 the Supreme Court of Canada overturned *Davidson v Ross*. Strong J in *McCrae v White* noted that *Davidson v Ross* was in direct conflict with a line of English authorities "extending back for more than 100 years." Strong J was not able to see how "it can be said that a creditor, who obtains payment ... as the direct result of ... pressure ... has obtained an unjust preference." *Davidson v Ross* carried to its logical conclusion simply meant that "no single creditor could obtain by means of pressure an actual payment ... without being liable to account to the other creditors." Such a "proposition ... has never yet been either embodied in a statutory form or propounded by judicial decision."[109] In subsequent decisions in 1885, 1890, and 1891 the Supreme Court of Canada continued to apply the doctrine of pressure under the provincial preference legislation. Coming full circle to the early cases that interpreted the *Insolvent Acts*, the Supreme Court concluded that a preference meant "a voluntary act on the part of the debtor."[110]

The doctrine of pressure had serious implications for both debtors and creditors. From the debtor's perspective, pressure sanctioned "pushing a debtor to the wall" and converted what might have been a temporary setback into "irretrievable insolvency," enabling a more assertive or aggressive creditor to collect on debts before others. The doctrine rewarded those creditors who were closely connected to the debtor, such as relatives or local creditors. These creditors were well placed to have knowledge of the debtor's demise before distant creditors. One author writing in the *Canada Law Journal* noted the unfairness of the doctrine of pressure. The ability of a creditor to obtain payment "by importuning his debtor depends largely upon mere accidents of locality ... A creditor who lives in the same town as his debtor is in a much more favourable situation for discerning the signs of approaching failure than one who lives at a distance. Upon foreign creditors, in particular, the doctrine of pressure weighs very hardly."[111]

The commercial press and Canadian Boards of Trade representing commercial interests trading at a distance opposed the doctrine of pressure. The application of the doctrine of pressure in one case prompted a Board of Trade to seek changes to the legislation. A court upheld a mortgage given by a debtor after the bank had pressed the debtor. The court held that the mortgage was valid, as the debtor entered into the transaction under pressure. The Board of Trade asked its delegates to bring the issue of pressure before the Dominion Board of Trade and "endeavour to have the law so worded that no creditor getting a mortgage under pressure " shall have a preference over creditors."[112]

Courts were important institutions that shaped the bankruptcy law debates. With all but *Davidson v Ross* upholding the doctrine of pressure and other courts simply interpreting the legislation in favour of the recipient creditor, local creditors achieved an extraordinary advantage under the bankruptcy statute. This factor, among others, raised the ire of creditors trading at a distance and in part contributed to the unpopularity of the legislation. Interest groups representing creditors who traded at a distance sought reforms to the legislation, and by the end of the 1870s they became engaged in a battle to prevent repeal.

5. Interest Groups

The conflict between local and distant creditors, which arose in most bankruptcy cases, translated into interest group lobbying efforts in Ottawa for reform, retention or repeal of the law. Speeches in Parliament illustrated a concern about the effect of bankruptcy law's demise on inter-provincial trade. In the House of Commons, a Member of Parliament suggested that it was not uncommon for merchants in Ontario and Quebec to send goods to the "distant provinces" in the west and east. If repeal was to occur and the common law system restored, "the local creditors would lay hold of the estate and creditors at a distance would be placed at a great disadvantage." Removing the *pro rata* distribution would mean "a serious blow would be struck at all credit, and injury would be inflicted on the people of the distant provinces and the commercial community as a whole."[113]

A Member from Cape Breton claimed that repeal "would prevent creditors living at a distance getting their share of the assets." He stated that efforts to increase inter-provincial trade would fail, "for no merchant in the West would give credit to a trader in the Maritime Provinces, or *vice versa* unless their interests were protected." Similarly, a Member from Quebec reminded his colleagues that Montreal merchants had advanced goods and credit goods "all over the Dominion." If bankruptcy law was repealed, "the nearest creditor would take out judgment and the estate would be fastened up until the demands satisfied."[114]

An 1877 publication also defended bankruptcy law on similar terms, noting that Canadian commerce had grown and encompassed Prince Edward Island, British Columbia and Manitoba. The author asked how creditors would protect themselves against local creditors without a bankruptcy law. The common law maxim of "first come, first served" always prejudiced distant creditors. If Parliament abolished the bankruptcy regime, creditors would be forced to pursue each debt to judgment. Further, abolition would force creditors to terminate much of their business in other provinces. The advantage of bankruptcy law was that it put everyone on the same footing and it did not permit unjust preferences to the detriment of all.[115]

The various Canadian Boards of Trade of the individual cities represented the merchants of these larger commercial centres. Throughout the 1870s these individual Boards sought to retain the federal bankruptcy legislation. Their efforts bear comparison to the developments in the United States. In the American context, one study argues that renewed demands for federal legislation in the late nineteenth century arose in response to a growth of inter-state trade and an increase in the number of creditors who experienced the problems of diverse state legislation. In the United States, the relative cost of seeking legislation declined as new national interest groups emerged to lobby for change.[116]

In 1869, the Montreal Board of Trade recognized that an insolvency regime was more effective than "the procedure authorized by the Common Law." However, the body also believed that the insolvency regime could be improved to ensure that fraud was punished "as a crime."[117] Throughout the 1870s, Boards of Trade kept in close contact with the Ministry of Justice over reform efforts,[118] for they feared repeal of the bankruptcy regime, as it would mean a return to the common law race to the debtor's assets. The Toronto Board of Trade wrote to Prime Minister Macdonald informing him that the Board was "unanimously of opinion" that repeal would be "most disastrous to business interests of the country." Boards of Trade had some success in delaying repeal throughout the 1870s. In 1872, the Montreal Board of Trade described the consequence of repeal of the *Insolvent Act*. The law would revert to the common law when the estate of an insolvent debtor could be reached only by an ordinary lawsuit, involving separate action by each creditor. This involved law costs and sheriff fees, "on the back of each creditor." Further, the debtor would "in many instances" make preferences "in favour of a portion of his creditors."[119] The Toronto and Montreal Boards of Trade convinced the Senate to block repeal in 1872.[120]

In 1873 and 1874, Boards of Trade persuaded the government to extend the 1869 Act rather than to allow it to expire.[121] Parliament delayed or withdrew repeal bills in 1877 in response to the efforts of the Montreal Board of Trade that urged amendment rather than repeal.[122]

The banking community also sought to retain a national law.[123] A representative from the Imperial Bank of Canada wrote to Macdonald and warned that if the *Insolvent Act* were to be repealed, "the present Government will be held responsible for all the evil effects."[124]

While these regional interest groups had some success in the 1870s, there was no unified national organization committed to lobbying Parliament to prevent repeal. The one national group that did emerge during this period, the Dominion Board of Trade (DBT), was itself divided over the merits of bankruptcy law. The DBT, which came into prominence during the 1870s, offered local Boards of Trade a national voice. The Board met in the parliamentary buildings to ensure access to Cabinet ministers, who routinely attended DBT meetings. The DBT clearly saw itself as a policy-generating body: "Of course our Commercial Parliament, as some have been pleased to call it, is purely suggestive or recommendatory but we seek to bring our views to bear on the government by respectfully placing before the Ministers the resolutions of the Board."[125]

The aim of the DBT was to "secure unity and harmony of action, in reference to commercial usages, customs and laws." In particular, the DBT wanted to ensure that there was a "united opinion" in the commercial community to ensure that Parliament would carefully consider financial and commercial matters. A review of the votes taken at the annual DBT meetings indicates that there were major divisions within the organization on the subject of bankruptcy law. As early as 1872, the DBT passed a resolution that concluded the *Insolvent Act of 1869* had been advantageous, and yet the DBT divided nineteen to thirteen over the issue.[126] Minutes of the 1873 meeting include a circular published by the Montreal Board of Trade that called for "united action of the mercantile community ... throughout the Dominion, for the continuance of the *Insolvent Act of 1869*."[127] By 1877, the debate over bankruptcy law included one member of the DBT seeking repeal.[128] In 1878, a Special Committee of the DBT divided on the issue of repeal. The Halifax, Ottawa and Levis Boards of Trade instructed their representatives on the Special Committee to vote for repeal. In the end, the DBT recommended that the Act be retained. Fears of return to the common law may have ultimately swung the vote in favour of continuance, as without bankruptcy legislation, "creditors living nearest to the debtor would have an advantage over those at a distance."[129]

In 1879, the DBT issued a comprehensive report recommending several amendments to the Act. However, two members of the special committee signed a separate statement indicating that if the amendments were not accepted, they would prefer repeal. Many members of the DBT spoke in favour of repeal, with some pointing to the example of the American repeal of the *Bankruptcy Act of 1867*[130] in 1878. A motion supporting repeal of the *Insolvent Act of 1875* was defeated by a ten-to-nine vote in the DBT meeting, foreshadowing the bitter debate that was to follow in the House of Commons.[131]

One of the most important votes took place in 1879. Members of the House of Commons rejected the *Insolvent Bill of 1879* and instead voted in favour of repeal. Faced with the House of Commons vote in favour of repeal, supporters of bankruptcy law in the Senate mounted an aggressive campaign to prevent the law's demise. A Senator tabled a petition that demanded the retention of the law: "The large cities of the Dominion, Montreal, and Quebec, St John, Toronto, Halifax and many others have large transactions beyond the mere province in which they are situated, and when the merchants of those cities go outside their own provinces they require a general law to regulate insolvency or bankruptcy, in order to make their transaction reasonably safe. If this Act is swept away they become subject to the local laws of the general provinces."[132] The Senate blocked repeal in 1879, but that action did nothing to delay the law's ultimate repeal the following year. In 1879, one Member of Parliament noted that the "vote in favour of the continuance of the Insolvent Law represented the great commercial thought to this country." The fact that Members of "almost every great commercial centre in the country voted in one direction" demonstrated that the "large preponderance of the commercial sentiment ... [is] in favour of the continuance of the Insolvent Law." Commercial interests lobbied Members of Parliament to retain the law. Members in the House received telegrams from Boards of Trade in Quebec, Hamilton and Toronto.[133]

In the end, divisions within the commercial community hampered the campaign to retain the federal law. A truly national and united commercial organization that was committed to national bankruptcy reform did not emerge until 1913.[134]

6. Conclusion

Ideas, interests and institutions led to the repeal of the federal bankruptcy legislation in 1880. The public and politicians divided over the key ideas underlying bankruptcy policy. The equitable distribution of assets provided the focal point of much of the public discourse. Equality competed unsuccessfully with the idea that debtors were entitled to arrange their affairs with local or family creditors. Debtors preferred local and family creditors at the expense of distant creditors and so, notwithstanding the existence of a bankruptcy regime, in practice debtors created what was in essence a scramble for assets. These unchallenged preferential transactions led to the unpopularity of the *Insolvent Acts*. Equality also had a fragile meaning from a judicial point of view. Courts interpreted the preference provisions in a way that favoured the preferred creditor, rendering ineffective one of the important tools available to the Assignee to uphold equality. The DBT and other urban Boards of Trade also represented prominent interests in the bankruptcy law debates. Commercial interests required a national bankruptcy law to protect distant creditors engaged in inter-provincial trade; ultimately, however, the DBT divided on the bankruptcy question and did not have sufficient influence to prevent repeal.

4

The Repeal of Bankruptcy Law 1867–1880: The Discharge

I think, beyond doubt that Titterington was on the 30th May [1878] hopelessly insolvent. He had been speculating largely in the Chicago produce market with the usual result, and although he may have cherished a visionary hope that fortune's wheel might yet turn in his favour, his real prospects were worse than those of a gambler making his last throw.

Morton v Nihan (1880), 5 OAR 20, pp. 24–5, Moss CJA

By 1874, Julius McCarty had established himself as Hamilton's largest lumber merchant, and his success extended to the political field. McCarty had been elected Alderman for the St Mary's ward. However, his accomplishments and reputation vanished overnight. The city "was startled" to read the headline "Hamilton: A Lumber Merchant Absconded – His Liabilities $150,000."[1] Rather than remaining in Hamilton to take advantage of recent bankruptcy legislation, McCarty "levanted,"[2] leaving numerous creditors unpaid. Facing the shame of the bankruptcy was not an option. On leaving Hamilton, McCarty left behind a letter telling his family that he had "left for good" and that he was a "ruined man." Once creditors examined their accounts, it became apparent that a bank and a man from nearby Waterdown were the "heaviest losers" in the McCarty affair. Witnesses last saw McCarty at the Hamilton train station leaving for the United States. After his departure, creditors discovered that McCarty had used what little money he had to "cover any of his friends who may have endorsed paper for him."[3] McCarty had simply paid off friends before other creditors.

McCarty's story was not unique in 1867–80. Even though Parliament had implemented a bankruptcy regime that offered prospects for a discharge, debtors often sought refuge outside of Canada rather than carry on as a "ruined man."[4] A bankruptcy law that provided for a discharge could be effective only where debtors and creditors accepted the very premise of forgiveness of debts. Absconding debtors underscored the fragile meaning of the discharge and contributed to the unpopularity of bankruptcy legislation. The McCarty affair also demonstrates that the legislative attempt to deal with creditors equitably could be undermined by the debtor. Payments to friendly creditors, before a debtor departed for the border, made a mockery of the bankruptcy principle of equal treatment of creditors. An absconding debtor, dissipating assets and leaving nothing to distribute, raised the important question of whether there should be a bankruptcy law at all.

The bankruptcy law discharge was one of the most contentious aspects of the legislation, and two distinct ideas were evident. On the one hand, it was unjust to burden the debtor with the shackles of debt for life. On the other hand, bankruptcy law interfered with the debtor's higher moral duty to repay all debts. Notions of forgiveness competed unsuccessfully with the idea that all debts had to be honoured. This chapter seeks to explain why repeal triumphed by examining the debate over the discharge.[5] Section 1 sets out the legislative context of the *Insolvent Act of 1869* and *1875*. Section 2 examines the arguments in favour of the discharge that were based on notions of forgiveness. Section 3 considers the arguments against the discharge. In the 1870s the idea that a debtor had an obligation to pay all debts without a discharge had a strong following. Section 4 examines the role of the farmers as an important interest group lobby, for they were not subject to the bankruptcy statute and they sought repeal on the basis that merchants could obtain a discharge, whereas the agricultural sector could not. Finally, section 5 discusses the role of the courts in interpreting the bankruptcy legislation. The courts' liberal interpretation of the legislation contributed to the unpopularity of the legislation.

1. The Legislative Framework

The judgment of *Cameron v Holland* explained that "the discharge absolutely frees and discharges [the bankrupt] from all liabilities whatsoever existing against him, and proveable against his estate."[6] However, the discharge provisions of the *Insolvent Act of 1869* illustrated society's deep mistrust of debtors. The *Insolvent Acts* did not apply to all debtors. The Acts of 1869 and 1875 only permitted traders to have access to the legislation. As Hargarty CJ noted in *Harman v Clarkson,* "Whoever is included in the term 'trader'... is within the Insolvent Law. No one else can be." By restricting the application of the Act to traders, Parliament limited the availability of the discharge to a narrow class of debtors. The Act gave "no definition or explanation" of the term *trader*, leaving the courts to work their way through the confused state of English jurisprudence.[7] A *trader* had been traditionally defined as a person "seeking to gain his living by buying and selling."[8] However, the few cases that interpreted the meaning of *trader* under the *Insolvent Act of 1869* were inconsistent and somewhat arbitrary. While the 1869 Act did not contain a definition of *trader*, the 1875 Act explicitly excluded a "farmer ... common labourer or workman for hire."[9] Therefore, a large segment of the Canadian working population was left outside the scope of the *Insolvent Acts.*

In order to obtain a discharge and be released "from all liabilities whatsoever,"[10] the debtor had to obtain consent from creditors representing a majority in number and three-quarters of the value of the debtor's liabilities.[11] However, before taking effect, the discharge had to be approved at a court hearing where dissenting creditors could appear and object to the confirmation of the discharge. Grounds of opposition included "[f]raud or fraudulent preference ... fraud or evil practice in procuring the consent of the creditors to the discharge ... fraudulent retention and concealment by the Insolvent of some portion of his estate."[12]

Even if creditors could not establish a proper ground, the court still retained discretion under section 103 to suspend the discharge for up to five years or issue a second-class discharge. Both a first- and second-class discharge released a bankrupt from his debts. However, the classification of discharges represented an official statement about the moral trustworthiness of a debtor.

Courts awarded a first-class discharge where the bankruptcy had arisen from unavoidable loss or misfortune.[13] The court granted second-class discharges when "the Insolvent has been guilty of misconduct in the management of his business, by extravagance in his expenses, recklessness in endorsing or becoming surety for others, continuing his trade unduly after he believed himself to be insolvent, incurring debts without a reasonable expectation of paying them ... or negligence in keeping his books and accounts."[14] This classification system had its origins in English law, which issued first-, second-, and third-class discharges between 1849 and 1861.[15]

James Edgar, author of an annotated text on the 1869 Act, noted that under the English statute a "certain stigma was deservedly attached" to a third-class certificate. (Canadian legislation provided for either a first- or second-class discharge.) In contrast, a first-class certificate "was justly prized by its possessor as a passport by which he might again enter into business with an untarnished reputation for honesty at least." John Popham, author of the competing text on the 1869 Act, offered a rationale for the class system: "It would seem but just there should be a distinction between the discharge given to an insolvent whose losses were unavoidable, and whose dealings were honourable; and that to another whose conduct bordered on recklessness or fraud, though insufficiently so to warrant a refusal of his discharge."[16] The classification of the discharge replicated ideas about debtors in the marketplace. Debtors failed through either misfortune or fraud.

Creditor consent was not always possible, and the Act provided a separate route to the discharge. After one year, debtors could apply for a judicial discharge. The one-year delay was considered a form of statutory punishment for the bankruptcy. However, creditors could effectively block this alternative route. A majority of the creditors representing three-quarters of the claims could apply to the court requesting suspension, or classification, or both. The court did not have any independent discretion on this issue and had to follow the direction of the creditors.[17]

The *Insolvent Act of 1875*, which permitted only involuntary bankruptcies, further restricted access to the discharge. One author saw "the increased stringency" of the discharge provisions as an improvement over the *Insolvent Act of 1869*. The Act of 1875 also required creditors to consent to a discharge and provided for second-class discharges, but the provisions made the discharge more difficult to obtain.[18]

Under the newly added section 58, a judge had the discretion to suspend or refuse the discharge altogether if it appeared that the dividend from the estate would not pay at least thirty-three cents on the dollar. Drawing on the concept that individuals should be responsible for the payment of their debts, "Anyone whose estate could not pay 33 cents in the dollar, who had not been overtaken by some unexpected calamity, had no right to be whitewashed or to receive credit again."[19]

The new provision, in the opinion of one commentator, "discouraged debtors from this immoral waste of other people's property." Previously there was no obstacle that prevented a debtor from obtaining a discharge when his assets were "utterly out of proportion to his liabilities." The Act of 1869 did not provide a debtor with any incentive to stop trading "in the earlier stages of his difficulties, so that his creditors might receive a productive estate to wind up."[20]

A judgment in a Wentworth County court file illustrates the rationale for the section 58 amendment. The county court judge believed that the "floodgates of dishonesty and fraud ... had been opened by the statutes of 1864 and 1869." The law was in such a state that it became the "rule and not the exception for an estate not to have anything [for] creditors." The ease with which debtors obtained a discharge induced "reckless trading and dishonest practices." Creditors sought some "barrier" that might be imposed against "the constant stream of discharges which were constantly passing through the courts to the injury of trade." Section 58 of the Act of 1875 "was the first to stop the current of commercial depravity." This was followed by a "more stringent provision in the same statute" in 1877.[21]

Notwithstanding the intent of the drafters, the thirty-three-cents-on-the-dollar test was ineffective, as courts refused to exercise their discretion and deny a discharge when the debtor's assets did not meet the minimum level. The *Journal of Commerce* reported in 1877 that it was "only in a vast minority of instances" where the Court was called upon to exercise its jurisdiction to refuse a discharge when the thirty-three-cent test was not met. Critics pointed to the discretionary power of the judge being exercised in a "compassionate spirit." The reality was that without a voluntary procedure, debtors continued to trade long after becoming insolvent. As a result, when a creditor finally forced a debtor into bankruptcy, the dividend rarely reached the thirty-three-cent level.[22] In 1877, Parliament amended the Act and imposed a requirement of a dividend level of fifty cents on the dollar before a debtor could obtain a discharge.[23]

The amendments did little to stop the flow of criticism. Some even objected to the provision, as it did not require debtors to pay all of their debts.[24] Others objected to the provision, as it interfered with the creditors' ability to set their own level of acceptable dividend: "Law has no right to dictate on this point that an insolvent should pay 10c, 25c, 33c, 50c, or 75c, on the dollar in order to obtain a discharge ... Law cannot and ought not to go into details on a point like this. It can only deal with broad principles. Every man must judge for himself in details and take the consequences of his folly or wisdom."[25]

When the Conservatives returned to power in 1878, they were uncertain how to proceed, as it became clear that their own party could not reach a consensus with the Liberals on whether to retain or repeal the legislation. In 1879, the Conservatives established a committee to study bankruptcy law.[26] The committee produced Bill 85, which would have made the discharge nearly impossible to obtain.[27] By the time Parliament appointed the 1879 Select Committee on Bankruptcy, the repeal option began to overwhelm reform options. The Committee's bill was a compromise that purported to appeal to the "repealers ... and [to] the champions of insolvency law and insolvency principles": "They had stripped the old Act of its evil as thoroughly as if they had repealed it, and had furnished the commercial community with what they did desire – a law by which the creditors might possess themselves of an insolvent's estate and fairly divide among themselves its proceeds."[28]

The Committee listed several evils associated with the bankruptcy regime, which had given rise to recklessness and extravagance in trade. Rather than inducing men to extricate themselves from financial difficulties through hard work, the *Insolvent Act of 1875* was available as an "easy process of starting anew in life, free from the load of debt." The Committee specifically intended to "diminish the facilities now possessed by a debtor for obtaining a discharge." In addition, it sought to increase the grounds of opposition to the discharge and to extend and increase the "precautions for ascertaining the conduct of the insolvent."[29]

The Committee's bill "struck the axe at the root of that evil" by requiring a debtor to obtain the consent of creditors representing four-fifths in number and four-fifths in value in order to obtain a discharge. Such a provision would have made it "impossible for [a debtor] to obtain his discharge as a matter of right, under any circumstances whatever, from the obligations he had voluntarily assumed." One Member of Parliament believed that under the four-fifths formula a debtor would "remain forever" the "victim" of creditors "incapable of becoming again a useful member of society, or of embarking in any enterprise whatever."[30] These proposed radical amendments did not satisfy the repeal camp. Bill 85 never became law; instead, Parliament opted to repeal the *Insolvent Act of 1875* in 1880,[31] and in the end, the shift from a four-fifths formula to repeal was an easy one for Parliament to make.

2. Forgiveness of Debt and the Discharge

Many believed that debts should be forgiven, as it was unjust to burden the debtor with the shackles of debt for life. One Member of Parliament claimed that "when a man made a clean breast of his affairs, and gave his estate honestly for the benefit of his creditors, he ought to have relief." Edward Blake argued that the discharge was "a wholesome provision which might be defended upon general principles." For another Member, the law's "first and principal object was the relief of the honest and unfortunate debtor." Even the modern terminology of "fresh start" found its way into the nineteenth-century debates.[32]

In a direct challenge to the idea that debtors failed through moral weakness, Members of Parliament argued that honest but unfortunate debtors deserved a discharge.[33] John Abbott claimed that the majority of debtors were honest. He asked, "[W]hy should a man who had been overwhelmed by a sudden depreciation in the value of produce – of pork, flour, butter ... or by the wreck of a ship containing his goods" be deprived of a discharge? Others argued that a man who fell into debt "through sickness or any other mishap ... should have the same means of getting free ... Why should he have no means of escape?"[34]

However, for nineteenth-century Parliamentarians, liberty was the central feature of the discharge, as one Letter to the Editor of the *Journal of Commerce* indicates: "Law ought to prevent the exercise of oppression and grant liberty to all to exercise their faculties so long as they do not interfere with the like liberty in others, therefore, it should protect the honest debtor who has been unfortunate, even though he be so through folly or bad judgment, and prevent his creditor from oppressing him."[35]

Debtors should not be kept "in a state of partial slavery." A discharge was a means to release debtors from their "shackles" and to prevent creditor "harassment."[36] No man should have "a mill stone around his neck" forever. However, it was more than just personal liberty that was at stake. The debtor was of no use to his community in a state of perpetual debt.[37] It was society that demanded a release of debts in order that the debtor could "become a larger contributor to the national wealth." The right of discharge did not belong, therefore, to the "poor debtor," but rather it was in the "public interest." The lack of discharge, therefore, had an economic impact. If there was no discharge, debtors who wished to remain in Canada would be forever dependent upon the will of creditors.[38]

There was another option. Debtors burdened with debts could leave the country.[39] One Member of Parliament claimed that if a debtor could not obtain his discharge in Canada, "he would follow his 500,000 fellow Canadians to the United States." Another referred to the lack of bankruptcy law in Ontario prior to Confederation, noting that "many useful members of society ... were obliged to leave the country, for judgments piled up one after another." Canadian debtors built up American industry, while the Canadian economy suffered.[40]

Nevertheless, the enactment of a national bankruptcy Act did not completely end the problem of fleeing debtors.[41] Given the negative connotations of financial failure and the possibility of receiving the official stigma of a second-class discharge, it is not surprising that debtors continued to leave Canada.[42] The Minister of Justice, Edward Blake, acknowledged in 1877 that some debtors continued to abscond to the United States; however, he claimed the problem was not as great with a bankruptcy statute. With a bankruptcy Act, debtors had a "hope of settlement," while without a bankruptcy discharge debtors "had no hope."[43] However, as the evidence below suggests, Blake's optimism was misguided.

Absconding was common, and the *Insolvent Acts* sought to specifically deal with the problem. Where a debtor engaged in one of the listed forms of misconduct under the 1869 Act, he "was deemed insolvent" and his estate was subject to compulsory liquidation.[44] The list included absconding or about to abscond "from any Province in Canada with intent to defraud any creditor,"[45] secreting or removing assets with the intent to defeat creditors and selling the main part of stock in trade without the consent of creditors.[46] Proof of one of these acts enabled a creditor to trigger an involuntary bankruptcy proceeding against the debtor. If the debtor did not file an assignment on his own but continued to trade or proceed with "the realization of his assets," the debtor's estate would "become subject to compulsory liquidation."[47] The Writ of Attachment that would issue under a compulsory liquidation empowered the Sheriff to seize the assets of the bankrupt.[48] The extent of the absconding problem can be measured by the number of creditors who sought to force their debtors into bankruptcy on the basis of an allegation of absconding.

Wentworth County records show that 8 per cent of debtors[49] fled the province rather than face the humiliation of bankruptcy.[50] Taking advantage of a relatively porous border, absconding debtors headed for destinations including Milwaukee, New York City, Lewiston and

Detroit.[51] While some debtors left with their families and their personal effects,[52] others left town as fast as they could, only to be joined by families later.[53] The shame of having to confront their families and the community with news of debt and default led debtors to flee. As noted in the introduction to this chapter, Julius McCarty chose to flee to the United States without his family rather than face the prospect of being known as a "ruined man."[54] S.L. Trumpeller, who fled to the United States, also felt shame. In a letter to his major creditor Trumpeller provided his motivation for his departure: "I cannot help myself out and ... can not stand to be dragged through the mire again so I [intend] to leave ... to pray you all go away."[55]

Absconding was not always a temporary solution for debtors; many debtors never intended to return to Canada. Evidence in county court files suggests that absconding was for some a permanent solution.[56] A sale of assets often signalled that the debtor did not intend to return. Debtors sold their goods or moved them beyond the reach of creditors before leaving. Simon Adams left for the United States, but before his departure he "sold, disposed of and removed large quantities of goods."[57] A few days before leaving, Adams was "selling ... his goods at almost any prices he could get for them" and offered to sell goods at half price to an acquaintance.[58] James Simpson, a creditor who had initiated proceedings against James Egan, swore in his affidavit, "Yesterday I went to the place where the said Defendant lately carried on business and was informed that he had sold out all his stock ... and had absconded from this Country and did not intend to come back."[59] The sale of stock by absconding debtors was such a problem that it led one court to warn creditors to "be more careful" in trusting debtors "with such very extensive stocks of goods."[60]

Leaving the shop unattended or unprotected was another sign that the debtor intended to leave for good. William Curry left Hamilton after selling assets but did little to protect his shop: "The store in which he recently carried on business in Hamilton presents every appearance of having been abandoned. The most valuable part of the stock having been removed and the store itself having been left open with no one in charge except a little girl who can give no satisfactory account of the defendant but states that she thinks he has gone away."[61]

Abandoning the personal residence also suggested that the debtor and his family had no interest in returning. Robert Yates of Wentworth County left his personal abode unoccupied, and it remained that way until the Official Assignee seized it.[62] Putting household furniture and effects up for sale similarly signalled that the debtor would remain out of the province. In one Wentworth County file, the auction notice was entitled "Extensive Auction of Elegant Household Furniture," which included the "contents of five bedrooms ... kitchen utensils," a rosewood piano and a family sewing machine. The auction notice concluded with a note that the listed items were "the property of a lady leaving the city."[63] Leaving with horses and carriage and clothes left "no intimation" about the debtor's return.[64] As debtors continued to abscond, there was recognition that if there was no bankruptcy statute in place, the problem would only be exacerbated. Without a bankruptcy statute in Canada, "the certain destiny of all who had any spirit or enterprise"[65] was the United States. Notwithstanding this reality, many continued to oppose the very notion of the discharge and called for repeal of the bankruptcy statute.

3. Opposition to the Discharge and the Moral Obligation to Pay

Opponents of the discharge appealed to the necessity of maintaining high business morals. Bankruptcy law did not encourage ethical standards as it created opportunities for fraud. The legislation "was now inflicting great damage on commercial men." "It had become so demoralising" that debtors could not operate a business without adopting "this mode of getting rid of their liabilities." Alexander Mackenzie, the leader of the Opposition, argued that the law "had been found eminently conducive to public immorality." Another Member of Parliament concluded that bankruptcy law "was conceived in sin, and whose fruits had been iniquity from first to last." Bankruptcy law impaired a sense of responsibility and rewarded debtors. It also caused commercial failure.[66]

The link between bankruptcy law and commercial immorality was derived from the fundamental principle that "he who owed should pay": "It was of the highest importance that we should admit the obligation of every man to pay the debts which he had legally incurred; that principle must rest at the very foundation of every well regulated and well governed community ... Any law of a general character which tended to impair that obligation ... was an unsound and impolitic law, and ought not to be enacted by any Parliament."[67]

Debts were governed, therefore, by more than a formal legal contract.[68] In Parliament many stood to defend the principle that debts should be repaid, as "[t]he very principle of the law was immoral."

Bankruptcy laws were "an unmitigated nuisance, a school of immorality and rascality." People should simply understand that "when they contracted debt they should be strictly held to the payment thereof." Every "law was unjust which did not force a man to carry out a contract." All men "should be made to feel the responsibility of their obligations, and not to be allowed to fall back upon the Insolvency Law." One Senator claimed, "Everyman should meet his obligations, and if there was any other principle preferable to that he would like to know it."[69] In the *Canadian Monthly*, an 1873 article claimed that "the creditor shall have the utmost farthing the debtor can pay." According to the *Monetary Times*, the principle that debts should be repaid was a higher law "which no man can annul." Founded upon an ethical obligation, the statute "could not dispense [the debtor's] conscience ... from paying his debts."[70]

For some,the bankruptcy discharge was a crime and an evil. The legislature was not justified in intervening in the contractual relationship between sellers and buyers by forcing the seller to give the buyer a discharge of a "just debt." Such intervention amounted to "legalized robbery." It was an act of "criminality" to put oneself "in the position of being unable to fulfill one's pecuniary promises." It was "legalized fraud" for a debtor to go through the "whitewashing" and come out better than before. The law protected the dishonest debtor while "he laughs in his sleeves at the misfortune of the man who was fool enough to trust in his honesty and fair dealing. It is this glaring evil which needs to be sternly met."[71] By 1878 the *Journal of Commerce* lamented the fact that "failure in business" was an "ordinary incident of everyday life."[72]

Creditors failed to see a reason to support bankruptcy legislation where their debtor had engaged in misconduct and they were left without a remedy. The firm of Dickie and Kennedy, suppliers of hoe broadcast seeders and drill and horse rakes, wrote to McMichael and Hughson complaining of the debtor's conduct: "Is it not a sham for you to treat us in the manner you have done about our spokes. Do you not feel mean or are you being that lowest of points of human depravity that you take such things as a matter of course. Remember you are going to pay for all this yet, you may treat us shabbily as you possibly can but you will have to suffer ... Now in the name of common sense why did you call on us at all or make any promises if it was not your intention to fulfill same ... We will not write or telegraph again." An importer similarly complained to the Official Assignee of the estate of J. Taylor, "We have had to do with a great many Estates. This is the worst swindle we have had – Taylor instead of being the honest & culpable young man ... is either a fool or a Knave possibly both in either case the penitentiary would be a very appropriate residence for him. We expect to lose money in business but do not care to be robbed by a worthless creature like Taylor and his relatives."[73]

The other side of the moral equation did not go unnoticed. Anticipating arguments based on forgiveness, and the need to restore a debtor as a productive member of society, the *Monetary Times* questioned whether or not it was always wise to return a debtor to his community.[74] The fact that some debtors might flee to the United States "would be the best possible thing for themselves and the public." Some might leave the country, but this "would be no loss, for the country has lost by their living in it." Society was better off without debtors "who have wasted other men's substance" and who were "a moral contagion in mercantile life."[75]

The moral imperative that debts should be repaid had obvious consequences for the discharge.[76] The conflict between the responsibility to repay debts and the discharge led the *Monetary Times* to claim that "it does not seem, prima facie, as if a discharge were an essential part of the Insolvent Act at all ..." The legal discharge "may be properly struck out of the Act altogether."[77]

Attitudes towards bankruptcy and debt reflected a more general concern about character and morality in business dealings during the 1870s and beyond. Success in business depended upon strong character. In a lecture given by the Cashier of the Bank of Toronto to the students of the British American Commercial College in Toronto, George Hague included character as one of the qualities to be "cultivated by a young man entering a commercial office." Character could be subdivided into, among other things, honesty, truthfulness, and promptness. An article in the *Monetary Times* claimed that there "is something better than money, which all businessmen should aim to secure, and that is character."[78]

One historian, who has examined the "Myth of the Self Made Man," argues that nineteenth-century "philosophers of success" emphasized "hard work, charity, and discipline. He who was successful was he who had shaped a moral life."[79] The *Monetary Times* similarly noted, "Fair dealing is to be preferred ... 'Do unto others' ... is a sound business maxim as well an obligatory injunction of the moral code." An individual who pursued legitimate interests "based on high moral principles, combined with untiring industry and strict economy," would possess a "place of competency and business independence."[80]

Michael Bliss's study of attitudes of Canadian businessmen from 1883 to 1911 also reveals that the moral character of business relations continued beyond 1880. Bliss concludes that "there was not one favourable reference to the straightforward goal of making money." He found no statements "advocating materialism, greed, or concentration on getting wealthy." However, there was nothing wrong with accumulation as long as the right methods were used. Bliss argues that "industry, integrity, and frugality were still the qualities without which success in life was impossible."[81]

According to an 1882 work, other characteristics of success in business included "self help, industry and energy, determination and talent; and these were supplemented by first, a lively sense of personal honour; secondly, tact, and unfailing serenity of temper; and thirdly, the happy art of inspiring and retaining friendship."[82]

The other side of the coin saw "blanket condemnations of luxury and extravagance." The success ethic "had little or nothing to do with making money, [and] everything to do with the cultivation of moral character."[83]

If strong character ensured success, failure was attributed to some moral weakness of the debtor. Personal misconduct explained business failure rather than downturns in the economy or misfortune. Failure implied a moral flaw such as the debtor's reliance upon alcohol. Common causes of mercantile failure included extravagance or imprudent purchases of unneeded items, speculation, overtrading, and intemperance. One author claimed extravagance caused eighty per cent of failures.[84] Extravagance inevitably led to a dismal result: "Then follow the neglect of business; the accumulation of bills; the protesting of notes; the stoppage of credit, the loss of confidence; the meeting of creditors; the visit of the sheriff's officer; piano gone, carpets and curtains gone; the man broken-spirited, broken hearted, the morning that shone out so promising, already dark and beclouded. Then in too many instances, the bottle, – then the grave."[85]

Other commentators equally blamed rash speculation as a grave sin.[86] Businessmen, entrusted with credit for legitimate purposes, invested in speculative ventures, "bringing upon others loss, perhaps suffering, and stamping themselves for all time to come as dangerous men whom it would be unsafe to trust." Merchants who gained through speculation did not escape the stigma. Riches acquired through folly and on the failures of others was "akin to money gained by gambling."[87] Other vices linked to speculation included fraud and embezzlement.[88]

Nineteenth-century Canadian novels also reveal contemporary attitudes towards debt and bankruptcy. In *At His Gates*,[89] the author tells of newspaper headlines proclaiming "Great Bankruptcy in the City – Suicide of a Bank Director." The story reported on the "wickedness and folly of men who without capital, or even knowledge of business, thus ventured to play with the very existence of thousands of people." The account went on to ask, "Could the unfortunate man who has hidden his shame in a watery grave look up this morning from that turbid bed and see the many homes which he has filled with desolation ... all the ruined households and broken hearts?" According to the author, the stigma of bankruptcy would simply follow the debtor wherever he travelled. Even "the son of a bankrupt could do nothing." The wife of a debtor, when hearing the news of her husband's pending bankruptcy, wondered "how much shame should she have to bear."[90]

4. Rural Opposition to Bankruptcy Law and the Farmers' Interest

Although there was a clear distinction between the opponents and supporters of bankruptcy law, it is important to note that this was not a disinterested debate of two abstract ideals. One particular interest group, the farming community, and rural MPs intervened in the debate and seized upon the anti-bankruptcy rhetoric to further a private interest. This was an important interrelationship between ideals and interests. While the moral obligation to repay all debts became part of the public discourse, it is important to ask whether any underlying interests relied on the normative public debate to their advantage. Trebilcock and Kelley remind us that the public discourse may actually "disguise the true interests and ideas at play."[91] Farmers and rural areas represented a high proportion of the population in the 1870s.[92] However, what specifically raised the ire of the rural community was the trader rule that excluded farmers from the *Insolvent Acts*. This limitation allowed merchants to escape from their obligations through a bankruptcy discharge, while farmers were specifically excluded from the Act. As farmers could not obtain the benefits of the Act, i.e. the discharge, rural MPs turned against the legislation.

The trader rule was said to differentiate between commercial and non-commercial debts. Traders required a special law, as they were regularly exposed to risk. Non-traders who borrowed did so out of extravagance and not necessity.[93] However, such a rationale was not accepted by the farming community and rural MPs. During the debates some Members of Parliament declared that they represented rural constituencies, had campaigned against the bankruptcy statute and would vote in favour of repeal.[94]

The inequity of the Act's non-application to farmers was exacerbated in a typical exchange between a farmer and a trader. A farmer, who sold grain to a miller on credit, risked having his claim extinguished by the miller's bankruptcy. Further, if the miller's bankruptcy led to the farmer's financial ruin, the trader rule prohibited the farmer from obtaining a discharge under the Act. Farmers obtained no benefits under the Act but were required to bear the loss if any of their debtors made an assignment in bankruptcy.[95]

The exclusion of farmers from the Act was held up as an example of class legislation that discriminated against the rural sector. However, in pointing out the unfairness of the exclusion of farmers, opponents of the trader rule did not call for a bankruptcy law of general application: the solution to the discrimination was repeal. Abolition of bankruptcy law would place the trader and the farmer "on an equality."[96] The criticism of bankruptcy law as class legislation[97] became a call for repeal in another name, but the demand for repeal continued to be expressed in traditional terms: "[T]he Act was most unpopular in the rural districts ... In the rural districts, the people were clamorous for its repeal. They could not tolerate a law ... [that] allowed [a debtor] to avoid paying all his debts; in which discrimination was made between different classes of society ... [Farmers] could not support that discrimination, and were willing ... [to] return to the good sound principle which bound every man to pay his legitimate debts."[98]

A Member of Parliament stated in 1877, "The belief of the men in rural districts had been that it was a piece of dishonesty, a crime, a sin for a man not to pay his debts ... He knew of villages where men would scorn to owe anything, and think it a crime if they did not pay their debts."[99]

One account of the repeal debates of the 1870s, written in 1913, summarizes the opposition to the trader rule: "These objections were urged more especially by members representing rural constituencies. Repeatedly it was pointed out by such members that the majority of their constituents, farmers, mechanics, and professional men, received no benefit from the Act, though compelled to bear their share of the loss resultant."[100]

There was a further reason why the rural sector opposed bankruptcy law: one Member of Parliament, a self-described farmer and representative of "the agricultural class," claimed that the farmer, like everyone else, was "subject to the uncertainties of life." Storms and hail could destroy crops, disease could "carry off flocks" and lightning could destroy his buildings. The law, however, offered no relief for his debts, which was a "fatal discrimination that the law sanctioned." He indicated that he would vote for repeal.[101]

These seasonal variations placed farmers' crops at risk. Over the course of a season, a farmer might experience temporary insolvency. Farmers feared a law that would enable creditors to force farmers into bankruptcy during periods of temporary insolvency. Late nineteenth-century bankruptcy reform proposals continued to restrict proceedings to traders, thereby protecting farmers from involuntary proceedings.[102] The *Bankruptcy Act of 1919* would eventually include a provision that prohibited creditors from initiating bankruptcy proceedings against a farmer,[103] and this remains the law today.[104]

5. The Courts and the Pro-Debtor Interpretation of the Legislation

The courts were an important institution and influenced attitudes towards the bankruptcy statutes. The general pro-debtor judicial interpretation of the *Insolvent Acts* explains the unpopularity of the legislation.[105] The pro-debtor interpretation of the legislation is evident on a number of different fronts. First, the reported cases suggest that many judges adopted a liberal approach to the discharge. Second, although the courts had the jurisdiction to award second-class discharges, very few were granted. Third, a number of courts tolerated collusion between debtors and creditors of the same family to enable an involuntary filing to be initiated.[106]

Liberal Interpretation of the Discharge Provisions

Parliament passed the *Insolvent Act of 1875* in reaction to the perception that debtors easily obtained a discharge under the *Insolvent Act of 1869*. In 1875, Parliament abolished voluntary proceedings, making it possible only for creditors to force debtors into bankruptcy. Further, the 1875 Act raised a new threshold for discharge applications. By imposing a thirty-three-cents-on-the-dollar test, it was hoped that fewer low-asset bankruptcy discharges would be granted. By 1877, the threshold had been raised to fifty cents on the dollar. The tenor of the legislation in

1875 and the amending Act in 1877 suggests that too many bankrupts were receiving a discharge under the 1875 Act.

The leniency of the courts is illustrated in *Re Lamb, An Insolvent*. Hagarty J on appeal concluded that the judge below "considered the insolvent's conduct to be reprehensible in not keeping proper books of account ... I think the learned [trial] Judge acted with extreme leniency, and possibly took a milder view of the bankrupt's misconduct than I should have done, judging wholly from the papers before me." Hagarty J believed that the legislation had done everything to "favour debtors and render the escape from liability as easy as possible to them." He was also of the view that "the very easy requirements of the Insolvent Act ... should be peremptorily insisted on, and proper punishment awarded to any breach of the trader's duties in conducting his business."[107] Notwithstanding Hagarty J's strong sentiments, he allowed the decision of the trial judge to stand.

In *Cameron v Holland*, the court had to consider whether a discharge should be barred when the bankrupt did not specify the nature and amount of debts in the statement of affairs. Such a statement would normally provide the court with guidance on which debts should be released. Adopting a "liberal construction" of the *Insolvent Act*, the court granted the discharge. The court was of the view that not granting a discharge for this reason would be taking a "very narrow and unreasonable view of the statute, and contrary to the policy and spirit of the insolvent laws ... [T]he Act of Parliament must have a reasonable construction. If the insolvent, being unable to set out the amount of the debt or claim of a particular creditor named in his schedule, sets it out in such a manner as cannot mislead that creditor, and leaves no doubt as to the debt or liability referred to, and the amount of which is capable of being determined by the creditor, in my opinion the insolvent substantially complies with the statute."[108] Rather than adopting a formalistic view of the statute and holding the lack of information against the debtor, the court interpreted the statute in a way that ultimately benefited the debtor.

The Ontario Court of Appeal in *Re Martin and English* also preferred a liberal rather than a technical interpretation of the statute: "Before the provisions of the Act are construed as inflicting a punishment so wholly disproportionate to the gravity of the offence, and so utterly repugnant to the sense of natural justice, the Court ought to be satisfied that the Legislature has spoken with no uncertain voice, and that its language is so express that we can only obey and wonder. If any other conclusion can be extracted without distortion of the language used, or the assignment of unreasonable and unlikely significations to words, it ought to be preferred."[109]

In *Re Garratt & Co.* the creditor argued that the debtor had engaged in fraud, because the bankrupt purchased goods from the creditor when the bankrupt "could not pay their debts in full." In a pro-debtor ruling, the court rejected the creditor's argument. The "mere fact" that the trader was insolvent at the time of purchase was not fraudulent, and such purchase "may be the very means of re-instating him and relieving him from difficulty." If such a "cramped and narrow rule" were established by the creditor, it would have the effect of deterring debtors "from attempting to right his fortunes." The creditor's principle would be "so disastrous to all ... creditors [and] debtors" and would "destroy [the] hope and confidence of traders." The court concluded that many traders who began with nothing transformed themselves into "self-made men." But such men could never start in business if the creditor's argument were upheld. Debtors would be forced to "stop at once whenever they met with a check by the failure of their bankers, the dishonesty of their debtors, by fire, robbery, or other superior agency."[110] Moral failure of the debtor was not within the court's list of the causes of failure. Failure was attributed to some external cause well beyond the control of the debtor.[111] The court concluded that "inability to pay is no more fraud, though it was thought so in former times when bankruptcy was esteemed a crime."[112]

Section 56 of the *Insolvent Act of 1875* listed grounds that disentitled the bankrupt to a confirmation of his discharge. For example, confirmation of the discharge was not possible if the bankrupt had entered into a fraudulent preference or failed to keep an account book showing receipts and disbursements of cash. As the Ontario Court of Appeal characterized it, "[W]here the insolvent had brought himself within any of the classes of conduct punishable under section 56, it was the imperative duty of the Judge to refuse the confirmation."[113] However, not all conduct falling under section 56 resulted in the bankrupt being denied a discharge. In *Re Bullivant* the Ontario Court of Appeal acknowledged that it was "extremely obvious that sound policy requires the courts not to relax" the cash book requirement. However, Moss CJA concluded that there were "degrees of culpability." The "plainest dictates of justice point to less severity where corrupt or fraudulent motives do not exist." Here the court suspended the discharge for three months, preferring to have the case "leniently dealt with, because the insolvent is free from any improper motive."[114]

Not all bankruptcy proceedings resulted in the granting of a liberal discharge. The *Insolvent Act of 1869* prohibited the debtor from obtaining the consent of creditors to the discharge by what the Act called a "fraud or evil practice." In these fraudulent circumstances the confirmation of the discharge was to be refused and the discharge was "set aside and annulled."[115] The judiciary invoked this provision and denied a discharge on the basis that "one is deserving of some punishment."[116] There are many instances where fraud was detected and a discharge was denied.[117] An Ontario judge concluded that if a debtor made an assignment having no assets whatsoever, "nor any expectation of any," such that the debtor had given up nothing before entering into bankruptcy, it was a "perfect mockery of the Insolvent Act." A no-asset assignment was not *bona fide* and was a "fraud of the Insolvent Act." A debtor may have "wastefully squandered all his estate in wanton extravagance" and "may laugh at his creditors, and become entitled to his discharge."[118]

Some judges even wondered whether it was worth having the statute on the books. One Nova Scotia judge pondered the utility of having the legislation at all if fraudulent behaviour was allowed to go unchecked: "It appears to me that if a trader can with immunity and impunity conduct his business as this insolvent is proved to have done, both positively and negatively, the provisions of the Insolvent Act are a dead letter, and had better be expunged from the statute-book." The case involved a debtor who failed to keep books and records and was "utterly ignorant of what his real financial condition is at any given period." The judge remarked that if "it can be judicially held that the laws made in the matter of insolvency ... have not been violated ... I am unable to recognize the usefulness of the legislation."[119]

Second-Class Discharges

The *Insolvent Acts of 1869* and *1875* enabled courts to issue second-class discharges,[120] which were intended as a signal to the commercial community that the debtor had engaged in some form of reckless conduct. However, a review of reported cases reveals only three instances in which an appellate court imposed a second-class discharge.[121] Courts were reluctant to make an order of second-class discharge. In one Nova

Scotia case, the court ordered a second-class discharge suspended by four months where the bankrupt had failed to keep proper books and records. The creditors appealed, seeking a stricter order. The appellate court confirmed the second-class order but extended the suspended period for a further four months.[122] In a second Nova Scotia case, the debtor stopped trading and transferred his stock to his daughter, who carried on the debtor's business with the debtor acting as a clerk. After ceasing his business, the debtor collected upon debts owed to him and paid nothing to creditors. The trial judge granted a first-class discharge and the creditors appealed. The appellate court ordered a second-class discharge suspended by two years.[123] In the third case, failure to keep a cash book resulted in a New Brunswick court ordering a second-class discharge.[124] Ontario county court records confirm the infrequency of the second-class discharge: a study of these unreported records discloses only a single instance of a second-class discharge between 1869 and 1880.[125]

Collusion

Ontario county court files also illustrate that judges did not strictly apply the *Insolvent Act of 1875*. Although it permitted only creditors to commence proceedings, the legislation became, in effect, a voluntary regime for many debtors. Even though the *Insolvent Act of 1875* had abolished the ability of a debtor to make a voluntary assignment to a friendly creditor, "the exercise of friendly influence was still rendered possible, and cases of unmerited lenience frequently occurred."[126] In other words, debtors and friendly creditors conspired to ensure that an involuntary proceeding would commence against the debtor.

This has a distinct parallel to earlier American bankruptcy legislation. The US *Bankruptcy Act of 1800* allowed only creditors to initiate proceedings; however, Bruce Mann's study of the American Act found both direct and indirect evidence of creditor collusion with the debtor to obtain an order of bankruptcy. For indirect evidence, Mann recorded the number of files in which a family member filed a bankruptcy claim against a relation. Mann notes that it is difficult to determine whether related creditors initiated the petition vindictively or compassionately; both motives are possible, but "the ones filed by fathers against sons bear the mark of one generation helping fallen members of the next to their feet."[127] In Canada, the *Insolvent Act of 1875* required the creditor who sought to initiate an involuntary proceeding against a debtor to complete an affidavit stating "that he or they are not acting in collusion with the debtor, or to procure him any undue advantage against his creditors."[128]

Notwithstanding the no-collusion affidavit, a study of Ontario county court insolvency procedure books illustrates that it was not uncommon for the court to accept a writ of attachment filed by a creditor with the same last name as the debtor. In Lanark County, 5.5 per cent of these files accepted by the courts fell into this category; in Huron County, 3.5 per cent; in Oxford County, 2.6 per cent; and in Lambton County, 0.5 per cent.[129] Filings by a father against a son are evident.[130] For example, William Henry Cooper filed against William Henry Cooper the younger on 6 March 1877, and by September of that year, the son received his discharge.[131] Women also played a role in the initiation of involuntary proceedings against a debtor with the same last name.[132] While appellate courts were prepared to censure collusion between related parties,[133] the county courts tolerated some level of collusion in the initiation of bankruptcy proceedings. County court acceptance of collusion may simply be an instance of lower court defiance of the principle of judicial hierarchy.[134]

The Press Reacts

The conduct of county court judges did not escape the scrutiny of the press. The *Daily Globe* complained that courts had adopted the practice of granting every petitioner a discharge, even where there was opposition by creditors. Insolvency law was "surely not intended chiefly to whitewash individuals and apply the sponge to the liabilities of defaulting debtors." An 1869 publication claimed that a debtor could get through his bankruptcy on such easy terms "as any calculating rogue can generally succeed in wresting from his reluctant creditors." An 1882 book pointed out that "the Courts granted discharges under the Act of 1875 in many cases too easily, trusting too much to the shewings made by the assignee ... or interpreting the Act too liberally, and though in other instances, judges adhered more closely to the actual letter of the provisions, discharges were still obtained which, in the opinion of merchants knowing well the merits of the insolvent, were undeserved by him."[135]

The press went beyond general attacks on the bankruptcy system and directly condemned bankruptcy judges on a more personal basis. The *Globe* dubbed county court judges "diminutive autocrats." An editorial in the Saint John *Morning Freeman* claimed that "County Court Judges are not always men who should be entrusted with the great discretionary powers the bill confers on them." In 1872, the *Monetary Times* complained about the conduct of judges in their interpretation of the legislation: "It would appear that the judges are directly blamable for the lax, not to say reckless way in which insolvency cases are disposed of." One periodical suggested reform to the judicial system of administering discharges, recommending that in Prince Edward Island the Supreme Court administer all bankruptcy matters and that all judges of that court should be Bankruptcy Judges. Further, a "fatal principle" in bankruptcy administration was that judges were paid according to a fee schedule rather than by salary. It was not fair to allow a judge's pay to "depend upon his decision, and that it is grossly unfair to creditors, and breeds in their minds jealousy and distrust."[136]

Although there was persistent anti-debtor rhetoric, county courts may have been responding to the other side of the debate. There was pro-debtor rhetoric, and county courts, being courts of first instance, may have been reflecting that aspect of public opinion. Theda Skocpol concludes, "Courts are profoundly rhetorical institutions bound to be affected by moral understandings deeply embedded in categories of political discourse."[137] County court judges may have been reflecting local legal attitudes and culture about debt.

The federal government appointed county court judges,[138] yet it seems that these judges were more in tune with local considerations rather than federal considerations. The drafters of the *Insolvent Acts* failed to take into account the possibility that county court judges may have taken a different view of the nature of debt and personal responsibility. When legal reformers fail to take into account the influence of local legal culture, there is a risk that the policy objectives of the national legislation may be frustrated. When local courts fail to adhere to the expectations of the drafters of the national legislation, "legal critics are given new material" to criticize "the ineffectiveness of ... formal rules." Therefore, local legal culture potentially "undercuts" legal reforms.[139]

The *Globe* explained the pattern of pro-debtor rulings: "[T]he county judge was, perhaps, too apt to take the view that the insolvent was a fellow townsman and a decent sort of citizen who ought not to be too hardly dealt with."[140] In an 1885 publication, E.R.C. Clarkson acknowledged that the *Insolvent Acts* allowed dishonest debtors to escape with a perfunctory application to a local judge. In part, the fault lay with county court judges who defeated the true intent of the legislation. According to Clarkson, judges allowed dishonest debtors to obtain their discharges and were "trammelled by sectional considerations." The solution lay in new legislation that would ensure that the power to grant the discharge would be vested in higher courts.[141] However, the idea that the discharge could protect creditor interests was not widely accepted until 1919. Those who sought bankruptcy reform struggled to overcome the idea that a debtor had a moral obligation to repay all debts.

6. Conclusion

The discharge was not only one of the most important provisions in the legislation, but also proved to be the most contentious. As the 1870s wore on, Parliament made the discharge more difficult to obtain. Two distinct ideas about the discharge competed in public discourse. On the one hand, honest debtors deserved a discharge from the millstone of debt, while on the other, debtors had a moral obligation to pay all debts. This higher responsibility was governed by more than mere contract. Notwithstanding a statutory discharge, many debtors chose to flee and abscond to the United States, suggesting that the moral obligation to repay all debts was more important than the nineteenth-century notions of forgiveness. Debtors chose to flee and avoid the shame of being a bankrupt, rather than wait for a discharge. In many instances, absconding debtors left Canada for good.

Rural opposition to bankruptcy legislation also contributed to the unpopularity of the legislation. Farmers were excluded from the legislation and were therefore ineligible to obtain a discharge. The farming interest as represented by rural MPs seized upon the anti-bankruptcy rhetoric to seek repeal of the legislation. Repeal also gained momentum as a result of the pro-debtor rulings by courts. Judges interpreted the legislation in a liberal manner and refused to utilize the sanction of the second-class discharge, except in a few cases. They also tolerated collusion between related creditors and debtors in involuntary proceedings.

5

The Role of Institutions 1867–1880

Why is a dishonest bankrupt like an honest poor man? – Because both *fail* to get rich.

[Montreal] Saturday Reader (6 July 1867) 284

Ideas and interests in part explain the repeal of the *Insolvent Acts*; however, it is also important to acknowledge the significance of institutions as having an autonomous influence on policy choice.[1] Institutional factors, and in some cases the failure of institutions, contributed to the demise of the bankruptcy legislation in 1880.[2] The absence of a strong government department responsible for the oversight of all bankruptcy matters was an important institutional factor. The Canadian regulatory state was yet to be formed, and political parties divided over the issue of repeal. Further, governments were not committed to reform. The weakness of the state inhibited the implementation of stable and lasting legislation.[3] Official Assignees, appointed to administer insolvent estates, were not supervised by any form of state apparatus, and their misconduct quickly became the focal point for those supporting repeal.

Federalism also affected policy direction.[4] Provincial jurisdiction over "property and civil rights" created the possibility of a provincial solution to a contentious subject. Ontario's proposal of a provincial law that distributed the debtor's assets on a *pro rata* basis without the controversial discharge provided Parliament with an opportunity to repeal the federal bankruptcy law. Section 1 considers the role of political parties and the state in the bankruptcy law debates, while section 2 examines bankruptcy administration and how Official Assignees contributed to the unpopularity of the bankruptcy statutes. The impact of federalism is considered in section 3.

1. Party Systems and the Role of the State

One possible explanation for the legislative pattern of bankruptcy lies in the realm of politics and the importance of political parties as an institutional factor. Political parties, dominant politicians and the timing of elections may offer a rationale for the change in legislation in 1875 and its subsequent repeal. In Canada, however, bankruptcy law was not a party issue, nor a matter of government policy. The governments of the day showed little interest in the legislation and mismanaged reform efforts. Bankruptcy law divided political parties and Cabinet.[5] The Conservatives sought to distance themselves from the *Insolvent Act of 1869*. As early as 1872, the Conservatives, who held power during the passage of the *Insolvent Act of 1869*, acknowledged that bankruptcy was not a government matter. The government showed little interest in the debate and lost a crucial repeal vote in the Commons. Only the action of the Senate staved off repeal in 1872.[6] When George-Étienne Cartier spoke for the government, he indicated that it "did not make it a Government question." Cartier feebly defended bankruptcy legislation and claimed that the *Insolvent Act of 1869* was only a temporary measure that was just beginning to be understood: "[T]he obvious course was to let the matter rest, and the Act could then expire in its natural course."[7]

At first glance, one might assume that the change in government from Conservative to Liberal in 1874 directly led to the enactment of the new *Insolvent Act of 1875*. However, again the *Insolvent Act of 1875* was not considered a government measure, and it was supported by a majority of Members from both sides of the House.[8] Edward Blake, a prominent member of the new Liberal Administration, summed up the traditional government position: "The position of all Governments on this question, as far as I know, from the time when it first came before the Legislature of old Canadas, and certainly since the Union, has been rather questionable ... It was never promoted by the government at all; the fact is that leading Members on both sides of the House have entertained conflicting views on the question for this law, and that, whether for good or ill, it has been one on which political lines have never been drawn, and on which divisions of a party have never taken place."[9]

During the campaign of 1878, many Members of Parliament "pledged themselves to unconditional repeal."[10] While in opposition, the Conservatives had been critical of the Liberal administration's handling of bankruptcy matters. These criticisms had found favour with the electorate during the election. Once returned to power in the election of 1878, the Conservatives found it difficult to support bankruptcy reform in the face of a strengthening repeal movement. In 1879 the government announced it would appoint a Select Committee to study bankruptcy reform but did so without committing the government in advance to any policy position.[11] Bill 85,[12] which was reported out of committee, was not considered a government matter. It was assumed that when the matter was put to a vote, "the Government would divide" on the bill. The *Journal of Commerce* reported in 1879 that it was well known "that differences of opinion prevail" among government Members on the subject of insolvency.[13]

In 1879, one Senator accused the government of being neutral throughout the whole debate, not having "spoken a word." The government "refuses to have policy in the matter, and pitches the whole subject over to a private member."[14] According to the *Monetary Times,* the government had "abdicated its functions and lost the control of the House."[15] By 1880 the *Monetary Times* simply reported the "policy of the Government is therefore repeal."[16]

The Conservatives in 1879 and 1880 were not willing to press bankruptcy reform and risk splitting party and electoral support, for there was insufficient backing in the community for either party to adopt bankruptcy reform as policy. As the repeal debates intensified in 1879 and 1880, the Conservatives decided not to push for legislative reform, particularly in the large number of rural ridings. MPs' responses to the bankruptcy law crisis no doubt involved a "political calculus" that considered the prospects for re-election in the context of a repeal or reform vote.[17] An analysis of the 1879 House of Commons repeal vote demonstrates the extent of the party divisions (see table 5.1).

Thus, parties divided over the repeal question, with a majority of MPs in both main parties voting in favour of repeal. Without government support for bankruptcy reform, there was little to stand in the way of the repeal movement. As an institutional factor, political parties played a weak role, as no major party supported retention of the law. There was little incentive for political parties or the government of the

Table 5.1: 1879, House of Commons: Repeal Bill, 5 May 1879[a]

MPs for Repeal	107	MPs against Repeal	55
Conservatives[b]	76	Conservatives[d]	30
Liberals	23	Liberals[e]	15
Others[c]	8	Other[f]	10

Notes:

[a] Commons Debates, 5 May 1879, 1783–4. For the background of each Member of Parliament, see CH Mackintosh, ed, *The Canadian Parliamentary Companion and Annual Register, 1879* (Ottawa: Citizen, 1879).

[b] Thirty-one MPs identified themselves as Liberal-Conservatives. John A. Macdonald's Conservative party had its roots in the pre-Confederation Liberal-Conservative Party, and many MPs continued to use the Liberal-Conservative label in the post–Confederation era. See Mackintosh, ed, *Canadian Parliamentary Companion*. See also Frank Underhill, "The Development of National Political Parties in Canada" in Dan Azoulay, ed, *Canadian Political Parties* (Toronto: Irwin Publishing, 1999) 65, pp. 67, 74. The Conservative vote also includes Independents (3), Protectionists (3), and National (1).

[c] The "Others" category includes Reformers (4), Independent (1), Nationalist (1), and unspecified (2).

[d] Three were also Independent, Protectionist, or Unionist. Twelve identified themselves as Liberal-Conservatives.

[e] One was also a Reformer.

[f] The "Others" category includes Independents (5), Reformers (3), and unspecified (2).

day to support such an unpopular measure. As discussed below, the administration of bankrupts' estates proved to be a major contributing factor in the law's unpopularity.

2. Bankruptcy Administration

The capacity of a political system can limit public policy developments. Political capacity includes the "the professionalism and expertise of the legislators and public administrators." In Canada, there was no separate bankruptcy office or department; bankruptcy law was not part of a larger regulatory state.[18] The absence of a strong government department committed to reform hastened repeal.

The Department of Justice had broad responsibility for bankruptcy. Most of the correspondence in the Department of Justice files concerned minor administrative matters rather than larger policy issues. However, without a separate bankruptcy department, those with a particular concern wrote directly to the Minister of Justice or to the Prime

Minister.[19] The correspondence included, for example, an appeal for legal advice from a bankrupt, demands for copies of legislation, and requests for legal advice from Official Assignees or other government departments.[20] No policy memoranda or papers could be located in the Justice Files.

Without any central control or supervision of bankrupts' estates, the day-to-day administration of the bankruptcy law was the responsibility of the Official Assignee (the equivalent to the modern day Trustee in Bankruptcy), who was responsible for making a distribution to creditors from the bankrupt's estate. The Official Assignee was considered to be "an officer of the Court" and was "accountable for the moneys, property and estates coming into his possession."[21] The Assignee held all the rights and powers of the bankrupt in relation to the bankrupt's property and was directed to wind up the estate by the sale of property and the collection of debts owing to the estate. The Assignee was also empowered to rescind agreements made in fraud of creditors.[22] Although creditors were unlikely to see much of a return on their claim on the bankruptcy, each estate provided a source of fees and profit for the Official Assignee.[23]

However, there was a disparity between the Official Assignee's standing and responsibilities under the legislation, and the reality of how the Assignee carried out those responsibilities. Official Assignees in many ways became the symbol of all that was wrong with the bankruptcy legislation. Assignees were to represent the interests of both the bankrupt and the creditors.[24] One author claimed that the Assignee was to stand "perfectly impartial and unbiased between insolvent and creditors." However, the relationship between Official Assignees and debtors led one paper to conclude that "collusion between the debtor and official assignee is possible and in fact often exists."[25] For example, in *Harvey v Cotter* the Official Assignee took an inventory of the bankrupt's property but then decided to allow the bankrupt to sell the property and pay creditors by instalments. The court held that the bankrupt's seizure of the goods for purposes of sale was an "illegal act."[26]

James D. Edgar, a leading author of *Insolvent Act* texts,[27] expressed concerns about the impartiality of Official Assignees. He was of the view that the law required more supervision of Official Assignees, since practice at the time had "a tendency to encourage conduct that, in a regular official administering of justice, would be called bribery and attributed, at least, to undue influence." According to Edgar, the Official Assignee was "often liberally paid by an insolvent." However,

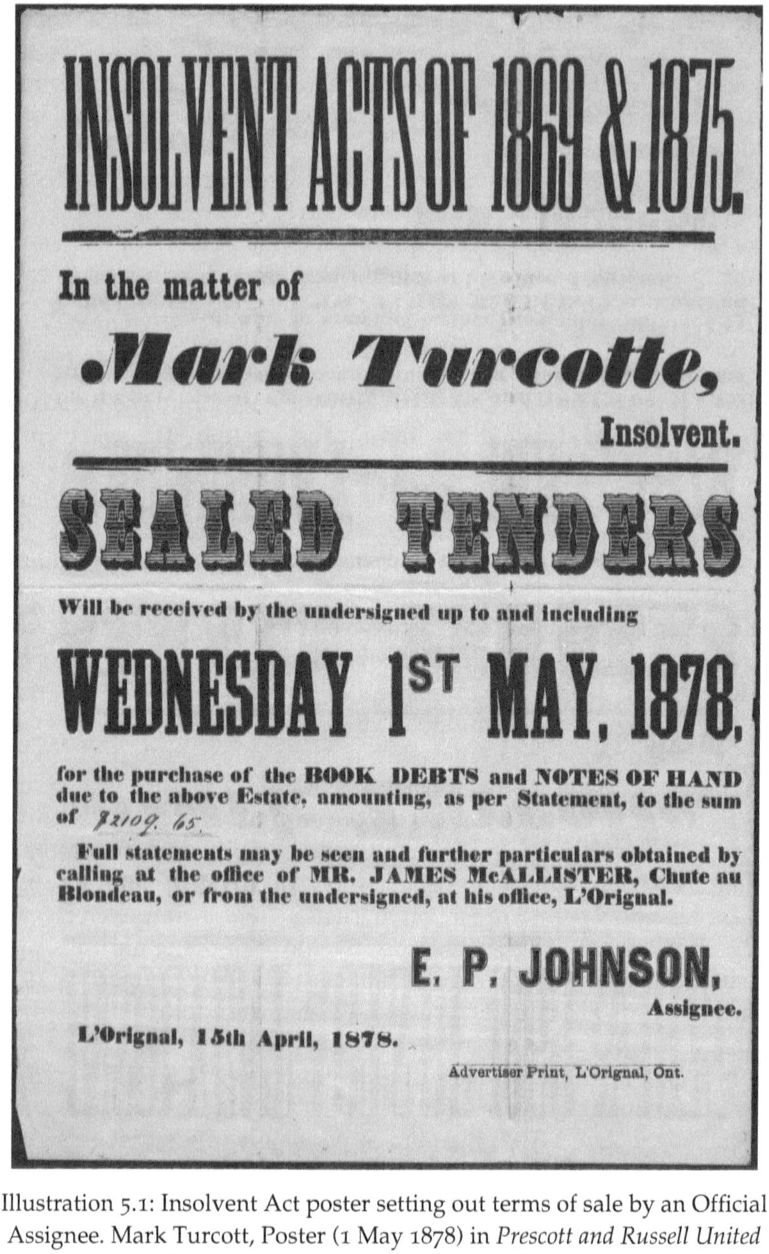

INSOLVENT ACTS OF 1869 & 1875.

In the matter of

Mark Turcotte,

Insolvent.

SEALED TENDERS

Will be received by the undersigned up to and including

WEDNESDAY 1ST MAY, 1878,

for the purchase of the **BOOK DEBTS** and **NOTES OF HAND** due to the above Estate, amounting, as per Statement, to the sum of $2109.65

Full statements may be seen and further particulars obtained by calling at the office of **MR. JAMES McALLISTER**, Chute au Blondeau, or from the undersigned, at his office, L'Orignal.

E. P. JOHNSON,
Assignee.

L'Orignal, 15th April, 1878.

Advertiser Print, L'Orignal, Ont.

Illustration 5.1: Insolvent Act poster setting out terms of sale by an Official Assignee. Mark Turcott, Poster (1 May 1878) in *Prescott and Russell United Counties County Court Insolvency Case Files*, AO (RG 22-4463).

the Assignee produced "no assets" and simply "'put [the bankrupt] through' in the shortest possible order." Thus, the Assignee considered himself "retained by the debtor, whom he regards in the light of a client or customer." Edgar concluded that unless "this evil is arrested ... the sooner the Act is repealed the better."[28] Another author also believed that there was a close relationship between the debtor and the Official Assignee. In many cases the Assignee became the paid agent of the debtor, "or rather the *pettifogging paid and unlicensed lawyer* of the insolvent ... it is easy to be seen that he will use every means in his power *to slip his client through*, regardless of creditors!"[29]

Creditors complained of inconsistent treatment by different Official Assignees. In one case, a creditor sold a set of scales to a debtor under a contract that enabled the creditor to seize the scales if the debtor defaulted. The debtor defaulted to the creditor and became a bankrupt. The creditor, entitled to the return of the scales notwithstanding the bankruptcy, asked the local Kent County Official Assignee to return them. When the Assignee did not, the creditor complained to the local Assignee about the delay, pointing out that in similar circumstances Toronto Assignees had returned scales without delay.[30]

In *Thomas v Hall*, the debtor, without any assets, made a voluntary assignment with the sole purpose of defeating a creditor. The court found the assignment to be fraudulent but focused on the misconduct of the Official Assignee. The judge could not "understand how any respectable gentleman filling the office of official assignee could ... assist the defendant in the perpetration of this fraud." The court concluded that if the Assignee had taken money in advance from the debtor to cover fees, "the acceptance of money" would be considered "as a very grave fraud." The long arm of the law was sufficient to "punish such conduct."[31]

Under the 1869 Act, local Boards of Trade or Chambers of Commerce appointed Official Assignees.[32] The idea behind this appointment scheme was to "confine the office to those who may enjoy the confidence of commercial men."[33] By 1875, the government assumed control over the appointment process, which quickly degenerated into a patronage scheme. There is little evidence that the government appointment process functioned as any form of supervisory mechanism. The ineffectiveness of Assignees led some to call for greater state intervention in the administration of bankruptcy estates or for all Assignee appointments to be made subject to a competency examination.[34]

After 1875, much of the Department of Justice's time was taken up

CANADIAN ILLUSTRATED NEWS.

TURN ABOUT IS FAIR PLAY.

The repeal of the Insolvency Law takes money from the official assignee and puts it in the hands of the lawyer. The impartial nurse finds one of the twins sufficiently gorged with pap, and therefore passes the bottle to the emaciated vociferator on the left.

C-072947

Illustration 5.2: "Turn about is fair play." A nurse, representing impartiality, holds a bottle representing the Insolvency Law. The repeal of the Insolvency Law takes money from the Official Assignee and puts it in the hands of the lawyer. The impartial nurse finds one of the twins sufficiently gorged with pap and passes the bottle to the emaciated vociferator on the left. *Canadian Illustrated News* 21:15 (10 April 1880) 240, LAC (reproduction copy no C-072947, control no ICON81011).

with filling the post of Official Assignee. According to the *Journal of Commerce*, appointments would now "be dictated more by political affinities than an appreciation of mercantile requirements."[35] The Department of Justice received numerous requests for appointments. It prepared countless lists of appointees, and it settled territorial disputes between feuding Assignees.[36] Even though Assignees were appointed by county or district,[37] Official Assignees competed for bankruptcy files. This led one Assignee to write to the Minister of Justice complaining that the bankruptcy file had been given to another Assignee who had "invaded my rights in this manner." One individual wrote to John A. Macdonald in 1878 warning that "having too many assignees causes them to use underhanded means towards each other to obtain payments."[38] An 1882 book noted that the government appointment system did not ensure qualified Assignees: "It fostered the creation of a number of assignees whose record, or whose general qualifications made them the most unlikely officers to carry out the meaning of the Act ... Some of the most illiterate men sprang into a position in which they were autocrats, and wielded their temporary facilities with a sharp eye to the accumulation of fees ... [T]he reckless creation and inefficiency of many assignees, under the Act of 1875, led up to the loosest interpretation of its provisions and practice, in many cases." Assignees were simply not qualified to "fully comprehend all the technicalities embodied in this Act" and were "merely broken down tradesmen themselves, and people are beginning to think the whole bankrupt law machinery is a humbug."[39]

After the declaration of a final dividend, the Act required the Assignee to prepare a final account for the court, including a statement of the amount of claims proved in the bankruptcy and the amount of dividends paid to creditors. Failure to submit the final account to the court resulted in a penalty not exceeding $100.[40] However, there was no sanction in the statute if the Assignee delayed in declaring a dividend. Creditors often complained of long delays between the commencement of proceedings and the actual receipt of a dividend.[41] The following chain of correspondence from the estate of W.H. Davy in Kent County illustrates the creditors' increasing frustration with having to wait on a dividend. Between January and July of 1879 the Official Assignee received numerous requests for a dividend.[42]

Letter of J. Segsworth & Co., Toronto, to H. Cuming, Official Assignee, 24 January 1879: "Toronto creditors are ... asking when they are going to get anything out of the Estate ... Will you please let me know."

Letter of A.B. Powell, London, to H. Cuming, Official Assignee, 1 April 1879: "We have never yet received any dividend in re W.H. Davy ... Kindly answer as to what was done in this matter as we have never yet had any word in regard to the affair."

Letter of Levy Bros. & Scheuer, Hamilton, to H. Cuming, Official Assignee, 11 April 1879: "Kindly inform whether we are to receive a dividend in re W.H. Davy how much about in the $ and when."

Letter of Carrier Marshall & Co, Toronto, to H. Cuming, Official Assignee, 28 May 1879: "Will you kindly advise us by return regarding the above Estate. Surely it is high time. We [are] never in receipt of [a] dividend. Information has some 6 mos. ago [been] given us to the effect that dividends were effected to be declared in about a month. Awaiting your reply."

Letter of Cronyn, Kew and Betts, Barristers, London, ON, to H. Cuming, Official Assignee, 3 June 1879: "Is there any prospect of a dividend being declared in this month? If something kindly advise us as to prospect."

Letter of H. Block to John Segsworth, 2 July 1879: "[I]t is now about 15 months since the Estate was placed in the hands of the Assignee which is certain[ly] ample time for liquidation and payment of claims, we have in no other instance ... been compelled to wait so long as in this case for our dividend ... [W]e would ask you to insist in some dividend being declared immediately."

Letter of A.B. Powell of London, to H. Cuming, Official Assignee, 24 July 1879: "No word yet of Dividend in re W.H. Davy – what about it – awaiting reply."

In the personal papers of James Langton, a bankrupt, numerous creditors complained about the delay in the declaration of a dividend. One creditor claimed that the estate had been in the hands of the Official Assignee for over a year and that all the creditor had received was "long letters." The creditor claimed that matters "cannot go on in this way much longer. If we do not hear from you soon with some money we [will be] taking legal measures to enforce a dividend."[43] The long delays ultimately led another creditor to commence an action against the Official Assignee for $50.[44]

The Assignee's fee was prescribed by legislation. Assignees were paid a commission on the net proceeds of the estate of 5 per cent on the first $1000, 2.5 per cent on amounts in excess of $1000 up to $5000 and 1.25 per cent for all amounts in excess of $5000.[45] Notwithstanding these strict and specific rules, creditors objected to the Assignee's fees. Critics charged that Assignees took larger fees than the legal profession and had no interest in representing creditors in no-asset cases. The Assignee's work consisted of merely "drawing papers, notices, attendances before the judge, drawing final order." Assignees and lawyers were "too rapacious," and it was in their "interest to prolong the proceedings and increase the expense ... Nobody gets paid." Official Assignees "took it all."[46] Critics blamed Assignees for throwing traders into bankruptcy because they "stood to make large fees as a result of the winding up of the business of these traders." One insolvent, having gone through bankruptcy four times in five years, claimed that he would have been wealthier if not for the "avariciousness" of the Assignee.[47] In the assignment of P. McKerral, a creditor challenged the fees associated with the estate: "Mr Cleghorn is much disappointed with the information given in the Dividend Sheet – you promised me to give full particulars of all the Real Estate sold – to whom sold – when sold and for what amount. Was the bill of your solicitor taxed? By what authority do inspectors value themselves $450 and how is your commission fixed. I must object to the dividend sheet unless I have full particulars by Wednesday next. Please therefore at once do what you promised me would be done."[48] There was no effective auditing of the Official Assignee's accounts, and the security required to be posted by Assignees was nominal.[49]

In specific cases, creditors objected to the Assignee's fees as well as fees charged by the Assignee's solicitor.[50] The Act sought to control costs by prohibiting an Assignee from acting as solicitor or agent for a particular creditor.[51] The object of the section was to "discourage the promotion of litigation ... by removing from the solicitor-assignee the temptation of embarking in it, with a view of making a profit for himself."[52]

The press also raised concerns about excessive fees.[53] Assignees had "killed the goose that laid the golden eggs, and merchants are consequently driven to accept even unreasonable offers of compromise rather than run the risk of losing it all."[54] The *Trade Review* claimed that many Assignees abused their office, and among the many Assignees there were "not a few black sheep ... who care little how the creditors of the Insolvent fare, so long as they secure their fees." Assignees occupied a "position of trust" and not for the "purpose of making fees for themselves." For those Assignees who abused creditors' trust, they should "speedily be turned out, and better men put in their places." In one instance, the creditors held an "indignation" meeting to censure the "delinquent" and to take steps to remove the Assignee.[55]

There was a sense that under the *Insolvent Act of 1875* the Official Assignees had benefited most of all.[56] The *Trade Review* noted that many complained about the way Assignees discharged their duties, and that while the *Insolvent Act* placed a great deal of power in the hands of Assignees, such powers were frequently "abused." As momentum grew in favour of repeal, the *Canada Law Journal* claimed that there would be few to "mourn the repeal of the Act, except an army of official assignees."[57]

A political cartoon published in the *Canadian Illustrated News* represents this best. Entitled "Othello's Occupation Gone!,"[58] the cartoon shows a "disconsolate official assignee" who had heard of the repeal of the *Insolvent Acts*. With his hat, gloves, and pipe strewn on the floor, and official papers littered everywhere, the Assignee, his head in his hand, contemplates his next career. A "To Let" sign hangs in his window, and a "Bankrupt Stock" notice is displayed on the wall.[59]

One such Assignee, fearing the prospects of unemployment, wrote to Prime Minister Macdonald on the eve of repeal, seeking another federal patronage appointment, perhaps in Customs, claiming, "I will be out in the cold should the Act be repealed."[60]

3. Federalism

If bankruptcy and insolvency law had been important enough to be included as a federal power, why did Parliament withdraw from this field in 1880? In part the answer can be found in the Constitution. While the grant of jurisdiction over bankruptcy and insolvency was exclusive, the provinces retained the right to regulate debtor-creditor matters generally under the "property and civil rights" jurisdiction.[61] The *BNA Act* created the possibility of some overlap in the regulation of debtors and creditors. Bankruptcy law therefore could not be separated from the important institutional factor of constitutional law. The ability of the provinces to pass legislation on more general debtor-creditor matters ultimately provided Parliament with a constitutional solution for the unpopular matter of bankruptcy law. The federal government's abandonment of bankruptcy legislation in 1880 and the provincial debtor-creditor legislation that followed suggests that consensus on the need for a national bankruptcy law did not survive long after Confederation. Despite the clear wording of the *BNA Act*, the federal government did not view bankruptcy law as a fundamentally important economic power.

The exclusive jurisdiction of the federal government over the field of bankruptcy and insolvency in section 91(21) of the *BNA Act* provided

Vol. XIX.—No. 19. MONTREAL, SATURDAY, MAY 10, 1879.

"OTHELLO'S OCCUPATION GONE!"

THE DISCONSOLATE OFFICIAL ASSIGNEE ON HEARING OF THE REPEAL OF THE INSOLVENCY LAW

C-072099

Illustration 5.3: "Othello's occupation gone!" The disconsolate official assignee on hearing of the repeal of the Insolvency Law. *Canadian Illustrated News* 19:19 (10 May 1879) 289, LAC (reproduction copy no C-072099, control no ICON80987).

supporters of a national law with a strong argument against repeal.[62] If Parliament repealed the national Act, the "[p]rovincial legislature would have no power to substitute anything else for it, not even a law to provide for the discharge from arrest of an unfortunate debtor." Provinces did not have jurisdiction over bankruptcy and insolvency, as "insolvency matters belonged to this Parliament exclusively."[63]

However, there was constitutional doubt. Even before the *Insolvent Act of 1869* had been passed, Prime Minister Macdonald admitted in private correspondence that he had discussions on the possible conflict between federal and local jurisdiction if Parliament adopted a national act.[64] During the 1870s many asserted that the federal law interfered with provincial jurisdiction. One MP argued that bankruptcy law impeded the "jurisdiction of the Local Legislatures."[65] Federal bankruptcy law, according to one author, threatened the Quebec civil code.[66]

Notwithstanding the number of challenges to federal authority, appellate courts consistently upheld the validity of the *Insolvent Acts*[67] and held that the statute should be applied uniformly throughout Canada.[68] In *Re Barrett*, Justice Burton of the Ontario Court of Appeal concluded that "it would lead to great difficulties if a different interpretation was given to the insolvent law in different localities." In *Crombie v Jackson*, the Upper Canada Queen's Bench held that "the exclusive legislative authority respecting bankruptcy and insolvency is vested in the Parliament of Canada, and there is no interference with property and civil rights beyond what has been considered to be expedient for the purpose of making the proceedings in insolvency more efficient."[69] Furthermore, the Nova Scotia Court of Appeal in *Kinney, Assignee v Dudman* held that "an Insolvent Act must necessarily conflict with previously existing legal rights, and insolvency is a subject over which the Dominion Parliament has the exclusive power of legislation so that a Dominion statute in relation to insolvency overrides all provincial enactments."[70]

The Privy Council in *Cushing v Dupuy* ruled that it would be "impossible to advance a step" in bankruptcy proceedings "without interfering with and modifying some of the ordinary rights of property ... It is therefore to be presumed, indeed it is a necessary implication, that the Imperial statute, in assigning to the Dominion Parliament the subjects of bankruptcy and insolvency, intended to confer on it legislative power to interfere with property, civil rights, and procedure within the Provinces, so far as a general law relating to those subjects might affect them."[71]

The Supreme Court of Canada later concluded that once a debtor becomes insolvent and proceedings are taken against him under bankruptcy legislation, "the provincial legislature ceases to have jurisdiction over his civil rights, either in relation to the disposition of his insolvent estate, or in relation to his dealings with his creditors."[72] In only one instance did a justice (in dissent) of an appellate court reach the conclusion that a provision of the Insolvent Act was *ultra vires*. Justice Westmore in *McLeod v Wright* concluded that while the "Dominion Parliament, doubtless had ample power to legislate upon bankruptcy and insolvency ... it had no right to legislate upon property and civil rights in this Province."[73] Notwithstanding the pro-federalism rulings, many began to think in terms of a political solution involving provincial legislation.

As the decade wore on, it became apparent that if the federal law were to be repealed, the provinces would play an important part in the regulation of debtor-creditor matters. For example, on three separate occasions the House of Commons debated amendments to bills that would have preserved some form of provincial autonomy. In 1872, an amendment to exempt the provinces of Nova Scotia and New Brunswick from the effects of the repeal bill of 1872 was proposed. While the amendment to exclude Nova Scotia and New Brunswick did not pass, John A. Macdonald was surprisingly open to the idea of allowing some provincial autonomy on the issue. He indicated that it was "perfectly open to the House to deal with the subject in one way with reference to Ontario and Quebec and in another way with reference to the Maritime Provinces."[74]

In 1875, a Member from British Columbia opposed the application of the *Insolvent Act of 1875* to his newly admitted province. He claimed that the application of the Act of 1875 to British Columbia "would be a step backwards."[75] Members from British Columbia feared that the application of a harsh law in their province would have the "effect of driving unfortunate men across to the States to find a home." A vote to exclude BC from the operation of the law failed in 1875.[76] Similarly, a Member suggested allowing the provinces to utilize their legislation for absconding debtors to supplement the provisions of a federal bill.[77] While Parliament defeated all three amendments, the debates foreshadowed the provincial solution that would emerge in 1880.

American experience provided an obvious parallel for Canadians looking for solutions to the bankruptcy issue. Even after the repeal of the *American Bankruptcy Act* in 1878, Canadians continued to monitor developments south of the border. Supporters of Canadian bankruptcy law noted that many American Boards of Trade petitioned Congress for re-enactment of a federal law. One Canadian Senator pointed to the new efforts in the United States to re-enact national bankruptcy legislation in 1880 and drew attention to the possible dangers of relying upon local legislation: "Congress is about to introduce a new one. The boards of trade in New York and Boston are busily engaged in drafting an insolvency act, and one of the leading commercial papers of the city of New York remarks that people are sick and tired of the grab system which had resulted from the repeal of the National Bankruptcy Law and the establishment of local state laws. I think that should be a warning to the people of Canada not to depend on local legislation in this matter."[78]

Canada also faced a similar problem if the national *Insolvent Act* were to be repealed. The common law of debtor-creditor relations rewarded the first diligent creditor, resulting in a race of diligence or "grab law." Only Quebec law provided for an equitable distribution of the debtor's assets.[79] However, the distribution of the debtor's assets was only one goal of bankruptcy law. The other central feature, the discharge, was no longer tolerated in nineteenth-century Canada; therefore repeal seemed inevitable. As releasing debts proved to be the most controversial issue in the federal law, some began to think in terms of provincial legislation that did not contain a discharge but sought to provide some form of equitable distribution of the debtor's assets. The *BNA Act* provided the possibility for provinces to ameliorate the effects of federal repeal by providing their own distribution scheme under their jurisdiction over property and civil rights. If all the common law provinces could be convinced to enact such legislation, a federal bankruptcy law would no longer be required.

In 1879, Oliver Mowat, the Liberal Premier of Ontario, raised the possibility of enacting provincial legislation with Alexander Campbell, the government leader in the Canadian Senate. As Mowat understood that "the Insolvent Law is likely to be abolished next session,"[80] he suggested a solution that separated the distribution of the debtor's assets from the discharge: "Is not the release of the debtor at the bottom of all the evils or supposed evils of the Act? And is not the machinery of the Act useful and desirable for the distribution of the estate equally?"[81]

Mowat indicated he had been considering a bill "which did not recognize priority between execution creditors ... for Upper Canada in case the abolition referred to takes place." He suggested that if provincial legislation was not viable, then the federal government should consider cancelling the discharge provisions of the Act and retain the distributive features.[82]

In 1879, the Senate delayed repeal of the *Insolvent Act* to allow the provinces to act. Ontario subsequently announced its intention to pass the *Act to Abolish Priorities Among Execution Creditors.*[83] Royal Assent was given to the Ontario Act on 5 March 1880, which was the day after the *Bill to Repeal the Insolvent Acts* was read for the third time.[84] The new provincial legislation required that creditors share rateably in the proceeds realized from the sale of the debtor's assets.[85] The provincial legislation provided only for the distribution of the debtor's assets without allowing a discharge. Provincial legislation could succeed, as the most controversial aspects of bankruptcy law had been removed.

Alexander Campbell, speaking in the Senate, confirmed that he had corresponded with the Premier of Ontario, "the result of which was the preparation of the [Ontario] Bill ... which is intended ... to meet any evils which might arise from the passage of the [repeal] Bill now before the House." He summarized the rationale for the Ontario legislation, "The law recently enacted by Ontario ... seeks to give ... a fair distribution of the assets of a debtor whose goods and chattels are taken in execution. Under the former laws of Ontario the first execution took everything."[86]

The timing of the Ontario Act was not a coincidence, as Charles Tupper would later confirm. In his speech in 1895 to the British Empire League in his capacity as the Canadian High Commissioner to the United Kingdom, former Prime Minister Tupper claimed that in 1879 the repeal of the 1875 Act was "purposively delayed by the action of the Senate for one year, to enable the provinces to adopt suitable legislation. Ontario immediately gave notice of that intention and passed legislation in 1880."[87] With the assistance of Ontario, Parliament "was glad to get out of the business of bankruptcy."[88]

If the federal division of powers made the repeal of bankruptcy law possible because of the tempering effects of provincial legislation, did federalism make repeal more likely? Members of the federal Parliament were well aware of the proposed Ontario legislation. Thomas Colby, who introduced the repeal bill in 1880, raised the possibility of an Ontario *pro rata* distribution law in his opening remarks.[89] The government was of the view that "it is better in the interests of commerce and of the public, to allow ... the Insolvency Law to be repealed and to let the effect of the repeal tempered as it will be by recent legislation in Ontario, be experienced."[90] According to a recent study, Members in the House of Commons repealed the federal Act, taking "comfort in the knowledge" that provincial legislation would "fill the void left by the federal abandonment of the field."[91] Without the possibility of provincial legislation, it would have been unlikely that the federal government would have opted for complete repeal. Like England, Parliament would have been forced to fashion some alternative solution. Providing the machinery for the distribution of the debtor's estate became a provincial role with the enactment of the Ontario *Creditors' Relief Act*. Federalism therefore contributed to the division of bankruptcy law into its two component parts, with the right of the debtor to obtain a discharge disappearing for almost forty years.

4. Conclusion

Institutions played an important role in bankruptcy law public policy developments. Despite the number of strong economic powers given to Parliament by the *BNA Act*, the regulatory state had not yet emerged. Bankruptcy law was not a matter of government policy. Further, political parties were not committed to bankruptcy as a reform measure, with parties splitting over the repeal question. Without a coalition of support within a political party or government, there was little to stop the repeal momentum. Bankruptcy administration also contributed to the law's demise. Although the legislation established the office of the Official Assignee, that office became the symbol of all that was wrong with bankruptcy law. Assignees' lack of expertise, delays in distributing dividends, and high fees all contributed to the law's unpopularity. Further, federalism allowed the federal government to abdicate responsibility over aspects of debtor-creditor relations to the provinces. The possibility of a provincial solution to the distribution problem made repeal an attractive solution for Parliament. Federalism contributed to the divorce of equitable distribution of assets from the discharge and made repeal of the federal Act possible. Not all Members saw provincial legislation as a safe solution. Some doubted the constitutionality of provincial legislation and feared endless appeals to the Supreme Court.[92] The impact of federalism and the rise of the provincial rights movement are considered in more detail in chapter 7, which covers the period 1880–1903.

PART TWO

1880–1903

6

Living with Repeal and the Failure of Federal Reform 1880–1903

[T]he real cause of delay in this matter is the inveterate tendency of Canadian politicians to shilly-shally, to weigh this vote against that, to temporize, and put off doing anything as long as they possibly can.

"The Insolvency Bill Fiasco," *Canadian Dry Goods Review*[1]

Parliament's action to repeal the *Insolvent Act of 1875* in 1880[2] left an immediate void in the federal field of bankruptcy and insolvency. During the period of 1880–1903, reform efforts took place at the provincial and federal level. The provinces sought to fill the gap by enacting provincial statutes in an attempt to establish an equitable distribution of assets and prohibit preferences, but there were limits to provincial jurisdiction and the provinces could not replicate a federal bankruptcy law. These limitations led many to suggest that Parliament should reinstate a national bankruptcy law. Under provincial law no discharge was available and a debtor could not be compelled to make an assignment. At the federal level, however, Parliament continued to review federal reform initiatives, debating twenty reform bills between 1880 and 1903. But by 1903 reform efforts exhausted themselves with no further bills being introduced in Parliament until 1918. Why were federal reform efforts between 1880 and 1903 such an abysmal failure? Part Two of this book considers this question.

Chapter 6 examines the legislative history of reform efforts at the provincial and federal levels. Prior studies that have accounted for the emergence of the *Bankruptcy Act of 1919* have focused largely on the fact that the new federal law provided a uniform solution to the problem of diverse provincial legislation that developed after 1880.[3] However, this interpretation ignores the fact that the provincial era did not transpire overnight.[4] It was not until 1903 that all the provinces had legislation that distributed the debtor's assets on a *pro rata* basis and prohibited preferential payments. During this time, it was not certain whether provincial legislation would adequately fill the gap or whether the federal government would take action to reinstate a uniform Act. Further, previous accounts that have explained the success of the *Bankruptcy Act of 1919* have ignored the fact that Parliament debated twenty reform bills between 1880 and 1903.[5] All bills failed and only two bore the imprint of government policy. The continued national debate reflected dissatisfaction with provincial reform efforts.

Chapter 6 also considers the important interrelationship between institutions and interest groups. Institutional factors constrained reform. The relative weakness of the state bureaucracy in proposing and implementing policy change[6] was an important factor in explaining the failure of federal reform. After 1880, federal governments continued to be indifferent towards bankruptcy policy; parties in power were unwilling to expend political capital on such a divisive issue, with the result that bankruptcy reform had no institutional backing by the government. This vacuum was filled by private interest groups such as Canadian urban Boards of Trade and foreign merchant groups, which played a major role in formulating bankruptcy law reform proposals by lobbying for change and submitting draft bills for Parliament to consider. Section 1 of this chapter examines the legislative history of provincial reform, while section 2 considers the failure of federal reform efforts.

1. Provincial Reform

The federal withdrawal from the field of bankruptcy and insolvency had a profound impact on debtor-creditor relations. Debtors were no longer able to receive a discharge through the operation of a statute. More importantly, through repeal, Parliament jettisoned the policy of equal treatment of creditors. Debtor-creditor matters reverted to the common law that rewarded the first execution creditor with priority of payment. This chaotic state of affairs created a race to the debtor's assets and favoured local creditors at the expense of distant or foreign creditors.[7] The common law race to the assets was further complicated by the absence of effective provincial legislation that prohibited preferential payments or transfers. If the federal government was unwilling to enact legislation, attention turned to what could be done at the provincial level within the provincial power of "property and civil rights."[8]

Given the race to obtain judgment and execution, questions arose "as to the relative exact minutes of time from which execution and assignment take effect." One Member of Parliament summed up the effect of repeal, "[T]here has been generally a race as to who can put a sheriff in possession of the assets of the insolvent first, and the consequences are that the man who is a little quicker and a little sharper than his next door neighbour will run away with perhaps the whole of the estate in order to make his debt."[9]

Without a federal Act, it was the "lawyers and sheriffs" who would "reap fat harvests," leaving creditors "at a grave disadvantage," and the race to the debtor's assets had an adverse impact on creditor behaviour. The *Monetary Times* indicated that the repeal would loosen the band of good faith between merchants and would "drive creditors to every sort of device to secure payments." Parliament's withdrawal from the field of bankruptcy and insolvency led to "sharp and unscrupulous conduct on the part of creditors seeking an advantage over each other, and to consequent bad faith and ill-feeling among merchants."[10]

Without a *pro rata* distribution scheme, creditors were forced to initiate separate enforcement proceedings. Once Parliament repealed the *Insolvent Act of 1875*, it soon became clear that the advantages of a collective system had been lost.[11] Unnecessary expenses were incurred "by separate proceedings taken by each creditor against a common debtor." Separate proceedings or the multiplicity of suits was more expensive than "there being one [bankruptcy] process by which ... assets might be distributed."[12] The *Monetary Times* published the story of fifteen creditors who had all taken the required legal steps to obtain judgments against the same debtor. Half of the assets of the debtor went to satisfy legal fees. According to the *Monetary Times*, a bankruptcy proceeding would have cost only about one-fortieth of the fees.[13] The solution to the "estate being squandered in ruinously expensive proceedings by each creditor on his own account" was to provide for *pro rata* distribution. Pointing to a case in which a debtor paid some creditors, leaving others "out in the cold," the *Monetary Times* proclaimed that "it will be strange if by the end of a twelve month, this country does not wake up to a realization of the mistake that has been made by the total repeal of the Bankrupt Law."[14]

Without a federal bankruptcy law or remedial provincial legislation, a debtor could refuse to make an assignment, thereby creating a race to see which creditor could place his execution in the hands of the Sheriff for enforcement. However, even the most vigilant creditor did not always succeed. A debtor could still defend proceedings, depriving a creditor of a quick judgment and an opportunity to enforce. By not defending the action of another, the debtor could in effect manipulate the race and prefer one creditor over another.[15] In the House of Commons, one Member of Parliament claimed that, as the law existed, "a merchant can allow a judgment to go against him by a favoured creditor, and in that way cut off all the others from any recourse against him."[16]

Although Ontario took quick steps to enact legislation to fill the void left by the repeal of the federal *Insolvent Act*, the provincial legislation did not take immediate effect. In what appeared to be an immediate solution for creditors, Ontario passed *An Act to Abolish Priorities Of and Amongst Execution Creditors* in 1880, the day after the federal repeal bill received third reading.[17] The Act, which became known as the *Creditors' Relief Act*, abolished priority among execution creditors and provided for a rateable distribution of the proceeds held by the Sheriff.[18] However, it did not come into effect until a date that was to be fixed by proclamation.[19] In fact, it did not come into force until 25 March 1884,[20] which meant that the inherent problems of the common law's race to the assets continued for some time in Ontario, even after the passage of the *Creditors' Relief Act*. The *Monetary Times*, impatient with the failure of the province to proclaim the Act, gave up hope that it would ever come into force and speculated that the Ontario government was waiting to see if the federal government would re-enact a national law. In effect, the *Monetary Times* proclaimed, without a bankruptcy law Canada was "enjoying a sort of interregnum, during which the old rule of 'first come, first served,' is applicable."[21]

It was not until 1903 that the remaining provinces enacted legislation providing for the *pro rata* distribution of debtors' assets.[22] Between 1880 and 1903, creditors faced the prospect of the common law race to debtors' assets in a number of different regions.[23]

The *Monetary Times* and the *Journal of Commerce* criticized the Ontario *Creditors' Relief Act* for its expense and its failure to deal with the major problem of preferential payments to favoured creditors.[24] According to the *Monetary Times*, debtors could pay related or friendly creditors with impunity: "[T]here is no machinery for setting aside prior preferential payments ... From all over the Province we hear of cases in which traders ... allow their friends to take judgments and sweep away all they have, while the suits of other creditors are staved off by every conceivable device ... All these things point to the one conclusion – viz: that a grave mistake was made when the bankrupt laws were repealed." There was no more "pernicious principle" than allowing an "insolvent debtor to give a preference to such of his creditors as he cares to favour."[25]

This problem led to calls for the abolition of preferences at the provincial level. Ontario enacted *An Act Respecting Assignments for the Benefit of Creditors* in 1885,[26] which improved upon an earlier pre-Confederation Ontario statute.[27] In addition to prohibiting preferences, the Act permitted a debtor to make an assignment of his or her assets to an authorized trustee for distribution to creditors.[28] Under section 9, an assignment under the Act took precedence over all judgments and incomplete executions. However, the legislation did not include a discharge. Further, a debtor could not be compelled to make an assignment.[29]

Only Manitoba followed Ontario's lead in 1885. Other provinces were much slower to enact legislation that prohibited preferences.[30] New Brunswick did not enact similar legislation until 1895 and Nova Scotia followed in 1898.[31] The lack of preference legislation in the Maritimes was a continual problem for foreign and distant creditors and created a demand for a federal law. Preferences were so common in the Maritimes that the *Journal of Commerce* urged merchants dealing in the region to transact business on a cash basis only.[32]

The *Journal of Commerce* referred to the slow progress of provincial reform as "feeble inefficient tinkerings of Provincial parliaments."[33] In many ways provincial laws were governed by local legal culture.[34] Many questioned the competence of county court judges: they were "old men" schooled "under the laws of twenty or thirty years ago," and it was hopeless to expect an interpretation of a radically new law from an intelligible perspective from judges "scattered over the country ... without any means of intercommunication."[35]

Provincial legislation came under attack as "unworkable" and expensive.[36] The *Monetary Times* cited a situation in which the estate realized $857 but the Assignee's fees amounted to $751. This was a most "outrageous thing," and the editorial suggested that the provincial Act should really be called "*Assignment for the Benefit of the Assignee.*"[37]

Provincial law was therefore slow to develop, and creditors had to cope with the common law race to the assets in many regions after repeal of the federal *Insolvent Act*. It took time before all provinces abolished priority of execution by adopting Ontario's *Creditors' Relief Act*. But this was not enough, as such legislation did not prohibit preferences, and provinces eventually responded by enacting preference legislation. However, as a result of constitutional constraints, provincial law did not contain any provision to release debts by a statutory discharge, nor could provincial legislation compel a debtor to make an assignment. These were features of a federal bankruptcy statute. Between 1880 and 1903 it became a question of whether provincial law could adequately fill the gap left by repeal or whether a new federal bankruptcy statute ought to be enacted.

2. Federal Reform Bills

At the same time as the provinces were seeking to pass legislation, Parliament debated the merits of reviving a national Act. The commercial community was not satisfied with the slow evolution of provincial law and began to demand new federal legislation.[38] Despite Parliament's rejection of bankruptcy law in 1880, private Members introduced numerous bills between 1880 and 1903. In all, Parliament debated twenty bills proposing some form of national bankruptcy regime between 1880 and 1903. But only two bills bore the imprint of government policy and every bill failed to garner sufficient votes in Parliament.[39] Federal reform efforts coincided with the slow progress of provincial legislation, and after 1903, bankruptcy law disappeared from the federal Parliamentary agenda until 1918.

Consistent with the policy of the 1870s, governments of the 1880s refused to make bankruptcy reform an official government matter. Federal bankruptcy policy was ambivalent and weak. In Canada, there was no institutional support for the development of bankruptcy as a public interest measure. In contrast, the English bankruptcy reforms of 1883 were initiated and implemented by a government with a strong policy direction: English civil servants formulated much of the policy expressed in the 1883 *Bankruptcy Act*. The English civil servants accepted that the state had a supervisory role to play. In England, a separate bankruptcy department was created, and it grew to become one of the largest departments in the civil service at the end of the nineteenth century. Bankruptcy law, in this new vision, was not just the concern of creditors; it affected the wider society.[40] This vision of bankruptcy law and the Canadian regulatory state did not emerge until after the turn of the century.[41] Passage of the Canadian *Bankruptcy Act* in 1919 coincided with an unprecedented growth of federal regulation during the First World War.

It became apparent soon after the repeal of the *Insolvent Act of 1875* that the government was not going to initiate any new bills. In 1883, a Member of Parliament, frustrated with the lack of the government's role, stated, "[I]t is about time the Government of the day took some share in the management of this extremely important trade question ... They allowed the old law to be repealed three years ago without taking sides upon it; they now permit any member who pleases to bring in bills and pass them to the second reading without affording an indication of their views."[42]

The *Journal of Commerce* proclaimed that the "Government ought to have a policy" on bankruptcy and to "maintain it as a unit." Instead of having prepared any government measure, "they have allowed private members to propose legislation." That was problematic because the government remained divided over how best to deal with private Member's bills.[43] A *Canada Law Journal* article suggested that bankruptcy law was sufficiently controversial to deprive it of the support of influential members of the governing party. Therefore, the success of the bill depended upon opposition votes: "No government, whether Liberal or Tory, will willingly expose itself to the risks of such a situation."[44]

As the government showed little initiative, a letter to the editor of the *Monetary Times* suggested that the drafting be privatized in order to come up with the best bankruptcy bill. The author proposed that Boards of Trade and the government establish a "substantial money premium." The money, amounting to $2000 or $3000, would be "awarded to whoever shall submit the best and most feasible suggestions for the most economical, speedy, and equitable settlement of insolvent estates. This would be an incentive for competent, experienced men to send in propositions or suggestions in a definite shape."[45] While Parliament never established a reward, Boards of Trade submitted numerous bills throughout this period.

Boards of Trade demanded a federal reform bill for a number of reasons. First, provincial law was not uniform. Second, many provinces did not prohibit preferences, leading to "sharp and unscrupulous conduct on the part of creditors seeking an advantage over each other." Third, provincial proceedings were costly and inefficient. However, without the assistance of the government, all of the private Member's bills were doomed to fail. Further, the Boards of Trade were not always united in their approach and had different views on the best form of legislation.[46]

Memories of the evils of the *Insolvent Act* discharge affected the tenor of debate during the 1880s. An 1883 survey of twenty-five leading bankers and merchants showed unanimity for some kind of legislation. However, they were divided on the question of whether a discharge was necessary.[47] Merchants simply could not agree on the form of a reform bill "on account of so many of them wishing to leave out the discharge altogether." The Tillsonburg Board of Trade's position was typical of many during this era: "[We] have no objection to a law providing for the cheap and rapid winding up of an insolvent estate equitably among all the creditors so none can make preferential claims but we are opposed to any law giving men a discharge from their debts without their paying some to satisfaction of others."[48]

Distribution and discharge continued to be viewed as separate issues, with most bills seeking to exclude or extremely limit the discharge. Between 1880 and 1885, Parliament debated eleven bills. Of the eleven, six bills did not contain a discharge provision. The *Journal of Commerce* called for Parliament to resuscitate a distribution scheme and "leave the evil [of the discharge] ... buried."[49] There was no apparent relationship between the discharge and distribution.

According to the *Monetary Times*, any attempt to link a distribution scheme with a discharge provision would result "in neither being granted." Those who were interested in ensuring a law providing for a distribution of assets could not afford to defeat that purpose by asking for legislation on the discharge as well.[50] It was far better to proceed by treating the two functions as separate issues. Once a federal distribution scheme was in place, the discharge could be dealt with in another bill. Merchants who sought a bankruptcy bill were "wise not to imperil" the distribution provisions by including a discharge. After all, the distribution of assets had "nothing to do" with the discharge. However, the absence of a discharge in federal reform bills did not go unnoticed. The *Globe* reported that such proposals would strip the debtor of all property and leave him penniless. The editorial suggested that where a debtor had given up everything to his creditors, "let him in justice as well as in mercy be relieved from liabilities and obligations which if they still burden him must render his future utterly worthless."[51]

A number of bills introduced between 1880 and 1885 proposed a compulsory bankruptcy regime without providing for a discharge. Each bill provided for a mechanism to liquidate and distribute the debtor's assets and prohibited preferential payments. For example, a Toronto MP introduced a distribution proposal in 1882.[52] The goal, as stated in the House of Commons, was to ensure a fair distribution of the assets of the insolvent and to ensure that a creditor with a prior execution would not have priority over subsequent execution creditors.[53] However, nothing in the bill would "force creditors into granting a discharge."[54] The Toronto and Montreal Boards of Trade, unhappy with the administrative provisions of the bill, drafted their own separate bills.[55]

Committees of the Toronto, Montreal, and Hamilton Boards of Trade met on 30 October 1883[56] with a "view to securing united action on the part of the mercantile community." The Boards of Trade met with Macdonald and the Ministers of Finance and Justice in late 1883, and the government gave "an assurance that the subject would engage consideration." However, the Boards received a further noncommittal reply after an additional meeting with Macdonald in late 1884.[57]

In 1885, a further joint proposal, "prepared under the direction of the Boards of Trade of Montreal, Toronto, Hamilton, and Winnipeg," was formally introduced in the House of Commons as Bill C-4.[58] In its original form, the bill provided for a comprehensive distribution scheme and prohibited preferences. Only creditors could initiate proceedings, as the Act did not provide for any voluntary scheme. The proposal specifically excluded the discharge. However, the exclusion of the discharge was controversial.[59] The government responded by appointing a Special Committee, but Macdonald later claimed in private correspondence, "[I]t is not a Government Committee and we do not supervise in any way its proceedings." The *Monetary Times* claimed that by appointing the Committee "the government has again shirked the responsibility of dealing with this question."[60]

The final form of the bill reported out of Committee in 1885 did include the right of a debtor to obtain a discharge. Inclusion of the discharge in the final Committee report created division among those who had been advocating reform. Those who had urged bankruptcy reform found that they could not support the measure as reported out of the Committee. "Leading merchants" said that they would have rather had the law remain the same than to have the country "exposed to the dangers ... [of] a discharge clause."[61] The Montreal Board of Trade believed that the discharge clause would "lead to a crowd of new assignments and provide discharges for an unworthy class of debtors."[62] Despite receiving further petitions and letters[63] in support for the bill, it was not debated further in the House of Commons,[64] but this did not end the flow of bankruptcy reform proposals.

By 1888 the Toronto Board of Trade, frustrated by the lack of federal action, submitted a petition to the government, which confirmed the role of private interest groups in the reform process. The petition stated, "The various Boards of Trade ... of the Dominion have spent a great deal of time and labour, and have incurred expense in framing a measure on the subject." In 1890, in response to a request for federal bankruptcy reform, Macdonald stated that no further action could be taken on the subject, as "so much difference of opinion exists."[65]

The death of Macdonald in 1891 paved the way for the Conservatives to embrace reform as a government matter. Macdonald's successor was Canada's leading insolvency expert. John Abbott, the drafter of the *Insolvent Act of 1864* and adviser to Macdonald on insolvency matters, became leader of the Conservatives and Prime Minister in 1891.[66] Abbott announced to representatives of wholesalers and manufacturers his intention to take charge of an insolvency bill,[67] and despite his brief tenure as Prime Minister, his initiative took hold.[68] In order to obtain feedback on insolvency reform in January 1893 the government established a committee of commercial men, and consultation continued through 1893 and into 1894. The government submitted a confidential draft to some of the Boards of Trade and the newly formed Canadian Bankers' Association.[69]

Some fourteen years after the repeal of the *Insolvent Act of 1875*, the federal government announced in the speech from the Throne on 19 March 1894 that an insolvency measure would be laid before Parliament.[70] For the first time bankruptcy reform would be a government matter. In the Senate, the government explained why it had introduced the bill: "[T]he commercial community of this Dominion ... have been pressing upon the Government for a number of years the necessity of passing an Insolvency Act, and the Government for a number of years have resisted it, until the pressure became so great that they believed it to be in the interest of the business community."[71]

Mackenzie Bowell, the Minister of Trade and Commerce, introduced the measure in the Senate and appointed a Select Committee so that bankers and Boards of Trade could make submissions on the bill. The Senate passed the legislation after great debate, but the House of Commons did not.[72]

The bill as presented was a comprehensive one[73] and provided for the administration of an insolvent's estate and for a discharge. However, there was no consensus on fundamental aspects of the bill, with debate focusing largely on the discharge and the trader rule. The scope of the legislation dominated the debates for days. Both the *Insolvent Acts of 1869* and *1875* had been restricted to traders (i.e. those who bought and sold) and thereby excluded the farming sector from the scope of the legislation. Almost all of the reform bills of the 1880s were similarly structured. In sum, there was little consensus on whether there should be an Act at all and if there was to be an Act there was little consensus on its scope or content. As one Senator summarized positions on the bill, "The members of this House may be divided into four classes with respect to their views on this measure. Some ... think that we should not have an insolvency law at all ... There is another class who think that if we are to have an insolvency law it should be limited strictly to the class who have asked for it, that is traders ... There is another class ... who think that all classes should come under the insolvency law, but that they should be all dealt with in the same manner ... then there is the fourth class ... who think that [traders] ... should be put in a worse position than any other section of the community."[74] With such fractured support for the bill, there was little prospect of it passing.

In 1894 the bill passed the Senate but failed to pass in the House of Commons, despite having the approval of the government. Although the official reason given for the lack of approval by the House of Commons was the lateness of the session,[75] failure in 1894 can be attributed in part to the efforts of the newly formed Canadian Bankers' Association.[76] While banks had been interested in insolvency legislation in the past, and some had in fact lobbied for a general federal law,[77] they united to form a new association in 1892.[78] On reviewing the draft bill, the banks objected to a provision that prejudiced their right to recover on negotiable paper from an insolvent debtor's estate.[79] Following the Senate debates, the Association passed a resolution at its 1894 annual meeting stating that it was "not prepared to affirm that a general Bankruptcy Act would be beneficial to the community at large."[80] The government reintroduced the measure in 1895 but did not press the matter, as there was little prospect for its success.[81] In 1895, the Senate voted to delay consideration of the bill, and it died on the order paper.[82]

With the election of Laurier and the Liberal government in 1896, there was the possibility that the new government would take new policy initiatives on bankruptcy. However, despite continued pressure from the Boards of Trade, Laurier's government took little interest in the matter. It offered no government bills and failed to support two private Member's bills drafted on behalf of the Montreal Board of Trade.[83]

As the century came to a close, Boards of Trade continued to debate bankruptcy policy. They held meetings to exchange ideas and proposed "to hold a conference of all Canadian Boards of Trade, with a view to making united representations to the Dominion Government."[84] Laurier's personal papers contain several direct appeals for a new law.[85] The Boards, continuing to be plagued by the provincial laws and the decline in foreign credit, arranged to meet directly with the government.[86] As the Montreal Board of Trade summed up the impact of the absence of a national law, "You doubtless become aware when visiting Great Britain of the unfavourable impression of Canadian business morality prevailing in commercial circles in that country owing to the absence here of a general insolvent law, and utterances in the trade journals there and intimations from business correspondents continue to show clearly how prejudicial to the Credit is the absence of legislation securing to creditors in Great Britain a fair share of a Canadian insolvent's estate."[87] However, despite these meetings the government failed to announce any new initiatives.

Therefore, in 1898 the Montreal Board of Trade prepared a bill. The Board wrote to Thomas Fortin, the MP who introduced the bill,[88] and demanded a national *pro rata* law, "a need emphasized by the fact that the system of preferential assignments prevalent in some provinces has rendered England and other European countries unwilling to give credit to Canadian Houses."[89] The bill provided the machinery for the distribution of the estate and included a discharge provision. The 1898 proposal applied to traders and did not allow voluntary proceedings.[90] Farmers obtained two advantages under the bill, and these changes reflected the continued important influence of rural Members of Parliament. First, since the bill applied only to traders, compulsory proceedings could not be taken against farmers. Farmers objected to a law of general application, as they feared a bankruptcy law that could be used against them during a period of seasonal insolvency.[91] Second, a new provision ensured that traders who did receive a discharge continued to remain liable for debts owed to farmers. It had always been a complaint of the farming community that they were unable to recover debts from bankrupt merchants.[92] In addition, the Bankers' Association succeeded in ensuring that the rights of banks would be safeguarded. The bill provided that nothing in the Act "shall interfere with, or restrict, the rights and privileges conferred upon banks and banking corporation by the Bank Act."[93]

However, what the bill lacked was government support. In a telegram to Laurier, Thomas Fortin asked "why [the] government cannot support the Insolvency Bill." In Parliament, Laurier stated that he did not want to make it a government measure because "it might be treated as [a] political measure, and above all things such a Bill should not be treated as a political one, but simply from a commercial point of view."[94] The 1898 bill did not progress beyond first reading. It was reintroduced in 1903,[95] but Laurier refused to support it, and if the House pursued the matter he would "ask the House to reject it."[96] Although private groups continued to lobby Laurier directly for reform,[97] he pointed to developments in the provinces as a reason not to pursue reform at the national level. Laurier's letter to James Crowe, a debtor in Erie, Pennsylvania, demanding federal reforms, summed up the Liberal Government's position. Laurier simply asserted that existing provincial legislation "seems to be satisfactory." [98] With that, Laurier closed a political chapter on the federal bankruptcy law reform debate.[99] Parliament did not debate any further bills until 1918.

3. Conclusion

Although the drafters of the *BNA Act* included bankruptcy and insolvency as a federal power, efforts to enact a permanent national bankruptcy regime after Confederation ended in failure with the repeal of the *Insolvent Act of 1875* in 1880. Perhaps the lack of success to reinstate a national bankruptcy law until after the First World War is hardly surprising. The overwhelming negative reaction to the two *Insolvent Acts of 1869* and *1875* most likely "poisoned the bankruptcy legislative well for years."[100] With repeal, the law reverted to the common law, which created a race to the debtor's assets. Creditors were also left without adequate provision to deal with preferences.

A provincial solution initially seemed promising as a way to fill the void left by repeal. In the end, provincial law was not comprehensive. Ontario's *Creditor's Relief Act*, which was passed on the heels of the federal Act's repeal, did not come into effect until four years later, and other provinces did not follow suit immediately. Similarly, it took time for provincial legislation on preferences to come into effect. Provincial law was not uniform, and it could not compel a debtor to make an assignment under provincial law. Finally, provincial law could not provide for a statutory discharge.

The flaws in provincial law led many urban Boards of Trade to demand federal reform. However, the absence of a strong government department and bureaucracy inhibited implementation of federal legislation. Unlike England, which had a civil service and new government department to support the *Bankruptcy Act of 1883*, bankruptcy law did not interest the Canadian Department of Justice, and most reform initiatives came from Canadian and foreign interest groups. Canadian bankruptcy reform had no institutional backing from the government. The lack of government action led private interest groups to become the chief source of bankruptcy reform proposals, as urban Boards of Trade drafted bills and submitted them to Members of Parliament to be introduced into the House of Commons. However, there was little consensus on the form of a reform bill, and urban Boards of Trade often divided over the reform question. Indeed, the variety of federal proposals generated mainly by Boards of Trade (which ranged from a bankruptcy law without a discharge; a bankruptcy law with a discharge; a bankruptcy law relying upon provincial legislation to distribute assets; or no bankruptcy law) made a stable outcome unlikely. David Skeel's recent work on the history of United States bankruptcy law demonstrates that where lawmakers hold "a multiplicity of views on a single subject ... irrational ... outcomes are likely."[101]

Skeel draws upon political science theory known as legislative cycling. He notes that if lawmakers have an "equal vote, and every option is available, the voting process may lead to chronically unstable results."[102] Using a hypothetical example of three senators voting on three policy options in the US context, Skeel predicts legislative cycling when there are multiple policy choices.

In the Canadian context, if MPs were presented with three policy options – bankruptcy law with a discharge (full bankruptcy), bankruptcy without a discharge (partial bankruptcy), and no bankruptcy law at all[103] – MPs would likely rank their choices in order of preference. Relying upon Skeel's model, if we were to hold a hypothetical vote by three MPs on the three policy choices, legislative cycling may occur. Assuming only two policy choices were presented on each vote, the following may occur: full bankruptcy may defeat partial bankruptcy and partial bankruptcy may defeat no bankruptcy law. However, the cycle would be complete with the possibility of no bankruptcy law defeating full bankruptcy law. If MPs continued to vote in accordance with their relative ranked preferences, "the votes would go around and around for ever – that is they would cycle."[104]

By the time the Canadian government initiated reform proposals in 1894–5, there was little consensus on the need for an Act. The election of

Laurier in 1896 sealed the fate of bankruptcy reform. Pointing to growing provincial legislation, Laurier saw no need to pursue reform at the federal level.

In part, the entrenchment of provincial legislation can be explained by the constitutional litigation of the 1890s. The impact of federalism is considered in chapter 7.

7

The Constitutional Question and the Impact of Federalism 1880–1903

Perhaps no decision of the Judicial Committee has been awaited with more interest.

A.H.F. Lefroy, "The Privy Council on Bankruptcy" (1894) 30:6 Canada Law Journal (NS) 182

Federalism also had a significant effect upon the legislative history of Canadian bankruptcy law.[1] The *BNA Act* provided the possibility that provinces might ameliorate the effects of federal repeal of the *Insolvent Act of 1875* by providing their own distribution scheme under their jurisdiction over property and civil rights. Similarly, provinces might enact legislation that prohibited preferences. If all the common law provinces could be convinced to enact such legislation, a federal bankruptcy law would no longer be required. The existence of a possible provincial solution provided the federal government with a strong reason not to push for the reform of a controversial subject at the national level.

The disinterest of the federal government in bankruptcy reform coincided with the rise of the provincial rights movement of the 1880s. However, unlike several of the more high-profile federal-provincial disputes of the provincial rights era, bankruptcy law was not a political battleground between Prime Minister Macdonald and the Ontario Premier Oliver Mowat. The federal government was content to allow the provinces to regulate debtor-creditor matters and to defer the constitutional question to the courts. Nevertheless, the jurisdictional issue was of great interest to creditors. By the late 1880s, for many the debate shifted away from substantive bankruptcy law to a discussion of the ambit of federal and provincial powers.

Between 1886 and 1893, several Ontario courts ruled on the validity of provincial legislation. The divided opinions of the Ontario Court of Appeal left the law in a state of confusion and inhibited reform at both the federal and provincial levels. The Privy Council did not resolve the uncertainty until its 1894 ruling in *Attorney-General of Ontario v Attorney-General for the Dominion of Canada*. The decision, which upheld the validity of provincial legislation, contributed to the further growth of provincial laws and largely ended federal reform efforts. Provincial law became entrenched as the primary means of regulating debtor-creditor matters. It was not until after the First World War that bankruptcy law again became a national issue. Federalism played a key institutional role in the legislative history of Canadian bankruptcy law.

In the 1880s and 1890s, the federal government came under increasing pressure to exercise its jurisdiction over bankruptcy and insolvency.[2] The *Journal of Commerce*, for example, pointed out that at Confederation a great deal of emphasis had been placed on the need to abolish local customary laws. In an 1899 editorial, the *Journal* commented on the state of provincial legislation: "Almost every Province in the Dominion has been cutting and patching at the various insolvent acts in such a way as to cause irritation and soreness and keep the country backward and divided. Instead of this, these petty inter-provincial business jealousies should be thrown to the wind and the general good of the country considered."[3]

Proponents of a uniform law pointed to the explicit wording in the *BNA Act* granting the federal government jurisdiction over bankruptcy and insolvency. In contrast, provincial laws regulating insolvency were "enacted by an authority which is hampered by limitations and doubts." It was "worse than useless" to allow provinces to deal with the matter, "since their action is hampered alike by lack of sufficient powers and the absence of all precedents." "Why were there national customs, insurance, banking, and railway statutes while insolvency matters had been abandoned to the provinces?"[4]

The period under study coincided with the growing conflicts between the provincial and federal governments on the limits of their respective constitutional grants of power. This conflict was personified in the contrasting positions taken by Oliver Mowat, Liberal Premier of Ontario, and the Conservative Prime Minister John A. Macdonald. These numerous constitutional disputes have been well documented by a number of scholars.[5] However, in contrast to the other areas of constitutional conflict, Macdonald showed little interest in the federal bankruptcy power and often referred to provincial legislation as a possible solution to the problem of insolvent debtors. Macdonald never formally challenged Mowat on the issue and was content to allow the provinces to regulate the area in the absence of federal legislation. For many, there was no other constitutional issue with real and tangible economic effects attached. Most participants in the economy were debtors or creditors in some form and watched impatiently as the jurisdictional question of bankruptcy stumbled its way through the 1880s and 1890s.

Despite pleas for federal action on the subject of bankruptcy law, Prime Minister Macdonald used provincial jurisdiction as a reason to delay federal reform. In 1882, in private correspondence, Macdonald questioned whether a federal bill, which provided only for the distribution of an insolvent's estate, was "within the competence of the Federal Parliament." In the House of Commons, Macdonald questioned whether or not an 1883 bankruptcy reform bill was an "interference with property and civil rights."[6]

Macdonald also used the constitutional question to deflect foreign pressure for federal reform. In 1884, he told a deputation from the London (England) Chamber of Commerce that "special difficulties were found to exist in Canada, owing to the concurrent powers of the Dominion and Local Legislatures." Macdonald pointed out that the federal Parliament had no right to interfere with provincial law affecting contracts, save for the exception of the federal power over bankruptcy and insolvency. As Parliament had no power to deal with preferences other than in a bankruptcy law, there was little action that it could take to address the growing problem of preferential payments. Therefore, preferences were to be left to the provinces to regulate. The federal government was "powerless to deal with the subject unless by the enactment of a general law of bankruptcy or insolvency."[7]

Macdonald was aware of developments at the provincial level but chose not to use the disallowance power.[8] Rather, the government was content to allow the judicial system to rule on the constitutional issue. For example, in 1886, the federal Minister of Justice recommended against the use of disallowance for the Ontario *Assignments Act*. It was "more than doubtful whether it is within the legislative authority of the provincial legislature." However, as the issue was pending before the courts, the question could "be more conveniently settled in that way than in any other."[9] Macdonald similarly refused to disallow other provincial statutes passed in Manitoba, Quebec and Nova Scotia, despite the fact that there was "great doubt as to the authority of a legislature to enact such laws as these, as they are in the nature of Insolvent Acts."[10]

In 1887, the provinces adopted a resolution at the Interprovincial Conference of Premiers[11] calling for an amendment to the *BNA Act* to expressly give the provinces the necessary jurisdiction to enact bankruptcy legislation in the absence of any federal law. Such an amendment was required because it was "doubtful" how far the provincial jurisdiction extended but, more importantly, it was in the "public interest that each province should be [at] liberty to deal with the matter subject to any federal law which may be thereafter enacted."[12]

As noted in chapter 5, there was little doubt about the constitutionality of the federal *Insolvent Acts.*[13] The Privy Council had resolved this matter in 1880.[14] However, what was in doubt was the scope of provincial powers to regulate in the absence of federal legislation. It was not long before several Ontario courts began to rule on the validity of the *Act Respecting Assignments and Preferences by Insolvent Persons,*[15] and early decisions upheld the constitutionality of the statute.[16] In 1888, the Ontario Court of Appeal agreed to hear arguments on four separate cases, and the outcome of the cases attracted national interest.[17]

On 20 March 1888, the Ontario Court of Appeal added to the uncertainty by issuing a split decision on the four concurrent appeals (referred to below as *Clarkson et al*).[18] All four cases dealt with the validity of *An Act Respecting Assignments for the Benefit of Creditors.*[19] The first part of the Act voided preferential transfers, while the second allowed a debtor to voluntarily make an assignment to a named assignee for the benefit of creditors. Assets were distributed on a *pro rata* basis. Assignees were given the exclusive power to set aside preferences. Further, section 9 provided that an assignment for the benefit of creditors took priority over all judgments and incomplete executions. No compulsory proceedings were available, and debtors did not receive a discharge of their liabilities. A debtor could "only be discharged from his debts so far as his estate pays them. All the rest he will continue to owe."[20]

In each of the appeals, an insolvent debtor had made a preferential transfer to a creditor prior to making an assignment for the benefit of creditors. The assignees, as plaintiffs, challenged the preferences under the Ontario statute. The defendants, the recipients of the preference, argued that the Ontario legislation was *ultra vires*. The four Justices of the Court of Appeal were "equally divided on the point."[21] Osler J held that the provincial legislation was *ultra vires*: "If one object of an insolvent Act be to insure uniformity in the distribution of the assets of the insolvent, it is not attained by legislation of this kind, under which, if within the competence of the local legislatures, the assets of the same debtor carrying on business in more than one province may be distributed upon as many different principles or systems as there are provincial Acts dealing with the question."[22]

While the country waited for a final resolution of the matter by a higher court, the interim was a "chaotic state of affairs, which assuming the Act to be *ultra vires*, allows the first-comer among claimants to be first served." The Ontario Court of Appeal's 1888 decision created, according to the *Journal of Commerce*, "a state of chaos" and was a "grave scandal." E.D. Armour, a Toronto lawyer and an editor of the *Canadian Law Times*, concluded, "In Ontario the law is in an unsatisfactory state. The leading decision [*Clarkson et al*] shows such a difference, such a variety, of opinion that it seems hopeless to reduce the different expressions of opinion to any definite form."[23]

After the split decision in *Clarkson et al*, in 1888 the Minister of Justice concluded that disallowance ought not to be used. Even though two Justices had upheld the validity of the provincial statute, and further appeals may have confirmed this view, the Minister of Justice declined to act. He concluded that the Act was "undergoing discussion before the courts of Ontario, and pending a decision" he did not advise the government to utilize the disallowance power.[24]

In 1891, the Ontario Court of Appeal added to the confusion by declaring section 9 of the Ontario Act *ultra vires* in *Union Bank v Neville*. The *Journal of Commerce* reported that the decision made "confusion worse confounded," while the *Monetary Times* advised that after the decision "it will be unsafe for insolvents to rely on the provisions of that statute."[25]

To clarify the matter, the Ontario government referred a question to the Court of Appeal: "Had the Legislature of Ontario jurisdiction to enact the 9th section of the Revised Statutes of Ontario, ch. 124, and entitled, 'An Act Respecting Assignments and Preferences by Insolvent Persons?'" In the reference case, the Court of Appeal concluded that section 9 was *ultra vires*.[26]

But the Court of Appeal decision did not settle the matter. The *Canadian Law Times* indicated, "No doubt the case will not end here." Many anticipated an appeal to the Privy Council. The *Canadian Law Times* optimistically predicted that the *Assignment and Preferences Act* as well as the *Creditors' Relief Act* would be struck down.[27] The files of the Department of Justice on the appeal to the Privy Council illustrate not only a confused state of affairs but also a desperate sense of urgency to end the constitutional uncertainty.

Three days after the Court of Appeal issued its ruling in the reference case, the Ontario Attorney General wrote to the Minister of Justice indicating that the provincial government was under pressure and needed a quick resolution of the matter. A letter to the Department of Justice asked that the solicitors representing the federal government in England request an immediate hearing and decision in the case.[28] However, by November 1893 the matter still had not been resolved and the Ontario Attorney General explained why they wanted a quick resolution: "[I]t is of great public importance to get a decision of the Privy Council at the earliest possible day. I understand that merchants and persons in business are looking very anxiously for it, and are in perplexity from the doubts which exist. I understand that the profession are also expressing like anxiety, because in the present unsettled condition of the question involved, they do not know how to advise their clients."[29]

Oliver Mowat, Premier of Ontario, was of the view that the Privy Council would appreciate the importance of the appeal if informed that the Ontario Act was the only effective substitute for a bankruptcy law in the province, given the inability of the federal government to agree on a new reform measure.[30] According to constitutional law scholar A.H.F Lefroy, "Perhaps no decision of the Judicial Committee has been awaited with more interest, at all events in the profession."[31] The Privy Council agreed to hear the matter in December 1893, and its subsequent decision ended the long period of constitutional uncertainty. The Privy Council upheld the validity of the provincial provision. However, there was more at stake than constitutional principle and doctrine.[32] While constitutional theory lay at the heart of the matter, the ruling had dire consequences for numerous creditors and merchants. "Real lobbyists and litigants," in the words of Blaine Baker, had a stake in the outcome.[33]

Edward Blake argued the appeal for the Attorney General of Ontario. Blake had earlier been the federal Liberal Minister of Justice. He had presided over the amendments to the *Insolvent Act of 1875* and was a leading Canadian constitutional lawyer in the post-Confederation era.[34] Blake raised a number of constitutional arguments, but more importantly, he made the members of the Privy Council aware of the practical implications of its ruling.[35]

The central question for Blake was not just the meaning of "bankruptcy and insolvency" in the constitution but rather the meaning of those terms in the absence of federal legislation. The earlier Privy Council case of *Cushing v Dupuy* had expressly stated that the *BNA Act* "intended to confer on [the federal government] the power to interfere with property, and civil rights, and procedure within the Provinces, so far as a general law relating to those subjects might affect them."[36] While *Cushing* seemed to carve out a great deal of potential for federal interference in provincial matters, for Blake the larger the area created for the federal power, "the more essential that it is that you should keep free the hands of the Local Legislature" to deal with property and civil rights until the federal power was exercised. Blake argued, "The more ample the power you assign to the Dominion Parliament to meddle with the sphere of the Local Legislature ... the more important it is to decide that at any rate until Parliament chooses to act the other Legislature shall not be disabled from acting."[37] According to Blake, the federal government urged an interpretation that would prohibit the provincial legislature from interfering while the Dominion was idle. This construction "would lead to obscurity and confusion and paralysis the moment it was adopted." It would "paralyze the action of the one Legislature without any attempt on the part of the other Legislature to act."[38]

Blake painted a contrasting image of the two branches of government. The federal government had not enacted any legislation since 1880. Further, "there has never since been any attempt to pass any fresh law." He stated to the Privy Council that it was unlikely that any federal legislation "will soon pass."[39]

Blake argued that the Constitution provided two mechanisms for federal action. First, the federal power of disallowance could have been used to prevent the provincial law from coming into force. Second, the Dominion government, "having determined upon the policy of Bankruptcy and Insolvency for themselves," could at any time intervene and pass federal legislation that would have put into abeyance the provincial statute. As neither option had been exercised, Blake characterized the Dominion attitude as "acting a little like the dog in the manger;

they will not act themselves. They will not take the food; nor do they propose to allow that it shall be obtained by anybody else."[40]

Provincial legislation had attempted to cure the "great evils" created by the repeal in 1880, such as the "game of grab," whereby individual creditors obtained unequal distributions. The federal policy of repeal, Blake told the English bench, bore "very hardly ... on foreign creditors and interfered with the general credit and interests of the country."[41]

Lord Herschell's eagerly awaited judgment concluded that the provincial legislation was valid. He concluded that assignments for the benefit of creditors had long been known under the common law and were independent of any system of bankruptcy and insolvency legislation. The validity of an assignment under the provincial law did not depend on the insolvency of the assignor. Further, having found that compulsory proceedings were an essential element of a bankruptcy and insolvency, the provisions of the provincial statute, "relating as they do to assignments purely voluntary, do not infringe upon the exclusive legislative power conferred upon the Dominion Parliament."

In the judgment, the Privy Council also ruled that the federal bankruptcy and insolvency power might necessarily include the regulation of matters within the provincial jurisdiction: "They would observe that a system of bankruptcy legislation may frequently require various ancillary provisions for the purpose of preventing the scheme of the Act from being defeated ... Their Lordships do not doubt that it would be open to the Dominion Parliament to deal with such matters as part of bankruptcy law, and the provincial legislature would doubtless be then precluded from interfering with this legislation inasmuch as such interference would affect the bankruptcy law of the Dominion Parliament."[42]

However, the Privy Council recognized that in the matter before them, there was no federal bankruptcy law. The absence of federal legislation clearly influenced the decision of the Privy Council:[43] "But it does not follow that such subjects, as might properly be treated as ancillary to such a law and therefore within the powers of the Dominion Parliament, are excluded from the legislative authority of the provincial legislature when there is no bankruptcy or insolvency legislation of the Dominion Parliament in existence."[44]

For constitutional scholars, the importance of the ruling was the clear statement that the federal government, in exercising its bankruptcy power, might deal with matters that would otherwise be within the competence of the provinces. Writing in 1894, Lefroy argued that in this aspect of the ruling, the Privy Council had carried out "the intention of the framers" of the *BNA Act*. The case, according to Lefroy, was one of the "first instances of the Dominion Parliament 'scoring' before the Privy Council."[45] However, what mattered more to creditors was the fact that the Privy Council had not invalidated the provision of the Ontario statute.

The decision enabled the provinces to continue on the path of provincial reform and removed the immediate need for federal reform.The decision actually preceded the introduction of the 1894 federal reform bill,[46] which marked the first time a government had officially backed an insolvency reform measure. However, the bill, which provided for involuntary proceedings against traders and a discharge, soon became entangled in the constitutional niceties of the Privy Council decision. On the first reading of the bill, the government admitted that it had not yet received an official copy of the Privy Council decision and did not have any further information than the brief press reports. When the bill next came up for debate, Members of Parliament quoted lengthy passages from the decision, and once the tenor of the decision became known, it spelled the end for the bill. It was urged that federal reforms be delayed for at least another twelve months to allow provinces to enact legislation in accordance with the decision of the Privy Council.[47]

After the Privy Council decision, attention in Parliament shifted to the provinces' ability to regulate the matter. The special needs,[48] or "the peculiar circumstances which may locally exist," could be accommodated by provincial legislation.[49] The interests of all were best served by the provinces exercising their jurisdiction over property and civil rights. In 1895, a Senator relied upon the Privy Council decision to oppose the reintroduction of a national bankruptcy bill in the Senate on the basis that the provincial reform path should be allowed to continue.[50] Charles Tupper, Canada's High Commissioner to England and later the Prime Minister who led the Tories to defeat in 1896, told the British Empire League on 4 December 1895 that "the recent decision of the Privy Council ... seems to have had the effect of stimulating local legislation on insolvency."[51] New Brunswick enacted preference legislation in 1895, followed by Nova Scotia in 1898.[52]

The election of the Laurier government in 1896 further strengthened the provincial cause. Laurier restored the tradition of federal non-involvement and allowed provincial reforms to take their natural course. By 1899, Laurier's government was systematically tracking the evolution of provincial legislation.[53] It was determined to prove that provincial legislation was adequate. In 1902, W.S. Fielding, the Minister of Finance, wrote to Charles Fitzpatrick, the Minister of Justice, and inquired about the state of provincial law. In his letter, Fielding referred to prior British complaints about cases where English creditors had "suffered severely" in the Maritime provinces: "Since that time, Provincial legislation respecting preferential assignments ... has, I think, largely, if not wholly, removed the difficulty. My impression is that the Provincial laws now cover the ground pretty fully."[54]

Laurier used the pending reforms in the provinces as the reason to bow out of the field.[55] In 1898, in response to the introduction of another private Member's bankruptcy bill, Laurier referred to the superior state of Quebec provincial law respecting insolvency. He argued that if other provinces followed, there would be no need for the federal government to legislate in the area.[56] By 1903, with provincial reforms firmly entrenched, there was no reason to press on with endless federal debates. Laurier ended the debate on the 1903 bill with a statement that clearly left the matter to the provinces: "[S]ince the matter has been brought to the attention of the House, most of the provinces have amended their laws with regard to insolvent estates and I understand that these are now pretty satisfactory except in one or two provinces. It is to be hoped that the provinces themselves will attend to this kind of legislation, and adopt laws of such a character as to be acceptable."[57]

The Privy Council ruling did not preclude federal action. Conversely, it clearly stated the wide ambit of the federal bankruptcy and insolvency power. However, the decision did offer the federal government a choice. By upholding the validity of the Ontario statute and enabling the provinces to regulate debtor-creditor matters in the absence of federal bankruptcy law, the ruling permitted the federal government to maintain the status quo of non-involvement. After 1903, no further bankruptcy reform bills were debated at the federal level until 1918.

Conclusion

Constitutional law played an additional role in the evolution of bankruptcy and insolvency law between 1880 and 1903. Despite the clear federal power over bankruptcy and insolvency law it was not certain whether federal or provincial legislation would prevail in the regulation of insolvent debtors. However, provincial legislation was slow to emerge and many regions tolerated preferences until the end of the century. The inadequacy of provincial legislation in many respects kept pressure on Parliament to re-enter the field. Boards of Trade continued to draft reform bills throughout this period in the absence of government interest.

Constitutional uncertainty, particularly between 1886 and 1894, inhibited federal and provincial reforms. Once the Privy Council ruled in 1894, it was open for the remaining provinces to institute reforms. Had the Privy Council ruled the other way, there is no doubt that legislative reform would have taken a different direction. A ruling against Ontario would have left provincial law in a state of chaos, leading to a more concerted effort for federal reform. In 1903, when Prime Minister Laurier shut the door on further federal reform initiatives, his decision to do so was justified on the basis that many of the provinces had legislation that adequately dealt with bankrupt estates. The possibility of a provincial solution removed the immediate need for reform during this period.

While the constitutional history of bankruptcy law helps to explain the failure of reform during this era, it is important to understand that the debate about bankruptcy law continued to involve competing ideas about the discharge and the distribution of assets. Both of these topics are considered in chapter 8.

8

The Bankruptcy Law Debates 1880–1903

The man who gives away his freedom is everlastingly bankrupt.

Lydia Leavitt & Thad W.H. Leavitt, *Wise or Otherwise* (Toronto: Wells Publishing, 1898) p. 35

The equitable distribution of assets and the discharge continued to spark debate after repeal. Ideas still mattered. All federal reform bills contained an equitable distribution of the debtor's assets and prohibited preferential payments, yet the idea of equality still remained controversial. Canadian Boards of Trade, and for the first time foreign creditor associations, lobbied for federal reform to overcome the deficiencies of provincial law.

The discharge also remained contentious. Throughout the 1880s, forgiveness competed unsuccessfully with the notion that a debtor had a moral obligation to repay all debts. What distinguished the post-repeal period from the 1870s was the increasing intensity of the public discourse over the merits of the discharge. The content of bankruptcy reform bills in this era reflected the discharge debate. There was little consensus over whether federal bankruptcy reform bills should contain a discharge. Many of the federal reform bills debated between 1880 and 1903 excluded a discharge. Ultimately, the moral obligation to repay debts triumphed, as all federal reform bills failed during this era. The debate over the discharge also intensified after the 1880 repeal of the

Insolvent Act of 1875 as debtors in increasing numbers absconded to the United States and other provinces. Without a statutory discharge, debtors had no incentive to remain in Canada.

Section 1 examines the debate over the equitable distribution of the debtor's assets while section 2 considers the discharge.

1. Preferences and the Distribution of the Debtor's Assets

The fair and equitable distribution of the debtor's assets continued to be controversial. Bankruptcy law offered a major advantage over the common law, as it provided a distribution of the debtor's assets to all creditors on a *pro rata* basis.[1] Distant creditors favoured a national bankruptcy law with its equitable distribution policy and the prohibition of preferences. Bankruptcy law reduced risks for distant creditors and destroyed local creditor advantage.[2]

The debate about bankruptcy law in many ways reflected two competing visions of the economy. Supporters of a national act appealed to the transformation of the economy. In the bygone era of local trade, transactions were of "very small character" and bankruptcy reform had not been so vital. However, with the "great advance we have made in trade and commerce," bankruptcy reform became essential.[3] It was important to establish uniform legislation because great distances separated many businesses. Manufacturers in the Atlantic region were interested in debtors' estates on the Pacific Coast.[4] One Member of Parliament stated, "We want a law that will govern this question from ocean to ocean."[5] Canada could not take advantage of the new opportunities for expanded trade until Parliament reformed the bankruptcy laws.

The confused state of the laws defeated the very purpose of the new railway infrastructure.[6] Monod's study of the evolution of shopkeepers traces the growth of the mass markets and the shift in distribution patterns away from merchants towards manufacturers with a more national outlook. In the 1880s and 1890s, major structural changes began in the distribution of goods, which included direct marketing, manufacturer controlled advertising and mass merchandising. By 1900, large department stores began to challenge independent shopkeepers. While some existed in the 1870s, by the 1890s the "power of their size" began to manifest itself. Chain stores were the fastest growing retail organization in early twentieth-century Canada. The railways not only offered a new distribution scheme for independent retailers; the lines also brought increasing competition from specialized stores, which threatened the independent proprietor.[7] The Canadian Manufacturing Association, in a 1900 letter to Laurier, noted that interprovincial and foreign trade of Canada had increased and was "steadily growing."[8] Thus, bankruptcy law was a necessary commercial statute designed to encourage and foster national markets.

Although the Canadian economy had undergone significant change, many areas continued to operate in traditional ways. Taylor and Baskerville note that, despite the growth of department stores and mail-order catalogues, many areas of Canada continued to be isolated from the changes. Outside central Canada, wholesalers and retailers continued to supply local markets in rural areas, and Monod's study shows that independent retailers did not disappear with the emergence of mass-market merchandisers.[9] This calls into question the axiom of business and economic historians that "the maturation of the industrial economy involved the destruction of the personal enterprise."[10]

Therefore the world of large corporations trading in mainly urban and national markets was yet to come. Even the completion of the transcontinental railway in 1885 did not overcome the vast political and social differences among the regions. Regional diversity was advanced as a positive element that should be preserved. Between 1875 and 1910, Canadian markets were small and scattered over great distances.[11] The Winnipeg Board of Trade's response to the Montreal Board's bill of 1892 illustrates how closely tied merchants remained to the rural economy: "The small merchants scattered throughout the country are dependent entirely upon the farmers, and they in turn have no source of income except their crops. Necessarily the merchant must give credit if he expects to do business, and his ability to meet his liability to the Wholesale Houses who supply him with goods, depends entirely upon the results of each harvest." In Manitoba and the Northwest Territories, business conditions did not allow for commerce to be carried out in accordance with the same strict principles that governed the established provinces. In the West, "distances were greater, the population very sparse, and the means of communication slow and exceedingly limited." The proposed insolvency bill required the institution of numerous legal proceedings, all of which were an expense, particularly when "the distance of the debtor's place of residence from the Court house would in Manitoba average at least 75 miles."[12] The requirement that the first meeting of creditors had to take place in the district where the debtor resides would involve a great expense to creditors, the majority of whom resided in Winnipeg. This might mean trips of 75 to 150 miles in order to attend a meeting of creditors. The census illustrates that the population continued to be predominantly rural, even as of 1901. The shift in favour of an urban population did not occur until after the First World War.[13]

Rural opposition to bankruptcy law continued to play an important role during this period. Members of Parliament pointed to "differences of opinion between the city and the rural constituencies on the subject." Upon repeal, only a few complaints emerged from rural Members, while urban Members demanded reform.[14] In 1885, the English Associated Chambers of Commerce interviewed Macdonald on his visit to England, who claimed that, despite pressures for federal reform, he had found it difficult to pursue the matter in the House of Commons.[15] The majority of the Members of Parliament "represented rural constituencies and they had all the prejudices of a rural population. The rural population did not like a bankruptcy act." Similarly, in 1885 the *Journal of Commerce* reported that the government would not succeed in passing Bill C-4, as representatives of rural districts "may make difficulty when the bill is before Parliament."[16] Notwithstanding the continued existence of local markets, it is clear that many were thinking along the lines of a more national economy. The efforts of Canadian Boards of Trade and foreign creditor associations to establish a national act to overcome the deficiencies of local laws is evidence of a growing sense of a national market, but the failure of Boards of Trade suggests that the national economy had not yet emerged. Further, institutional factors such as the lack of government support and federalism impeded reform.

The premise of the equal treatment of all creditors contained in a bankruptcy Act ran counter to the notion of individual responsibility and the higher obligation to repay all debts. An 1885 publication (located in the Macdonald papers) suggested that creditors who sought to rely upon a *pro rata* distribution neglected "honesty and integrity," and that there should be "no special law" dealing with a distribution of assets. The anonymous author claimed, "God had established ... economic laws, which if we ignore will bring upon a society of devastation." Legislators could not eliminate "the consequences of any infringement of God's eternal laws."[17] In a letter to Macdonald, another individual explained that the first to initiate proceedings "may take all he can find and leave other creditors to take whatever they can get." Provincial law discriminated "in favour of local creditors to the detriment of those more distant."[18]

The equal distribution of assets also contradicted the concept of offering assistance to a local friend or family member, which lay at the heart of more traditional forms of business. Preferences were therefore consistent with older forms of business. The *Journal of Commerce* in an 1893 editorial argued that traditional or "old fashioned business" was based on the premise that "a trader effected most of his dealings with his friends and near neighbours, and it was they who counselled him during his career and gave him support – that only an outsider could go the length of bringing his affairs to a crisis by some unfriendly act – that friends and near neighbours must be thought of first in times of peril."[19]

Many tolerated preferences, as it promoted "home trade ... and to prevent the over-running of territory by new and venturesome competitors."[20] In considering the relationship between distant creditors and preferences, the *Journal of Commerce* observed, "The drawing of provincial boundaries created domains within which residents had privileges that outsiders could not claim. Thus preferences became engrafted on our business systems in some of the Provinces." Preferences therefore "naturally excite the ire of creditors at a distance."[21]

Indeed, there was a further reason to excuse preferences in favour of close friends or neighbours. Often loans from close connections were loans of compassion without the stipulation of interest. Loans of this category were fundamentally different than the purchase of goods on credit or a bank loan that carried interest. A borrower who received a compassionate loan was under a "moral obligation ... to return the thing borrowed – or if it be of a nature to become merged in his business, then a preference seems a natural equivalent to its non-return."[22]

The practice of preferring local or family creditors came into conflict with the interests of distant creditors. Nova Scotia, which did not abolish preferences until 1898, was often singled out as a troublesome province for creditors. The *Monetary Times* claimed that Ontario and Quebec merchants who sold goods into Nova Scotia found that the debtor often "made an assignment to some Bluenose friend ... giving preferences to local creditors." Similarly, in New Brunswick, "a debtor classifies his debts into four classes – first, to clerks, second, to his relatives, third, debts owing to Canadians, and fourth, debts owed to the English."[23] The President of the Montreal Board of Trade pointed out in a speech during the 1897 annual meeting that the evil of provincial law was the preferences given to one or two friends. He used an example of a debtor in the Maritimes who made payments to seven friends and local creditors, to the detriment of the thirty-two other creditors who received nothing.[24]

As discussed in chapter 6, Canadian Boards of Trade, representing commercial interests that extended credit across regions, submitted numerous bills to Parliament. The Boards of Trade had also been active during the 1870s, but in the 1880s and the 1890s they stepped up their efforts. However, new to the scene were foreign creditors, who also lobbied for the restoration of a Canadian bankruptcy law. English merchants, who believed they were dealing with their "own kindred on similar principles of mercantile morality as are legalized in the United Kingdom," soon discovered that the state of provincial law operated to their detriment.[25] As early as 1881, English merchants submitted a petition to Prime Minister Macdonald indicating that "creditors, especially at a distance are practically at the mercy of the dishonest debtor." Thus, foreign merchants and Canadian wholesalers were "unable to protect their own claims against the scheming and rascality of dishonest debtors."[26]

Between 1880 and 1903 there was significant English interest in the state of Canadian bankruptcy law, and Prime Ministers Macdonald and Laurier received pleas from English merchants.[27] But despite petitions, resolutions of English and Canadian associations, articles in English journals, and direct meetings with politicians,[28] Parliament made little headway in enacting a federal law. In particular, English creditors complained about preferential payments to local creditors.[29] In 1884, the Home Trade Association of Manchester submitted a petition to Macdonald which claimed that "creditors and especially those at a distance are practically at the mercy of the debtor, experience having shown that there is no available means of preventing debtors from disposing all their assets by preferential payments or otherwise to prevent Canadian creditors depriving the general body of creditors of a fair participation in the estates of such debtors."[30]

In 1885, Macdonald justified the appointment of the Parliamentary Special Committee by pointing to the fact that "the commercial classes in England ... have specially referred to what was alleged to be the opportunity to traders of granting undue preferences." In a meeting of the British Empire League in 1894 to discuss the state of Canadian Insolvency laws, a member posed a problem: "A warehouseman either in England or in Canada might have done business with his Canadian customer for years ... but he could not be certain when he sold him a parcel that before the time came to pay for the goods the customer might not have given a preferential claim, or made a preferential assignment covering the merchant's goods in payment of an old debt, or to his bankers."[31]

Charles Tupper, a Conservative Member of Parliament and former High Commissioner to England, stated that he had been approached by English merchants: "I had occasion again and again to listen with great mortification to statements made by commercial men in [London] ... pointing out ... the losses they had sustained, because a few parties in Canada had obtained their property and were enabled to divide it among their friends and others." A Member of Parliament in 1903 referred to several complaints by English merchants who indicated that "there was ... no protection to them when they sold goods to Canadians, because, in the event of failure, the Canadian creditors gobbled up the estate and there was practically nothing left for anybody."[32]

Distance proved particularly problematic for English merchants who could not compete with American creditors. The *Journal of Commerce* claimed, "Propinquity ... permit[s] the American seller to see his customer personally, or through his travellers and thus size up his character, surroundings, and standing." A letter from the Canadian High Commissioner in England to the Minister of Justice raised a similar concern: "What is implied by this statement is, that the American trader has better means of protecting himself than the British trader. ... [T]he American trader being so much nearer, knows sooner tha[n] his English competitor what is going on in this country; and the absence of a general and effective insolvency law enables the American creditor to get an advantage over the British trader, in the event of any assignment or insolvency proceedings."[33] To protect themselves, British firms insisted upon more cumbersome and expensive terms of trade, which led Canadian importers to favour trading with American firms.[34]

Not only did greater distances render collection difficult, but creditors also had to familiarize themselves with the patchwork of provincial laws. Foreign creditors were "perplexed and exasperated" in having to consult numerous provincial statutes. One author writing in 1898 suggested that legal advisers to overseas creditors were "obliged to take a preliminary course in the geography of Canada" before rendering an opinion. The author continued, "When a merchant in London or Berlin, or it may be in Australia, or Hong Kong, desires to know what security he will have that his goods will not be taken to pay the home creditors of his debtor, and leave the foreigner in the lurch, it must be obvious that it would be of the greatest importance that he should be able to deal with the Dominion as a unit."[35]

The absence of a national law increased the cost of credit and the price of goods. In attempting to sell their goods across Canada, Canadian importers faced the perennial problem of losing out to local creditors.[36] Further, the absence of national legislation increased the cost of goods, and all imports bore the double "impost" of risk premium.[37] The British merchant added on to the price to reflect the risk of trading into Canada, and Canadian wholesalers who resold the imported goods also added on a premium for the risk of inter-provincial trade. A letter to Prime Minister Macdonald claimed that Canadian merchants were being economically squeezed at both ends of their transactions.[38]

Efforts to expand British trade were like "whipping the horses of a coach while 'slippers' are left on the wheels." The English Associated Chambers of Commerce told Macdonald that unless Parliament enacted a bankruptcy law, "it would be a great impediment to trade between Great Britain and the Dominion of Canada." The standard form petition from English merchants demanding a federal bankruptcy law claimed that if the current state of affairs continued, it would "seriously impair the general commercial credit of the Dominion to the great injury of the common interests of the country."[39]

2. The Discharge

The discharge often dominated the Parliamentary debates during the period of 1880–1903. Despite strong opposition to the discharge, forgiveness of debt was a common theme. Those who had been subject to the uncertainties of the market or who suffered from sickness or other mishap deserved a discharge and an opportunity to start again.[40] The lack of a discharge prevented the unfortunate debtor "from becoming a free man and being set on his feet again." One Member of Parliament claimed that it would be better "if insolvent debtors were allowed to start afresh." A letter to Prime Minister Macdonald warned that debtors with executions "hanging over their heads" could never do business again "nor start life again." A letter to Laurier complained of the "thousands and tens of thousands of men, women and children who are groaning under the iron heels of debts and mortgage covenants." A further letter to Laurier lamented that the lack of a discharge rendered fathers "helpless or brokenhearted."[41]

According to a Letter to the Editor of the *Monetary Times*, the absence of a discharge simply resulted in a "civil lynch law" whereby creditors took all means short of violence to persecute the debtor in order to recover the amount owed.[42] Many debtors had little choice but to flee to the United States. Even with a discharge under the *Insolvent Acts*, absconding debtors had been a problem in the 1870s, as debtors fled to avoid the stigma or shame of bankruptcy, and the absence of a federal discharge after 1880 created an additional incentive to flee to the United States.[43] Members of Parliament pointed to the increasing problem of fleeing debtors. Creditors who insisted upon their "pound of flesh" had the effect of "driving many a man out of the country to do business in the United States." Without a discharge, the debtor had no option but to "go to a new country where he can make a fresh start without having around his neck the millstone of debt which he cannot throw off in Canada." Macdonald acknowledged that as no debtor could obtain a statutory discharge, he was liable to be followed "to all parts of Canada and the US ... A debtor was a slave to his creditor." In Toronto, one lumber merchant reported that 306 families obtained United States Consular certificates so as to be able to enter the US with their household goods duty-free. The merchant claimed that nine out of ten people left because "they were so heavily involved in debt that not even hope was left [to] the poor wretches." The Auer Incandescent Light Manufacturing Company of Toronto wrote to Laurier, claiming that if a debtor fails, "he may as well leave the country."[44]

However, sympathy for exiled debtors was not the sole reason to support the discharge. The problem of absconding debtors had a detrimental impact on the Canadian economy. Fleeing debtors meant the loss of "our good but unfortunate trading population." Driving "men out of the country" was a loss and not a gain to the community. One company, concerned with the extent of migration to the United States, wrote to Laurier and claimed that "an Insolvent Act would reclaim so much good active brain power, and that it would be equal almost, if not quite as good as one year's immigration to Canada."[45]

While support for a discharge was often framed in terms of the underlying value of forgiveness and sympathy for an unfortunate debtor, the credit community had a particular interest in seeking bankruptcy legislation that contained a discharge. Members of Parliament remarked that it was not debtors who demanded bankruptcy reform.[46] This suggests that creditor interest groups may have been relying upon the public discourse of forgiveness to advance the cause of bankruptcy reform, as the absence of the discharge had negative consequences for creditors. For example, the inability of debtors to obtain a release of their old debts meant fewer customers for creditors wishing to sell goods on credit.[47] Further, the lack of discharge drove debtors to "means flavouring of trickery and deception" in order to re-establish their livelihood. In an effort to avoid the enforcement of a judgment, the debtor or the assets often disappeared. The intensity of competition between creditors increased dramatically without a bankruptcy law. Without a discharge, "it is in the power of one vindictive creditor to hinder the debtor from making further restitution to his other creditors. Is this wise or right?"[48] Thus the absence of a discharge had a direct impact on creditor interests.

In 1885, ERC Clarkson, a Toronto accountant and one of the drafters of the 1883 Toronto Board of Trade bill,[49] published an outline of the advantages of a bankruptcy regime. In referring to the discharge, Clarkson recognized the need to guard against the contingencies of business. A number of uncontrollable factors affected businesses, and the discharge was a form of statutory insurance: "Commerce flourishes by circumstances, contingent, transitory, almost as liable to change as the wind ... Failure may be caused by the insolvency of others, by errors of judgment, by many causes, which one cannot control, and yet we may be honest, have the dearest and strongest ties to stimulate our exertions, and fail." A debtor was "subject to vast fluctuations and influenced by occurrences which no human foresight can estimate, provide against, or avoid."[50]

However, in outlining the advantages of a bankruptcy regime, Clarkson made it clear that the legislation served creditor interests. He argued that the legislation was "more calculated to protect the creditor than the debtor." While the discharge offered a debtor "an avenue of escape from the positive slavery of irretrievable debt," it also provided a "wider and more practical means of detecting and punishing fraud." Clarkson acknowledged that the prior legislation seemed to allow dishonest debtors to escape with a perfunctory application to a local judge. In part, the fault lay with county court judges who defeated the true intent of the legislation. The solution lay in new legislation that would ensure that the power to grant the discharge would be vested in higher courts.[51] However, the idea that the discharge could protect creditor interests was not widely accepted until 1919. Those who sought bankruptcy reform struggled to overcome the notion that a debtor had a moral obligation to repay all debts.

In 1880, Thomas Ritchie, President of the Belleville Board of Trade and one of the chief opponents of bankruptcy law, sent Macdonald a publication entitled "Insolvency Laws." Ritchie began with the premise that all "legislation of every country and every age relating to insolvency was wrong." Bankruptcy law interfered with natural law, as it relieved individuals of the consequences of their own responsibilities. This resulted in a "widespread evil." He proposed, "Teach men to recognize that there are laws above them and that these *must* be obeyed, whatever earth or hell may say to the contrary. If they break these laws they shall suffer for it, that they will suffer for it whether they break them knowingly or unknowingly ... [Y]et do not legislate to relieve them from the natural consequences of their own acts, or you will bring greater evil on the land and multiply suffering and loss to thousands of others. Insolvency reform would 'carry us back to darkness and chaos.'"[52]

In a subsequent 1885 publication, entitled *Fallacy of Insolvency Laws and their Baneful Effects*, Thomas Ritchie claimed that statutory law should be "framed as to lead men to observe the laws of nature ... and observe the obligations they are naturally under to their fellow men." The state simply had no right to pass any law that would "tempt men" to break their obligations or "to disregard the duties and responsibilities of their condition in life, and this all insolvency laws practically do." Bankruptcy law ran counter to man's higher obligations in life: "[A]ll insolvency laws are wrong ... on account of being in direct conflict with the constitution of things, the established order under which we live, furnishing occasion and opportunity for men to overlook their responsibilities and neglect their obligations to God and to their fellow men."[53]

Throughout the 1880s and 1890s, Members of Parliament continued to make the argument that debtors had a responsibility to repay debts: "[E]very man ought to be responsible for his liabilities, and ought to pay his debts ... I do not think it is right for the representatives of the people in any Parliament in the world to interfere to protect any man from the consequences of failing to pay the debts which he has contracted; it is unfair to men who have dealings with each other." Why should Parliament interfere and "make it legal for a man not to pay his debts"? In an open letter to Parliament, published in the *Toronto World*, the author was of the view that "no special law should be enacted to interfere with the debtor and creditor." The parties should be governed by "general law" and be left to settle their own affairs on the basis of their own contractual terms.[54]

The notion of moral obligation was "a good and sound principle, an old principle [and] a very moral principle against which nobody can say anything." A debtor who went into business knowing that the policy of the law was to provide a discharge did not have the "same moral incentive to pay his debts in full as if the law recognized his obligation to do so." The discharge provisions were an "evasive repeal" of the requirement to pay debts in full, as bankruptcy law weakened the "moral effect" of the obligation to repay creditors.[55] Opponents of the discharge argued that debtors had the option to approach their creditors to obtain a consensual discharge. Only responsible debtors obtained extensions from their creditors. Others were blameworthy and did not deserve special treatment.[56] After all, the majority of those who failed were "men who spend their evenings in saloons [and] who spend their days at horse races and in idleness."[57] The solution of creditor forgiveness was consistent with the view that debtor-creditor affairs were a private matter. The discharge compelled creditors, against their will, to accept part payment for settlement of the entire debt.[58] The basis of legislation in civilized countries had been "never to impair contracts which have been legitimately made under existing laws."[59]

Character continued to play an important role. Bankruptcy law shifted the fundamental base of credit decisions: "The practical effect of an insolvency law is to shift the only *just* grounds on which credit ought to be dispensed, namely integrity and ability of the recipient, to the *false* ground furnished by the *assurance* of getting an equal division of the assets of a debtor in case of insolvency. Who does not recognize the far reaching evils of such a result?"[60]

Without a bankruptcy law, creditors had to "know the character of the man to whom he is ... to sell goods. He examines carefully, as he does not give credit further than he has good reason to believe is safe."[61] In a letter to Macdonald, Thomas Ritchie claimed that under a bankruptcy regime credit was not dispensed on the basis of "financial ability to pay, business qualifications, integrity and honesty."[62] Opponents of bankruptcy legislation also pointed out that the discharge encouraged reckless speculation. After repeal, traders without any commercial standing could obtain credit from foreign sellers and import goods in a speculative venture. This had the effect of harming established importing houses. Trade should be based upon sound business principles and character rather than reckless speculation. The discharge therefore encouraged recklessness in trade and enticed inexperienced men into business. Ritchie claimed, "[I]mporters with very limited capital, and often with none at all, are enabled and permitted to speculate illegitimately on the capital of others to the great embarrassment and injury of those other importers who are striving to do an honest and fair business in proportion to their means." And in a separate letter to Macdonald, Ritchie argued that bankruptcy law would cause "overtrading and speculation," especially in Montreal and Toronto, and "greatly embarrass honest and legitimate trade throughout the Dominion."[63]

"Ridiculous competition" not only caused the downfall of the inexperienced new entrants but also led to the demise of established businesses.[64] It was therefore better that the discharge not be enacted, for its enticement would lead to the failure of many.[65] The repeal of the law had "restored confidence and induced men of capital to invest amongst us as they felt assured they would not be wiped out by a lot of bankrupt speculators."[66] It is not surprising that many celebrated the exodus of debtors to the United States. To the charge that the country was losing valuable traders, opponents of the discharge argued that it was better for the country that dishonest debtors left.[67] Repeal gave those "who are the fittest to remain" an opportunity to rid the economy of "the weak and incapable men."[68]

Although there was no bankruptcy law in effect during this period, late nineteenth-century novels reflected negative attitudes towards bankrupts. In Carrie Harris's *Cyril Whyman's Mistake* a son proposed to the daughter of a bankrupt and asked his mother to accept his fiancée into the family. His mother declined and ordered her son to "break his engagement at once." After all, the fiancée was tainted with the bankruptcy of her father. The mother refused to "receive the daughter of a defaulter, who had cowardly ended his life rather than face the consequences of his crimes, as a member of her family."[69] Harris explores a similar theme in *A Modern Evangeline*. In this second novel, Evangeline was engaged, but when her father died, it was discovered that his financial affairs "were in a fearfully involved state." Instead of being a wealthy heiress, Evangeline would "come to her new home a penniless bride." The mother of the groom therefore opposed the match of her son to the "pauper daughter of the defunct bankrupt."[70]

Sarah Tytler's *Logie Town* explores the social stigma associated with financial failure, as the character Adam undergoes a transformation following the destruction of his mills. Since the failure, he was "rapidly losing caste." Adam had fallen on "evil days and evil ways, until his very looks were undergoing a deterioration. His handsome, bluff manliness was growing coarse and swaggering, with touches, here of brazen defiance, there of wheedling deceit." Although there was some public sympathy for Adam, "sympathy could not repair a bankrupt's shattered fortunes, or clear his damaged reputation from an ugly suspicion of fraudulent and felonious practices, with the sword of justice suspended over his head."[71]

In the end it was this portrait of a bankrupt that won out. The absence of a discharge in many reform bills signalled the continued unpopularity of releasing debtors from their obligations. A debtor's moral obligation to repay all debts became the more important idea during this era.

3. Conclusion

Ideas continued to remain important in the debate over bankruptcy reform. The distribution of assets remained a focal point in the bankruptcy law debates. The arguments of distant creditors in favour of a federal reform Act during this period were not new. In the 1870s urban Boards of Trade had demanded the retention of a national law, and the 1880s and 1890s saw increasing lobbying by Canadian Boards of Trade. However, what was new to this era was the first intervention of foreign creditors into the debate. Canadian and foreign interest groups sought national legislation that eliminated local advantage by seeking to restore the *pro rata* division of assets and legislation that would prohibit the granting of preferences to local or friendly creditors. Despite pressure from distant and foreign creditors, federal legislation seemed only a remote possibility, and provincial legislation, designed to cure the problem of preferences, was not immediately forthcoming. As discussed in chapter 6, lobbying fell on deaf ears because there was no federal institutional backing for reform as a government measure. In addition, as considered in chapter 7, federalism and constitutional litigation played a role in entrenching provincial law as the means to deal with insolvent debtors.

Notions of forgiveness competed unsuccessfully with the more dominant idea of a moral obligation to repay all debts. Canada was not ready for a bankruptcy discharge. Not all bankruptcy bills contained a discharge, and the bills that did include one failed to garner enough votes in Parliament. The debate over the discharge was inherently linked to the problem of absconding debtors. Whereas in the 1870s debtors fled to avoid the shame of bankruptcy proceedings, after 1880 there was little incentive for an overburdened debtor to remain in Canada. Finally, some creditors came to realize that the absence of the discharge had a detrimental impact on their interests. The discharge provided incentives for debtors to co-operate and reduced fraud. However, that claim failed in the face of the argument that the discharge itself encouraged fraud. It would not be until 1919 that a majority of creditors came to recognize that the discharge could also protect their interests. This transformation of the discharge is considered in chapter 9.

PART THREE

1903–1919

9

Reform Achieved: The *Bankruptcy Act of 1919*

The discharge is the key to the efficiency of a Bankruptcy Act, as the Court is enabled ... to bring its influence in favour of a high standard of commercial morality to bear directly on the debtors."

A.C. McMaster, "The Bankruptcy Act" (1912–13) 2 Canadian Chartered Accountant 236

As requested by the Honourable Arthur Meighen, I enclose you herewith a copy of the Credit Men's Journal containing a draft Bankruptcy Act which I have prepared during the winter months at the request of the [Canadian Credit Men's Trust Association].

H.P. Grundy to C.J. Doherty, Minister of Justice (21 June 1917) in Department of Justice Papers, vol 213, file 1081)

The *Bankruptcy Act of 1919* re-established a national bankruptcy law after nearly forty years. It created the framework for much of twentieth- and twenty-first-century Canadian bankruptcy law.[1] The new *Bankruptcy Act of 1919* marked an important event in "Canada's legal history." After the long regime of provincial legislation, the Act was "a very radical change" in debtor and creditor relationships.[2] The Act contained several important provisions that improved upon provincial legislation and the prior federal *Insolvent Acts*. The legislation allowed creditors to initiate compulsory bankruptcy proceedings and permitted formal composition proceedings.[3] Unlike the *Insolvent Act of 1875*, the *Bankruptcy Act of 1919* allowed debtors to voluntarily file for bankruptcy. More importantly, the new federal legislation allowed debtors to apply for a discharge and obtain a release of their debts. Provincial law did not offer a statutory discharge. This chapter examines the period from 1903 to 1919 and offers an explanation for the success of the federal legislation.

Insight into why the legislation passed at this time may be gleaned from the private correspondence of future Prime Minister Arthur Meighen. At least one lawyer anticipated that the new legislation would provide a source of patronage. W.M. Crichton, a Winnipeg barrister, wrote to federal Cabinet Minister Arthur Meighen[4] seeking some form of government employment. Crichton asked Meighen whether "it may be possible that some appointment may be made in connection" with the new Bankruptcy Act. Crichton asked for a "remunerative" appointment. While Meighen indicated he would keep the request in mind, he doubted "anyone will be regularly appointed." The only person that Meighen believed might be appointed was H.P. Grundy, who "did an immense amount of work in the preparation of the Act."[5] Grundy, of the Manitoba Bar, had been retained by the Canadian Credit Men's Trust Association (CCMTA) to draft a new bankruptcy bill, and the legislation reflected the impact of this private interest group.

Parliament's achievement can be explained in part by the influence of new national interest groups that pressed for reform. The Canadian Bar Association (CBA) and the CCMTA lobbied for a new federal bankruptcy Act. Although passed as a government measure, the origins of the Act can be traced to the drafting efforts of Grundy on behalf of the CCMTA, which took place during a time of economic change and the important institutional[6] factor of an emerging regulatory state during the war.[7] The federal government assumed an ever-increasing role in regulating the economy, and bankruptcy reform coincided with that changing role. The war provided the federal government with an opportunity to reassert its authority over the field of bankruptcy and insolvency. However, this was not a complete triumph for the bankruptcy and insolvency power under the Constitution. Federalism continued to play a role in that Grundy was only partially successful in establishing uniformity. On the issue of bankruptcy exemptions, property that the debtor could retain in a bankruptcy, Grundy deferred to the provinces to legislate.

While important, these factors do not completely explain the emergence of the legislation in 1919. It is unlikely that reform would have occurred unless there was transformation of attitudes towards the discharge. The discharge was no longer perceived as an evil, as in the nineteenth century, but was now proclaimed as a necessary form of business regulation. The new acceptability of the discharge also reflected the underlying interests of creditors who demanded reform. The *Bankruptcy Act of 1919* had little to do with concepts of debtor rehabilitation. Canada opted for a discharge because it met the legal needs of the credit community, and provincial legislation did not adequately deal with debtors. The absence of compulsory proceedings and of a discharge created collection difficulties for creditors, as debtors often engaged in deceptive conduct. Creditors came to accept the necessity of the discharge as a means of improving the standard of debtor conduct and as a way to enhance their collection efforts.

The new attitude towards the discharge suggests that 1919 was a world very different from the preceding period of 1880–1903. Section 1 provides an overview of some of the economic changes that occurred in the period leading up to 1919. The debate over bankruptcy reform took place within the context of growing industrialization and urbanization. Further, 1913 marked the end of a boom in the Canadian economy and the start of a significant economic downturn, and after 1913 the bankruptcy reform question could no longer be ignored. Section 2 examines the problems created by provincial legislation and the impact of federalism, whereas section 3 discusses the rise of the regulatory state during the war. Section 4 analyses the role of interest groups, and the chapter concludes with section 5, which explains why the bankruptcy law discharge became more acceptable in this period.

1. The Economic Context

Although Parliament debated numerous reform proposals between 1880 and 1903, after 1903 bankruptcy law disappeared from Parliament's agenda until 1918. The absence of activity after 1903 can be explained in part by the shifting cycles of the economy. Canada experienced an economic boom between 1897 and 1912,[8] which coincided with the disappearance of bankruptcy law debates. Laurier simply allowed the provinces to regulate debtor-creditor matters without federal interference, and a prosperous economy provided Laurier with a rationale to support the provincial status quo.

Pleas for national bankruptcy legislation reflected a concern for missed opportunities in a buoyant economy, as is illustrated by one merchant's 1907 letter to Prime Minister Laurier. The author demanded a national bankruptcy law to allow exiled debtors the chance to return to Canada: "It seems ... a most disgraceful and cruel state of things, that in the case of an honest debtor, getting into difficulties it may be through no fault of his own, or from any cause whatever he cannot get a discharge and a chance to recover himself and pay his just debts, but he may be hounded for life by any unsatisfied creditor ... Now when the times are prosperous in Canada, these people cannot return to share in the good times without the risk of any small success being taken from them by creditors still holding judgements against them."[9]

But Laurier refused to proceed with bankruptcy reform. In an earlier letter to another merchant, he claimed that there was no immediate need for bankruptcy legislation: "The country is so prosperous just now that your request is the only one in that sense that I have received during the last twelve months and I am pretty sure the moment would be very inopportune to act on your suggestion. As you wanted me to give you a frank answer, I have just given it to you as frank as it possibly could be."[10]

However, 1913 marked the beginning of a sharp recession. The tide of industrial optimism reversed. Capital investment from abroad fell.[11] As credit tightened, industrial production slowed, resulting in serious unemployment in urban areas. Credit restrictions had severe consequences in rural areas. Banks refused to extend loans, and mortgage companies threatened foreclosure, leading to a flight to the cities as "[f]armers, their sons, their tenants and hired men, along with a continuing flood of immigrants ... poured into the cities to join the growing ranks of urban unemployed in the fruitless search for work." As a result, land prices plummeted.[12]

Statistics for the number of commercial failures from 1902 to 1918 show a period of relative stability from 1902 to 1912. However, the number of failures rose in 1913 and dramatically increased in 1914 and 1915 (see figure 9.1).[13]

If the economic boom had removed the issue of bankruptcy law from the public mind, the downturn of 1913 clearly re-established the matter for debate.[14] By 1914, *Saturday Night* reported that "the news that Hon. C.J. Doherty, Minister of Justice, is contemplating the enactment of a Federal Bankruptcy Act for the relief of insolvent debtors comes none too soon."[15]

However, it was not just the downturn in the economy that paved the way for new legislation. The structural changes that had occurred in the Canadian economy during the boom years prior to 1913 were

Figure 9.1: Number of Commercial Failures in Canada 1902–18

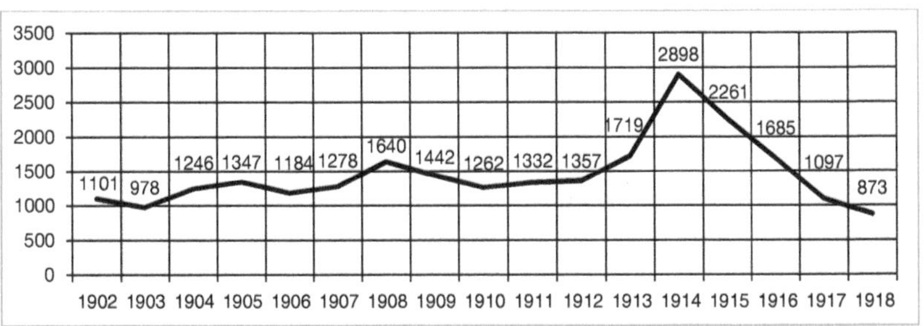

also significant.[16] Rapid industrialization occurred on an unprecedented scale. National manufacturing companies emerged, and large retail department stores began to dominate Canada's central cities. New national distribution networks emerged as mail-order houses and department stores grew in number.[17] After the turn of the century, corporations began to take on an ever-increasing role.[18] In 1909, a major merger movement began as larger national companies emerged out of the consolidation of smaller local enterprises.[19] Transcontinental rail links forged inroads into new markets.[20] The dichotomy between local and distant creditors that had dominated the debates in the nineteenth century gave way to more firms trading in the emerging national economy. This paved the way for new national interest groups.

The population of Canada dramatically increased after the turn of the century as well. Between 1881 and 1901, it increased by 24 per cent.[21] However, between 1901 and 1921, it grew by 64 per cent.[22] The decline in the percentage of the rural population was matched with a concern in the farming community of declining political influence and that legislative policies in the future would represent urban interests.[23]

The new rural-urban population ratio was reflected in the parliamentary debates. In the nineteenth century, rural opposition was a chief impediment to bankruptcy reform, but in 1919 there were few rural-based objections to the bankruptcy bill. While farmers did obtain one benefit under the Act (they could not be forced into bankruptcy), this issue was not the focus of the debates in 1918–19.[24] Instead, discussion turned to the urban concerns of retailers, wage-earners, and professionals, such as doctors and lawyers.

For example, the Retail Merchants' Association opposed the exclusion of wage-earners from compulsory proceedings. Retailers faced the unpleasant prospect of their own bankruptcy at the behest of wholesalers without being able to force their own customers into bankruptcy because of the wage-earner exclusion.[25] While wage-earners could make a voluntary bankruptcy filing, section 8 of the new Act prevented creditors from petitioning wage-earners into bankruptcy.[26] Others were concerned with the plight of professionals under the Act. One Senator argued that there was no need to extend bankruptcy law to "lawyers, doctors, ministers, gentlemen who are commonly known as capitalists, public men, judges, and various other persons who are not traders, but whose credit is largely based on moral grounds."[27]

It is within this economic context that new national interest groups emerged to demand uniform commercial legislation. These economic changes did not make federal bankruptcy reform inevitable in 1918–19; rather, they made it more possible. One study of bankruptcy reform in Europe draws a specific connection between economic development and legislative change.[28] If reform was made more possible, one might ask why reform took place at the federal rather than the provincial level.

2. The Difficulties with Provincial Legislation and the Initial Constraints of Federalism

By 1903 provincial regulation of debtor-creditor matters was well established.[29] Provincial legislation shared several common elements. Under provincial statutes, debtors made voluntary assignments to authorized trustees who liquidated the debtor's assets for the benefit of the creditors. The legislation prohibited unjust preferences and abolished priority between execution creditors. Authorized trustees distributed the debtor's assets on a *pro rata* basis.

One of the largest organizations of authorized assignees or trustees to emerge under the provincial regimes was the CCMTA.[30] The CCMTA identified at one of its meetings "four defects or omissions" in the provincial legislation:

> *Firstly*, the lack of uniformity relating to insolvency laws in Canada; *secondly*, the absence of machinery for compelling an insolvent debtor under certain circumstances to turn over to a trustee for creditors his property for pro rata distribution among creditors (involuntary bankruptcy); *thirdly*, the ratification by the court of composition and extension agreements when approved by a certain majority of creditors (say 75 per cent) thereby binding the minority; and *fourthly*, the right of an honest but unfortunate debtor to obtain his discharge.[31]

The listed defects had significant consequences for creditors. For example, the lack of compulsory proceedings in provincial legislation prevented a creditor from forcing a debtor to turn over his or her assets. The most significant defect in provincial legislation was the inability of the debtor to obtain a discharge,[32] which created collection problems for creditors. Debtor misbehaviour led to a growing acceptance among creditors that some legislative reform was required. Individual enforcement under provincial law was "a most wasteful method of procedure both as to costs and to the amount realised on property through a sheriff's sale."[33]

While the economic boom in the early part of the twentieth century provided the federal government with ample reason not to raise the bankruptcy issue, federalism also operated as an initial constraint on reform. The provincial model had become so entrenched that by the time the need for new legislation was raised, the initial response was to look to provincial reform. Originally, the CCMTA did not envisage national legislation and instead sought uniformity in provincial legislation.[34] A 1913 letter from the President of the CCMTA to the Minister of Justice revealed that it initially proposed a "National Assignment Act" based upon Manitoba legislation. The CCMTA therefore passed a resolution in 1916 that "the Canadian Bar Association be asked to draft out a uniform assignments act for submission to all the provinces." But the CCMTA eventually abandoned the concept of pursuing uniformity at the provincial level in favour of a new federal law.[35] Provincial jurisdiction did not extend to compulsory proceedings or allow a discharge.[36] These two key concerns of the CCMTA thus constitutionally necessitated a federal bill. Switching to federal reform allowed the CCMTA to lobby one government rather than all the provinces.

However, efforts to introduce a uniform federal bankruptcy statute could not avoid the impact of federalism. Provincial law would ultimately shape the content of the *Bankruptcy Act of 1919*. In the absence of a national bankruptcy statute, provincial exemption statutes provided a source of debtor relief that enabled debtors to shelter items such as food, clothing, and tools of trade from an execution creditor who sought to enforce a judgment. The types and values of exempt property varied across the country. Exemptions ranged from a rather meagre fifty-dollar list of items in Prince Edward Island to the generous 160-acre homestead exemptions in the Canadian west.[37] Bankruptcy law also traditionally allowed debtors to retain exempt property. For example, by 1914 English bankruptcy exemptions extended to "the tools (if any) of his trade and the necessary wearing apparel and bedding of himself, his wife and children, to a value, inclusive of tools and apparel and bedding, not exceeding twenty pounds in the whole."[38]

However, in a significant departure from the notion of uniformity, the *Bankruptcy Act of 1919* relied upon provincial exemption law to determine the types and values of personal – and in some cases real – property that a debtor might retain in a bankruptcy.[39] Rather than specifying a minimal level of exempt property in the bankruptcy statute in a national list, the policy choice in 1919 ensured that there would be no uniformity of bankruptcy exemptions in Canada. At a time when Parliament was seeking to establish a national uniform bankruptcy law, provincial law prevailed on exemptions.

There are several reasons that explain the policy choice to incorporate provincial exemptions laws into the *Bankruptcy Act* in 1919. First, the provincial model found in the 1919 Act was consistent with provisions found in the earlier *Insolvent Acts*. Second, and perhaps more importantly, the diversity of provincial exemption laws precluded the adoption of a uniform bankruptcy exemption regime in 1919. The generous homestead exemptions in Manitoba, Saskatchewan and Alberta and the absence of similar regimes in other provinces would have made it difficult for Grundy to draft some form of compromise acceptable to each region, and reconciliation of the provincial lists would have been nearly impossible. The starting point for Parliament in 1919 was the old and very different provincial exemption laws that had been enacted at various times and in response to various needs.[40]

The diverse exemption statutes did not escape the attention of the legal profession. A 1914 article in the *Canada Law Journal* highlighted some of the differences in the provincial exemption statutes:

> It is scarcely necessary to emphasize further how great the contrast between a western and an eastern province. Thousands of dollars exemption in the west one finds reduced to hundreds in the east, across the Atlantic to a mere bagatelle. While clothing is exempt in Ontario, the exemption of furniture is on a critically exact detailed list, the exemption of food gives the judgment debtor a chance to live 30 days, but his food must be cheap.
>
> The exemption of cattle and domestic fowl suffers similar shrinkage, the exemption of tools and implements likewise, and while there is a slight pampering in the way of bees, there is no provision running up into the thousands for land and buildings in Ontario.

The article noted that as of 1914 in Canada there was "no uniform standard ... fixing the execution debtor's exemption rights." Further, "[t]he western provinces are liberal, the execution creditor thinks too liberal: the older provinces are more exacting and give less offence to the execution creditor." The article offered several reasons for the wide differences. The western provinces required "the honest worker whether he has ... execution creditors or not" and were "making a clean start with equal rights to debtor and creditor." In the western provinces "many a healthy, honest, but unfortunate, worker with a family may there once again hold up his head and have a home for his wife and children. Those lusty developing provinces, it is said, need the industrial influx; the unfortunate citizen needs whereon to lay his head." Far from criticizing the lack of uniformity, the article praised the western provinces while criticizing the "strict eastern provinces" for knowing "little" and caring "less about the policy of developing exemption laws."[41]

Provincial exemption law as it stood at the time that H.P. Grundy began to draft the new *Bankruptcy Act* was diverse and likely impossible to harmonize. Indeed, an editorial in the *Canada Law Journal* suggests that reconciliation of the varied approaches in England and the provinces would not have been possible: "The history of law of such exemptions in England, in the eastern provinces of Canada, and in the west, is interesting. It would be a keen criticism, on the score of fair play, against the various law districts of the empire to urge that the right to exemption is based on the same standard in all those law districts. If it is, one has trouble to reconcile the law of exemptions in a typical western province with that enforced in eastern provinces and still more in England."[42]

The Canadian *Bankruptcy Act of 1919* opted to rely upon provincial exemptions rather than establish a national exemption provision. Section 25 provided that

> [t]he property of the debtor divisible amongst his creditors (in this Act referred to as the property of the debtor) shall not comprise the following particulars:
> ...
> (ii) Any property which as against the debtor is exempt from execution or seizure under legal process in accordance with the laws of the province within which the property is situate and within which the debtor resides.[43]

The entrenchment of provincial law made it difficult to avoid the effects of federalism in 1919.

When Parliament debated the bankruptcy bill in 1919, some Members of Parliament continued to see merit in the idea of reforming provincial legislation. Rather than introducing an elaborate federal bill, one Senator suggested that Parliament "pass a short act to the effect that any debtor who had complied properly and honestly with the terms of the provincial Act should be entitled to receive a discharge."[44] Another Senator pointed out that machinery already existed for the distribution of debtors' estates at the provincial level that could be used "economically without creating another system of vast bankruptcy machinery."[45]

Other Members of Parliament, rather than advancing the specific merits of provincial reform, chose to attack the constitutionality of the federal bill. When Parliament debated the bankruptcy bill in 1919, there was a specific acknowledgment that the federal structure of the constitution had posed unique problems for bankruptcy reform in Canada: "Only this Parliament can pass a bankruptcy law which will have uniform force and effect throughout the Dominion. One difficulty in the way is the fact that there is so many legislative jurisdictions in this country. In Great Britain, the Bankruptcy Act is a comparatively simple thing, there being but one central authority for the United Kingdom. But in Canada there is the Dominion Parliament, as well as nine provincial legislatures, and during the last forty years all the provincial legislatures have made some attempt to pass laws approximating very nearly to bankruptcy and insolvency laws."[46]

The introduction of new federal legislation, after a long period of provincial regulation, led to inevitable challenges to federal jurisdiction: "My honourable friend speaks of England having legislated in a much wider manner. Of course, Great Britain is not a federation, and is not bound by a written constitution. Great Britain can cover the whole ground. But our claim is that under the Constitution with powers divided so fairly between the provinces and the Dominion, this Act may trespass upon provincial rights."[47] The federal bankruptcy bill was attacked in Parliament on several occasions on the basis that it interfered with provincial jurisdiction over property and civil rights.[48] One MP argued that the bankruptcy bill was a "direct infringement of civil rights in the province of Quebec. I do not see how this law and our law in Quebec can be reconcilable."[49]

The entrenchment of provincial law for nearly forty years and the absence of federal legislation no doubt gave rise to these constitutional arguments. These arguments were given little weight in the face of the clear wording of the federal bankruptcy and insolvency power in the *BNA Act*.[50] The Solicitor General, in introducing the bill in 1919, reminded Parliament that "under s 91 of the British North America Act, the question of bankruptcy and insolvency is one of the questions which was left to the jurisdiction of the Dominion of Parliament." The Solicitor General made it very clear that the scope of "provincial powers were exceedingly limited"[51] in that provincial legislation did not permit a creditor to force a debtor into bankruptcy or provide for a discharge.[52] The Solicitor General admitted that the bill proposed to infringe upon property and civil rights but maintained it was a permissible infringement. He reminded the House of Commons that "the British North America Act says that to this extent we may infringe upon property and civil rights."[53] The Solicitor General claimed that the federal government "was not seeking to infringe on the rights of any province more than is necessary to give effect and validity to the particular legislation now in question."[54] The advantages of a single federal Act outweighed the prospects for coordinated reform at the provincial level. However, this factor alone does not explain the success of the *Bankruptcy Act of 1919*. Its passage coincided with the rise of the Canadian regulatory state.

3. The Impact of the War and the Growth of Federal Regulation

The attempts to justify the use of the federal bankruptcy and insolvency power must be considered in the context of the changing role of the government during the war, for the very need for bankruptcy legislation was linked to the effects of the war and its aftermath. S.W. Jacobs, who introduced the bill in 1918, described it as a "war measure." Jacobs reminded the House that when the war came to an end, Canada had to be prepared for "the struggle and of the readjustments that will have to be made."[55] The Retail Merchants' Association, in its submission to the Parliamentary Special Committee, also recognized the significance of the war to the debate over bankruptcy reform: "It appears to us that during the present commercial strain, owing to the war, as well as after the war is terminated, provision should be made whereby an honest debtor should be able to secure a release from debts in which he may have become entangled through misfortune or through no fault of his own." It was not just the war itself that led to greater government intervention. Many anticipated the realities of the aftermath of the war before the conflict came to a close. A Vancouver importer and wholesaler believed that "post war economic conditions may be so serious that it will be more necessary than ever to have the Act enforced at that time." The importer believed that with the "disbandment of the army" and the growing responsibility of the government, it was essential that Parliament pass the legislation.[56]

However, the *Bankruptcy Act of 1919* was not just a war measure or a response to the aftermath of war. Parliament's adoption of the *Bankruptcy Act of 1919* must be considered in light of the unprecedented growth of government regulation in the Canadian economy. The war pushed the state into increasing its influence over commerce. For example, the Union government created boards and agencies to help coordinate the economy during the war, including the Fuel Control Office, the War Trade Board, the War Purchasing Commission, the Food Board and the Railway War Board.[57] In addition, the 1914 *War Measures Act* gave Cabinet broad powers to make orders or regulations necessary "for the security, defence, peace, order and welfare of Canada."[58] S.W. Jacobs complained that Parliament was "practically being superseded by Orders in Council."[59] The war legitimized various forms of government intervention. While some thought that the state had gone too far, others viewed it as just the beginning of an increased role for the state.[60]

Industries that supported the war effort, such as munitions, faced the possibility of collapse following the end of the conflict.[61] Many of the provinces enacted debt moratorium legislation to deal with the economic problems of the war.[62] While the number of commercial failures dropped towards the end of the war,[63] many feared the impact of the removal of the moratorium legislation.[64] By 1918, "the free-wheeling economic activity and business practices of the pre-war years had been replaced by government regulation."[65] Federal health and education measures did not draw any resistance from the provinces.[66]

At the same time as Parliament considered the bankruptcy bill, another major piece of legislation was also being contemplated. In 1919, the government appointed a special Parliamentary Committee to investigate the problem of the escalating cost of living. The deliberations of the committee led to the enactment of the *Board of Commerce Act, 1919*[67] and the *Combines and Fair Prices Act, 1919*[68] in 1919. The legislation created the Board of Commerce, which could limit profits and fix prices with the goal of stabilizing the cost of living. The Board was responsible for, in the words of one historian, "exposing the villainous retail profiteers, encouraging production, and bringing down high prices." The Board of Commerce was "a direct assertion of the new, more activist role sought by many for the state in the interests of the public."[69]

Thus, bankruptcy reform must also be considered in the context of the new role of the federal government that emerged during the war. The re-emergence of bankruptcy law as a reform issue coincided with the outbreak of the war in 1914. The war allowed the federal government to reassert its authority over the field of bankruptcy and insolvency and justify intervention on a national basis. Federal reform occurred with the institutional backing of government support, which was a missing ingredient in many of the prior reform proposals. Such government support enabled the legislation to have a lasting legacy. However, reform in 1919 did not represent a purely public initiative, as the origins of the legislation can be traced to the private sector. Interest groups took advantage of the new regulatory state to ensure that their reform measure passed.

4. The Role of Interest Groups

It was within the context of a growing national economy and the emerging regulatory state that new interest groups took up the challenge of bankruptcy reform. Private interest groups had a direct influence over the *Bankruptcy Act of 1919*.[70] The CCMTA not only lobbied for reform but also had a direct influence over the content of the *Bankruptcy Act of 1919*. Although debtors had a vested interest in the outcome of bankruptcy reform, there was no national voice that represented debtors scattered across the country. Parliament preferred to rely upon well-informed and concentrated interest groups that advocated bankruptcy reform.[71]

Early reform efforts focused on the idea of uniformity. The CBA and the CCMTA advocated an end to the diversity of provincial legislation. Arguments for more uniform insolvency laws were not new and had been raised in the nineteenth and early twentieth centuries. However, as a result of increasing difficulties that businesses encountered with the variety of provincial assignment laws, the idea of uniformity took on added importance in the twentieth century.[72] Uniformity would do "away with the old feudal idea which in some parts of Canada would seek to prevent outsiders from having similar rights to those of their own province." Bankruptcy legislation was required "owing very largely to the fact that nearly all business concerns of any importance now do an interprovincial business."[73] Diverse regulation added to the cost of credit. Before extending a loan, foreign creditors had to familiarize themselves with the various provincial regimes.[74] The Solicitor

General warned Parliament that English exporters claimed that unless something was done to reform insolvency proceedings in Canada, "it is ultimately going to injure our credit."[75]

The CBA's original constitution of 1914 adopted uniformity as one of its goals.[76] The President of the CBA, James Aikins,[77] was said to have launched the movement for uniform commercial legislation in a speech to the CCMTA in 1914. Aikins "touched off a spark that was instantly fanned into flame, and the agitation ... will be spread throughout the Dominion from coast to coast." He called for uniformity in many areas of commercial law, including bankruptcy.[78]

Aikins identified the unique Canadian problem that led to dissimilarity in provincial legislation: "Our provinces are far flung, and feelings of mistrust, lack of sympathy or cordiality ... which may have happened between the respective bodies of citizens in the different provinces, arise very largely from the fact that the separated communities do not know or understand each other, or their aims or ideals."[79]

Provincial boundaries were only "artificial or imaginary lines [and] should not be allowed to interfere with the free working of principles which are in their nature universal."[80] Aikins warned that "a provincial spirit, a spirit of isolation and exclusive selfishness, would in time mean national atrophy and retrogression." A national group of lawyers was best suited to deal with the uniformity issue: "Expense must necessarily be incurred in employing persons who understand the law to make a study of the comparative legislation of our provinces and to frame such bills as will mould into uniformity those divergent provincial laws on business subjects."[81] While the CBA was not ultimately responsible for presenting a draft bill to Parliament, the Association was instrumental in advancing the idea of uniformity.[82]

The other significant national interest group to emerge at this time was the CCMTA, which was formed as an organization of wholesalers and manufacturers who "banded together for mutual protection and assistance along all lines that have any bearing whatever upon credit." Its activities included "furnishing complete and accurate reports on the standing of any customer" and securing "improved legislation."[83] Under provincial assignment statutes, debtors made assignments to authorized trustees who liquidated the debtors' assets for the benefit of the creditors. One of the largest firms of authorized assignees or trustees was the CCMTA.[84] However, under the provincial assignment statutes, the interests of the trustee organizations became invariably linked to the interests of creditors. The lack of uniformity of provincial legislation was a key problem identified by the CCMTA.[85]

The CCMTA originally sought the assistance of the CBA to draft uniform assignment acts for submission to the provinces. However, the CCMTA was concerned that legislation drafted by the CBA would not protect the CCMTA's interests.[86] Thus the CCMTA retained H.P. Grundy, a solicitor from Winnipeg, and "instructed him to draft a bill based upon creditor control and retaining the essential features of the provincial Assignment ... Acts."[87] As Grundy explained his retainer, "The subject has been discussed at the meetings of the Legislative Committee and the National Council of the [CCMTA] during the past two years and finally at its last Legislative Committee meeting the writer was requested to undertake the work of drafting an Act which would give the commercial interests of Canada the benefit of the usual provisions in similar acts of other countries as to 'involuntary bankruptcy' and the 'discharge of an honest debtor,' but would on the other hand eliminate the heavy expense and delays complained of by the commercial interests in England, United States and Australia."[88] Grundy prepared a memorandum for the CCMTA outlining the principles of his proposed bill that provided for uniformity, involuntary bankruptcy, composition proceedings and a discharge.[89]

He presented his draft bill to the Minister of Justice on 21 June 1917[90] and later sent a detailed eleven-page letter explaining the provisions of his bill.[91] According to Grundy, "Generally speaking the draft Act is based upon the English Act."[92] The mere presentation of the bill to the government did not, of course, guarantee its passage. More important matters, such as the war, distracted the government, and the government did not take any action during 1917.[93] Therefore, direct lobbying and interest group pressure played a role in ensuring that the initiative was not lost once the government received the bill. The extent of the lobbying efforts further illustrates the significance of the bill to the CCMTA.

S.W. Jacobs, a Member of Parliament who had been studying bankruptcy reform for the Liberal Party,[94] introduced the bill the following year[95] as a non-government measure. All members of the government expressed support for the bill and agreed to appoint a Parliamentary Special Committee. However, "it was not the intention to allow the bill to become law this Session. What was desired was that members of the public interested in such a measure should thus have an opportunity this year to become familiar with its terms and at a later session if the draft measure proved agreeable to the financial interests generally it might become law."[96]

On 10 April 1918, the House of Commons appointed a Special Committee to review the bill. The Special Committee heard from wholesalers, retail trade associations, accountants, commercial travellers, bankers and lawyers. Grundy attended, representing the CCMTA, but his role went beyond that of solicitor, as he was called to explain the bill.[97] The bill was allowed to stand until the following session. With his clients concerned about whether any action would be taken on the committee report, Grundy sent an urgent telegram to Jacobs asking if the House of Commons had adopted the committee's recommendation to reprint and widely distribute the bill. Jacobs assured Grundy that much interest had been expressed in the bill and that it looked "as if [at the] next session it will go through as one of the first measures."[98]

The war-time Union government, led by Robert Borden, introduced the bankruptcy bill on 6 March 1919, and the House debated the second reading on 28 March.[99] However, the debate was suspended and weeks passed without any activity on the bill. Word leaked out that the government was considering shelving the bill, with one source claiming it was due to the opposition of the banks.[100] Grundy's response indicated his clients' disappointment over the potential defeat of their privately drafted bill. Grundy wrote to Jacobs, "I have heard some rumours that the Government may not have the time to put through the Act at this session, and if such is the case the parties whom I represent will be very greatly disappointed. They have spent a lot of time and money getting the Act into shape, and it is a measure which will be of great benefit to Canada, and they feel, I know, that the measure should be pressed through." In closing his letter to Jacobs, Grundy suggested that Jacobs see some of the Ministers in order to save the bill.[101] Some "agitation from without," such as a resolution from the CCMTA, was also required.[102]

Grundy additionally represented the Toronto Board of Trade and met with the Solicitor General on 25 April 1919, strongly urging "that an effort be made to have the bill passed at the present session." Grundy noted that he did not believe that the bill would pass unless "strong pressure is brought to bear not alone upon the Government but on the Members of Parliament." He suggested a joint resolution of the Toronto and Montreal Boards of Trade be forwarded to the government and urged that the Boards at once notify their members by wire that the legislation should be passed.[103] Debate resumed in the House of Commons on 1 May 1919. The bill passed later that year as a government measure and came into effect on 1 July 1920.[104]

The law in its final form reflected the concerns of private interests and the specific interests of the CCMTA. Members of the CCMTA, who had experience with administering provincial assignment estates, were well placed to take up work under the new bankruptcy regime. Administration of bankruptcy estates was to be carried out by the private sector through the office of a trustee in bankruptcy.[105] Authorized trustees were appointed by the Governor in Council after the candidate submitted an application to the Secretary of State. The Act provided no guidelines on the necessary skills required of individuals to become a trustee. The Act simply stated that it permitted the Governor in Council to appoint "sufficient fit and qualified persons to be trustees in bankruptcy." The Act required applicants to state in the application particulars of "qualifications, ability and previous business experience."[106]

While Grundy's bill was based upon English legislation, Grundy made "one important variation in principle: ... Under the English practice a debtor would file a voluntary petition in bankruptcy asking the court to declare him a bankrupt and to make a receiving order. I propose to eliminate the expense and delay of the procedure of England by adopting the procedure established in most of the provinces under the various Assignments Acts, that is making an assignment direct to a trustee. There seems to be no real reason why a debtor who wishes to turn over his property to his creditors for pro rata distribution should have to incur the expense of making an application to the court."[107]

Grundy sought to retain trustee control over voluntary proceedings rather than follow the English model of requiring a court application by the debtor. Provincial assignment Acts did not require court applications by the debtor, and Grundy sought to retain this element of provincial procedure in the bankruptcy bill. Under Grundy's bill, on the making of a voluntary assignment, the property of the debtor vested in the trustee who was charged with the administration of the debtor's estate.[108] This procedure protected the interests of trustees and the CCMTA by ensuring that jurisdiction over voluntary proceedings lay in their hands. The voluntary procedure enhanced the standing and reputation of trustees. On the issue of voluntary assignments Grundy succeeded in preserving the status quo, which was necessary for sustaining the support of trustees. If Grundy had changed the voluntary assignment procedure and followed a court model, he would have risked alienating the trustee community that had emerged under provincial assignment statutes. Grundy wisely chose not to disturb this aspect of provincial law, arguing that there was a "certain amount of danger in adopting the Act of another country as a foundation and remodelling it to make it apply to different customs and conditions existing in the country of its adoption." After all, "it is always better not to change the laws of a country to any greater extent than is really necessary."[109]

The success of the bill can be attributed partially to the CCMTA, who initiated the drafting of the legislation and then followed its progress through Parliament. The importance of the bill to the CCMTA is reflected in their lobbying efforts. The final version of the legislation sought to retain some of the beneficial aspects of provincial law. It also provided for compositions, compulsory bankruptcy and discharge. While the government re-entered the bankruptcy field and enacted public legislation, private interests had significantly shaped the law. Those private interests sought and obtained a law that included a discharge. What explains the transformation of the discharge from a nineteenth-century evil to a commercial necessity?

5. Twentieth-Century Values: The Transformation of the Discharge

Provincial legislation did not contain "the right of an honest but unfortunate debtor to obtain his discharge."[110] The acceptability of the discharge at the federal level in 1919, however, did not entirely represent the triumph of forgiveness or concerns for the rehabilitation of the debtor. Simply put, the discharge became acceptable in 1919 because it satisfied the interests of creditors. The 1919 Act should not be viewed as a triumph for debtors' rights. After all, only two provinces abolished imprisonment for debt before the *Bankruptcy Act of 1919* came into force.[111]

Some of the public rhetoric continued to focus on the evil of bankruptcy legislation and the forgiveness of debt. However, unlike in the nineteenth century, these ideas did not dominate the public discourse. In 1918, an anonymous author published *A Protest against the Bankruptcy Act Now before the Dominion Parliament*, to coincide with the introduction of the bankruptcy bill in Parliament. The publication reminded readers that when the old *Insolvent Acts* were in force in the nineteenth century, "bankruptcy was rampant and notorious throughout the country." On repeal, "a marked change for the better speedily took place." Trade proceeded on a "juster and safer basis." Notwithstanding the negative sentiment towards bankruptcy, the publication did not contain arguments that a debtor had a moral obligation to repay all debts. In fact, the author conceded that "it is a benevolent purpose" to provide for a discharge of an honest debtor "who through no fault of his own" had become unable to pay his creditors in full. The author questioned only whether such a discharge provision could distinguish between honest and unfortunate debtors and "bad men."[112] The negative aspects of *A Protest against Bankruptcy* did not reflect widespread attitudes towards bankruptcy law in 1918 and 1919,[113] and its arguments were not replicated in the House of Commons.

The theme of forgiveness carried forward into 1918–19. *Saturday Night*, for example, lamented the fact that Canada was "practically the only civilized country which has not a Bankruptcy Court with powers to free a man from a financial burden he is unable to bear."[114] Another author claimed that without a bankruptcy act a man had debts "hanging around his neck like a mill stone depriving him of ambition." Without a bankruptcy law, the "human heart cannot be expected to struggle on."[115] In the absence of a federal bankruptcy discharge, a debtor was required to pay his debts in full "if he has the means at any time in his lifetime to do so."[116] However, in the twentieth century, public rhetoric tended to shift away from strict notions of forgiveness. Notwithstanding that rehabilitation had been the dominant theme of supporters of bankruptcy law in the nineteenth century, it was not the most important rationale for the inclusion of a discharge in the *Bankruptcy Act of 1919*. There was a growing recognition that a discharge would operate in the interests of creditors.

The reasons in favour of the discharge in 1919 bear a striking resemblance to the origins of the discharge in England. While the original English bankruptcy statute of 1543[117] established many of the principal elements of bankruptcy legislation, no discharge was available by statute in England until 1705.[118] The bankruptcy discharge is often viewed as one of the essential elements of modern bankruptcy law, as it allows debtors to obtain a release of their debts.[119] However, when one examines the historical context of 1705, it is clear that debtor rehabilitation was not the prime motivating factor behind the legislation.[120] The discharge was aimed at "the recovery of the most assets for the benefit of the creditors."[121] Therefore, the English Parliament was not motivated by generosity to debtors.[122] Rather, creditor interests lay at the heart of the English reform, and the change had only a limited beneficial effect on most debtors.[123] As Emily Kadens has demonstrated, eighteenth-century English creditors were struggling to see that if all promises to pay were fully enforced then debtors would lose their incentive to earn in the face of debt. Indeed, such a regime led debtors to cheat. Conversely, if the discharge provided an incentive for debtors to disclose, in theory, debtors should be less inclined to cheat.[124] Between 1867 and 1919 Canadian creditors faced a similar challenge in recognizing these truths.

In Canada, the large numbers of individuals heavily burdened with debt were of no use to creditors as new customers, as it was "no advantage to creditors to have a debtor die poor." A wholesaler who conducted business in Ontario and the four Western provinces wrote to the Department of Justice and complained of the lack of individuals who were able to enter into business: "In the West, with large numbers of young men who have joined the forces, it is necessary for the proper carrying on of business here that a number of the older men should go back into business, but as a result of unwise Real Estate speculation, many of these are tied up with old judgments and debts that they cannot under any circumstance ever pay."[125]

More specifically, without a discharge, debtors tended to engage in "crookedness and deception" designed to thwart the collection efforts of creditors. Debtors continued to flee to the United States, and Canadian debtors could be found "in every leading city of the American Union."[126] In 1917, the Liberals adopted a resolution in favour of a national discharge. They pointed to the "hundreds of bright young men [who] have gone to the United States because there is no opportunity for them to recover themselves financially."[127] The number of exiled debtors had an impact on the business of creditors. The lack of a discharge deprived Canada of "active and enterprising individuals." If there had been a proper bankruptcy law, they would have "remained at home and would now be taking part in the development of Canada."[128] In a letter to Laurier, a merchant pointed out that the absence of a discharge "annihilated ... thousands of good business men throughout Canada." Debtors were simply "helpless on account of unscrupulous creditors and some very spiteful." Without a bankruptcy law, men had no choice but to "remain practically idle."[129]

Debtors sequestered assets and arranged their affairs so as to become judgment proof.[130] Debtors could operate their businesses in the name of a wife or corporation, and writs of execution simply became valueless when debtors had taken these steps.[131] In a letter to the Department of Justice, one creditor complained that "by the time we obtain judgement and the Sheriff makes the seizure, the bulk and most desirable portion of the assets ... have been disposed of." Merchants saw the advantages of the bankruptcy bill from a creditor perspective. A Winnipeg wholesale boot and shoe merchant wrote to the Minister of Justice and claimed that "any legislation that will assist in the conservation of wealth by prohibiting the dissipation of same by unworthy debtors should ... have your enthusiastic and unstinted support." The Quebec Board of Trade wrote to Prime Minister Borden in 1913 noting that European nations claimed that the absence of a bankruptcy law encouraged "fraudulent trades."[132]

Without a discharge, the debtor became "absolutely cornered" and then proceeded to cheat general creditors for the benefit of "his friends and family."[133] Without a formal statutory release of debts, "the question of discharge rest[ed] wholly [as] a matter of bargain between a debtor and his creditors." One author suggested that the bargain led to the following result: "These conditions have permitted avaricious creditors, seeking preferment, to penalize, if not prevent, an unfortunate debtor from obtaining a discharge, except upon terms or special treatment accorded to them; at the same time, they have allowed debtors, who have committed fraud, to bargain with their creditors individually, and frequently to obtain discharges at rates which have left them with profit, thus providing an incentive to them to again commit fraud as a method of making money at the expense of creditors."[134] Debtors attempted to deal with the lack of a discharge by seeking the signatures of all of their creditors to a composition agreement. Any special treatment given to holdout creditors adversely affected the level of dividend paid to the other creditors.[135] Creditors privately decided to release a debtor on self-interested motives rather than on larger public policy goals such as the reduction of fraud. Inevitably creditors granted dishonest debtors a release:[136] "It seems to me, in considering the matter of discharge, that one of the chief faults of the present law, and of some of the previous Acts, is that too often, through the selfishness of creditors looking only to their own immediate interests, or what they think to be their immediate interest, men are discharged, or allowed to make composition and settlements, who, speaking commercially, at any rate, if not legally, would be much better sent to jail."

In discussing the Grundy bill, S.W. Jacobs noted that it did not call for creditors to approve discharges; rather, it required official court approval:[137] "Under the bill it is recognized that the Court, seized of all the circumstances, would be in a better position to decide as to whether the debtor should be given his discharge, than creditors whose interest in the Estate is in many cases too immediate and personal to permit unbiased judgment." The discharge therefore came to be viewed not as an interference with a debtor's moral obligation to pay all debts, but rather as a new regulatory feature that would come to benefit creditors. The courts would therefore assume a function that creditors had been unable to carry out. In an address to the Institute of Chartered Accountants, A.C. McMaster emphasized the importance of the discharge: "The discharge is the key to the efficiency of a Bankruptcy Act, as the Court is enabled ... to bring its influence in favour of a high standard of commercial morality to bear directly on the debtors." Some saw regulating the conduct of the debtor as a broader matter of public policy: "[I]t must be the duty of the court to decide the extent to which the debtor has been responsible for his own misfortune, and where it is shown that the disordered state of his business is brought about through no dishonesty or wilful negligence, the law ought to consider it a matter of public policy to see that after a certain length of time the debtor is once more permitted to engage in business on his own account."[138]

Therefore, creditors found judicial supervision of discharges acceptable. It replaced the unworkable system of individual creditors granting releases to debtors.[139] A court-supervised system satisfied creditors who were trying to conduct business in the emerging national economy. The regime allowed for the courts to subsume control over debtors. Creditors, particularly those trading at a national level, had never been effective at controlling debtor misconduct. It was also hoped that the discharge would have the effect of stemming the tide of fleeing debtors to the United States and curtailing debtor misconduct more generally.

The honest but unfortunate debtor came to replace the evil and untrustworthy character of the nineteenth century. The CCMTA, in its original analysis of the defects of provincial legislation, demanded a "right of an honest but unfortunate debtor to obtain his discharge."[140] A properly drawn discharge provision could filter out the difference between the two types of debtors, thereby making a discharge broadly acceptable. One manufacturer wrote to the Department of Justice,[141] "We believe that there are many good business men in Canada who have had the misfortune to get into firm difficulties by unforseen circumstances over which they had no control and if given a reasonable chance to again succeed in business life they will make good. When a man has given up all honestly and honourably we think he should be released from all further obligations."

A distinction was drawn between debtors who failed through "no fault of their own" and "dishonest and incompetent traders [who] should be stigmatized as undischarged bankrupts." Those who had "wilfully wrecked" their business were not deserving of a discharge. A debtor was entitled to a discharge only if he had been "an honest man," his insolvency was a result of "causes beyond his control" and he cooperated with the trustee.[142]

The 1915 Ontario Commission on Unemployment recognized financial failure as a wider social problem. It claimed that, in the past, personal causes of unemployment had received disproportionate attention. A modern economy necessarily involved unemployment. The Commission concluded that unemployment was not primarily the fault of the unemployed. As Owram notes, their conclusion pointed to more government intervention.[143] A bankruptcy statute that granted relief to the honest but unfortunate debtor became acceptable.

The provisions adopted by Parliament in 1919 reflected the honest/dishonest distinction and the concern for improving the standard of business, which creditors acting on their own had been unable to achieve. They also reflected creditor concern for a conservative discharge. According to Grundy, "Generally speaking you will find that the debtors will not in all cases receive their discharge as a matter of course but conditions on which a debtor receives this great benefit are carefully safeguarded. The result being that hereafter a business man will be honest and careful in his business methods not only because it is right and proper for him to be so but also because it will pay him." As one author, commenting on the newly enacted provisions, interpreted the new discharge provisions, "If he had been an honest man, and if his insolvency has been occasioned by causes beyond his control, and if he deals frankly and fairly with his official trustee in bankruptcy, he may, at any time after his estate has passed into the possession of his trustee in bankruptcy, make an application for discharge."[144]

Therefore, the transformation of the discharge did not represent an entirely disinterested shift in values. Underlying the demands for reform lay specific creditor interests. The *Bankruptcy Act of 1919* met the needs of the credit community. In 1918 and 1919, debate in Parliament proceeded upon the basic assumption that a discharge was an essential part of any bankruptcy system, and there was little debate on the fundamental question of whether it was right to release a debtor from his or her obligations. Many were prepared to acknowledge that the primary function of bankruptcy legislation was to discharge the debtor. H.P. Grundy stated that discharge was one of three main reasons for a bankruptcy act.[145] S.W. Jacobs wrote that the discharge was said to be "the very soul of a Bankruptcy Act." In introducing the bill, Jacobs claimed that "the main purpose of a Bankruptcy Act ... is to see to it that a debtor ... obtains a discharge." The following year in Parliament, the Solicitor General stated that the "one great object to be attained by a Bankruptcy Act in Canada is the discharge of the honest debtor."[146] There were no objections to these statements of general principle, and the fact that they went unchallenged is noteworthy and contrasts to earlier nineteenth-century debates. Behind these statements of general principle lay broader concerns about the protection of creditors. In contrast, the discharge had been challenged in the nineteenth century on the basis that debtors had a moral obligation to repay debts. But in 1918 and 1919 Parliament did not debate the specific discharge provisions of the new bankruptcy bills. Instead, it focused on a clause-by-clause analysis of other more technical matters and constitutional issues. The discharge had therefore been transformed from a nineteenth-century evil to an essential form of business regulation.

In fact, the CCMTA instructed Grundy to draft a bill that would "carefully guard the granting of discharges."[147] The CCMTA and its solicitor, in reviewing the need for a discharge, made "careful inquiries and investigations" of foreign bankruptcy Acts, and the English discharge provisions provided the perfect model for the new Canadian bill: "It was found, on examining the provisions of the English Act and upon making inquiries among the creditor class in England, that the discharge provisions contained in the English Act gave satisfaction to the public at large, to both the creditor and the debtor class. They are very conservative and the dishonest debtor has not much of a chance. The honest debtor has."[148]

Grundy made it clear that the new legislation was not a debtors' Act. The intention of the legislation was that "discharges shall not be obtained readily by debtors where business methods are below the standard fixed by the requirements of the Act." Grundy ensured that creditor interests would be protected and the abuses that occurred under the provincial laws would be cured: "[I]f the judges follow the same conservative course which has been adopted by the English Bankruptcy Judges very few abuses will arise."[149] The willingness to embrace English bankruptcy legislation as the perfect model for the discharge was consistent with the general trend in the Canadian common law legal community at that time to accept laws and ideals from the Empire as worthy of emulation.[150]

The court-supervised discharge regime clearly distinguished between an honest but unfortunate debtor and a debtor who had engaged in misconduct. However, the statute did not entitle the bankrupt to a discharge "as of right."[151] The Act only permitted debtors to make application for a discharge any time after being adjudged bankrupt or making an assignment. There was no automatic discharge through the lapse of time. If debtors failed to make an application, they would remain a bankrupt indefinitely.[152] The discharge application was at the court's discretion. The court, on hearing the debtor's application, could grant or refuse an absolute order of discharge or suspend the operation of the order for a specified period. Alternatively the court could make an order conditional upon payment of a portion of the debtor's after-acquired earnings.[153] Bankruptcy legislation, therefore, was "just and generous to the honest and unfortunate trader" and "penalizes the incompetent and dishonest."[154]

In some cases the judge did not have the discretion to grant an absolute discharge, "even if the judge thought it appropriate to make such an order."[155] If any of the listed factors set out in section 59 were proven, the bankrupt was not entitled to an absolute discharge. The court was required to refuse, suspend or make a conditional order of discharge.[156] Section 59 listed factors that focused on the debtor's conduct and whether or not the debtor's insolvency was attributable to circumstances for which the debtor could be held responsible. Relevant factors included:

- failing to keep proper books,
- continuing to trade after knowing to be insolvent,
- failing to account for any loss of assets,
- making a frivolous defence to a creditor's action,
- bringing a frivolous action,
- making an undue preference,
- incurring liabilities with a view to making his assets equal to fifty cents in the dollar,
- previously being bankrupt, or
- being guilty of any fraud or fraudulent breach of trust.[157]

The ultimate discretion for the granting of the discharge lay with the courts and not creditors. However, the Act permitted the trustee or creditors to object to the bankrupt's application for discharge.

It was the duty of the court "to decide the extent to which the debtor has been responsible for his own misfortune."[158] Where there was no dishonesty or wilful negligence, it was a matter of public policy that the court granted a discharge. The courts would therefore assume a function that creditors had been unable to carry out. The private remedy of individual creditor release encouraged dishonest competition among creditors. The private release did not operate as a check on debtor misconduct, as creditors sought their immediate best deal and did not concern themselves with the larger public goal of improving commercial morality: "Under the bill it is recognized that the Court, seized of all the circumstances, would be in a better position to decide as to whether the debtor should be given his discharge, than creditors whose interest in the Estate is in many cases too immediate and personal to permit unbiased judgment."[159] After all, a discharge was not simply a matter between a debtor and his creditors but was a matter in which the "community is also vitally interested."[160] Creditors were willing to give up this role of monitoring debtor behaviour in favour of a judicial system that provided better control over debtors. At its core, therefore, the new discharge provisions reflected the honest but unfortunate conceptualization of the discharge. Jacob Ziegel argues that the Act's rehabilitative goals were "heavily compromised," since the legislation did not guarantee a fresh start.[161]

Was creditor acceptance of judicial supervision of discharges surprising, given the nineteenth-century pro-debtor interpretation of the *Insolvent Acts*? There are several reasons why creditors were willing to accept a judicial system by 1919. First, the judicial interpretation of the *Insolvent Acts* was not raised in the debates leading up to the passage of the *Bankruptcy Act of 1919*. The *Insolvent Acts* played little or no role in the shaping of the *Bankruptcy Act of 1919*. The nineteenth-century statutes were distant memories when Parliament came to debate the new legislation in 1919. Second, judicial discretion in 1919 was trusted because it provided an improvement on the near forty-year period of no federal bankruptcy law. During that time creditors were unable to obtain contractual concessions from debtors, because there was no mandatory collective regime to make the debtor and other creditors cooperate. Finally, creditors trusted judicial discretion in 1919 because this system had been in place in England since 1883 and appeared to work well. Much of the *Bankruptcy Act of 1919* was based upon the English statute of 1883.

The move from the nineteenth-century notion that all debts must be repaid to the *Bankruptcy Act of 1919*, which contained a discretionary discharge regime, was an important development. Campbell argues that for a new paradigm to be implemented a number of factors must occur. First, the new program of legislation must be economically viable, in that it solves economic problems that are consistent with the country's economic structure. Second, the new policy option must not threaten key interest groups. Finally, once the new policy is tested and it works, it will become "institutionalized."[162]

These three factors may be applied to the evolution of bankruptcy law in Canada. The *Bankruptcy Act of 1919* was consistent with the economic structure of Canada. For the first time in more than forty years, Canada adopted a national uniform bankruptcy statute, which replaced the diverse and patchwork quilt of provincial law on debtor-creditor matters that operated between 1880 and 1919. As noted in this chapter, the Canadian economy was moving in a national direction in the period leading up to the enactment of the 1919 Act. The new legislation solved the economic problem associated with diverse provincial legislation. Further, the new bankruptcy statute in 1919 did not threaten key interest groups. In fact, the CCMTA lobbied for change and benefited from the enactment of the *Bankruptcy Act of 1919*.

Hall also argues that paradigm shifts will occur under certain circumstances. The "movement from one paradigm to another is likely to be preceded by significant shifts in the locus of authority over policy." The battle for policy control will end only when "the supporters of a new paradigm secure positions of authority over policymaking." Policy shifts are likely to occur when there have been instances of policy experimentation and policy failure. Where a paradigm is incapable of adapting or dealing with "anomalous developments,"[163] policy failure will occur. This will undermine the existing paradigm and pave the way for a paradigm shift.

Hall's insights also may be considered in light of policy developments in Canada. By 1919 there was a shift in the locus of power in relation to policy development. The CBA and the CCMTA dominated the debates on bankruptcy reform. The CCMTA retained a solicitor to draft a bankruptcy bill, which ultimately became the *Bankruptcy Act of 1919*. The Act may also be considered as a response provincial reform law that was incapable of dealing with the pressing need for a national bankruptcy statute. Provincial law was not uniform and did not provide for a discharge. The failure of provincial reform opened the door for a paradigm shift and the implementation of the *Bankruptcy Act of 1919*.

6. Conclusion

For several reasons, the *Bankruptcy Act of 1919*[164] must be considered Canada's first modern bankruptcy statute. The legislation included a compulsory bankruptcy provision,[165] allowed debtors to make composition agreements[166] and distributed assets on a *pro rata* basis. Unlike the *Insolvent Act of 1875*, the *Bankruptcy Act of 1919* permitted voluntary proceedings, and debtors no longer needed to qualify as a trader to obtain access to the legislation. Importantly, the *Bankruptcy Act* enabled debtors to apply for a statutory release of their debts for the first time in nearly forty years. However, it was not a late twentieth- or early twenty-first century bankruptcy statute. Notwithstanding the significant improvements in the law and the fact that it applied to corporations, the statute remained concerned largely with liquidation of debtors' estates. Corporate reorganizations as we know them today were well beyond the vision of the drafters of the *Bankruptcy Act*.[167]

Nevertheless, in its time the *Bankruptcy Act of 1919* was a significant milestone in the history of Canadian bankruptcy law. Canada was at last joining the United States and England as a nation with a permanent bankruptcy regime. Further, the federal government finally fulfilled the aims of the drafters of the *BNA Act* by enacting national and stable bankruptcy legislation. While the source of the law can be traced to the private sector, Parliament had finally enacted a bankruptcy statute as a government matter. This enabled important institutional support for future growth of bankruptcy law as a public matter.

The re-emergence of bankruptcy law as a national reform issue in Canada prior to the war can be explained in part by the economic downturn in the economy beginning in 1913. Further, the industrialization and urbanization of the Canadian economy in the years leading up to 1919 coincided with the growth in new national lobby groups and their increasing frustration over the proliferation of non-uniform provincial law. The impact of the institutional factor of the growth of the federal regulatory state during the war cannot be ignored. The growing regulatory state provided the CCMTA with an opportunity to press for reform in a time when the government was already committed to growing the size of the state. However, it would be wrong to characterize the *Bankruptcy Act of 1919* as a new form of government regulation initiated by the state, designed to protect the interests of debtors. While the *Bankruptcy Act of 1919* emerged from the public institution of Parliament, private interests significantly shaped the law: it was drafted and promoted on behalf of the CCMTA, which largely represented creditors and assignees under provincial law. Moreover, not all aspects of the legislation involved making changes to the provincial model. The CCMTA sought to preserve beneficial provisions of the provincial legislation. It is unlikely, however, that the *Bankruptcy Act of 1919* would have come into existence unless there had been a new consensus over the discharge.

The transformation of the discharge represented more than a shift in values. By 1919, creditors recognized the discharge as part of the larger bankruptcy scheme that enhanced collection goals. The nearly forty-year absence of the discharge provided numerous examples of debtors engaging in deceptive or fraudulent conduct under defective provincial legislation. The CCMTA, which had gained prominence during the provincial era, was well placed to recognize the needs of creditors and ensured that the bill contained a discretionary discharge that was aimed at controlling the conduct of debtors. The discharge released individuals from the burden of debt and returned them to the community of borrowers. Further, statutory regulation of discharges served the public interest as well as creditors' interests by protecting the community from dishonest debtors. Creditors acting individually had not been able to monitor debtor conduct effectively under the provincial regimes. The new discharge provisions maintained the rights of creditors. Bankruptcy reform succeeded because creditors recognized that it was in their interests to have a discretionary discharge regime supervised by the courts.

10

Conclusion

But alas for human hopes! How often do we find the glittering treasure we have followed, when at last we have it all secure, it has suddenly collapsed, like an empty bauble."

Carrie J. Harris, *Cyril Whyman's Mistake* (Toronto: William Bryce, 1894) p. 70

1. Bankruptcy Reform Through the Lens of Ideas, Interests and Institutions

One business historian suggests that "fraud and success are not easy to separate ... some players in business often find themselves on the borderline of legality when they have the pitfalls of failure in mind."[1] In 1880, Parliament repealed the *Insolvent Act of 1875* in response to the growing perception that bankrupts engaged in fraudulent behaviour, but it was not clear that additional legislative reform would cure the problem of deviant bankrupts. In an 1880 letter to Prime Minister Macdonald, Thomas Ritchie declared that opting for further bankruptcy reform would "carry us back to darkness and chaos."[2] Ironically, repeal of the *Insolvent Act of 1875* extended that darkness and chaos until Parliament enacted the *Bankruptcy Act of 1919*. In the interregnum, creditors had to deal with the ambiguity of the common law and the constitutional uncertainty of provincial legislation.

The study of bankruptcy law "inevitably bring[s] to the foreground all the many evils of capitalism."[3] In the nineteenth century, the inefficient *Insolvent Acts* provided ample opportunity for debtors, creditors and even Official Assignees to engage in the plundering of the bankruptcy regime. Under the *Insolvent Acts*, debtors believed that they were entitled to arrange their affairs with local or related creditors. They simply ignored the equality principle, ensuring that favoured creditors would be paid first. Although the *Insolvent Acts* prohibited transactions of this kind, courts interpreted the preference provisions in a way that favoured the preferred creditor, rendering ineffective one of the important tools available to the Assignee to uphold equality. Favourable arrangements with family or local creditors led to the unpopularity of the *Insolvent Acts*, leaving many to question the merits of continuing with a bankruptcy regime. The evils of capitalism also included the corruption of Official Assignees and the collusion between debtors and creditors in an involuntary bankruptcy proceeding. Discharge applications did not provide the necessary deterrent for debtor misconduct, as the courts interpreted the provisions in a liberal way that favoured the debtor. However, this was not the story that the drafters of the *BNA Act* had anticipated in 1867.

Bankruptcy and insolvency was one of the many important economic powers granted to Parliament under the *BNA Act* in 1867, but Parliament did not effectively utilize this federal power until the passing of the *Bankruptcy Act of 1919*,[4] which would form the basis of a permanent bankruptcy regime for twentieth- and twenty-first-century Canada. In the nineteenth century, bankruptcy law was not readily accepted. The *Insolvent Acts of 1869* and *1875* marked Canada's first foray into the field of bankruptcy and insolvency, but it was a tenuous entrance at best. Between 1869 and 1880, the House of Commons debated ten separate repeal bills. The original *Insolvent Act of 1869* was passed as a temporary four-year measure and was limited to traders. The *Insolvent Act of 1869* raised the ire of the credit community, because a debtor could easily make a voluntary bankruptcy filing and obtain a discharge.

In 1875, Parliament abolished voluntary proceedings, and in subsequent amendments it further restricted access to the discharge. However, amendments did not satisfy the Members of Parliament calling for repeal. The repeal movement, which began soon after the 1869 Act came into effect, culminated in 1880 with the repeal of the *Insolvent Act of 1875*. But the issue was far from exhausted. Between 1880 and 1903, Parliament debated a number of bankruptcy reform bills. Only two bills bore the imprint of government policy, and none garnered sufficient votes in Parliament.[5]

In 1919, after a near forty-year absence from the fray, Parliament reasserted its jurisdiction over bankruptcy and insolvency and passed what many believed to be an essential form of business regulation. The *Bankruptcy Act of 1919* applied to all types of debtors, both individual and corporate. It allowed both voluntary and involuntary proceedings and enabled debtors to apply for a discharge. The consensus in 1919 on the desirability of a national bankruptcy act containing a discharge stands in stark contrast to the debates of the nineteenth century. What had been deemed an evil and immoral form of regulation in the nineteenth century became a commercial necessity by 1919.

Why Canada repealed bankruptcy legislation in 1880 and did not pass a national uniform statute until 1919 has been the central question of this book. Opposition to nineteenth-century bankruptcy law, the absence of federal legislation for nearly forty years and the success of the 1919 Act can be explained by examining how ideas, interests and institutions affected legislative change.

Bankruptcy law at its core is concerned with distributing the debtor's assets equitably and providing the debtor with a discharge. These two central goals dramatically interfered with the common law debtor–creditor relationship. The collective nature of bankruptcy proceedings and the distribution of the debtor's assets on an equal basis were central to the debate. Bankruptcy law's interference with the traditional common law scramble for the debtor's assets affected the specific interests of local and distant creditors. Much of the debate in the nineteenth century focused on the morality of the discharge and whether it interfered with a debtor's higher obligation to repay debts. Therefore, bankruptcy law represented a distinct divergence of interests between local and distant creditors over the advantages and disadvantages of a *pro rata* distribution and a conflict of values over the morality of the discharge. Institutional factors such as federalism and the emerging regulatory state also had an independent effect on the legislative history. Thus, the book has focused on ideas, interests and institutions to demonstrate the role that they played in shaping Canadian bankruptcy reform.

Equitable Distribution of the Debtor's Assets

Creditors who traded across regional boundaries focused on the equitable distribution of assets, first to prevent repeal of bankruptcy law during the 1870s, and after 1880 to call for reinstatement of bankruptcy law, which offered a major advantage over the common law, as it provided a distribution of the debtor's assets to all creditors on a *pro rata* basis. In contrast, the common law system of "first come, first served" rewarded local creditors who acted quickly and disadvantaged creditors who traded at a distance. Such distant creditors favoured a national bankruptcy law and its equitable distribution policy that prevented local creditors from seizing all of the debtor's assets. Bankruptcy law, by abolishing the common law race and prohibiting preferences, reduced risks for foreign creditors and destroyed local creditor advantage. Throughout the 1870s, Members of Parliament warned that repeal would have grave consequences for inter-provincial trade. Merchants would refuse to extend credit or ship goods across distances if Parliament repealed the law.

Express support for a bankruptcy law in the 1870s came from the urban Boards of Trade in Toronto and Montreal, which sought to prevent repeal and had some success in delaying the law's demise. The Dominion Board of Trade, a national organization representing local Boards, also advocated for the retention of the law. However, not all agreed with the goal of uniform national legislation. The Dominion Board of Trade was itself divided over the issue, and repeal suggests that the national vision of the economy was premature and that some creditors may have preferred to trade under the common law system.

After 1880, bankruptcy law did not disappear from the Parliamentary agenda, as national and increasing numbers of foreign creditors continued to demand uniform legislation. Foreign merchants complained that it was common practice for Canadian creditors to benefit at the expense of overseas creditors. Both Macdonald and Laurier received numerous pleas and petitions from overseas merchants seeking a national bankruptcy law that prohibited debtors from making preferential payments. Not all provinces took immediate steps to prohibit preferences.

The premise of equal treatment of creditors ran counter to the notion of offering assistance to a local friend or family member, which lay at the heart of more traditional forms of business. Many provinces continued to tolerate preferences, as they justly rewarded local enterprise at the expense of outsiders and foreigners. Loans to family members or friends were fundamentally different from credit obtained from businesses or banks, and preferences were expected where a neighbour or family member had extended credit.[6] The failure of federal bills throughout the 1880s and 1890s, and the slow pace of provincial reform to prohibit preferences, suggests that localism remained an important influencing factor and further implies that many arguments against the bankruptcy discharge on the basis of moral obligation may have concealed local interests seeking to retain the advantages of the common law.

The success of the *Bankruptcy Act of 1919* reflected a fundamental shift between local and distant creditor interests. New national interest groups emerged just prior to the First World War to demand uniform legislation. As more firms engaged in inter-provincial trade, there was a decided shift in the expected benefits of national uniform legislation.[7] Uniformity would do away with the older notion that outsiders did not have the same rights as those within the province,[8] and by 1919, numerous businesses stood to benefit from a national law. Further, the emergence of new national interest groups, such as the CBA and the CCMTA, provided the means for an effective lobbying effort. The CBA led the general call for uniformity of all commercial legislation, and the CCMTA seized upon the bankruptcy issue and retained a lawyer to draft new legislation.[9] The advantages of a national uniform legislation could no longer be denied.

The Discharge

In the nineteenth century, the discharge proved to be the most contentious reform issue. The discharge provisions of the *Insolvent Acts of 1869* and *1875* were based upon creditor consent, and the requirements for obtaining consent became more stringent as the decade progressed. While both Acts allowed debtors to apply for a discharge, the court had the discretion to award either a first- or second-class discharge. The classification system permitted the courts to pass judgment on the moral trustworthiness of the debtor. The call for repeal in 1880 was directly linked to the discharge. Many argued that releasing debtors from their obligations was not a proper role for the state.

One cannot understand Parliament's actions without examining the underlying ideas about the discharge. Two distinct positions were evident. On the one hand, debtors required a fresh start, and it was unjust to burden a person with debt for life. Honest but unfortunate debtors deserved a discharge and the opportunity to start again, and forgiveness of debt was advocated for those who had been subject to the uncertainties of the market or who suffered from sickness or other mishap.

On the other hand, notions of forgiveness competed unsuccessfully with the idea that all debts had to be honoured. The common claim heard in Parliament from the 1870s through to the end of the century was that bankruptcy law encouraged commercial immorality – a link that was derived from the fundamental obligation to repay debts. Bankruptcy law therefore interfered with this higher value. No law should lead a debtor to betray one's duty to one's fellow man; debt was a private matter to be worked out between the parties.[10] There was a perception that bankrupts were simply fraudulent.

If repeal and the continued failure of federal reform bills between 1880 and 1903 can be attributed to the unpopularity of the discharge and its challenge to the higher obligation to repay debts, it is significant to note that by 1919 opposition to the discharge largely disappeared. The paradigm regarding the debtor's discharge had changed. While notions of commercial morality dominated the debates of the nineteenth century, after the war the discharge was an accepted feature of the bankruptcy statute. Statements in the House of Commons that emphasized the fundamental importance of the discharge were not challenged. However, that is not to say that the fraudulent debtor view had disappeared completely; the discharge in 1919 did not represent an altruistic measure for the benefit of debtors. Rather, creditors came to realize that the absence of a discharge hampered collection because debtors had an incentive to misbehave. An organized and knowledgeable interest group, the CCMTA, presented Parliament with a comprehensive bankruptcy bill that contained a discharge.[11] Parliament enacted the discharge in 1919, because it was in the interests of creditors. This acceptance of the discharge as an essential aspect of bankruptcy regulation in Canada in the twentieth century parallels earlier developments in the United States and England.[12]

Institutions

Institutional factors had an independent effect on policy direction. Parliament debated bankruptcy law within the framework of federalism and the emerging regulatory state. During the 1870s there was little sense that bankruptcy law was part of a larger regulatory state. It was never adopted as a government reform measure and there was no specialized government department responsible for the legislation. As a regulatory measure, bankruptcy law had no institutional backing in the nineteenth century. While the Department of Justice had broad responsibility for the legislation, there was little support for the law as a public policy measure. Official Assignees had broad responsibility for bankruptcy administration, with little supervision. Creditors mistrusted Assignees who charged excessive fees and delayed in declaring a dividend. The negative fallout from Assignee misconduct contributed to the unpopularity of the *Insolvent Acts*. The Department of Justice and the Prime Minister were more concerned with sorting out patronage appointments to fill the position of Official Assignee than with Assignee conduct.

In contrast, the English reforms of 1883 were initiated and implemented by a government with a strong policy direction. Senior civil servants formulated much of the policy expressed in the 1883 Act, and they accepted that the state had a supervisory role to play. Bankruptcy law, in this new vision, was not the concern just of creditors but of society at large.[13] This newer concept of bankruptcy law in Canada did not emerge until the passage of the 1919 Act, which coincided with unprecedented growth of federal regulation during the war. In Parliament, the bill was justified as an important war measure to deal with the economic dislocation following the end of the conflict.

The courts also played an important role in shaping bankruptcy law debates. Although there was a strong sentiment that a debtor had an obligation to repay all debts, nineteenth-century courts tended to favour a liberal interpretation of the bankruptcy statute that weighed in the debtor's favour, particularly in discharge applications. These judicial decisions also contributed to the unpopularity of the *Insolvent Acts*. Courts also tolerated collusion in involuntary proceedings under the *Insolvent Act of 1875*. Judges allowed family creditors to initiate proceedings against the debtor in order to allow the debtor to obtain access to the discharge. The preference jurisprudence shows a distinct pattern of courts interpreting the legislation in favour of the preferred creditor and against the Official Assignee, which had the effect of undermining the equality principle. Finally, the Official Assignee became a symbol of all that was wrong with the *Insolvent Acts*.

Federalism also had a significant impact upon the legislative history of Canadian bankruptcy law. The division of powers and the ability of the provinces to regulate debtor-creditor matters provided Parliament with the option to abandon a controversial subject. Repeal in 1880 coincided with Ontario's enactment of a *Creditors' Relief Act* to provide for an equal distribution of the debtor's assets. Federalism took on a more significant role after 1880, as the bankruptcy law debate shifted to a discussion over the scope of federal and provincial powers. Between 1886 and 1893, several Ontario courts ruled on the validity of provincial legislation.[14] The divided opinions of the Ontario Court of Appeal left the law in a state of chaos and inhibited federal and provincial reform. It was not until 1894 that the Privy Council resolved the uncertainty with its ruling in *Ontario (AG) v Canada (AG)*. The decision upheld the validity of provincial legislation and contributed to the further growth of provincial laws and largely ended federal reform efforts until after the First World War. Provincial law became entrenched as the primary means of regulating debtor-creditor matters. It would take the war and the efforts of a new national lobby group to shift the focus away from provincial regulation.

The period of study coincides with the rise of the provincial rights movement at the end of the nineteenth century. The more highly publicized disputes between Ontario and Ottawa contrast with Macdonald's tacit acceptance of provincial regulation of debtor-creditor matters. The repeal of the federal Act and the adoption of the Ontario *Creditors' Relief Act* followed correspondence between Oliver Mowat and Macdonald's government leader in the Senate. After 1880, Macdonald did not take issue with provincial legislation and expressly chose not to use the power of disallowance. In 1883, in the House of Commons, he cast doubt on a private Member's bill on the basis that it might interfere with provincial jurisdiction, and in 1884 Macdonald raised jurisdictional complexities as a means to deflect foreign demands for reform.[15] Bankruptcy law was a controversial subject, and the ability of the provinces to pass debtor-creditor legislation provided Macdonald and subsequently Laurier with a valid excuse not to proceed with federal legislation. Macdonald's explicit decision not to challenge provincial jurisdiction in this area is worthy of attention and illustrates that not every jurisdictional issue of this era was part of a confrontational strategy with the provinces.

2. Other Explanations for Legal Change

While ideas, interests and institutions provide an explanatory framework for Canadian bankruptcy reform, one might consider whether other theories of legal change apply to the Canadian setting. Canada's pattern of legislation and repeal followed by other legislation raises the possibility of drawing a comparison to the United States. Congress enacted short-lived bankruptcy statutes in 1800, 1841 and 1867 before adopting a permanent Act in 1898.[16] David Skeel argues that "a small assortment of political factors – including the rise of organized creditor groups and the countervailing influence of populism, together with the emergence of the bankruptcy bar – set a pattern that has characterized U.S. bankruptcy law for over a century and shows no sign of decline."[17]

Skeel's work covers a much broader period, analysing events up to the late twentieth century. However, one can draw a parallel between the Canadian *Bankruptcy Act of 1919* and the US *Bankruptcy Act of 1898*. Both statutes established a permanent bankruptcy regime in their respective countries after periods of legislation and repeal. Further, on both sides of the border organized creditor groups "created a demand for bankruptcy legislation."[18] In Canada, interest groups demanded federal reforms. In the nineteenth century the Dominion Board of Trade and later, during the First World War, the CCMTA lobbied for comprehensive bankruptcy reform. However, Skeel identifies a factor that was not present in Canada. In the United States the "pro-debtor forces ... had a crucial restraining effect on ... creditors' bankruptcy proposals."[19] In Canada there was no such countervailing populist movement or the existence of pro-debtor lawmakers. The Canadian *Bankruptcy Act of 1919* was a creditors' Act in many respects.

The broad similarity between the Canadian *Bankruptcy Act of 1919* and the *English Bankruptcy Act of 1914*[20] raises the possibility that legal origins theory offers an explanation for the ultimate format and scope of the Canadian 1919 Act. Legal origins scholars[21] emphasize that "differences in legal rules and regulations are accounted for to a significant extent by legal origins." Thus, distinct legal traditions (i.e. common law vs civil law systems) matter, and these distinctions explain "why legal rules differ."[22] As one critic of legal origins summed it up, legal origins "are supposed to have emerged in a given historical context and to have then crystallized: they are interpreted as some essential hardcore identity, which would lie beyond the reach of either economic or political competition."[23] One might expect Canada to follow English patterns of legislative reform under a legal origins theory.

However, legal origins theory does not explain the evolution of Canadian bankruptcy law. First, it is comparative theory that seeks to explain differences in legal rules across many countries and different legal systems. Second, a recent comparative study of European bankruptcy laws for the period of 1808–1914 concluded that "continent wide evolutions" were "linked to the process of capitalist development." Economic development was "much more important than country-specific features."[24] While the *Bankruptcy Act of 1914* ultimately influenced the Canadian reforms in 1919, it should be noted that the UK 1914 reforms were only a consolidation of the earlier landmark English reforms in 1883. It must be remembered that Canada was without a national law for nearly forty years, during which time Canada could well have adopted the English Bankruptcy Act of 1883.

After repeal of federal bankruptcy law, Canada chose to ignore the English 1883 reforms, instead charting its own course of provincial law and constitutional uncertainty. In the late nineteenth and early twentieth century, Parliament held running debates on the merits of re-establishing a new national law, all the while disregarding English law reforms of 1883. Although Canada and England shared a common background and heritage in bankruptcy law, the two countries did not have a common vision about bankruptcy law until 1919. Even then, as discussed in chapter 9, the drafter of the Act did not readily copy every English provision. The failure of legal origins to explain Canadian bankruptcy reform suggests that other factors, like economic development, cannot be ignored. As noted in chapter 9, the enactment of the *Bankruptcy Act of 1919* coincided with important economic changes and the growth of the government.[25]

Path dependence might also explain why Canada ultimately chose to follow English law in 1919. When policymakers are faced with a choice, path dependence suggests that the decision-makers will adopt what is familiar rather than adopt something new and untried.[26] In other words, path dependence "describes how the reinforcement of a given set of arrangements over time raises the cost of changing them." A related concept is historical institutionalism, which assesses "the concepts of self-reinforcing mechanisms and high switching costs." This allows for a better understanding of "the 'stickiness' of certain institutional and political arrangements."[27]

The near forty-year reign of provincial law between 1880 and 1919 demonstrates elements of path dependence. The institutionalization of the provincial regime proved "difficult to dislodge."[28] The debate over bankruptcy reform in 1918–19 also exhibited elements of path dependence. Initially, interest groups sought reform at the provincial level, and when provincial reform became unworkable, efforts shifted to the national level. However, provincial law still had an influence, as the drafter of the federal reform bill allowed the provinces to set bankruptcy exemptions.

Parliament based the *Bankruptcy Act of 1919* on the English *Bankruptcy Act of 1914*. Did path dependence play a role in the choice of a model statute? After all, the *Bankruptcy Act of 1919* was a significant departure from the Canadian *Insolvent Acts* of *1869* and *1875*. Those nineteenth-century statutes had failed and were a distant memory by 1919. Further, English law was a familiar source. Blaine Baker's study demonstrates that in turn-of-the-century Ontario, provincial law libraries replaced Upper Canadian law books with English legal digests, treatises and case reporters. He argues, "One reason for this literary and professional transformation was waxing Ontarian and British interest in an ascending Empire, in which law was to be a major link." There was a "turn-of-the-century enthusiasm for things British."[29] As Jacob Ziegel notes with respect to the *Bankruptcy Act of 1919*, "[T]here appears to have been a general willingness to continue to live with the structure, principles and philosophy inherited from the British sources."[30]

3. The Legacy of the Bankruptcy Act of 1919

The *Bankruptcy Act of 1919* established a lasting legacy. The 1919 Act "still provides the conceptual framework for the current Bankruptcy and Insolvency Act."[31] Beyond the conceptual framework, a number of provisions have remained unchanged. For example, the decision to leave the definition of bankruptcy exemptions to the provinces remains to this day. Although reforms have been proposed to provide for an optional federal exemption list, the 1919 decision to allow the provinces to define the scope and extent of bankruptcy exemptions remains firmly entrenched.[32]

Further, the discharge provisions in the *Bankruptcy and Insolvency Act* continue to be influenced by the *Bankruptcy Act of 1919*. Today, the court may not grant an absolute discharge on proof of any of the facts listed in section 173.[33] That list, which includes such factors as omitting to keep books of account or trading while knowing to be insolvent, is virtually identical to a list of factors that the courts considered under the *Bankruptcy Act of 1919*.[34]

The *Bankruptcy Act of 1919* and an amending Act of 1920 also influenced the current law on preferences.[35] Under the current *Bankruptcy and Insolvency Act* creditors may no longer provide evidence of pressure as a defence in response to a trustee's attempt to set aside a preferential payment.[36] The origins of this policy can be traced to 1919–20. As discussed in chapter 3, in the nineteenth century, the doctrine of pressure had undermined the ability of the Official Assignee to set aside preferences under the *Insolvent Acts*. Pressure enabled the creditor to retain the preferred payment. While the 1919 bill proposed to eliminate the doctrine of pressure as a defence, commercial groups and the banking industry objected to the abolition of the doctrine. Commercial groups advocated retention of the doctrine of pressure, which, if invoked, would enable the creditor to retain the benefit of the transaction. Commercial lobby groups persuaded Parliament to retain the doctrine of pressure for the *Bankruptcy Act of 1919*. However, in a 1920 amending Act, Parliament abolished pressure[37] and that position remains to this day. The current *Bankruptcy and Insolvency Act* does not permit creditors to provide evidence of pressure as a defence in a preference action by the trustee.[38] However, the attempt to abolish the doctrine of pressure has met with mixed success. Notwithstanding the statutory abolition of the doctrine, some courts have given credence to a creditor diligence defence in preference actions. In the case law there is no clear distinction between pressure and creditor diligence, nor is there any discernible test for what constitutes creditor diligence.[39]

Finally, one goal of the *Bankruptcy Act of 1919* was to establish a federal and uniform regime over all bankruptcy matters. On the one hand, the 1919 Act purported to overcome the inconsistent and diverse provincial statutes that had emerged during the absence of a national bankruptcy statute. However, on the other hand, the new federal bankruptcy statute did not mean an immediate end to the provincial legislation. The enactment of the *Bankruptcy Act of 1919* created a "complex and nonharmonious overlay of federal and provincial legislation,"[40] which remains today. There has been no attempt to reconcile overlapping provincial and federal legislation. For example, a trustee in bankruptcy may rely upon section 95 of the *Bankruptcy and Insolvency Act* and the Ontario *Assignments and Preferences Act*[41] to challenge a preferential transaction.[42]

While the *Bankruptcy Act of 1919* continues to influence bankruptcy matters today, the *Insolvent Acts of 1869* and *1875* should not become mere footnotes in the history of Canadian bankruptcy law, for they provide a perspective on debt and credit in nineteenth-century Canada. Both Acts failed to provide any form of comprehensive protection for insolvent debtors, because only individuals engaged in buying and selling were eligible for bankruptcy.[43] Individuals operating businesses that bought and sold goods were important to the Canadian economy, yet the *Insolvent Acts* of the nineteenth century provided only rudimentary protection to them. Furthermore, farmers and wage-earners were offered no protection under the Acts. Parliament did little to protect insolvent traders during the 1870s and then abandoned them altogether by repealing the *Insolvent Act of 1875*. The tendency for nineteenth-century Canadian governments to intervene and subsidize failing infrastructure projects stands in contrast to their unwillingness to adopt comprehensive bankruptcy legislation providing for the discharge of debtors. It will be the task of future historical studies to take into account the limited range of legal options available to the financially troubled debtor before 1919.

Notes

Chapter 1

1 James Crowe, Erie, PA, to Wilfrid Laurier (18 December 1909) in Laurier Papers, LAC (MG 26-G) [hereafter Laurier Papers] (reel C-884, pp. 163911–13).

2 See David A. Skeel Jr, *Debt's Dominion: A History of Bankruptcy Law in America* (Princeton: Princeton University Press, 2001) ch. 1.

3 James Crowe to Wilfrid Laurier (18 December 1909); Wilfrid Laurier to James Crowe, Erie, PA (21 December 1909) in Laurier Papers (reel C-884, p. 163913).

4 Editorial, "Shall We Have a Bankruptcy Law?" (1858) 4 UCLJ 2, pp. 3–4; Editorial, "A Bankruptcy Law Required" (1863) 9 UCLJ 141, pp. 141–2; Editorial, "Colonial Bankruptcy Law" (1861) 7 UCLJ 165; Editorial, "Bankruptcy and Insolvency" (1861) 7 UCLJ 10; Editorial, "The Act Respecting Insolvency" (1864) 10 UCLJ 225.

5 Thomas H. Jackson, *The Logic and Limits of Bankruptcy Law* (Cambridge, Mass: Harvard University Press, 1986) p. 7.

6 *Insolvent Act of 1869; Insolvent Act of 1875*. Section 149 of the *Insolvent Act of 1875* repealed the *Insolvent Act of 1869* as of 1 September 1875.

7 See chapter 2 below.

8 *An Act to repeal the Acts respecting Insolvency now in force in Canada*, SC 1880, c 1. The *British North America Act*, s 91(21), granted the federal Parliament jurisdiction over bankruptcy and insolvency. In 1919, Parliament passed the *Bankruptcy Act of 1919*.

9 Alan Watson, "Legal Change: Sources of Law and Legal Culture" (1983) 131:5 U Pa L Rev 1121, p. 1123.

10 Ninette Kelley & Michael Trebilcock, *The Making of the Mosaic: A History of Canadian Immigration Policy* (Toronto: University of Toronto Press, 1998) p. 12; Michael Trebilcock et al, *The Law and Economics of Canadian Competition Policy* (Toronto: University of Toronto Press, 2003) p. 12; Skeel, *Debt's Dominion*, p. 15 (ideology played an important factor in US bankruptcy law debates). David Skeel concludes that creditor interest groups, lawyers and bankruptcy judges had a significant influence on the shape of US bankruptcy law.

11 Kelley & Trebilcock, *Making of the Mosaic*, p. 11; Stephen Skowronek, *Building a New American State: The Expansion of National Administrative Capacities, 1877–1920* (New York: Cambridge University Press, 1982) p. ix.

12 Federal jurisdiction under the *BNA Act*, s 91(21) extended to bankruptcy and insolvency. The inclusion of both terms in the *BNA Act* was an attempt to avoid a dispute over the scope of the power. *R v Chandler* (1869), 12 NBR 556, p. 561 (CA). See John Honsberger, "The Nature of Bankruptcy and Insolvency in a Constitutional Perspective" (1972) 10:1 Osgoode Hall LJ 199, pp. 199–200.

13 In England, there was another important distinction between bankruptcy and insolvency. Until 1861, only traders could take advantage of bankruptcy legislation, leaving non-traders to become dependent upon insolvency legislation for relief. Prior to Confederation, some provinces enacted both bankruptcy and insolvency statutes. Peter Oliver, *"Terror to Evil Doers": Prisons and Punishments in Nineteenth-Century Ontario* (Toronto: University of Toronto Press, 1998) pp. 49, 50, 55–8. After Confederation some provinces enacted insolvency statutes. See C.R.B. Dunlop, *Creditor-Debtor Law in Canada*, 2nd ed (Toronto: Carswell, 1995) pp. 97–8. This survey focuses on bankruptcy statutes and does not consider insolvency statutes.

14 *McWhirter v Thorne* (1869), 19 UCCP 302, para 1. See also *Re Hurst, an Insolvent* (1876), 6 PR 329 (UC Pract Ct) para 1; *Green v Swan* (1872), 22 UCCP 307, para 25.

15 See Ian P.H. Duffy, *Bankruptcy and Insolvency in London During the Industrial Revolution* (New York: Garland, 1985) p. 304, who criticizes economic historians for describing the bankruptcy rates without making reference to the legal definition. See also W.J. Jones, *The Foundations of English Bankruptcy: Statutes and Commissions in the Early Modern Period* (Philadelphia: American Philosophical Society, 1979) p. 6.

16 For example, Norrie and Owram state that in the recession of 1913 unemployment rose, land prices tumbled and "bankruptcies sky-rocketed."

Kenneth Norrie & Douglas Owram, *A History of the Canadian Economy* (Toronto: Harcourt Brace, 1991) p. 414.

17 See e.g. *Shields v Peak* (1883), 8 SCR 579; V. Markham Lester, *Victorian Insolvency: Bankruptcy, Imprisonment for Debt and Company Winding-Up in Nineteenth-Century England* (Oxford: Clarendon Press, 1995) p. 8.

18 Scarboro, "A Question under the Bankrupt Law," Letter to the Editor, (1867) 3 Can LJ (NS) 193, p. 194; Lester, *Victorian Insolvency*, pp. 37–8. The *pro rata* principle was established as early as 1543, but it was not until 1705 that the discharge became part of English bankruptcy law. See Emily Kadens, "The Last Bankrupt Hanged: Balancing Incentives in the Development of Bankruptcy Law" (2010) 59:7 Duke LJ 1229.

19 There is a large modern literature on the nature of the fresh start. See e.g. Jackson, *Logic and Limits of Bankruptcy Law*; Karen Gross, *Failure and Forgiveness: Rebalancing the Bankruptcy System* (New Haven: Yale University Press, 1997) pp. 91–113; Margaret Howard, "A Theory of Discharge in Consumer Bankruptcy" (1987) 48:4 Ohio St LJ 1047.

20 W.S. Holdsworth, *A History of English Law* (London, UK: Methuen, 1925) vol 8, p. 230; Charles Jordan Tabb, "The Historical Evolution of the Bankruptcy Discharge" (1991) 65:3 Am Bank LJ 325, p. 328; Louis Edward Levinthal, "The Early History of English Bankruptcy Law" (1919) 67:1 U Pa L Rev 1, p. 13. It was this very feature of the common law that led the English Parliament to enact the first bankruptcy statute in 1543. (UK), 34 & 35 Hen VIII, c 4, s 1. See Kadens, "Last Bankrupt Hanged," p. 1241; *The Case of the Bankrupts* (1584), 2 Co Rep 25, 76 ER 441 (KB).

21 See e.g. *Beekman v Jarvis* (1847), 3 UCQB 280; *Topping v Joseph* (1859), 1 E & A 292 (UC Err App); *Rowe v Jarvis* (1863), 13 UCCP 495; *Bank of Montreal v Munro* (1864), 23 UCQB 414.

22 The stay of proceedings has been recognized as one of the fundamental principles of modern bankruptcy law. On the reasons why there must be a mandatory collective proceeding, see Jackson, *Logic and Limits of Bankruptcy Law*.

23 The conflict between local and distant creditors is explored in US literature. See Tony A. Freyer, *Producers versus Capitalists: Constitutional Conflict in Antebellum America* (Charlottesville: University of Virginia Press, 1994) pp. 9, 11, 21, 38, 85–7 (exploring the conflict between the local "associational economy" and corporate and mercantile enterprises tied more directly into the national market).

24 See Dennis C. Mueller, *Public Choice III* (New York: Cambridge University Press, 2003) p. 1. On the role of interest groups in US bankruptcy law, see Skeel, *Debt's Dominion*, pp. 14–15.

25 Kelley & Trebilcock, *Making of the Mosaic*, p. 9. See also Skeel, *Debt's Dominion*, p. 15.

26 Mueller, *Public Choice III*, p. 1. See also Kelley & Trebilcock, *Making of the Mosaic*, p. 9.

27 David A. Skeel Jr, "Public Choice and the Future of Public Choice–Influenced Legal Scholarship" (1998) 50:3 V and L Rev 647, p. 651. See also Skeel, *Debt's Dominion*, pp. 14–15.

28 *Ibid.*

29 Caroline Hughes Tuohy, "National Policy Studies in Comparative Perspective: An Organizing Framework Applied to the Canadian Case" in Laurent Dobuzinskis, Michael Howlett & David Laycock, eds, *Policy Studies in Canada: The State of the Art* (Toronto: University of Toronto Press, 1996) 317, p. 319. Ideology matters when a broad mass of people have a weak preference and the preference is the same for most people; see Mark Roe, *Strong Managers, Weak Owners: The Political Roots of American Corporate Finance* (Princeton: Princeton University Press, 1996) p. 27. See also Skeel, *Debt's Dominion*, p. 15.

30 Peter A. Hall, "Policy Paradigms, Social Learning, and the State: The Case of Economic Policymaking in Britain" (1993) 25:3 Comparative Politics 275, p. 279. See also Margaret Weir, "Ideas and the Politics of Bounded Innovation" in Sven Steinmo, Kathleen Thelen & Frank Lonstreth, eds, *Structuring Politics: Historical Institutionalism in Comparative Analysis* (Cambridge, UK: Cambridge University Press, 1992) 188.

31 Hans Wehberg, "Pacta Sunt Servanda" (1959) 53:4 AJIL 775.

32 Kelley & Trebilcock, *Making of the Mosaic*, p. 9.

33 Mariana Prado & Michael Trebilcock, "Path Dependence, Development, and The Dynamics of Institutional Reform" (2009) 59:3 UTLJ 341, p. 355; Paul Pierson & Theda Skocpol, "Historical Institutionalism in Contemporary Political Science" in Ira Katznelson & Helen V. Milner, eds, *Political Science: The State of the Discipline* (New York: Norton, 2002) 693, p. 696.

34 Kathleen Thelen & Sven Steinmo, "Historical Institutionalism in Comparative Politics" in Steinmo, Thelen & Lonstreth, eds, *Structuring Politics* 1, p. 2, citing G. John Ikenberry, "Conclusion: An Institutional Approach to American Foreign Economic Policy" in G. John Ikenberry, David A. Lake & Michael Mastanduno, eds, *The State and American Foreign Policy* (Ithaca, NY: Cornell University Press, 1988) 219, pp. 222–3. See also Daniel Béland, "Ideas, Interests and Institutions: Historical Institutionalism Revisited" in André Lecours, ed., *New Institutionalism: Theory and Analysis* (Toronto: University of Toronto Press, 2005) 29.

35 Theda Skocpol, *Protecting Soldiers and Mothers: The Political Origins of Social*

Policy in the United States (Cambridge, Mass: Harvard University Press, 1992) p. 41; Ellen M. Immergut, "The Theoretical Core of the New Institutionalism" (1998) 26:1 Politics & Society 5, p. 17.

36 André Lecours, "New Institutionalism: Issues and Questions" in Lecours, ed, *New Institutionalism* 3, p. 6.

37 R. Kent Weaver & Bert A. Rockman, "Assessing the Effects of Institutions" in R. Kent Weaver & Bert A. Rockman, eds, *Do Institutions Matter? Government Capabilities in the United States and Abroad* (Washington, DC: Brookings Institution Press, 1993) 1, p. 32; David Brian Robertson, "Politics and the Past: History, Behaviouralism, and the Return to Institutionalism in American Political Science" in Eric H. Monkkonen, ed, *Engaging the Past: The Uses of History Across the Social Sciences* (Durham: Duke University Press, 1994) 113.

38 Skowronek, *Building a New American State*, p. 27; Lecours, "New Institutionalism," p. 6.

39 Skowronek, *Building a New American State*, p. ix; Weaver & Rockman, eds, *Do Institutions Matter?*; Daniel R. Ernst, "Law and American Political Development, 1877–1938" (1998) 26:1 Reviews in American History 205.

40 Theda Skocpol, "Reply: Against Evolutionism – Social Policies and American Political Development" (1994) 8:1 Studies in American Political Development 140, p. 142; Douglass North, *Institutions, Institutional Change and Economic Performance* (New York: Cambridge University Press, 1990) p. vii.

41 See e.g. Scarboro, "Assignees in Bankruptcy Matters – The Operation of the Act," Letter to the Editor, (1868) 4 Can LJ (NS) 83, p. 84; Quinte, "Insolvent Acts – Assignees," Letter to the Editor, (1868) 4 Can LJ (NS) 101; Union, "The Insolvent Act of 1864 – Assignees," Letter to the Editor, (1868) 4 Can LJ (NS) 131.

42 Skowronek, *Building a New American State*, p. 27.

43 See similar results under the US Bankruptcy Act of 1800. Bruce H. Mann, *Republic of Debtors: Bankruptcy in the Age of American Independence* (London, UK: Harvard University Press, 2002) pp. 228–39.

44 Lecours, "New Institutionalism," p. 6; Leslie A. Pal, "Missed Opportunities or Comparative Advantage? Canadian Contributions to the Study of Public Policy" in Dobuzinskis, Howlett & Laycock, eds, *Policy Studies in Canada* 359, p. 367.

45 RSO 1880, c 78.

46 [1894] AC 189 (PC).

47 RSO 1887, c 124.

48 Peter A. Hall & Rosemary C.R. Taylor, "Political Science and the Three

New Institutionalisms" (1996) 44:5 Political Studies 936, p. 942. See also Thelen & Steinmo, "Historical Institutionalism in Comparative Politics," p. 3 (institutions are "never the sole 'cause' of outcomes").

49 See e.g. *Re Cobourg & Peterborough Railway* (1869), 16 Gr 571 (UC Ch). On the issue of corporate reorganization prior to Confederation in Ontario, see R.C.B. Risk, "The Nineteenth-Century Foundations of the Business Corporation in Ontario" (1973) 23:3 UTLJ 270, p. 295.

50 *Insolvent Act of 1875*, s 1.

51 *Act respecting Insolvent Banks, Insurance Companies, Loan Companies, Building Societies, and Trading Corporations*, SC 1882, c 23; RSC 1886, c 129.

52 This term is borrowed from Lester, *Victorian Insolvency*, p. 8.

53 Risk, in his study of the law and the economy of Ontario from 1841 to 1867, stated that "the legislature, not the courts, made the major changes in legal policy." See R.C.B. Risk, "A Prospectus for Canadian Legal History" (1973) 1:2 Dal LJ 227, p. 244.

54 *Clarkson v Ontario Bank* (1888), 15 OAR 166; *Union Bank v Neville* (1891), 21 OR 152 (CA); *Re Assignments and Preferences Act, Section 9* (1893), 20 OAR 489; *Ontario (AG) v Canada (AG).*

55 John McLaren has recently called for the legal historical project to investigate "the status role and motives of those who create, apply and enforce the law." He argues that such work should consider "the history of legislation and its promoters and sponsors." John McLaren, "The Legal Historian, Masochist or Missionary? A Canadian's Reflections" (1994) 5:1 Legal Education Review 67, p. 78.

56 See James D. Edgar, *The Insolvent Act of 1869; with Tariff, Notes, Forms, and a Full Index* (Toronto: Copp, Clark & Co, 1869); John Popham, *The Insolvent Act of 1869; with Notes and Decisions of the Courts of Ontario and Quebec; Together with the Rules of Practice and the Tariff of Fees for the Provinces of Ontario, Quebec, Nova Scotia, and New Brunswick* (Montreal: Dawson Brothers, 1870); James D. Edgar & F.H. Chrysler, *The Insolvent Act of 1875, with an Introductory Chapter; Notes, Forms, Tariffs of Ontario, Quebec, and New Brunswick; and a Full Index* (Toronto: Copp, Clark & Co, 1875); Hugh MacMahon, *The Insolvent Act of 1875, including Full Notes to Each Section, Tariff of Costs, Index, and List of Cases* (Toronto: Willing & Williamson, 1875); Ivan Wotherspoon, *The Insolvent Act of 1875: with the Rules of Practice and Tariffs of Fees in Force in the Different Provinces of the Dominion* (Montreal: Dawson Brothers, 1875); Samuel Robinson Clarke, *The Insolvent Act of 1875, and Amending Acts* (Toronto: R Carswell, 1877); William Wilson, *Analyse et index de l'Acte de faillite de 1875* (Ottawa: Maclean Roger, 1875).

57 Louis Edward Levinthal, "The Early History of Bankruptcy Law" (1918) 66:5–6 U Pa L Rev 223.

58 Jones, *Foundations of English Bankruptcy*; Levinthal, "Early History of English Bankruptcy Law"; E. Welbourne, "Bankruptcy Before the Era of Victorian Reform" (1932) 4:1 Cambridge Historical Journal 51; Julian Hoppit, *Risk and Failure in English Business, 1700–1800* (New York: Cambridge University Press, 1987); Duffy, *Bankruptcy and Insolvency in London*; Craig Muldrew, *The Economy of Obligation: The Culture of Credit and Social Relations in Early Modern England* (Hampshire, UK: Macmillan, 1998); Julian Hoppit, "Attitudes to Credit in Britain, 1680–1790" (1990) 33:2 Historical Journal 305; Margot C. Finn, *The Character of Credit: Personal Debt in English Culture, 1740–1914* (Cambridge, UK: Cambridge University Press, 2003); Barbara Weiss, *The Hell of the English: Bankruptcy and the Victorian Novel* (Lewisburg: Bucknell University Press, 1986).

59 Lester, *Victorian Insolvency*.

60 Charles Warren, *Bankruptcy in United States History* (Cambridge, Mass: Harvard University Press, 1935); Peter Coleman, *Debtors and Creditors in America: Insolvency, Imprisonment for Debt, and Bankruptcy, 1607–1900* (Madison: State Historical Society of Wisconsin, 1974).

61 Skeel, *Debt's Dominion*. For a further account of the twentieth century, see Louis Hyman, *Debtor Nation: The History of America in Red Ink* (Princeton: Princeton University Press, 2011).

62 Mann, *Republic of Debtors*; Edward J. Balleisen, *Navigating Failure: Bankruptcy and Commercial Society in Antebellum America* (Chapel Hill: University of North Carolina Press, 2001); Elizabeth Lee Thompson, *The Reconstruction of Southern Debtors: Bankruptcy After the Civil War* (Athens, Ga: University of Georgia Press, 2004); Bradley Hansen, "Commercial Associations and the Creation of a National Economy: The Demand for Federal Bankruptcy Law" (1998) 72:1 Business History Review 86; Richard C. Sauer, "Bankruptcy Law and the Maturing of American Capitalism" (1994) 55:2 Ohio St LJ 291.

63 Scott A. Sandage, *Born Losers: A History of Failure in America* (Cambridge, Mass: Harvard University Press, 2005).

64 For the political history of US bankruptcy law, see Warren, *Bankruptcy in United States History*. On the ideological divide, see Robert Weisberg, "Commercial Morality, the Merchant Character and the History of the Voidable Preference" (1986) 39:1 Stan L Rev 3, pp. 60–1; Sauer, "Bankruptcy Law and the Maturing of American Capitalism," pp. 298, 339.

65 Balleisen, *Navigating Failure*, p. 14.

66 Coleman, *Debtors and Creditors in America*, p. 248. This theme is also identified in Jérôme Sgard, "Do Legal Origins Matter? The Case of Bankruptcy Laws in Europe 1808–1914" (2006) 10:3 European Review of Economic History 389.

67 Skeel, *Debt's Dominion*, p. 2.

68 Karen Gross, Marie Stefanini Newman & Denise Campbell, "Ladies in Red: Learning From America's First Female Bankrupts" (1996) 40:1 Am J Legal Hist 1.

69 On the attention given to investment in public infrastructure in Canada, see Stephen McBride, "The Political Economy Tradition and Canadian Policy Studies" in Dobuzinskis, Howlett & Laycock, eds, *Policy Studies in Canada* 49, p. 51.

70 Michael Bliss, *Northern Enterprise: Five Centuries of Canadian Business* (Toronto: McClelland & Stewart, 1987) pp. 172, 180–2; Graham Taylor & Peter A. Baskerville, *A Concise History of Business in Canada* (Toronto: Oxford University Press, 1994) pp. 168–9.

71 Norrie & Owram, *History of the Canadian Economy*, p. 438.

72 See e.g. *An Act to authorize and provide for the winding up of the Consolidated Bank of Canada*, SC 1880, c 46; *An Act to authorize and provide for the winding up of the Stadacona Bank*, SC 1880, c 48; *An Act to make provision for the winding up of insolvent incorporated Fire or Marine Insurance Companies*, SC 1878, c 21; *An Act to grant relief to the Canada Agricultural Insurance Company*, SC 1878, c 38; *An Act to confirm and give effect to a certain agreement between the Government of Canada, and the Great Western Railway Company*, SC 1869, c 61.

73 Norrie & Owram, *History of the Canadian Economy*, p. 438.

74 There are studies that examine failure of small firms. See e.g. Douglas McCalla, *The Upper Canada Trade 1834–1872: A Study of the Buchanans' Business* (Toronto: University of Toronto Press, 1979) pp. 135–48; David G. Burley, *A Particular Condition in Life: Self-Employment and Social Mobility in Mid-Victorian Brantford* (Montreal and Kingston: McGill-Queen's University Press, 1994) pp. 103–26, 187–90. However, these studies do not consider the legislative framework that regulated bankrupts.

75 For a broad historical overview of English, European, American and Canadian bankruptcy and insolvency legislation, see Micheline Gleixner & Michael J. Bray, "La gestion des risques des créanciers et la réhabilitation des débiteurs surendettés: objectifs contradictories ou complémentaires?" (March 2013), online: Office of the Superintendent of Bankruptcy Canada <http://www.ic.gc.ca/eic/site/bsf-osb.nsf/eng/home>.

76 Walter Stewart, *Belly Up: The Spoils of Bankruptcy* (Toronto: McClelland & Stewart, 1995), ignores the fact that Parliament repealed the legislation in 1880. Margot Priest & Aron Wohl, "The Growth of Federal and Provincial Regulation of Economic Activity, 1867–1978" in W.T. Stanbury, ed, *Government Regulation: Scope, Growth, Process* (Montreal: Institute for Research on Public Policy, 1980) 69, p. 119.

77 However, see Louis-Joseph de la Durantaye, *Traité de la faillite en la province de Québec à l'usage des praticiens et des commerçants* (Montreal: Chez l'auteur, 1934); John Honsberger, "Bankruptcy Administration in the United States and Canada" (1975) 63:6 Cal L Rev 1515; Albert Bohémier, *La faillite en droit constitutionnel canadien* (Montreal: Les Presses de l'Université de Montréal, 1972) p. 101; Canada, *Report of the Study Committee on Bankruptcy and Insolvency Legislation* (Ottawa: Queen's Printer, 1970) [hereafter Canada, "Tassé Report"] p. 14.

78 Evelyn Kolish, *Nationalismes et conflits de droits: le débat du droit privé au Québec, 1760–1840* (Quebec: Hurtubise HMH, 1994); R.C.B. Risk, "The Golden Age: The Law About the Market in Nineteenth-Century Ontario" (1976) 26:3 UTLJ 307; Philip Girard, "Married Women's Property, Chancery Abolition and Insolvency Law: Law Reform in Nova Scotia, 1820–1867" in Philip Girard & Jim Phillips, eds, *Essays in the History of Canadian Law: Nova Scotia*, vol 3 (Toronto: University of Toronto Press, 1990) 80.

79 Edgar, *Insolvent Act of 1869*, pp. 33–4.

80 Weaver & Rockman, "Assessing the Effects of Institutions," p. 32; Skowronek, *Building a New American State*, p. 27; Lecours, "New Institutionalism," p. 6.

81 Pal, "Missed Opportunities or Comparative Advantage?," p. 367 (on the importance of federalism).

82 Federalism also affected the evolution of American bankruptcy law. See F. Regis Noel, *A History of the Bankruptcy Clause of the Constitution of the United States of America* (Gettysburg: Gettysburg Compiler Print, 1918); Douglass G. Boshkoff, "Limited, Conditional, and Suspended Discharges in Anglo-American Bankruptcy Proceedings" (1982) 131:1 U Pa L Rev 69, p. 111; Thomas E. Plank, "The Constitutional Limits of Bankruptcy" (1996) 63:3 Tenn L Rev 487.

Chapter 2

1 Ivan Wotherspoon, *The Insolvent Act of 1875: with the Rules of Practice and Tariffs of Fees in Force in the Different Provinces of the Dominion* (Montreal: Dawson Brothers, 1875) p. v.

2 *Insolvent Act of 1869*, s 154.

3 1869: Bill, *An Act to repeal the Act respecting Insolvency*, 2nd Sess, 1st Parl, 1869.
1871: Bill, *An Act to repeal the Insolvency Laws now existing in the Dominion*, 4th Sess, 1st Parl, 1871.
1872: Bill C-3, *An Act to repeal the Insolvency Laws*, 5th Sess, 1st Parl, 1872.

1877: Bill C-2, *An Act to repeal the Insolvency Laws now in force in the Dominion of Canada*, 4th Sess, 3rd Parl, 1877; Bill C-39, *An Act to repeal the Insolvent Act of 1875, and all Acts passed in amendment thereof*, 4th Sess, 3rd Parl, 1877.

1878: Bill C-2, *An Act to repeal the Insolvency Laws now in force in the Dominion of Canada*, 5th Sess, 3rd Parl, 1878.

1879: Bill C-15, *An Act to repeal the Acts respecting Insolvency now in force in the Dominion*, 1st Sess, 4th Parl, 1879; Bill C-22, *An Act to repeal the Insolvent Act of 1875, and to make provision in lieu thereof*, 1st Sess, 4th Parl, 1879; Bill C-85, *An Act to repeal the Insolvent Act of 1875, and the Acts amending it, and to make provision for the liquidations of the estates of Insolvent Debtors*, 1st Sess, 4th Parl, 1879.

1880: Bill C-2, *An Act to repeal the Acts respecting Insolvency now in force in Canada*, 2nd Sess, 4th Parl, 1880. This last Bill received Royal Assent and became *An Act to repeal the Acts respecting Insolvency now in force in Canada*, SC 1880, c 1.

4 *An Act to repeal the Acts respecting Insolvency now in force in Canada*, SC 1880, c 1. The *BNA Act* granted the federal Parliament jurisdiction over bankruptcy and insolvency (s 91(21)).

5 The *BNA Act* is now known as the *Constitution Act, 1867* (UK), 30 & 31 Vict, c 3, reprinted in RSC 1985, App II, No 5. This book will use the *BNA Act* throughout.

6 For the division of powers at Confederation and the reasons for assigning bankruptcy to the federal government see Bohémier, *La faillite*; Pierre Carignan, "La compétence législative en matière de faillite et d'insolvabilité" (1979) 57:1 Can Bar Rev 47; Richard Risk & Robert C. Vipond, "Rights Talk in Canada in the Late Nineteenth Century: 'The Good Sense and Right Feeling of the People'" (1996) 14:1 LHR 1; D.E. Thomson, "Bankruptcy Law in Canada" (1894) 1 Barrister 39, pp. 39–40; D.E. Thomson, "Bankruptcy Legislation in Canada" (1902) 1:4 Can L Rev 173, p. 174.

7 *BNA Act*, s 91(21). In the United States the federal power was limited to "Uniform laws on the subject of Bankruptcies." US Const art I, § 8. This generated constitutional litigation: *Sturges v Crowninshield*, 17 US (4 Wheat) 122 (1819); *Ogden v Sauders*, 25 US (12 Wheat) 213 (1827). By including both terms, the drafters sought to avoid similar constitutional disputes in Canada. *R v Chandler*, p. 561.

8 Bohémier, *La faillite*, pp. 19–25. On the importance of uniformity, see *Dupont v La Cie de Moulin* (1888), 11 LN 225 (Qc Sup Ct), p. 227; *Re Barrett* (1880), 5 OAR 206, para 13, Burton J, dissenting.

9 *BNA Act*, s 92(13); s 92(16); On the issue of potential overlap between fed-

eral and provincial powers, see Dale Gibson, "Development of Federal Legal and Judicial Institutions in Canada" (1996) 23:3 Man LJ 450, p. 471; J.A.C. Cameron, "Annotation: Bankruptcy Act of Canada, 1920" (1920) 53 DLR 135, p. 137; J.H. Greenberg, "The Bankruptcy Law in Canada" (1931) 5 Journal of the National Association of Referees in Bankruptcy 118.

10 Book Review of *The Insolvent Act of 1869; with Tariff, Notes, Forms, and a Full Index* by James D. Edgar, (1870) 6 Local Ct Gaz 31; Letter to John J.C. Abbott (5 March 1869) in Department of Justice Papers, LAC (RG 13-A-2) [hereafter Department of Justice Papers] (vol 557, file 703).

11 Bliss, *Northern Enterprise*, p. 249. On the impact that economic shocks have in shaping bankruptcy laws, see Paolo Di Martino, "The Historical Evolution of Bankruptcy Law in England, the US and Italy up to 1939: Determinants of Institutional Change and Structural Differences" in Karl Gratzer & Dieter Stiefel, eds, *History of Insolvency and Bankruptcy from an International Perspective* (Huddinge: Södertörns högskola, 2008) 263, p. 274.

12 Commercial Failures, 1873–1885

Year	# of failures
1873	994
1874	966
1875	1,968
1876	1,728
1877	1,892
1878	1,697
1879	1,902
1880	907
1881	635
1882	787
1883	1,379
1884	1,308
1885	1,247

The statistics do not represent official numbers of bankruptcies under the *Insolvent Acts*. Rather they are based upon reports published in the *Monetary Times*. The statistics are drawn from Gaétan Gervais, "Le commerce de détail au Canada: 1870–1880" (1980) 33:4 Revue d'histoire de l'Amérique française 521, p. 552, which are based on statistics reproduced in the *Monetary Times*.

13 William Wickliffe Johnson, *Sketches of the Late Depression; Its Cause, Effect and Lessons* (Montreal: J Theo Robinson, 1882), p. 8.
14 S.W. Jacobs, "A Canadian Bankruptcy Act: Is it a Necessity?" (1917) 37:8 Can LT 604, p. 605.
15 See e.g. Colin Hay, "Ideas, Interests and Institutions in the Comparative Political Economy of Great Transformations" (2004) 11:1 Review of International Political Economy 204, p. 207.
16 Skeel, *Debt's Dominion*, p. 32.
17 Commons Debates, 26 February 1877, 281 (Barthe).
18 During the repeal debate of 1879, Girouard made reference to a petition published in the British press calling for the repeal of all bankruptcy laws in England. Further, Girouard referred to the new reform efforts being undertaken by the English Lord Chancellor, who introduced a reform Bill in 1879. *Ibid.*, 29 April 1879, 1602 (Girouard). This English Bill appeared to influence the Canadian Select Committee of 1879. "The Insolvency Law," *Journal of Commerce* 8:4 (14 March 1879) 110. For a review of the reform efforts of the 1870s and 1880s in England, see Lester, *Victorian Insolvency*, pp. 183–4.
19 James Bicknell, "The Advisability of Establishing a Bankruptcy Court in Canada" (1913) 33:1 Can LT 35, p. 43.
20 Commons Debates, 10 November 1867, 87–8 (Abbott); Montreal Board of Trade, Council Minutes (10 December 1867) in Montreal Board of Trade Papers, LAC (MG 28 III 44) [hereafter Montreal Board of Trade Papers] (reel M-2785, pp. 407–8).
21 House of Commons, Select Committee, "Third Report of the Select Committee on Bankruptcy and Insolvency" in Commons Journals, 1st Parl, 1st Sess, vol. 1 (17 April 1868) A5 [hereafter House of Commons, "Third Report"], p. 8. Also reported in (1868) 4:2 LCLJ 47.
22 See e.g. *Commentaries on the Present Bankrupt Act in a Series of Letters Addressed to the Editor of the Morning Courier* (Montreal: Lovell and Gibson, 1848); Editorial, "Shall We Have a Bankruptcy Law?" (1858) 4 UCLJ 2, pp. 3–4; Scarboro, "Assignees in Bankruptcy Matters," p. 84; Editorial, "Bankruptcy and Insolvency" (1861) 7 UCLJ 10, p. 11; Editorial, "A Bankruptcy Law Required" (1863) 9 UCLJ 141; Editorial, "The Act Respecting Insolvency" (1864) 10 UCLJ 225, p. 226; E.T. Bromfield, *Practical Hints to the Retail Merchant, or How to Make a Business Successful: With an Appendix Containing Advice to Embarrassed Debtors and Remarks on the Present Law of Bankruptcy in Canada* (Toronto: E.T. Bromfield, 1869) (CIHM microfiche series no 53131); Union, "Insolvent Law of 1864 – Assignees"; Quinte, "Insolvent Acts – Assignees."

23 County Clerk of Huron to County Clerk of Elgin (30 October 1867) [enclosure] in *Resolution of Corporation of County of Huron at June Session, 1867, Goderich, Ont*, AO (CIHM no 53355).
24 Scarboro, "Assignees in Bankruptcy Matters," p. 84; "The Working of a Bankruptcy Act," *Trade Review* 3:6 (22 February 1867) 82. "Debtor and Creditor," *Trade Review* 4:7 (14 February 1868) 102.
25 Carman Miller, "Sir John Joseph Caldwell Abbott" in *Dictionary of Canadian Biography*, <http://www.biographi.ca/en/bio/abbott_john_joseph_caldwell_12E.html>. See also Paul P. Hutchison, "Sir John J.C. Abbott: Barrister and Solicitor" (1948) 26:6 Can Bar Rev 934, p. 944.
26 John A. Macdonald to John J.C. Abbott (5 May 1868) in Macdonald Papers, LAC (MG 26-A) [hereafter Macdonald Papers] (vol 1, file 718, reel C-26); John A. Macdonald to Charles Stathers (28 May 1868) in Macdonald Papers (vol 1, file 727, reel C-26).
27 Commons Debates, 21 April 1869, 36 (Macdonald); *ibid.*, 4 May 1869, 173–4 (Macdonald).
28 See two annotated texts: Edgar, *Insolvent Act of 1869*; Popham, *Insolvent Act of 1869*.
29 *Insolvent Act of 1869*, Preamble.
30 *Insolvent Act of 1869*. Section 155 provided that it was to remain in force for four years. The law was extended by SC 1873, c 2 and SC 1874, c 46.
31 Bill, *An Act to repeal the Act respecting Insolvency*, 2nd Sess, 1st Parl, 1869; Bill, *An Act to repeal the Insolvency Laws now existing in the Dominion*, 4th Sess, 1st Parl, 1871; Bill C-3, *An Act to repeal the Insolvency Laws*, 4th Sess, 1st Parl 1872.
32 Commons Debates, 3 April 1871, 830; *ibid.*, 26 April 1872, 163–4; Senate Debates, 23 May 1872, 789–90 (Holmes). For a discussion of the repeal issue, see "Proposed Repeal of the Insolvency Laws," *Monetary Times* 5:41 (19 April 1872) 826; "Opposition to the Insolvent Act," *Monetary Times* 5:43 (3 May 1872) 867–8. On the extent of the division in public opinion, see RMF, "Legislation Upon Insolvency" (1873) 2:5 Canadian Monthly and National Review 419.
33 *Insolvent Act of 1869*, s 155.
34 Edgar, *Insolvent Act of 1869*, pp. 33–4.
35 Commons Debates, 9 June 1869, 685. In *Duncan v Smart* (1874), 35 UCQB (CA) 532, a banker and exchange money broker who bought and sold American currency was held to be a trader. In *Harman v Clarkson* (1872), 22 UCCP 291, an innkeeper was held not to be a trader. In *Thomas v Hall* (1874), 6 PR 172 (UC Pract Ct), a barber was held not to be a trader.
36 *Insolvent Act of 1869*, s 1. Former English statutes and older English cases

had developed a detailed and somewhat confusing jurisprudence on the definition of trader: Edgar, *Insolvent Act of 1869*, pp. 33–6. On the definition of trader, see The Hon J.J.C. Abbott, *The Insolvent Act of 1864 with Notes together with the Rules of Practice* (Quebec: George Desbarats and Malcolm Cameron, 1864) pp. 1–10; D Girouard, "Can a Person Who Ceased to be a Trader Before Passing of the *Insolvent Act of 1869*, Take Benefit of the Act" (1872) 2:1 RCLJ 65; D. Girouard, "Can a Trader without Assets Make an Assignment?" (1872) 2:1 RCLJ 63.

37 *Insolvent Act of 1869*, s 3; Popham, *Insolvent Act of 1869*, pp. 36, 41.

38 Edgar, *Insolvent Act of 1869*, p. 38.

39 Huron County Court Insolvency Procedure Book, 1864–85, AO (RG 22-2466) [hereafter Huron County Court Insolvency Procedure Book]; Lambton County Court Insolvency Procedure Book, 1865–80, AO (RG 22-2764) [hereafter Lambton County Court Insolvency Procedure Book]; Lanark County Court Insolvency Minute Books, AO (RG 22-2873) [hereafter Lanark County Court Insolvency Minute Books]; Oxford County Court Official Assignee's Insolvency Docket Books, 1865–9, AO (RG 22-3965) [hereafter Oxford County Court Insolvency Docket Books]; Peel County Court Insolvency Minute Book, 1867–80, AO (RG 22-4163) [hereafter Peel County Court Insolvency Minute Book]; Perth County Insolvency Docket Books, 1871–79, AO (RG 22-4264).

40 Edgar & Chrysler, *Insolvent Act of 1875*, p. xxix; Honsberger, "Bankruptcy Administration in the United States and Canada," p. 1528.

41 Commons Debates, 19 February 1875, 239 (Fournier).

42 *Insolvent Act of 1875*, s 148.

43 Royal Assent on 8 April 1875. Five separate publishers released annotated versions of the statute. Edgar & Chrysler, *Insolvent Act of 1875*; MacMahon, *Insolvent Act of 1875*; Wotherspoon, *The Insolvent Act of 1875*; Clarke, *Insolvent Act of 1875*; Wilson, *l'Acte de faillite de 1875*. A shorter publication was also released: see C. Beausoleil, *La loi de faillite* (Montreal: Plinguet, 1877).

44 Beausoleil, *La loi de faillite*, p. 2.

45 Book Review of *The Insolvent Act of 1875, including Full Notes to Each Section, Tariff of Costs, Index, and List of Cases* by Hugh MacMahon, (1875) 11 Can LJ (NS) 259; Commons Debates, 19 February 1875, 239 (Fournier). See also Wotherspoon, *Insolvent Act of 1875*, p. 38.

46 "[T]he abrogation of the power of voluntary assignments ... is the greatest change effected by the present Act." Wotherspoon, *Insolvent Act of 1875*, p. vi. See "The New Insolvent Act," *Daily Globe* (31 August 1875) 2; *Insolvent Act of 1875*, ss 3, 9. "Some Provisions of the New Insolvent Act," *Monetary*

Times 9:10 (3 September 1875) 265–6. A debtor could still make an assignment, but Parliament removed the voluntariness of the procedure. First, a creditor had to make a formal demand to a debtor to make an assignment. If the debtor failed to make an assignment, his or her estate became subject to the liquidation provisions of the Act. Parliament anticipated attempts by debtors to persuade friendly creditors to issue formal demands. The Act required creditors to file an affidavit indicating that they were not "acting in collusion with the debtor." *Insolvent Act of 1875*, s 4.

47 Wotherspoon, *Insolvent Act of 1875*, p. 38. One author called the law reactionary: de la Durantaye, *Traité de la faillite*, p. 25. See also Bohémier, *La faillite*, p. 11.

48 MacMahon, *Insolvent Act of 1875*, p. ix.

49 Bill C-39, *An Act to repeal the Insolvent Act of 1875* 4th Sess, 3rd Parl, 1877; Bill C-2, *An Act to repeal the Insolvency Laws*, 4th Sess, 3rd Parl, 1877.

50 Bill C-2, *An Act to repeal the Insolvency Laws*, 5th Sess, 3rd Parl 1878.

51 Bill C-15, *An Act to repeal the Acts respecting Insolvency*, 1st Sess, 4th Parl, 1879; Bill C-22, *An Act to repeal the Insolvent Act of 1875*, 1st Sess, 4th Parl, 1879; Bill C-85, *An Act to repeal the Insolvent Act of 1875*, 1st Sess, 4th Parl 1879.

52 Bill C-2, *An Act to repeal the Acts respecting Insolvency*, 2nd Sess, 4th Parl, 1880. This last bill received Royal Assent and became *An Act to repeal the Acts respecting Insolvency now in force in Canada*, SC 1880, c 1.

53 E. Sills to John A. Macdonald (12 March 1879) in Macdonald Papers (vol 356, file 156502–5, reel C-1715).

54 Bicknell, "Advisability of Establishing a Bankruptcy Court in Canada," p. 43.

55 Commons Debates, 7 March 1879, 189 (McDonald, Pictou). An initial vote by the committee indicated nine Members in favour of amendment, and eight Members for repeal; *ibid.*, 29 April 1879, 1594 (Colby).

56 Bicknell, "Advisability of Establishing a Bankruptcy Court in Canada," p. 44. For second reading, see Commons Debates, 30 April 1879, 1627: 117 votes in favour of second reading of repeal Bill, 60 votes against second reading. See "Insolvent Act Repeal," *Monetary Times* 12:45 (2 May 1879) 1359; Commons Debates, 5 May 1879, 1783–4. See Editorial, (1879) 15 Can LJ (NS) 119; Editorial, (1879) 15 Can LJ (NS) 146.

57 Senate Debates, 9 May 1879, 459, 537.

58 Bill C-2, *An Act to repeal the Acts respecting Insolvency*, 2nd Sess, 4th Parl, 1880. See Commons Debates, 19 February 1880, 105 (Bechard).

59 Senate Debates, 12 March 1880, 152; 1 April 1880, 219. See *An Act to repeal the Acts respecting Insolvency now in force in Canada*, SC 1880, c 1.

Chapter 3

1 *Roe v Smith* (1868), 15 Gr 344, p. 345 (UC Ch).

2 *Ibid.*, p. 347. In a separate ruling the court held that the Official Assignee was not in a position to set aside the transaction, as the payment was made in the United States. The ruling created an incentive to follow debtors into the United States and receive payment south of the border.

3 For a discussion of the US experience and the problem of preferential payments to local and family creditors, see Balleisen, *Navigating Failure*, pp. 90–4; Charles Jordan Tabb, "A Century of Regress or Progress? A Political History of Bankruptcy Legislation in 1898 and 1998" (1999) 15:2 Bankr Dev J 343, p. 357 (national law neutralized advantages of creditors receiving preferential payments); Skeel, *Debt's Dominion*, p. 36; Mann, *Republic of Debtors*, pp. 34, 48–9.

4 The common law race and the equal treatment of creditors applied to unsecured creditors. Where a creditor held a security interest, either by a chattel mortgage or a mortgage on real property, the creditor could look to that security interest. See Mann, *Republic of Debtors*, pp. 15, 49.

5 See e.g. *Beekman v Jarvis*; *Topping v Joseph* (1859), 1 E & A 292 (UC Err App); *Rowe v Jarvis* (1863), 13 UCCP 495; *Bank of Montreal v Munro*.

6 *Gottwalls v Mulholland* (1864), 15 UCCP 62, p. 73 aff'd (1866), 3 E & A 194 (UC Err App). See also *McPherson v Reynolds* (1857), 6 UCCP 491, p. 495.

7 See *Insolvent Act of 1869*, ss 56, 58; *Insolvent Act of 1875*, ss 80, 82. See e.g. First and Final Dividend Sheet in the estate of Re P. McKerral (31 October 1878) in Kent County Court Insolvency Files, 1874–1881, AO (RG 22-2675) [hereafter Kent County Court Insolvency Files]. See also *Bullen v Harding* (1871), 13 NBR 499, p. 501 (SC).

8 *An Act Against Such Persons as do Make Bankrupts*, 1542–43 (UK), 34 & 35 Hen VIII, c 4.

9 Levinthal, "The Early History of Bankruptcy Law," p. 235.

10 (UK), 34 & 35 Hen VIII, c 4, s 1. See Kadens, "The Last Bankrupt Hanged," p. 1241 (one of defining elements of the statute was the ratable distribution of the assets).

11 *The Case of the Bankrupts* (1584), 2 Co Rep 25.

12 Kadens, "Last Bankrupt Hanged," p. 1240.

13 Yet both statutes created an exception to the equality principle. The *Insolvent Act of 1869*, s 67, and the *Insolvent Act of 1875*, s 91 (see also amendment found in SC 1877 (40 Vict), c 41, s 22) provided a special priority for arrears in wages to be paid ahead of unsecured creditors. However, just as there appeared to be broad support for the equality principle among

supporters of bankruptcy law, the wage-earner exception also appeared to be "widely accepted." Wage-earner priority sparked little debate and was rarely an issue before the courts. Changes to the wage priority provisions did not come about because of "active lobbying by workers, employers or creditors." Rather, amendments were the result of drafters copying English law. The opposition to bankruptcy law cannot be explained by wage priority. Eric Tucker, "The Recurring Dilemma of Wage Priority in Bankruptcy" in Eric Tucker, *Labour Law's Recurring Regulatory Dilemmas* (2012) [unpublished, archived at Western University, Faculty of Law] p. 16.

14 Editorial, "Shall We Have a Bankruptcy Law?," p. 4; Editorial, "Bankruptcy Law Required"; Editorial, Act Respecting Insolvency," p. 226.

15 This has been recognized in modern bankruptcy literature. See Jackson, *Logic and Limits of Bankruptcy Law*, pp. 7–27.

16 *Burland v Larocque* (1867), 12 LC Jur 292 (QB); *Insolvent Act of 1869*, s 59; *Insolvent Act of 1875*, s 16. See also *Wallace v Bossom* (1876–7), 11 NSR 419 (SC) (judgment and execution obtained after bankruptcy not valid).

17 *Bullen v Harding*, p. 501. Edgar, *Insolvent Act of 1869*, p. 62; See *Insolvent Act of 1869*, ss 56, 58; *Insolvent Act of 1875*, ss 80, 82.

18 Abbott was clearly Macdonald's right-hand man on the bankruptcy file. See John A. Macdonald to John J.C. Abbott (22 May 1868) in Macdonald Papers (vol 514/3, reel C-26, p. 718): "May I invite your consistent attention to the Act in question so that I may introduce it in … the early part of the next session."

19 Commons Debates, 11 May 1869, 259 (Abbott). See also "Proposed Repeal of the Insolvency Laws," *Monetary Times* 5:42 (19 April 1872) 826 (fearing a return to the old rule of "first come, first served"); "Shall the Insolvent Act Be Repealed?," *Monetary Times* 12:37 (7 March 1879) 1116; "Insolvent Act Repeal," *Monetary Times* 12:46 (9 May 1879) 1389.

20 Edgar, *Insolvent Act of 1869*, p. 128. *Insolvent Act of 1869*, s 116 provided that the Official Assignee prevailed over uncompleted executions. See also *Insolvent Act of 1875*, s 16.

21 Lynne E. Richardson, "Young, James" in *Dictionary of Canadian Biography*, online: <http://www.biographi.ca/en/bio/young_james_1835_1913_14E.html>.

22 Commons Debates, 26 February 1877, 304 (Young).

23 *Ibid.*, 296 (Macdonald); *ibid.*, 27 March 1878, 1447 (Young); *ibid.*, 3 April 1877, 1111 (Blake); *ibid.*, 7 March 1879, 213 (McDonald, Pictou).

24 Beausoleil, *La loi de faillite*, p. 6; "The Insolvency Law," *Monetary Times* 10:35 (23 February 1877) 962.

25 J. Gibbons to Robert Service & Co (13 January 1880) in Haldimand County

Court Insolvency Files, 1879–80, AO (RG 22-1272) [hereafter Haldimand County Court Insolvency Files].

26 William Kemp to Messrs Adams & Co. London, 7 May 1879; *Re W.M. Kemp*, May 1879, Writ of Attachment, in Kent County Court Insolvency Files (box 244754).

27 The legislation did not promote absolute equality. The statutes recognized the superior rights of secured creditors to enforce their claims. See *Insolvent Act of 1869*, s 60 and *Insolvent Act of 1875*, s 82.

28 *Shaw v Massie* (1871), 21 UCCP 266, p. 269. See also *Fowler v Perrin* (1866), 16 UCCP 258, p. 262; *Re Barrett*, p. 216; *McWhirter v Thorne*, p. 309; *Harvey v Cotter* (1873), 9 NSR 161, p. 165 (CA); *Rumsey v Hare* (1877), 12 NSR 4 (CA); *Mason v Hamilton* (1872), 22 UCCP 411, p. 416; *Davidson v Ross* (1876), 24 Gr 22, pp. 50–1 (UC Err App); *Keays v Brown* (1875), 22 Gr 10, p. 15 (UC Ch); *Dever v Morris* (1873), 14 NBR 270 (SC).

29 *Adams v McCall* (1866), 25 UCQB 219, p. 226. See also *Re Hurst*, p. 330.

30 *Brown v Wright* (1874), 35 UCQB 378, p. 381.

31 *McLeod v Wright* (1877), 17 NBR 68, para 63 (SC (Eq App)), Allen CJ. See also *Re Barrett*, p. 216; *Payne v Hendry* (1873), 20 Gr 142, para 1 (UC Ch).

32 *Milloy v Kerr* (1879), 8 SCR 474, p. 495. See also *Jones v Kinney* (1884), 11 SCR 708, p. 714.

33 Ian M. Drummond, *Progress Without Planning: The Economic History of Ontario From Confederation to the Second World War* (Toronto: University of Toronto Press, 1987) p. 3.

34 Norrie & Owram, *History of the Canadian Economy*, p. 277. The 1871 census reports that in Ontario, 49 per cent of those stating an occupation indicated farming. Douglas McCalla, *Planting the Province: The Economic History of Upper Canada, 1784–1870* (Toronto: University of Toronto Press, 1993) p. 219. For a study of the occupations of Canadians in 1871, see Gervais, "Le commerce de détail au Canada."

35 Canadian Population, 1880 (Millions)

Year	Urban	Rural
1871	0.7	3.0
1881	1.1	3.2
1891	1.5	3.3
1901	2.0	3.4
1911	3.3	3.9
1921	4.4	4.4

Richard Pomfret, *The Economic Development of Canada* (Toronto: Methuen, 1981) p. 53.

36 Bliss, *Northern Enterprise*, p. 286.

37 Taylor & Baskerville, *A Concise History of Business in Canada*, p. 230.

38 Ben Forster, "Finding the Right Size: Markets and Competition in Mid- and Late Nineteenth-Century Ontario" in Roger Hall, William Westfall & Laurel Sefton MacDowell, eds, *Patterns of the Past: Interpreting Ontario's History* (Toronto: Dundurn Press, 1988) 150, p. 154.

39 *Kalus v Hergert* (1876), 1 OAR 75. For a discussion of distant vs local creditors in the context of the US Bankruptcy Act of 1841, see Balleisen, *Navigating Failure*, pp. 90–4.

40 "Mercantile Summary," *Monetary Times* 11:39 (22 March 1878) 1111; "Mercantile Summary," *Monetary Times* 14:21 (19 November 1880) 580; "100 Cents in the $," Letter to the Editor, *Monetary Times* 10:25 (15 December 1876) 678.

41 "Mercantile Summary," *Journal of Commerce* 5:21 (11 January 1878) 625.

42 *Re Jones* (1868), 4 PR 317, p. 326 (UC Pract Ct). Edward Balleisen argues that in the context of preferential payments "[f]inancial obligations to relatives or close business associates generally carried more weight than debts that resulted from more impersonal commercial transactions." Balleisen, *Navigating Failure*, p. 94.

43 *Parke v Day* (1875), 24 UCCP 619, pp. 620, 622.

44 Affidavit of George Patterson, Solicitor for Plaintiff (21 June 1876), #391 *William Irvine v William Thompson*, Writ of Attachment (18 November 1876) in Wentworth County Court Insolvency Files, 1864–80, AO (RG 22-5762) [hereafter Wentworth County Court Insolvency Files] (box B244576).

45 "A Failure with its Lessons," Letter to the Editor, *Monetary Times* 9:16 (8 October 1875) 438.

46 Statement of Duncan at Meeting of Creditors (10 December 1879), *Re Duncan* in Kent County Court Insolvency Files (box 244754).

47 *Re Gearing* (1879), 4 OAR 173, p. 175. In this particular case a creditor filed a writ of attachment against Mrs Gearing compelling a bankruptcy. The court acknowledged that under certain circumstances a married woman may become a bankrupt. In this case, even though Mrs Gearing held property in her name and was entitled to dispose of it as she saw fit, the property was never employed in trade separately from her husband and thus she was never a trader.

48 Affidavit of Official Assignee (16 May 1878), #449 *Charles Cameron and John Proctor v Richard Morgan, John Malloy individually and member of firm Mor-*

gan, Malloy and Malcolm in Wentworth County Court Insolvency Files (box B244579, container 21).

49 Examination of Joseph Wilson (15 February 1879), #485 *Kenneth McKenzie and Edmund Power, Montreal v Joseph Wilson* in Wentworth County Court Insolvency Files (box B244581, container 23).

50 See e.g. #459 *John Proctor v Mary Ann O'Byrne*, Writ of Attachment (13 December 1879) in Huron County Court Insolvency Procedure Book.

51 Lori Chambers, *Married Women and Property Law in Victorian Ontario* (Toronto: University of Toronto Press, 1997) p. 9. Under the common law doctrine of coverture, women had no separate property rights. See Karen Pearlston, "Married Women Bankrupts in the Age of Coverture" (2009) 34:2 Law & Soc Inquiry 265. On the impact of the legislative reforms and the enhanced role of businesswomen see Peter Baskerville, *A Silent Revolution: Gender and Wealth in English Canada, 1860–1930* (Montreal and Kingston: McGill-Queen's University Press, 2008).

52 Chambers, *Married Women and Property Law*, p. 121. Baskerville notes that legislative reforms in Ontario and British Columbia made it more difficult for spouses to transfer property to defraud creditors. Baskerville, *Silent Revolution*, p. 7.

53 *McLeod v Wright*, para 30.

54 *Insolvent Act of 1869*, s 89; *Insolvent Act of 1875*, s 133.

55 Most courts were of the view that the provision required proof of the debtor's intention. See *McWhirter v Thorne*, p. 309; *Newton v Ontario Bank* (1868), 15 Gr 283, p. 289–90 (UC Err App); *Creighton v Merchants' Bank* (1882), 15 NSR 139, p. 145 (SC). That view was not universally accepted, as some courts emphasized the overall effect of the transaction. See *McLeod v Wright*, para 32; *Payne v Hendry*; *Davidson v Ross*.

56 *Insolvent Act of 1869*, s 89. The provision also stated that if the transfer or payment was made within thirty days of the commencement of the bankruptcy, the transaction was presumed to have been made in contemplation of bankruptcy. See *Insolvent Act of 1875*, s 133.

57 *Insolvent Act of 1869*, s 90; *Insolvent Act of 1875*, s 134. Under this provision the Assignee had to establish that the creditor had "probable cause" for "believing" that the debtor was "then unable to meet his engagements in full." See e.g. *Cochran v Chipman* (1876–7), 11 NSR 254 (SC).

58 Where there was evidence of a transfer of goods to a creditor within the thirty-day period prior to bankruptcy, it gave the Official Assignee good reason to formally examine the bankrupt with a view to setting aside the transaction. See e.g. Affidavit of Official Assignee (14 June 1874), #278 *Re Alex Milne*, Voluntary Assignment (21 March 1874) in Wentworth County Court Insolvency Files (box B244645).

59 Affidavit of William Reid, Plaintiff (23 June 1876), #374 *William Reid & N. Galbraith v Robert Griffith*, Writ of Attachment (23 June 1876) in Wentworth County Court Insolvency Files (box B244576).
60 Order Confirming Discharge (22 April 1880), *Re Gibbons* in Haldimand County Court Insolvency Files; Affidavit of A Cosforth (3 April 1876), #342 *Frank Samuel & Lewis Samuel v Joseph Morrison*, Writ of Attachment (12 November 1875) in Wentworth County Court Insolvency Files (box B244648).
61 Statement of Watson at Meeting of Creditors (22 October 1879), *Re George Watson* in Kent County Court Insolvency Files (box 244754); #350 *Thomas Wilson, Walter Bastable, Alexander Barrie and Daueau McFarland v John McKay* [nd] in Wentworth County Court Insolvency Files (box B24469).
62 "The Insolvent Act," *Trade Review* 5:16 (16 April 1869) 246.
63 *Creighton v Merchants' Bank*, p. 146; *Murphy v Stadacona Bank* (1879), 5 QLR 321, p. 322 (Sup Ct) (interpreting s 134 of the *Insolvent Act of 1875*).
64 *Godkin v Beech* (1876), 10 NSR 261, p. 268 (SC). A discharge obtained by fraud was void. *Griffiths v Perry* (1881), 6 OAR 672.
65 *Pineo v Gavaza* (1887), 20 NSR 249, para 3 (SC).
66 *Kalus v Hergert*, pp. 75, 81.
67 See e.g. *McGregor v Hume* (1869), 28 UCQB 380.
68 *Mathers v Lynch* (1868), 27 UCQB 244, p. 253, citing *Deacon on Bankruptcy*, vol 1, p. 8.
69 *Bell v Rickaby* (1877), 3 QLR 243 (QB, Appeal Side), aff'd on other grounds (1878), 2 SCR 560.
70 *Smith v McLean* (1878), 25 Gr 567, p. 269 (UC Ch).
71 *Royal Canadian Bank v Kerr* (1870), 17 Gr 47, p. 68 (UC Ch).
72 *Newton v Ontario Bank*, p. 299.
73 Affidavit of Defendant (10 April 1873), *Adam Hope, Charles Hope & Robert Weuyss v Henry Walker, plumber*, Writ of Attachment (5 April 1873) in Wentworth County Court Insolvency Files (box B244643).
74 See e.g. *McEdwards v Palmer* (1878), 2 OAR 439 (CA); *Ex parte Jones* (1878), 18 NBR 136, pp. 139–40 (SC). Even where a debtor sold his entire stock and trade to a creditor and absconded the next day, the Ontario Court of Appeal held that there was insufficient evidence to show that the debtor sold the stock in contemplation of insolvency. The court found that the debtor did not intend to commit fraud or prefer the creditor. See *Lewis v Brown* (1884), 10 OAR 639; See also *Patterson v Kingsley* (1878), 25 Gr 425, p. 431 (UC Ch).
75 *McCrae v White* (1883), 9 SCR 22, pp. 25, 26. On the narrow interpretation of a similar provision in the US Bankruptcy Act of 1841, see Balleisen, *Navigating Failure*, p. 111.
76 *Insolvent Act of 1869*, s 89; *Insolvent Act of 1875*, s 133.

77 Affidavit of Defendant (10 April 1873), *Adam Hope, Charles Hope & Robert Weuyss v Henry Walker, plumber,* Writ of Attachment (5 April 1873) in Wentworth County Court Insolvency Files (box B244643); Affidavit of Robert Griffith (24 June 1876), #374 *William Reid & N Galbraith v Robert Griffith,* Writ of Attachment (23 June 1876) in Wentworth County Court Insolvency Files (box B244576); *Re John Hennessy* [nd] in Wentworth County Court Insolvency Files (box B244645).
78 *Churcher v Johnston* (1874), 34 UCQB 528, p. 539.
79 *Smith v Hutchinson* (1878), 2 OAR 405, pp. 408, 412.
80 *Nelles v Paul* (1879), 4 OAR 1, pp. 5, 6.
81 Anthony Duggan & Thomas GW Telfer, "Voidable Preferences" in Stephanie Ben-Ishai & Anthony Duggan, eds, *Canadian Bankruptcy and Insolvency Law: Bill C-55, Statute c.47 and Beyond* (Toronto: LexisNexis, 2007) 145. In Quebec the doctrine of pressure did not operate. See *Bell v Rickaby,* p. 252 (Dorion CJ dissenting).
82 C.B. Labatt, "The Doctrine of Pressure" (1899) 35:10 Can LJ (NS) 322, p. 323; *Re Hurst,* para 39; *Allan v Clarkson* (1870), 17 Gr 570, p. 571 (UC Ch).
83 *Ex parte Topham* (1873), LR 8 Ch App 614 cited in *McFarlane v McDonald* (1874), 21 Gr 319 (UC Ch). Thus where a debtor entered into contract with a creditor to make a payment, the payment was not voluntary, as the debtor simply had no choice: *Hersee v White* (1869), 29 UCQB 232.
84 Labatt, "Doctrine of Pressure," p. 322.
85 *Johnson v Fesenmeyer* (1858), 25 Beav 88, p. 93, cited in *Royal Canadian Bank v Kerr,* p. 67; *Tucker v Young,* [1877] Man R temp Wood 186, p. 202 (QB); *Gordon v Young* (1866), 12 Gr 318, pp. 319–20 (UC Ch).
86 *Allan v Clarkson,* p. 571; Labatt, "Doctrine of Pressure," p. 356.
87 *Newton v Ontario Bank,* p. 295; *Royal Canadian Bank v Kerr; Tucker v Young.* However, some courts set aside transactions on the basis that the transaction would disable the trader's ability to carry on business, whether or not there was pressure. *McWhirter v Royal Canadian Bank* (1870), 17 Gr 480 (UC Ch); *Re Hurst,* p. 334.
88 *Campbell v Barrie* (1871), 31 UCQB 279, p. 293; *Re Hurst,* p. 333.
89 *McWhirter v Thorne,* p. 310; *Campbell v Barrie,* p. 293; *Re Hurst,* p. 333.
90 *Keays v Brown.*
91 *Tucker v Young,* p. 203.
92 R.S. Cassels, "Mercantile Preferences," Note, (1891) 11.3 Can LT 61.
93 *The Bank of Toronto v McDougall* (1865), 15 UCCP 475.
94 *Campbell v Barrie,* pp. 282, 293.
95 *Clemmow v Converse* (1869), 16 Gr 547, p. 552 (UC Ch); *Re Hurst,* p. 332.
96 *Davidson v Ross,* p. 58, Burton J.

97 *Ibid*, p. 61, Patterson J.
98 On the differences between an effect and an intention test from a modern perspective, see Thomas GW Telfer, "Voidable Preference Reform: Shifting Rules, Standards and Goal Posts: A New Zealand Perspective" (2003) 12:2 Int'l Insol Rev 55.
99 *Davidson v Ross*, p. 80, Moss J.
100 *Ibid.*, p. 58, Burton J.
101 *Ibid.*, p. 87, Moss J. The effect of the decision was to overrule four earlier cases that had held that transfer under pressure was valid (*ibid.*, p. 70, Patterson J). See *Campbell v Barrie*; *Archibald v Haldan* (1871), 31 UCQB 295; *McFarlane v McDonald*; *Keays v Brown*.
102 *Davidson v McInnes* (1876), 24 Gr 414, p. 421 (UC Ch). See also *McLeod v Wright*, para 46 (also holding that intention not required).
103 "Securities Given by Debtors," *Monetary Times* 10:17 (10 October 1876) 450, p. 451.
104 *McEdwards v Palmer*.
105 *Smith v Hutchinson*, p. 407.
106 *Suter v Merchants Bank* (1877), 24 Gr 365 (UC Ch); *Cook v Rogers* (1879), 26 Gr 599, p. 606 (UC Ch).
107 *Nelles v Bank of Montreal* (1881), 28 Gr 449, p. 453 (UC Ch), aff'd (1882), 7 OAR 743; *Smith v McLean*, p. 569; Labatt, "Doctrine of Pressure," p. 351.
108 *Brayley v Ellis* (1882), 1 OR 119, p. 123 (Ch), aff'd (1884), 9 OAR 565; *Totten v Bowen* (1882), 8 OAR 602, p. 610. In *Brayley v Ellis* (1884), 9 OAR 565, a majority of the Ontario Court of Appeal accepted the doctrine of pressure. In contrast, Patterson J dissented, pointing out the merits of *Davidson v Ross*. See also *Martin v McAlpine* (1883), 8 OAR 675; *Slater v Oliver* (1884), 7 OR 158, pp. 159–60 (HCJ (Ch Div)).
109 *McCrae v White*, pp. 30, 31. See also comments of Gwynne J, who suggested that comments in *Davidson v Ross* were merely *obiter dicta*, *ibid.*, p. 33.
110 *Long v Hancock* (1885), 12 SCR 532; *McLean v Garland* (1885), 13 SCR 366; *Molson Bank v Halter* (1890), 18 SCR 88; *Stephens v McArthur* (1891), 19 SCR 446. See *ibid.*, p. 453, Strong J.
111 Labatt, "Doctrine of Pressure," p. 356.
112 "The Insolvency Laws," *Monetary Times* 7:26 (26 December 1873) 610.
113 Commons Debates, 26 February 1877, 304 (Workman).
114 *Ibid.*, 28 February 1877, 364 (Laflamme); *ibid.*, 26 February 1877, 308 (Mackay, Cape Breton); *ibid.*, 28 February 1877, 364 (Laflamme).
115 Beausoleil, *La loi de faillite*, p. 6. For similar views, see Commons Debates,

28 February 1877, 358 (Landerkin); *ibid.*, 27 March 1878, 1433 (Wood); *ibid.*, 28 February 1877, 364 (Laflamme).

116 Compare Hansen, "Commercial Associations."

117 Petition of Council of the Montreal Board of Trade to Governor General of Canada (20 April 1869), in Secretary of State Papers, LAC (RG 6-A-1) [hereafter Secretary of State Papers] (vol 6, file 852).

118 W.J. Patterson, Montreal Board of Trade, to E. Blake, Minister of Justice (28 March 1876), in Department of Justice Papers (vol 36, file 1876-420).

119 J. Morrison, President, Toronto Board of Trade, to John A. Macdonald (1 March 1800), in Macdonald Papers (reel C-1748, p. 169691); Petition of the Boards of Trade, of Banking Institutions, and of Merchants and Manufactures of Montreal (30 April 1872) in Secretary of State Papers (vol 11, file 704).

120 Senate Debates, 23 May 1872, 783 (Campbell).

121 "Two Important Measures," *Monetary Times* 6:37 (14 March 1873) 796; Dominion Board of Trade, Annual Meeting, 1874 at 13. The action by the Toronto Board of Trade in securing the extension was acknowledged in a letter: see William Thomson, President Toronto Board of Trade, Letter to the Editor (3 November 1873) in "Insolvent Act," *Monetary Times* 7:19 (7 November 1873) 438.

122 See Commons Debates, 26 February 1877, 293 (Blake).

123 Petition to Governor General of the Dominion of Canada (February 1880), in Department of Justice Papers (vol 46, file 1880-347). The signatories included the Bank of Montreal, Merchants Bank of Canada, La Banque du Peuple, Molson's Bank, Québec Bank and seventy-two individuals, corporations or businesses.

124 D.R. Wikes, Imperial Bank of Canada, Toronto, to John A. Macdonald (5 May 1879), in Macdonald Papers (reel C-1716, pp. 165219–22).

125 DBT, Annual Meeting 1874, p. 27, DBT Annual Meetings, MG28-III44, LAC [hereafter DBT Annual Meeting].

126 DBT, Annual Meeting 1872, appendix, pp. 75–7.

127 DBT, Annual Meeting 1873, pp. 112–20.

128 DBT, Annual Meeting 1877, p. 158.

129 DBT, Annual Meeting 1878, p. 191.

130 See Skeel, *Debt's Dominion*, ch. 1.

131 DBT, Annual Meeting 1879, pp. 25–36, 159–77. Again a reminder was given of the evils of the common law: "The moment there was a judgment against a man, there were creditors from Toronto, Hamilton, Montréal and other places all trying to get the better of each other" (p. 174).

132 To support his claim of the detrimental impact of local legislation, Ryan read a letter from the solicitor of the British North American Bank, who claimed that the common law would result in a return to a race to the debtor's assets. Senate Debates, 8 May 1879, 514 (Ryan).

133 Commons Debates, 5 May 1879, 1776 (Bechard). He asked if the commercial sector demanded such a law, as evidenced by the many telegrams from the Boards of Trade in Quebec, Hamilton and Toronto: "[W]hy should the representatives of the rural districts say 'you shall not have it [?]'"; *ibid.*, 29 April 1879, 1602 (Colby).

134 See chapter 9, below.

Chapter 4

1 The undated news clipping was located in the bankruptcy file #265 *Bank of British North America v Julius McCarty* (23 March 1874) in Wentworth County Court Insolvency Files (box B244645).

2 *Ibid.* The *Concise Oxford English Dictionary* identifies the word as an archaic expression for absconding or leaving debts unpaid. *The Concise Oxford English Dictionary*, 12th ed, *sub verbo* "levanted."

3 Affidavit of Attorney for Plaintiff (24 March 1874), #265 *Bank of British North America v Julius McCarty* (23 March 1874) in Wentworth County Court Insolvency Files; news clipping [nd], #265 *Bank of British North America v Julius McCarty* (23 March 1874) in Wentworth County Court Insolvency Files (box B244645).

4 Affidavit of Attorney for Plaintiff (24 March 1874), #265 *Bank of British North America v Julius McCarty* (23 March 1874) in Wentworth County Court Insolvency Files (box B244645).

5 See Thomas GW Telfer, "Ideas, Interests, Institutions and the History of Canadian Bankruptcy Law, 1867–1880" (2010) 60:2 UTLJ 603.

6 *Cameron v Holland* (1870), 29 UCQB 506, p. 509. The liabilities had to be listed in the bankrupt's statement of affairs presented at the first meeting of creditors. See *Standard Bank of Canada v Johnson* (1877), 42 UCQB 16, pp. 19–20 (HCJ (QB)).

7 *Harman v Clarkson*, pp. 295, 292; *Insolvent Act of 1869*, s 1. Edgar, *Insolvent Act of 1869*, pp. 33–6. Abbott, *Insolvent Act of 1864*, pp. 1–10; Girouard, "Can a Person Who Ceased to be a Trader"; Girouard, "Can a Trader without Assets Make an Assignment?"

8 Statute 21 (UK), James I, c 19, s 2, cited in Edgar, *Insolvent Act of 1869*.

9 In *Duncan v Smart* a banker and exchange money broker who bought and sold American currency was held to be a trader. In *Harman v Clarkson* an

innkeeper was held not to be a trader. In *Thomas v Hall* a barber was held not to be a trader. *Insolvent Act of 1875*, s 1. For a review of the English case law on the meaning of *trader*, see Clarke, *Insolvent Act of 1875*, pp. 14–20.

10 *Insolvent Act of 1869*, ss 94, 98. See *Austin v Gordon* (1872), 32 UCQB 621.

11 *Insolvent Act of 1869*, s 94. The Act also provided a separate regime that allowed debtors to enter into a deed of composition, which, in effect, allowed debtors to reach a settlement with their creditors. If there was a deed, the estate was reconveyed to the debtor, and debts were paid in accordance with the deed. In contrast, a discharge released the debtor from all debts, and creditors received a *pro rata* dividend. For a detailed description of the operation of the discharge provisions, see William H. Kerr, "Deeds of Composition and Discharge Between Co-Partners and their Creditors under the *Insolvent Act of 1869*" (1871) 1:2 RCLJ 171.

12 *Insolvent Act of 1869*, s 101.

13 See Popham, *Insolvent Act of 1869*, p. 138.

14 *Insolvent Act of 1869*, s 103.

15 See Popham, *Insolvent Act of 1869*, p. 138.

16 Edgar, *Insolvent Act of 1869*, p. 120; Popham, *Insolvent Act of 1869*, p. 138.

17 *Insolvent Act of 1869*, s 105; *Re Robert Holt and John Gray* (1867), 13 Gr 568, p. 569 (UC Ch); *Insolvent Act of 1869*, s 107.

18 Wotherspoon, *Insolvent Act of 1875*, pp. vii, 175. The discharge provisions in the *Insolvent Act of 1875* are found in ss 49–66. See Clarke, *Insolvent Act of 1875*, pp. 161–2.

19 Commons Debates, 25 March 1875, 912 (Paterson). For an excellent overview of how the 1875 discharge provisions worked, see Commons Debates, 3 April 1877, 1091 (Colby). See also "Some Provisions Of The New Insolvency Act," *Monetary Times* 9:10 (3 September 1875) 266.

20 Edgar & Chrysler, *Insolvent Act of 1875*, pp. xxix–xxx.

21 #350 *Thomas Wilson, Walter Bastable, Alexander Barrie and Daueau McFarland v John McKay* [nd], in Wentworth County Court Insolvency Files (box B24469).

22 "Tricks in Trade," *Journal of Commerce* 5:9 (19 October 1877) 269; Commons Debates, 26 February 1877, 292, 293 (Blake). The *Monetary Times* suggested the 50 per cent dividend as early as 1875. See "Some Provisions of the New Insolvent Act," *Monetary Times* 9:10 (3 September 1875) 265.

23 SC 1877, c 41, ss 14, 15.

24 "Minor Defects in the Solvent Act," *Monetary Times* 12:42 (11 April 1879) 1274; "The Bankrupt Law, and the Collection of Debts," *Monetary Times* 11:29 (11 January 1878) 812. See speeches of Mitchell and Paterson, Commons Debates, 3 April 1877, 1094–6.

25 "Experience," Letter to the Editor (5 March 1877), *Journal of Commerce* 4:4 (9 March 1877) 116.
26 Bicknell, "Advisability of Establishing a Bankruptcy Court in Canada," p. 43.
27 Under Bill C-85, *An Act to repeal the Insolvent Act of 1875, and the Acts amending it*, 1879, s 44, consent of creditors representing four-fifths in number and four-fifths in value was required.
28 Commons Debates, 29 April 1879, 1599, 1605 (Girouard).
29 The *Journal of Commerce* reproduced a memorandum attached to the report of the Parliamentary Committee. "The Insolvent Law," *Journal of Commerce* 8:9 (18 April 1879) 274. The *Monetary Times* criticized the Committee for not tabling its full report. "Insolvent Act Amendment," *Monetary Times* 12:43 (18 April 1879) 1304.
30 Commons Debates, 29 April 1879, 1597 (Colby); *ibid.*, 29 April 1879, 1596 (Colby); *ibid.*, 1620 (MacDonnell). See Bill C-85, *An Act to repeal the Insolvent Act of 1875, and the Acts amending it*, 1879, s 44.
31 *An Act to repeal the Acts respecting Insolvency now in force in Canada*, SC 1880, c 1.
32 Commons Debates, 11 May 1869, 258 (Bodwell); *ibid.*, 24 April 1872, 136 (Blake); *ibid.*, 3 April 1877, 1105 (Macdonnell). "When a man failed honestly the law should step in and distribute his property among his creditors, and then he should be allowed to take a fresh start." Senate Debates, 22 May 1872, 744 (Wark).
33 Commons Debates, 26 February 1877, 305 (Paterson).
34 *Ibid.*, 11 May 1869, 262 (Abbott); *ibid.*, 20 March 1875, 829 (Orton).
35 "Experience," Letter to the Editor (5 March 1877), *Journal of Commerce* 4:4 (9 March 1877) 116.
36 Senate Debates, 18 June 1869, 357 (Sanborn); *ibid.*; Commons Debates, 7 March 1879, 210 (Domville); Senate Debates, 22 May 1872, 744 (Wark).
37 Commons Debates, 2 May 1872, 286 (Anglin); *ibid.*, 21 April 1869, 36 (Macdonald).
38 "The Insolvent Act," *Trade Review* 3:28 (26 July 1867) 434; Commons Debates, 3 April 1877, 1111 (Blake); *ibid.*, 1105 (Macdonnell).
39 On the ability of American debtors to avoid creditors by leaving town, see Balleisen, *Navigating Failure*, pp. 170–3.
40 Commons Debates, 24 March 1875, 880 (Bunster); *ibid.*, 26 February 1877, 286 (McDougall); *ibid.*, 7 March 1879, 211 (Ross, West Middlesex).
41 "The Insolvency Bill," *Nation* (5 March 1875).
42 Burley's study of Brantford indicates that those who failed often could not face the public shame. Many fled, and some even committed suicide rather

than confront creditors, friends and families with their financial failure. Burley, *Particular Condition in Life*, pp. 176–7.

43 Commons Debates, 26 February 1877, 296 (Blake); 304 (Young).

44 *Insolvent Act of 1869*, s 13.

45 *Ibid.*, s 13(a).

46 *Ibid.*, s 13(b)(c)(i).

47 *Ibid.*, s 17.

48 *Ibid.*, ss 23, 24.

49 Wentworth County Court Insolvency Files.

50 See e.g. *Sarah Catherine Birley v Lewis D. Birley*, Writ of Attachment (3 July 1879) in Wentworth County Court Insolvency Files (box B24482, container 24).

51 #305, *Joseph Chemer & Havier Chemer v James Ball*, Writ of Attachment (19 April 1875) in Wentworth County Court Insolvency Files (Milwaukee); Affidavit of David Garson (20 December 1875), (box B244646); #341 *Bank of British North America v Robert Yates & David Garson*, Writ of Attachment [nd], in Wentworth County Court Insolvency Files (box B24468) (New York) (box B24469); #416 *Cassandra Wisker v James Barnes*, Writ of Attachment (23 May 1877) in Wentworth County Court Insolvency Files (Lewiston, NY) (box B244578, container 20); #413 *John Wood v John Callaghan*, Writ of Attachment (8 May 1877) in Wentworth County Court Insolvency Files (Detroit) (box B244578, container 20).

52 Affidavit of George Beach, Book Keeper (23 March 1874), #266 *Alexander Harvey, John Stuart & Thomas MacPherson v William Curry*, Writ of Attachment (24 March 1874) in Wentworth County Court Insolvency Files (box B24465).

53 Affidavit of Sheriff (24 March 1873), #226 *George Taylor & Francis Ninety v Daniel Murphy*, Writ of Attachment (14 March 1873) in Wentworth County Court Insolvency Files (box B244643).

54 #265 *Bank of British North America v Julius McCarty* (23 March 1874) in Wentworth County Court Insolvency Files (box B244645).

55 Trumpeller, Merchant Tailor, to Hughes Bros (3 July 1879) in Affidavit of Patrick Hughes (4 July 1879), #503 *Patrick Hughes & Bernard Hughes trading as Hughes Bros v S.L. Trumpeller*, Writ of Attachment (3 July 1879) in Wentworth County Court Insolvency Files (box B244581, container 23).

56 *Cf.* Affidavit of insolvent Peter Fraser in application for discharge (15 September 1883), #359 *Canadian Bank of Commerce v Peter Fraser*, Writ of Attachment (24 April 1876) in Wentworth County Court Insolvency Files (box B24469) in which the debtor left the province and family on three occasions in search of work, only to return to Wentworth County.

57 Affidavit of Moses Silverfreud, an acquaintance of Defendant (25 April 1872), #212 *Henry Nerlish, Peter Baker & Charles Dougherty v Simon Adams*, Writ of Attachment (25 April 1872) in Wentworth County Court Insolvency Files (box B244643). See also Affidavit of John Barry, Solicitor for the Plaintiffs (5 June 1872), #212 *Henry Nerlish, Peter Baker & Charles Dougherty v Simon Adams*, Writ of Attachment (25 April 1872) in Wentworth County Court Insolvency Files (box B244643).

58 Affidavit of Moses Silverfreud, an acquaintance of Defendant (25 April 1872), #212 *Henry Nerlish, Peter Baker & Charles Dougherty v Simon Adams*, Writ of Attachment (25 April 1872) in Wentworth County Court Insolvency Files (box B244643).

59 Affidavit of James Simpson (14 December 1875), #339 *James Simpson & James Stewart v James Egan*, Writ of Attachment (14 December 1875) in Wentworth County Court Insolvency Files (box B24468). See also *Buchanan v Smith* (1870), 17 Gr 208 (UC Ch).

60 *Re Smith, an Insolvent* (1867), 4 PR 89, p. 92 (UC Pract Ct).

61 Affidavit of George Beach, Book Keeper (23 March 1874), #266 *Alexander Harvey, John Stuart & Thomas MacPherson v William Curry*, Writ of Attachment, in Wentworth County Insolvency Files (box B24465).

62 Affidavit of David Garson (20 December 1875), #341 *Bank of British North America v Robert Yates & David Garson*, Writ of Attachment [nd] in Wentworth County Insolvency Files (box B24468).

63 Affidavit of Birkett (4 April 1879), #494 *William Birkett & John Bell v William Stodgson*, Writ of Attachment [nd] in Wentworth County Court Insolvency Files (box B244581, container 23).

64 *Colwell v Robertson* (1877), 17 NBR 481, p. 481 (CA). However, *cf.* the judgment of Allen CJ, p. 486.

65 "Insolvent Debtor's Act," *Trade Review* 5:1 (1 January 1869) 4.

66 Commons Debates, 19 April 1869, 24 (Magill); *ibid.*, 11 May 1869, 253 (Mackenzie); *ibid.*, 7 March 1879, 202 (Rymal). "The effect of the law was to draw men into bankruptcy and create recklessness in the way of conducting business – in fact demoralize the whole community." Senate Debates, 28 May 1872, 789 (Kaulback).

67 Commons Debates, 7 March 1879, 206 (Houde); *ibid.*, 20 March 1875, 815 (Maclennan).

68 "Regarding verbal and written promises lightly is one of the most common and dangerous mistakes into which our traders fall. Aside from the moral question involved, the merchant who indulges this vice throws away that which is of the utmost value to him … Once established a reputation for negligence and recklessness in regard to one's obligations, the

very essence of credit is gone." "Broken Promises," *Monetary Times* 5:6 (11 August 1871) 107.

69 Commons Debates, 28 February 1877, 359 (Mousseau); *ibid.*, 25 March 1875, 918 (Rymal); *ibid.*, 7 March 1879, 199 (Huntington); *ibid.*, 25 April 1872, 156 (Magill); Senate Debates, 22 May 1872, 746 (Sanborn).

70 RMF, "Legislation Upon Insolvency," p. 422; "Dominion Board of Trade," *Monetary Times* 6:30 (24 January 1873) 622; Commons Debates, 7 March 1879, 206 (Houde). "While a debtor might go through insolvency or make a compromise with his creditors for 50c on the dollar and be legally absolved from his liabilities, still, under the higher law, the moral law, he should pay every dollar of his debts." *Ibid.*, 3 April 1877, 1094 (Paterson).

71 "The Insolvent Act," *Trade Review* 3:28 (26 July 1867) 434; *ibid.*; "Need of An Amended Insolvent Act," *Trade Review* 5:8 (19 February 1869) 117; "The Insolvent Act," *Trade Review* 5:16 (16 April 1869) 246; *ibid.*

72 "Some Characteristics of the Age," *Journal of Commerce* 5:26 (15 February 1878) 781.

73 Dickie & Kennedy, The Buckeye Spring Hoe Broadcast Seeder and Drill and Horse Rakes to McMichael and Hughson (4 June 1877), *Re McMichael & Hughson*, Assignment (23 June 1877) in Kent County Court Insolvency Files (box 244754); A. Watts, Importer, Brampton, to H. Cuming, Official Assignee (18 August 1878), *Re J. Taylor*, Assignment (19 April 1877) in Kent County Court Insolvency Files (box 244754).

74 "Is it not, therefore, to the detriment of the community, and not to its benefit, to facilitate their getting into business again?" "A New Insolvency Law," *Monetary Times* 7:46 (15 May 1874) 1163. In a later editorial the *Monetary Times* suggested that of the 1500 or so who failed in 1875, it was far better if they never returned to business: "And it is only mistaken kindness to help them back." See "Failures in 1875," *Monetary Times* 9:19 (5 November 1875) 519.

75 "The Insolvency Law," *Monetary Times* 10:35 (23 February 1877) 962; *ibid.*; "Business Morality," *Monetary Times* 3:40 (20 May 1870) 628.

76 "Proposed Repeal of Insolvency Laws," *Monetary Times* 5:41 (19 April 1872) 826; "Two Important Measures," *Monetary Times* 6:37 (14 March 1873) 796. The latter article suggested amendments to "render the release of the dishonest and extravagant more difficult to obtain."

77 "The Insolvency Law," *Monetary Times* 10:35 (23 February 1877) 962; *ibid.*; see also "Shall the Insolvent Act be Repealed?," *Monetary Times* 12:37 (7 March 1879) 1116; "Insolvent Act Repeal," *Monetary Times* 12:40 (28 March 1879) 1209.

78 "Hints to Young Men on Preparation for Business," *Monetary Times* 6:21 (22 November 1872) 412.

79 Allan Smith, "The Myth of the Self-made Man in English Canada, 1850–1914" (1978) 59:2 Canadian Historical Review 189, pp. 203–4.

80 "Over-Reaching in Business," *Monetary Times* 7:11 (12 September 1873) 249; *Chicago Journal of Commerce*, reprinted in *Monetary Times* 3:40 (20 May 1870) supplement, p. xii. Risk states, "[E]ach individual was to be responsible for his own economic fate, even though one transaction or a lifetime of disadvantage made that fate a cruel one." Risk, "Golden Age," p. 338.

81 Michael Bliss, *A Living Profit: Studies in the Social History of Canadian Business, 1883–1911* (Toronto: McClelland and Stewart, 1974) pp. 16–18.

82 Johnson, *Sketches of the Late Depression*, p. 21.

83 Bliss, *Living Profit*, pp. 20, 32.

84 "The Hurry to Get into Business," *Monetary Times* 6:15 (11 October 1872) 289. In this article the author claims that one cause of failure is rushing "unthoughtfully" into business when not prepared. Johnson, *Sketches of the Late Depression*, p. 25; "Overtrading," *Monetary Times* 5:27 (12 January 1872) 550; "Causes of Mercantile Failures," *Monetary Times* 6:7 (16 August 1872) 124. See also "Why So Many Fail in Business," *Chicago Journal of Commerce*, reprinted in *Monetary Times* 4:29 (3 March 1871) 564.

85 "Causes of Mercantile Failures," *Monetary Times* 124.

86 Johnson, *Sketches of the Late Depression*, p. 26.

87 "Causes of Mercantile Failures," *Monetary Times* 124; *Chicago Journal of Commerce*, reprinted in *Monetary Times* 3:40 (20 May 1870) supplement, p. xii. See also "Business and Gambling," *Monetary Times* 4:1 (19 August 1870) 6.

88 One author claimed that the causes of fraud and embezzlements were "speculation, gambling and fast living." See "Recent Crimes and Their Moral," *Monetary Times* 5:13 (29 September 1871) 246.

89 Margaret Oliphant, *At His Gates* (Toronto: Hunter, Rose, 1872). Margaret Oliphant lived on the edge of debt and insolvency. See Julianne Smith, "Private Practice: Thomas De Quincey, Margaret Oliphant, and the Construction of Women's Rhetoric in the Victorian Periodical Press" (2004) 23:1 Rhetoric Review 40, p. 49.

90 Oliphant, *At His Gates*, pp. 111, 112, 233, 328, 403.

91 Kelley & Trebilcock, *Making of the Mosaic*, p. 9.

92 Pomfret, *Economic Development of Canada*, p. 53.

93 For a summary of the rationale of the rule, see RMF, "Legislation Upon Insolvency," p. 422.

94 Commons Debates, 27 March 1878, 1449 (Little), 1451 (Bourbeau); *ibid.*, 7 March 1879; *ibid.*, 203 (Hesson), *ibid.*, 204 (Oliver). Mr Methot, who described himself as representing "a rural district," had promised during the

election campaign that "he would do all in his power to have this Insolvency Act repealed." *Ibid.*, 204 (Methot).

95 See *ibid.*, 20 March 1875, *ibid.*, 810 (Mills), *ibid.*, 812 (Colby), *ibid.*, 813 (Oliver); *ibid.*, 23 April 1872, 123 (Oliver).

96 *Ibid.*, 20 March 1875, 821 (Ryal); *ibid.*, 25 February 1880, 222 (McCuaig).

97 Rural opposition to bankruptcy law was an issue in the election of 1878, and "rural constituencies ... looked to this Government to carry out the repeal of this law which they looked upon as class legislation." *Ibid.*, 7 March 1879, 209–10 (McCallum).

98 *Ibid.*, 220 (Bechard). One Member of Parliament claimed, "The almost unanimous opinion of the people of the rural districts in this country was in favour of repeal." *Ibid.*, 29 April 1879, 1618 (Cameron).

99 *Ibid.*, 26 February 1877, 299 (Workman).

100 James Bicknell, "Advisability of Establishing a Bankruptcy Court in Canada," p. 46.

101 Commons Debates, 7 March 1879, 217 (Landry).

102 See e.g. Bill C-84, *An Act respecting Insolvency*, 3rd Sess, 8th Parl, 1898. The US Bankruptcy Act of 1898 protected farmers against involuntary bankruptcies. See David Ray Papke, "Rhetoric and Retrenchment: Agrarian Ideology and American Bankruptcy Law" (1989) 54:4 Mo L Rev 871, p. 877. (The provision was designed to protect the "precarious position of farmers in the interdependent economy," p. 881.)

103 *Bankruptcy Act of 1919*, s 8.

104 *Bankruptcy and Insolvency Act*, s 48. See Stephanie Ben-Ishai & Virginia Torrie, "Farm Insolvency in Canada" (2013) 2 *Journal of the Insolvency Institute of Canada* 33.

105 Appellate courts did not always adopt a consistent pro-debtor or pro-creditor approach to interpretation. See e.g. *Forrester v Thrasher* (1882), 2 OR 38, p. 44 (QB); *Re Hill* (1882), 7 OAR 694.

106 On the tendency of judges to favour debtors under the US Bankruptcy Act of 1841 see Balleisen, *Navigating Failure*, pp. 114–15.

107 *Re Lamb, An Insolvent* (1866), 4 PR 16 (UC Pract Ct).

108 *Cameron v Holland*, pp. 513, 514.

109 *Re Martin and English* (1880), 5 OAR 647, p. 650.

110 *Re Garratt & Co.* (1869), 28 UCQB 266, pp. 269–71.

111 *Cf. Standard Bank of Canada v Johnson* (debtor who failed to do what the statute makes necessary for his own protection "has only himself to blame if there be no protection," p. 21).

112 *Re Garratt & Co*, p. 271.

113 *Re Gooding* (1880), 5 OAR 643, pp. 643–4.

114 *Re Bullivant* (1880), 5 OAR 638, p. 641, 642; *cf. Re Hill.* The court had the power to suspend the discharge for a period not exceeding five years or order a second-class discharge: *Insolvent Act of 1875*, s 57.
115 *Insolvent Act of 1869*, s 101.
116 *Re Jones*, p. 329.
117 *McLean v McLellan* (1870), 29 UCQB 548.
118 *Thomas v Hall*, pp. 174, 175.
119 *Re Hutchinson, Insolvent* (1877), 12 NSR 40, pp. 42, 43 (CA).
120 *Re Gooding*, p. 645.
121 *Re Mooney, Insolvent* (1876–7), 11 NSR 563 (CA); *Re Donald Matheson* (1872–5), 9 NSR 538 (SC); *Gilbert v Girouard* (1878), 18 NBR 148 (SC).
122 *Re Mooney.*
123 *Re Donald Matheson.*
124 *Gilbert v Girouard.*
125 In *Adam Rutherford Bell v George McPherson*, a second-class discharge was ordered on 3 June 1887. *Adam Rutherford Bell v George McPherson*, Writ of Attachment (26 June 1876) in Lanark County Court Insolvency Minute Books.
126 Johnson, *Sketches of the Late Depression*, p. 46.
127 Mann, *Republic of Debtors*, pp. 232–3. See generally Mann, pp. 228–39. Collusion between debtors and creditors was also common in England under an involuntary regime. See Kadens, "Last Bankrupt Hanged," pp. 1248–9.
128 *Insolvent Act of 1875*, s 4.
129 Lanark County Court Insolvency Minute Books; Huron County Court Insolvency Procedure Book; Oxford County Court Insolvency Docket Book; Lambton County Court Insolvency Procedure Book. The Peel County sample was too small to include in the statistics listed above. Peel County Court Insolvency Minute Book.
130 #518, *John Gamble Geddes the Elder v John Gamble Geddes the Younger*, Writ of Attachment (7 January 1880) in Wentworth County Court Insolvency Files (box B24483, container 25).
131 *William Henry Cooper v William Henry Cooper the Younger*, Writ of Attachment (6 March 1877) in Huron County Court Insolvency Procedure Book.
132 See e.g. *Agnes Buchan v Charles Buchan*, Writ of Attachment (15 May 1879) in *Huron County Court Insolvency Procedure Book*. Female creditors also remained active in filing writs of attachment against non-related debtors: see e.g. #433 *Elizabeth Coulthard v William Allan*, Writ of Attachment (1 May 1879) in Huron County Court Insolvency Procedure Book.
133 See e.g. *Parke v Day*.

134 Evan H. Caminker, "Why Must Inferior Courts Obey Superior Court Precedents?" (1994) 46:4 Stan L Rev 817, p. 820. On the discretion of lower courts, see Pauline T. Kim, "Lower Court Discretion" (2007) 82:2 NYUL Rev 383.

135 "Bankrupts in Court," *Daily Globe* (24 February 1872) 2; Bromfield, *Practical Hints to the Retail Merchant*, p. 31; Johnson, *Sketches of the Late Depression*, p. 46.

136 "Farmers and Insolvency Laws," *Globe* (25 December 1884) 4; Editorial, *Morning Freeman* (17 June 1869) 2; "Proposed Repeal of the Insolvency Laws," *Monetary Times* 5:41 (19 April 1872) 826; "The Bankrupt Court," *Broad-Axe* 1:4 (14 March 1871) 18; *ibid.* See also Editorial, *Morning Freeman* (17 June 1869) 2.

137 Skocpol, *Protecting Soldiers and Mothers*, p. 371.

138 T.G. Zuber, *Report of the Ontario Courts Inquiry* (Toronto: Queen's Printer, 1987) p. 21.

139 Teresa A. Sullivan, Elizabeth Warren & Jay Lawrence Westbrook, "The Persistence of Local Legal Culture: Twenty Years of Evidence from the Federal Bankruptcy Courts" (1994) 17:3 Harv JL & Pub Pol'y 801, p. 804.

140 "The Law of Insolvency," *Globe* (11 April 1892) 4.

141 E.R.C. Clarkson, *Bankruptcy Legislation* (Toronto: 1885) pp. 4–8.

Chapter 5

1 Weaver & Rockman, eds, *Do Institutions Matter?* For an overview of the historical literature in this area, see Ernst, "Law and American Political Development." See also Hansen, "Commercial Associations." Broad economic change may influence policy direction over time. However, institutional factors may have an autonomous influence on policy choice. On the interplay between macroeconomic change and state structures, see Lawrence C. Dodd & Calvin Jillson, "Conversations on the Study of American Politics: An Introduction" in Lawrence C. Dodd & Calvin Jillson, eds, *The Dynamics of American Politics: Approaches & Interpretations* (Boulder: Westview Press, 1994) 1, p. 10.

2 See Telfer, "Ideas, Interests, Institutions and the History of Canadian Bankruptcy Law, 1867–1880."

3 The professional expertise of the legislators and public bureaucracy affects the capacity of the political system to implement stable and lasting policies. On the capacity of the political system, see Robertson, "Politics and the Past," p. 137. On the importance of state expertise, see Weaver & Rockman, "Assessing the Effects of Institutions," p. 32.

4 Federalism is acknowledged as an important institutional factor in Weaver & Rockman, "Assessing the Effects of Institutions," p. 31; and Robertson, "Politics and the Past," p. 137. Historical studies have acknowledged the importance of federalism in the United States. See e.g. Harry N. Scheiber, "Federalism and the American Economic Order, 1789–1910" (1975) 10:1 Law & Soc'y Rev 57; Freyer, *Producers Versus Capitalists.*

5 In 1878, the *Journal of Commerce* noted that the subject was not one of "party character; indeed the insolvent law is objected to by members of both parties." "The Insolvent Law," *Journal of Commerce* 6:11 (3 May 1878) 312. The Conservatives held office from 1867 to 1873, winning the elections of 1867 and 1872, and were forced to resign in November 1873. The Liberals won the election of 1874 and held office until 1878, when the Conservatives were returned to power. See J. Murray Beck, *Pendulums of Power: Canada's Federal Elections* (Toronto: Prentice Hall, 1968) pp. 1–37.

6 Commons Debates, 25 April 1872, 162 (Cartier); *ibid.*, 134 (J.H. Cameron); Editorial, "The Insolvency Acts" (1872) 8 Local Ct Gaz 65.

7 Commons Debates, 25 April 1872, 162 (Cartier).

8 It "was forced on the House by a powerful majority of gentlemen on both sides of the House." Commons Debates, 26 February 1877, 306 (Dymond).

9 *Ibid.*, 289 (Blake).

10 "Insolvent Act Repeal," *Monetary Times* 12:46 (9 May 1879) 1389. Commons Debates, 7 March 1879, 204 (Methot). Bicknell, "Advisability of Establishing a Bankruptcy Court in Canada," pp. 43–4.

11 Commons Debates, 7 March 1879, 216 (Landry).

12 Bill C-85, *An Act to repeal the Insolvent Act of 1875 and the Acts amending it*, 1879.

13 Commons Debates, 28 April 1879, 1576 (Mcdonald, Pictou); see "The Insolvent Law," *Journal of Commerce* 7:29 (7 February 1879) 785; "The Insolvency Law," *Journal of Commerce* 8:4 (14 March 1879) 110.

14 Senate Debates, 9 May 1879, 536–7 (Wark, Brown).

15 "Insolvent Act Repeal," *Monetary Times* 12:45 (2 May 1879) 1359; See also "Insolvent Act Repeal," *Monetary Times* 12:46 (9 May 1879) 1389. The *Monetary Times* accused the government of shirking their responsibility. See "Bankrupt Law," *Monetary Times* 3:13 (19 September 1879) 356.

16 "Repeal of the Bankrupt Law," *Monetary Times* 3:36 (27 February 1880) 1018. The timing of the elections, however, affected the repeal movement. Efforts to repeal bankruptcy law failed just prior to the elections of 1872 and 1878. In 1872 a majority of government Members were opposed to repealing bankruptcy law "on the eve of a general election." Commons

Debates, 25 April 1872, 162 (Cartier). See "The Insolvent Amendment Bill," *Monetary Times* 10:37 (9 March 1877) 1027.

17 See Skowronek, *Building a New American State*, p. 12.

18 Robertson, "Politics and the Past," p. 137.

19 See e.g. Dame C. Labelle to the Minister of Justice (15 June 1878) in Department of Justice Papers (vol 41, file 1878-849).

20 E.W. Chipman to Edward Blake (17 March 1876) in Department of Justice Papers (vol 36, file 414); A.J. Fortrin to H. Renaryd (26 May 1876) in Department of Justice Papers (vol 37, file 675); S.K. Mathews to Edward Blake (1 February 1877) in Department of Justice Papers (vol 38, file 140); Department of Public Works to Department of Justice (14 November 1877) in Department of Justice Papers (vol 39, file 1194).

21 *Insolvent Act of 1875*, s 28(b).

22 *Ibid.*, ss 38, 39.

23 On the opportunities for profit arising from the process of bankruptcy, see Balleisen, *Navigating Failure*.

24 See e.g. *Re Andrews, An Insolvent* (1877), 2 OAR 24.

25 Scarboro, "Assignees in Bankruptcy Matters," p. 84; Editorial, *Morning Freeman* (17 June 1869) 2.

26 *Harvey v Cotter*, p. 164.

27 Edgar, *Insolvent Act of 1869*; Edgar & Chrysler, *Insolvent Act of 1875*.

28 J.D. Edgar, "The Insolvency Laws," Letter to the Editor, *Daily Globe* (19 April 1869) 2.

29 Scarboro, "Assignees in Bankruptcy Matters," p. 84 [emphasis in original]. *Cf.* position of an Official Assignee who claims that the office offers a "neutral position ... [that qualifies] him for negotiating a settlement." An Official Assignee, "The Bankrupt Act," Letter to the Editor, *Daily Globe* (12 April 1869) 2.

30 C. Wilson & Son, Standard Scale Manufacturers, Toronto, to W. Cuming, Official Assignee (4 November 1879), *Re Boughner* (26 February 1879) in Kent County Court Insolvency Files (box 244754).

31 *Thomas v Hall*, p. 175.

32 *Insolvent Act of 1869*, s 31; Popham, *Insolvent Act of 1869*, p. 60. John Abbott advised the Montreal Board of Trade that they had "an unlimited discretion as to the persons they appoint." John J.C. Abbott to Montreal Board of Trade (14 September 1869) in Montreal Board of Trade Papers (reel 2785, MB V, p. 152).

33 Popham, *Insolvent Act of 1869*, p. 60.

34 W.M. Munro, "The Bankruptcy Question," Letter to the Editor, *Daily Globe* (23 February 1874) 2.

35 "The Insolvency Law," *Journal of Commerce* 1:1 (20 August 1875) 10. See also "The *Insolvent Act of 1869*," *Monetary Times* 6:25 (20 December 1872) 493; "The Insolvent Act," *Monetary Times* 8:35 (26 February 1875) 977. It was not long before Members of Parliament raised the issue of patronage. Commons Debates, 27 March 1878, 1444 (Young).

36 For a specific example, see Petition of Toronto Merchants for Appointment of John Clark to the Office of Official Assignee [nd] in Department of Justice Papers (vol 37, file 847). Those who had acted as Official Assignees under the former Act did not hesitate to make direct application for reappointment. See e.g. Georges Hyacinthe to Governor General of Canada (9 April 1875) in Department of Justice Papers (vol 33, file 1875-307).

37 *Insolvent Act of 1875*, s 27.

38 Thomas Bowerman to Minister of Justice (1 March 1877) in Department of Justice Papers (vol 38, file 1877-246); A. Morris to John A. Macdonald (2 November 1878) in Macdonald Papers (reel C-1714, pp 162398–403).

39 Johnson, *Sketches of the Late Depression*, pp. 46–7, 45; Scarboro, "Insolvent Acts – Assignees," Letter to the Editor, (1868) 4 Can LJ (NS) 159, p. 159.

40 *Insolvent Act of 1875*, ss 47, 48.

41 See e.g. *Re Girdlestone* (14 February 1879) in Kent County Court Insolvency Files (box 244754).

42 *Re W.H. Davy* (28 February 1878) in Kent County Court Insolvency Files (box 244754). Only a select few letters have been reproduced. See also *Re Girdlestone* (14 February 1879) in Kent County Court Insolvency Files (box 244754).

43 W.E. Ewan & Son, Wholesale Clothiers, to J.H. Delemare (12 June 1878) in *James Langton Fonds* (F 176, MU 1696), AO.

44 "Special Summons in the First Division Court of the Provincial County of Hamilton" (3 February 1877), *John Johnson v JH Delamere as Official Assignee of estate of James Langton* in James Langton Fonds (F 176, MU 1695).

45 *Insolvent Act of 1875*, s 43.

46 Scarboro, "Insolvent Acts – Assignees," p. 159; Bicknell, "Advisability of Establishing a Bankruptcy Court in Canada," p. 45; *ibid.*

47 Jacobs, "Canadian Bankruptcy Act: Is it a Necessity?," p. 605; "Zeke Trimble on the Insolvency Laws," *Diogenes* 2:2 (21 May 1869) 11 (CIHM microfiche series no. 8-06209).

48 Fraser & Fraser, Barristers, London, Ont, to H. Cumming, Official Assignee (4 November 1878), *Re P. McKerral*, Assignment (8 December 1873) in Kent County Court Insolvency Files (box 244754).

49 James Bicknell, "The Advisability of Establishing a Bankruptcy Court in

Canada" (Address delivered before the Ontario Bar Association, [nd]) (1913) 49:4 Can LJ (NS) 81, p. 86.

50 Fraser & Fraser, Barristers, London, Ont, to H. Cumming, Official Assignee (4 November 1878), *Re P. McKerral*, Assignment (8 December 1873) in Kent County Court Insolvency Files (box 244754). See also *Re Botsford* (1871), 22 UCCP 65.

51 *Insolvent Act of 1875*, s 32.

52 *Agnew v Ross* (1879), 8 PR 67 (UC Pract Ct).

53 "The New Insolvent Bill," *Daily Globe* (4 May 1869) 2.

54 "No Alternative," *Journal of Commerce* 5:10 (26 October 1877) 804.

55 "Official Assignees," *Trade Review* 5:38 (17 September 1869) 583.

56 "Notes From the Capital," *Mainland Guardian* (28 May 1879) 3.

57 "Official Assignees," *Trade Review* 5:38 (17 September 1869) 583; Editorial, "Repeal of Bankruptcy Law in United States" (1878) 14 Can LJ (NS) 189.

58 See William Shakespeare, "*Othello, the Moor of Venice*" in Michael Neill, ed, *Othello: The Oxford Shakespeare* (New York: Oxford University Press, 2006), act III, scene iii, 1, p. 304.

59 "Othello's Occupation Gone!" *Canadian Illustrated News* 19:19 (10 May 1879) 289, LAC (reproduction copy no C-072099, control no ICON80987).

60 A.W. Roberts, Port Perry, to John A. Macdonald (19 February 1880) in Macdonald Papers (reel C-1748, p. 169522–4).

61 *BNA Act*, s 92(13). See also *BNA Act*, s 92(16). On the issue of potential overlap, see Gibson, "Development of Federal Legal and Judicial Institutions in Canada," p. 471; Cameron, "Annotation: Bankruptcy Act of Canada, 1920," p. 137.

62 Edward Blake, a prominent member of the Liberal Party, reminded the House that the federal government had "exclusive jurisdiction over both bankruptcy and insolvency." Commons Debates, 9 June 1869, 680 (Blake).

63 *Ibid.*, 2 May 1872, 282 (Houde); *ibid.*, 5 May 1879, 1769 (Girouard).

64 John A. Macdonald to C. Cameron (31 May 1868) in Macdonald Papers (vol 11, file 786, reel C-26).

65 Commons Debates, 5 May 1879, 1779 (Vallee). "Insolvent Act and Amendments," *Journal of Commerce* 6:8 (12 April 1878) 239.

66 D. Girouard, "Le droit constitutionnel du Canada" (1871) 1:2 RCLJ 189, 263, p. 272.

67 *Jones v Kinney*, p. 718; *Ex parte Bejeau* (1874), 15 NBR 200 (SC); *Crombie v Jackson* (1874), 34 UCQB 575; *Kinney, Assignee v Dudman* (1876), 11 NSR 19 (CA); *Re Frederick B.K. Marter* (1882), 15 NSR 412 (CA); *Re Barrett; Vanwart v Shepherd* (1878), 18 NBR 225 (SC).

68 *Re Perks* (1870), 13 NBR 120, p. 126 (SC).

69 *Re Barrett*, p. 210; *Crombie v Jackson*, p. 579.
70 *Kinney, Assignee v Dudman* (1876), 11 NSR 19, p. 26 (CA). See also *Vassie v Vassie* (1882), 22 NBR 76 (SC (Eq App)) in which the plaintiff alleges that the bankruptcy statute was *ultra vires*.
71 *Cushing v Dupuy* (1880), 5 AC 409, pp. 415, 416 (PC).
72 *Shields v Peak*, p. 589.
73 *McLeod v Wright*, paras 149–51 (SC (Eq App)), Wetmore J. See also *Robinson v Ellis and Carter* (1879), 19 NBR 6 (SC).
74 Commons Debates, 17 May 1872, 266 (Macdonald).
75 Commons Debates, 20 March 1875, 809 (DeCosmos). On pre-Confederation bankruptcy law in the colonies of British Columbia and Vancouver Island, see British Columbia 1865 ordinance, *An Ordinance to Amend the Law Relative to Bankruptcy and Insolvency in British Columbia*. See *Insolvent Act of 1875*, s 149. For Vancouver Island, see 1862 *An Act to Declare the Law Relative to Bankruptcy and Insolvency in Vancouver Island and its Dependencies*. See *Insolvent Act of 1875*, s 149.
76 Commons Debates, 20 March 1875, 809 (DeCosmos).
77 *Ibid.*, 5 May 1879, 1773 (Robertson).
78 *Ibid.*, 19 February 1880, 107 (Cameron); Senate Debates, 11 March 1880, 141 (Hope).
79 In Quebec, creditors could rely on the Code of Civil Procedure. See Duncan, *The Law and Practice of Bankruptcy* (Toronto: Carswell, 1922), p. 20. See also House of Commons, Select Committee, "Third Report," p. 8. See also Thomson, "Bankruptcy Legislation in Canada" (1894) 1:1 Barrister 29.
80 Oliver Mowat to Alexander Campbell (20 October 1879) in Alexander Campbell Papers, AO (M-22) [hereafter Alexander Campbell Papers]. See also "Incoming Correspondence, 1855–1892" in Alexander Campbell Fonds, Series F 23-1, AO (reel MS-10279) [hereafter Alexander Campbell Fonds].
81 Oliver Mowat to Alexander Campbell (20 October 1879) in Alexander Campbell Papers. See also "Incoming Correspondence, 1855–1892" in Alexander Campbell Fonds.
82 Oliver Mowat to Alexander Campbell (20 October 1879) in Alexander Campbell Papers.
83 British Empire League, *Canadian Insolvency Legislation: Report of Meeting of the League held on Wednesday, December 4th, 1895, including a statement by the Hon Sir Charles Tupper* (London, UK: Commerce Print, 1895).
84 The 1970 Study Committee on Bankruptcy and Insolvency Legislation suggests that the coincidence "appears not to be accidental." Canada, "Tassé Report," p. 14. The federal repeal bill was given Royal Assent on 1 April

1880. See British Columbia Law Reform Commission, *Report on Creditors' Relief Legislation: A New Approach* (Vancouver: BC Law Reform Commission, 1979) [hereafter BCLRC, *Creditors' Relief Legislation*] p. 6.

85 "The Creditors' Relief Act," *Journal of Commerce* 10:2 (27 February 1880) 47; "The Creditors' Relief Act," *Monetary Times* 13:36 (27 February 1880) 1019. Current secondary sources, however, point out that the Act was far from perfect and was not an effective replacement for a bankruptcy law. See Dunlop, *Creditor-Debtor Law in Canada*, p. 548; Ontario Law Reform Commission, *Report on the Enforcement of Judgment Debts and Related Matters*, part 5 (Toronto: Ministry of the Attorney General, 1983) [hereafter OLRC, *Enforcement of Judgment Debts*] p. 5.

86 Senate Debates, 10 March 1880, 124 (Campbell). "The Creditors' Relief Act," *Monetary Times* 13:36 (27 February 1880) 1019. See Editorial, (1880) 16 Can LJ (NS) 69.

87 British Empire League, *Canadian Insolvency Legislation.*

88 John D. Honsberger, "Philosophy and Design of Modern Fresh Start Policies: The Evolution of Canada's Legislative Policy" (1999) 37:1–2 Osgoode Hall LJ 171, p. 178.

89 Commons Debates, 19 February 1880, 104 (Colby). The *Monetary Times* reported on the possibility of an Ontario Law about one month before Colby's speech. *Monetary Times* 13:30 (16 January 1880) 839.

90 Senate Debates, 10 March 1880, 124 (Campbell). See "The Creditors' Relief Act 1880," *Journal of Commerce* 10:2 (27 February 1880) 47.

91 J. Murray Ferron, "The Bankruptcy Court and Administration in Ontario" (1990) 24:2 L Soc'y Gaz 130.

92 Commons Debates, 19 February 1880, 108 (McCuaig); 109 (Weldon). The *BNA Act* deprived the provinces "of all authority to deal with insolvency; and as long as this doubt exists, appeals to the Supreme Court will unavoidably follow." *Ibid.*, 25 February 1880, 223 (McCuaig). See also Senate Debates, 10 March 1880, 125 (Scott); *ibid.*, 11 March 1880, 142 (Lewin). Lewin suggested that a year of litigation would be lost on the jurisdictional issue. The constitutionality of the Creditors' Relief Act was questioned as early as 1880. See "Creditors' Relief Act: Is it Constitutional?," *Monetary Times* 13:46 (7 May 1880) 1321.

Chapter 6

1 Enclosed in letter from S.G. Little, Dry Goods and Clothing Etc., to Wilfrid Laurier (16 May 1898) in Laurier Papers, LAC (MG 26-G) [hereafter Laurier Papers] (reel C-756, pp. 22341–2).

2 Although repeal took effect on 1 April 1880, the repeal statute, *An Act to repeal the Acts respecting Insolvency now in force in Canada*, SC 1880, c 1, s 1, provided that the Assignee was able to continue proceedings where the estate had vested in the Assignee prior to 1 April 1880. See *Clarkson v White* (1882), 4 OR 663, p. 671 (HCJ (Ch Div)).
3 Ferron, "Bankruptcy Court and Administration in Ontario," p. 131; Honsberger, "Bankruptcy Administration in the United States and Canada," p. 1529; Canada, "Tassé Report," pp. 15–16; Lewis Duncan, "The Operation and Effect of the Bankruptcy Act" (Address to the Toronto Bankers' Educational Association, 22 February 1922), (1922) 29:4 Journal of the Canadian Bankers' Association 502, p. 503; E Heaton, ed, *The Commercial Handbook of Canada of Interest to Traders Investors and Intending Settlers* (Toronto: 1905) pp. 31–2.
4 Sources that ignore this fact include Duncan, *Law and Practice of Bankruptcy*, p. 20; OLRC, *Report on the Enforcement of Judgment Debts*.
5 See list of bills 1880–1903 in the bibliography.
6 See e.g. Weaver & Rockman, eds, *Do Institutions Matter?* For an overview of historical literature in this area, see Ernst, "Law and American Political Development." See also Hansen, "Commercial Associations." On the capacity of the political system, see Robertson, "Politics and the Past." On the importance of state expertise, see Weaver & Rockman, "Assessing the Effects of Institutions," p. 32.
7 For a discussion of provincial legislation, see Duncan, *Law and Practice of Bankruptcy*, p. 21; Thomson, "Bankruptcy Legislation," p. 176.
8 The state of provincial legislation is summarized in a series of Department of Justice memoranda. See Department of Justice Papers (vol 2310, file 23/1902); *ibid.* (vol 2311, file 117/1902). See Charles Fitzpatrick, Minister of Justice, to Lord Strathcona, High Commissioner for Canada in London (30 January 1903) in Department of Justice Papers (vol 2310, file 23/1902); Charles Tupper in British Empire League, *Canadian Insolvency Legislation*, p. 6; Editorial, "Insolvency Legislation" (1899) 35:6 Can LJ 179, p. 180.
9 "The Confusions of Modern Insolvency Law," *Monetary Times* 16:9 (1 September 1882) 235; Commons Debates, 29 March 1882, 608 (Robertson, Hamilton).
10 "Insolvent Act Repeal," *Monetary Times* 12:46 (9 May 1879) 1389, 1390; "Creditors' Relief Act," *Monetary Times* 13:39 (19 March 1880) 1111; Thomson, "Proposed Bankruptcy Bill," p. 560.
11 For a discussion of this point from a modern perspective, see Jackson, *Logic and Limits of Bankruptcy Law*.

12 "Distribution of Insolvent Estates," *Journal of Commerce* 17:8 (12 October 1883) 240.
13 "Bankruptcy Laws," *Monetary Times* 15:40 (31 March 1882) 1206; "Bankruptcy Distribution," *Journal of Commerce* 16:10 (27 April 1883) 1165.
14 "Bankruptcy Distribution," *Journal of Commerce* 16:10 (27 April 1883) 1165; "No Insolvent Law," *Monetary Times* 13:45 (30 April 1880) 1293.
15 C.F. Fitzpatrick to Wilfrid Laurier (28 January 1903) [enclosure: "A Comparative View of English and Canadian Insolvency Legislation"] in Laurier Papers (reel 797, pp. 69605–19).
16 Commons Debates, 6 March 1883, 119 (White, Cardwell). One merchant wrote to Macdonald and claimed that it was unjust that one creditor may take all that "he can get and leave other creditors to take whatever they can get." Charles Julyan to John A. Macdonald (27 January 1884) in Macdonald Papers (reel C-1765, pp. 192552–5).
17 *The Creditors' Relief Act*, RSO 1880, c 10. "By a coincidence that appears not to be accidental, the *Bill to Repeal the Insolvency Acts* was read for the third time on 4 March 1880, while on 5 March 1880, assent was given, in Ontario, to '*An Act to Abolish Priorities Of and Amongst Execution Creditors*.'" Canada, "Tassé Report," p. 14.
18 On the prior regime of priority of executions and the new regime introduced by the Act, see *Re Assignments and Preferences Act, Section 9*, p. 501, MacLennan JA.
19 "Creditors' Relief Act," *Monetary Times* 13:39 (19 March 1880) 1111.
20 *Administration of Justice Act, 1884*, SO 1884, c 10, s 3 (Assented to 25 March 1884); Commons Debates, 5 May 1887, 283 (Edgar).
21 "What Law Instead of the Insolvent Act?," *Monetary Times* 13:42 (9 April 1880) 1201; "Without a Bankruptcy Law," *Monetary Times* 14:3 (16 July 1880) 67.
22 Quebec law was not in need of reform, as existing civil law provided for a distribution of the debtors' assets. In Quebec, creditors could rely on the Code of Civil Procedure. See Duncan, *Law and Practice of Bankruptcy*, p. 20; House of Commons, "Third Report," p. 8. See also Thomson, "Bankruptcy Legislation," p. 176.
23 Manitoba: *The Queen's Bench Act*, SM 1895, c 6; British Columbia: *Creditors' Relief Act, 1902*, SBC 1902, c 17; Nova Scotia: *Creditors' Relief Act*, SNS 1903, c 14; New Brunswick: *Creditors' Relief Act*, SNB 1902, c 3; Alberta: *Creditors' Relief Act*, SA 1910(2), c 4; NWT: *The Creditors' Relief Ordinance*, Ord No 25 1893. See OLRC, *Enforcement of Judgment Debts*, vol. 5, pp. 5–6. See also BCLRC, *Creditors' Relief Legislation*, p. 7.
24 "Bankruptcy Legislation," *Monetary Times* 18:43 (24 April 1885) 1199; see

also "Distribution of Insolvent Estates," *Journal of Commerce* 18:18 (2 May 1884) 600.

25 "Without a Bankruptcy Law," *Monetary Times* 14:3 (16 July 1880) 67; "Bankrupt Laws," *Monetary Times* 14:23 (3 December 1880) 639.

26 SO 1885, c 26. The Act was amended by *An Act to amend the Act Respecting Assignments for the Benefit of Creditors*, SO 1886, c 25; *An Act to make further provisions respecting Assignments for the Benefit of Creditors*, SO 1887, c 19 and consolidated as RSO 1887, c 124. Bicknell, "Advisability of Establishing a Bankruptcy Court in Canada," p. 40.

27 For a legislative history of this Act, see Edward Blake's argument before the Privy Council in *Ontario (AG) v Canada (AG)*, [1894] AC 189 (PC) p. 191; Melvin A. Springman et al., *Frauds on Creditors: Fraudulent Conveyances and Preferences* (Toronto: Carswell, 1994) pp. 4-3–4-5. The pre-Confederation statutes were reported in the consolidation of the Ontario statutes in 1877. See *An Act Respecting the Fraudulent Preferences of Creditors by Persons in Insolvent Circumstances*, RSO 1877, c 118, and amended by *Administration of Justice Act, 1884*, SO 1884, c 10, s 3.

28 Canada, "Tassé Report," pp. 15–16; "Bankruptcy Legislation," *Monetary Times* 18:43 (24 April 1885) 119.

29 Duncan, *Law and Practice of Bankruptcy*, pp. 21–2.

30 Ontario: *An Act Respecting Assignments For the Benefit of Creditors*, SO 1885, c 26; Manitoba: c 45 (1885); Northwest Territories: No 49 (1888); British Columbia: c 12 (1890); New Brunswick: c 6 (1895); Nova Scotia: c 11 (1898); Prince Edward Island: c 4 (1898); Saskatchewan: c 25 (1906); Alberta: c 6 (1907). See Duncan, *Law and Practice of Bankruptcy*.

31 New Brunswick: c 6 (1895); Nova Scotia: c 11 (1898).

32 "Insolvency Legislation," *Journal of Commerce* 24:19 (13 May 1887) 1060; "Insolvency Legislation," *Journal of Commerce* 25:17 (28 October 1887) 802.

33 "Insolvency Legislation," *Journal of Commerce* 24:19 (13 May 1887) 1060.

34 See Sullivan, Warren & Westbrook, "Persistence of Local Legal Culture," p. 804. See discussion in chapter 4 on local legal culture.

35 "Creditors Relief Act," *Monetary Times* 13:40 (26 March 1880) 1144.

36 "Bankruptcy Legislation in Ontario," *Journal of Commerce* 22:13 (26 March 1886) 765; see also "Insolvency Legislation," *Journal of Commerce* 22:17 (23 April 1886) 1020 where the Journal pointed out that there was no means to secure control of a debtor's estate that was in danger of being dissipated.

37 "A Specimen – But Not a Model Estate," *Monetary Times* 22:16 (19 October 1888) 448.

38 Jacobs, "Canadian Bankruptcy Act: Is it A Necessity?," pp. 605–6. See e.g. "Resolution re Insolvency Law," British Columbia Board of Trade to

Secretary of State (4 January 1888) in Department of Justice Papers (vol 1870, file 1888-45).

39 See list of bills 1880–1903 in bibliography.

40 See Lester, *Victorian Insolvency*, pp. 207–13, 221, 304 (discussing the role of the civil service).

41 See R.C.B. Risk, "Lawyers, Courts, and the Rise of the Regulatory State" (1984) 9:1 Dal LJ 31, p. 33.

42 Commons Debates, 6 March 1883, 121 (Casey). See also "Insolvent Estates," *Journal of Commerce* 11:9 (15 October 1880) 276 (urging the government to have its own policy rather than allow private members to introduce bills).

43 "Insolvent Estates," *Journal of Commerce* 11:19 (15 October 1880) 276.

44 B. Russell, "Provisions of the British North America Act for Uniformity of Provincial Laws" (1898) 34:14 Can LJ (NS) 513, p. 525.

45 Biz, "Insolvency Legislation," Letter to the Editor (9 February 1883), *Monetary Times* 16:33 (16 February 1883) 907. See also J. Ponsonby Sexton, Barrister of the Province of Québec & I.H. Pignolet, Counsellor at Law of the State of New York and Barrister of Québec, to John A. Macdonald (12 April 1883) [enclosure: Outline of Proposed Bankruptcy Act] in Department of Justice Papers (vol 56, file 1883-701).

46 Thomson, "Proposed Bankruptcy Bill," p. 560. For further details of the united Board of Trade Bill, see Editorial, "The Proposed Bankruptcy Bill" (1884) 4:2 Can LT 62. The Montreal Board of Trade issued a circular calling upon other local Boards to express their views on an Insolvency Act. Further, the Toronto Board of Trade referred the matter to its new Council. See "Insolvency," *Monetary Times* 16:31 (2 February 1883) 851–2; "Insolvency Legislation," *Monetary Times* 17:15 (12 October 1883) 405.

47 "Insolvency Legislation," *Journal of Commerce* 15:26 (9 February 1883) 810. The paper reported that those who were favourable to the discharge were inclined to make it conditional upon the payment of fifty cents on the dollar.

48 E.B. Greenshields, President of Montreal Board of Trade, Letter to the Editor (11 January 1893) in "Bankruptcy Legislation," *Journal of Commerce* 36:3 (20 January 1893) 101; J. Cauchon, Tillsonburg Board of Trade, to John A. Macdonald (3 March 1885) in Macdonald Papers (reel C-1770, pp. 199648–50).

49 "Insolvency Legislation," *Journal of Commerce* 10:14 (21 May 1880) 422.

50 "Insolvency," *Monetary Times* 16:31 (2 February 1883) 851.

51 "Distribution of Insolvent Estates," *Journal of Commerce* 16:12 (11 May 1883) 1233; "Bankruptcy Legislation," *Daily Globe* (3 January 1884) 4.

52 The bill was later reintroduced in 1883, 1884 and 1885. Bill C-136, *An Act for the equitable distribution of Insolvents' Estates*, 4th Sess, 4th Parl, 1882; Bill C-9, *An Act to provide for the equitable distribution of Insolvents' Estates*, 1st Sess, 5th Parl, 1883; Bill C-79, *An Act for the equitable distribution of Insolvents' Estates*, 2nd Sess, 5th Parl, 1884; Bill C-33, *An Act for the equitable distribution of Insolvents' Estates*, 3rd Sess, 5th Parl, 1885.

53 Commons Debates, 29 March 1882, 607 (Beaty). The bill as presented in 1883 provided that assets were to be distributed on a *pari passu* basis (s 27(3)) and prohibited fraudulent preferences (s 73).

54 Commons Debates, 29 March 1882, 607 (Beaty). Not all accepted the exclusion of the discharge. A copy of Mr Beaty's bill found in the Macdonald Papers include this handwritten notation: "This Act makes no provision for the discharge of the debtor ... No Act of the kind should pass without such a provision." Copy of Bill C-9, 1883 [with handwritten markings] in Macdonald Papers (reel C-1487, no 11012) p. 1.

55 The Montreal Board of Trade had, as early as 1882, passed a formal resolution that deplored the absence of a law for distributing insolvent estates. "Concerning a Bankrupt Law," *Monetary Times* 15:41 (7 April 1882) 240. "Insolvency," *Monetary Times* 16:38 (16 March 1883) 1063; H.W. Darling, President of Toronto Board of Trade, Letter to the Editor (24 March 1883), *Monetary Times* 16:39 (30 March 1883) 1095; "Insolvent Estates," *Journal of Commerce* 16:4 (16 March 1883) 972. The Montreal bill was introduced into the House of Commons in 1883 and again in 1884. Bill C-99 (1883); Bill C-71 (1884). The Toronto Board of Trade bill was never introduced in Parliament. See Toronto Board of Trade, *An Act to Provide for the Equitable Distribution of Insolvent Debtors' Estates, Prepared in Compliance with a Resolution passed by the Board of Trade of the City of Toronto* (Toronto: June 1883).

56 See "Insolvency Legislation," *Journal of Commerce* 18:3 (18 January 1884) 80.

57 "Insolvency Legislation," *Monetary Times* 17:18 (2 November 1883) 488; "Insolvency Legislation," *Journal of Commerce* 17:19 (28 December 1883) 608; *Monetary Times* 18:25 (18 December 1884) 696.

58 Bill C-4, *An Act to provide for the distribution of the Assets of Insolvent Debtors*, 3rd Sess, 5th Parl, 1885. The Toronto Board of Trade joined with other boards to pressure the government to enact a federal bankruptcy Act. See G.H. Stanford, *To Serve the Community: The Story of Toronto's Board of Trade* (Toronto: University of Toronto Press, 1975) p. 43; Kenneth McKenzie, President, Winnipeg Board of Trade, to John A. Macdonald (24 March 1885) in Macdonald Papers (reel C-1565, p. 61874).

59 Thomson, "Proposed Bankruptcy Bill"; Editorial, "Proposed Bankruptcy Bill."

60 Sir John A. Macdonald to Messrs Senton & Pignolet (20 February 1885) in Macdonald Papers (vol 23, reel C-34, no 116); "Bankruptcy Legislation," *Monetary Times* 18:38 (20 March 1885) 1058.
61 Commons Debates, 5 May 1887, 288–9 (Curran). See Bill C-4 as reported out of the Select Committee, *An Act to provide for the distribution of the assets of Insolvent Debtors*, 3rd Sess, 5th Parl (1885), s 44.
62 "Montreal Board of Trade Council Annual Reports: 44th Annual Report, 1888" in Montreal Board of Trade Papers (reel M-2804, p. 14).
63 Montreal Board of Trade to John A. Macdonald (30 March 1885) in Macdonald Papers (reel C-1770, no 200056); petition from a series of Quebec Banks (30 March 1885) in Macdonald Papers (reel C-1497, no 11073); Winnipeg Board of Trade to John A. Macdonald (24 March 1885) in Macdonald Papers (reel C-1565, no 61874). The Montreal Board of Trade sent a deputation to Ottawa to urge that the Committee Bill become a government measure. See "Insolvency Legislation," *Journal of Commerce* 20:13 (27 March 1885) 448.
64 Bill C-4 was also reintroduced in 1886 as Bill C-93, *An Act to provide for the distribution of the assets of Insolvent Debtors*, 4th Sess, 5th Parl, 1886. Bill C-93 was not debated in 1886. Commons Debates, 22 April 1885, 1280. Other bills were also introduced in 1885. An additional proposal was also introduced in 1885. See Bill C-32, *An Act respecting Insolvency*, 3rd Sess, 5th Parl, 1885. Bill C-32 also included a discharge provision, but it was not debated.
65 Petition of the Toronto Board of Trade to the Dominion of Canada in Parliament (7 March 1888) in Macdonald Papers (reel C-1566, p. 63195); John A. Macdonald's Office to W.B. Snetsinger (3 May 1890) in Macdonald Papers (vol 27-A, reel C-36, no 92).
66 Abbott, *Insolvent Act of 1864*. On Abbott, see Miller, "Sir John Joseph Caldwell Abbott," <http://www.biographi.ca/en/bio/abbott_john_joseph_caldwell_12E.html>; Hutchison, "Sir John J.C. Abbott," p. 944.
67 See "An Insolvency Act Wanted," *Monetary Times* 27:18 (3 November 1893) 543.
68 Following the death of Macdonald, the Conservatives changed leaders four times. Their leadership problems may have contributed to the failure of government reform: John Abbott 1891–2; John Thompson 1892–94; Mackenzie Bowell 1894–6; Charles Tupper 1896. Shortly after relinquishing the leadership to John Thompson, John Abbott died on 24 November 1892, leaving the Conservatives without essential leadership on this issue.
69 "An Insolvency Act Wanted," *Monetary Times* 27:18 (3 November 1893) 543; "Third Annual Meeting of the Association (26, 27 July 1894)" (1894)

2:1 Journal of the Canadian Bankers' Association 5; Editorial "Insolvency Legislation" (1898) 5:4 Journal of the Canadian Bankers' Association 437; Lash address to the Canadian Bankers' Association in "Proceedings of the Third Annual Meeting of the Association (26, 27 July 1894)" (1894) 2:1 Journal of the Canadian Bankers' Association 23.

70 Senate Debates, 19 March 1894, 4.

71 *Ibid.*, 18 April 1894, 248 (Bowell); W.M. Proudfoot, "An Insolvent Law," Note, (1894) 14:12 Can LT 305, p. 306.

72 Charles Tupper in British Empire League, *Canadian Insolvency Legislation*, p. 5. The Reports of the Senate Committee were located but they contain no minutes of evidence or list of witnesses. Bill C-152, *An Act Respecting Insolvency*, 4th Sess, 7th Parl, 1898. On the role of Boards of Trade, see Stanford, *To Serve the Community*.

73 Bill S-C, *An Act respecting Insolvency*, 4th Sess, 7th Parl (1894); "An Insolvency Act," *Monetary Times* 27:32 (9 February 1894) 990; Thomson, "Bankruptcy Legislation in Canada," p. 176.

74 Senate Debates, 14 June 1894, 556 (Power).

75 See *ibid.*, 30 April 1895, 108 (Bowell); Charles Tupper in British Empire League, *Canadian Insolvency Legislation*, p. 5.

76 See Charles Tupper in British Empire League, *Canadian Insolvency Legislation*, pp. 5, 6. See also "An Insolvency Law for Canada" in Laurier Papers (reel C-752, no 18052). See also "Proceedings of the Seventh Annual Meeting of the Canadian Bankers' Association (26, 27 October 1898)" (1899) 6:2 Journal of the Canadian Bankers' Association 103, p. 107.

77 Imperial Bank of Canada to John A. Macdonald (2 June 1880) in Macdonald Papers (reel C-1749, no 171099); Imperial Bank of Canada to John A. Macdonald (5 May 1879) in Macdonald Papers (reel C-1716, no 465219). See Petition from a series of Quebec Banks (30 March 1885) in Macdonald Papers (reel C-1497, no 11073).

78 "Report of the Proceedings of the First Annual Meeting (19 May 1892)" (1892) 1 Journal of the Canadian Bankers' Association 309, p. 311.

79 Banks insisted upon ranking for the full amounts of all notes that they held, which would mean that in the majority of cases the banks would be paid in full, to the exclusion of other debtors. "Montreal Board of Trade Council Reports, Annual Report 1894" in Montreal Board of Trade Papers (reel M-2804, p. 20); Lash address to the Canadian Bankers' Association, (1894) 2:1 Journal of the Canadian Bankers' Association 23, p. 26.

80 "Proceedings of the Third Annual Meeting of the Canadian Bankers' Association (26, 27 July 1894)" (1894) 2:1 Journal of the Canadian Bankers' Association 5, pp. 50–1.

81 The 1895 bill was introduced in the Senate as Bill S-A, *An Act respecting Insolvency*, 5th Sess, 7th Parl, 1895. See Charles Tupper in British Empire League, *Canadian Insolvency Legislation*, p. 5; "Proceedings of the Fourth Annual Meeting of the Canadian Bankers' Association (11, 12 September 1895)" (1895) 3:1 Journal of the Canadian Bankers' Association 15, pp. 18–19. See also "Report of the Quebec Board of Trade on the Insolvency Bill of 1894 for the Dominion" (24 November 1897) in Department of Trade and Commerce Papers, LAC (RG 20-A-1, vol 1191, p. 6).

82 See Senate Debates, 29 May 1895, 164; Charles Tupper in British Empire League, *Canadian Insolvency Legislation*, p. 6.

83 See e.g. Montreal Board of Trade Council Annual Reports, Annual Reports 1896, 1897, 1898, 1899, 1900, 1901 which all contain resolutions urging federal reform. Montreal Board of Trade Papers (reels 2804, 2805). For a general discussion of the 1898 and 1903 bills, see Jacobs, "Canadian Bankruptcy Act."

84 For details of the proposed meeting, see "Insolvency Legislation," *Monetary Times* 31:28 (7 January 1898).

85 All following correspondence is directed to Wilfrid Laurier and can be found in Laurier Papers. See e.g. Auer Incandescent Light Mfg Co (11 September 1896), (reel C-742, no 6905); Vancouver Board of Trade (11 November 1897), (reel C-751, no 17837); Soclean Chemical Co (9 August 1907), (reel C-850, no 127611); Christie and Co (17 February 1906), (reel C-850, no 107231); Montreal Board of Trade (7 January 1897), (reel C-752, no 18593); Resolution of Prince Albert Board of Trade (15 April 1898), (reel C-756).

86 "An Insolvency Act," *Monetary Times* 31:32 (4 February 1898) 1024.

87 Montreal Board of Trade to Wilfrid Laurier (10 March 1897) in Laurier Papers (reel C-752, p. 18597).

88 See Bill C-84, *An Act respecting Insolvency*, 1898; Commons Debates, 17 March 1898, 2004; Montreal Board of Trade Council Annual Reports, Annual Report 1898 in Montreal Board of Trade Papers (reel 2804, pp. 49–50). See also Fortin to Laurier (13 May 1899) in Laurier Papers (reel C-765, no 33524).

89 Commons Debates, 17 March 1898, 2008 (Fortin reading from letter of Montreal Board of Trade).

90 Bill C-84, *An Act respecting Insolvency*, 3rd Sess, 1898, cls 27–34, 3.

91 See discussion of this point in chapter 4. See also *Bankruptcy Act of 1919*, s 8. See Ben-Ishai & Torrie, "Farm Insolvency in Canada."

92 Bill C-84, *An Act respecting Insolvency*, 1898, cl 38; Commons Debates, 17 March 1898, 2014 (Fortin).

93 Bill C-84, *An Act respecting Insolvency*, 1898, cl 113. Commons Debates,

17 March 1898, 2019 (Fortin). This section has been continued into Canada's modern-day legislation. *Bankruptcy and Insolvency Act*, s 212. See "Proceedings of the Seventh Annual Meeting of the Canadian Bankers' Association (26, 27 October 1898), p. 107.

94 Thomas Fortin to Wilfrid Laurier (12 May 1899) in Laurier Papers (reel C-765, nos 33487, 33524-6); Commons Debates, 17 March 1898, 49 (Laurier). On the lack of progress on the bill, see Russell, "Provisions of the British North America Act," p. 523.

95 See Bill C-53, *An Act respecting Insolvency*, 3rd Sess, 9th Parl (1903).

96 Commons Debates, 18 May 1903, 3248 (Laurier).

97 See e.g. resolution cited in "Equitable Insolvency Laws," *Monetary Times* 36:2 (11 July 1902) 47; "Canadian Insolvency Law," *Monetary Times* 36:7 (15 August 1902) 208; Resolution of the Canadian Manufacturers' Association (18 April 1899) in Laurier Papers (reel C-765, no 33017); Representative of the Toronto Board of Trade to Wilfrid Laurier (25 March 1900) in Laurier Papers (reel C-774, no 43391).

98 Wilfrid Laurier to James Crowe, Erie, PA (21 December 1909) in Laurier Papers (reel C-884, p 163913). See chapter 1.

99 While no bills were introduced, some groups did not give up the fight: see Montreal Board of Trade to Wilfrid Laurier (8 March 1904) in Laurier Papers (reel C-809, no 83171); Montreal Chamber of Commerce to Wilfrid Laurier (21 March 1905) in Laurier Papers (reel C-821, no 95879).

100 Tabb, "Century of Regress or Progress?," p. 354 (describing a similar failure of the United States to enact a national bankruptcy law after the repeal of the *Bankruptcy Act* of 1867).

101 Skeel, *Debt's Dominion*, p. 28.

102 Skeel relies upon Kenneth Arrow, *Social Choice and Individual Value* (New York: John Wiley, 1951). See Skeel, *Debt's Dominion*, pp. 29–30.

103 Bankruptcy, relying upon provincial legislation for a distribution scheme, has been eliminated for purposes of discussion.

104 Skeel, *Debt's Dominion*, p. 30.

Chapter 7

1 See Thomas GW Telfer, "A Canadian 'World Without Bankruptcy Law': The Failure of Bankruptcy Reform at the End of the Nineteenth Century" (2004) 8:1 Austl J Leg Hist 83.

2 "Bankruptcy," *Journal of Commerce* 30:11 (14 March 1890) 592: "The Dominion government has practically abandoned one of its chief prerogatives to the provinces."

3 "Faulty Insolvency Legislation," *Journal of Commerce* 28:16 (19 April 1889) 655; "Faulty Insolvency Legislation II," *Journal of Commerce* 28:17 (26 April 1889) 693.

4 "Federal Insolvency Legislation," *Monetary Times* 39:15 (6 October 1905) 429–30; "Bankrupt Laws," *Monetary Times* 14:23 (3 December 1880) 640; Commons Debates, 17 March 1898, 2024 (Monk). See also "Insolvency," *Monetary Times*, 16:29 (19 January 1883) 795.

5 Ramsay Cook, *Provincial Autonomy, Minority Rights and the Compact Theory, 1867–1921* (Ottawa: Queen's Printer, 1969) p. 1; R.C.B. Risk, "Canadian Courts Under the Influence" (1990) 40:4 UTLJ 687, p. 696; Paul Romney, *Mr Attorney: The Attorney General for Ontario in Court, Cabinet, and Legislature, 1791–1899* (Toronto: University of Toronto Press, 1986) pp. 242–55; Risk & Vipond, "Rights Talk"; William Lahey, "Constitutional Adjudication, Provincial Rights, and the Structure of Legal Thought in Late Nineteenth-Century New Brunswick" (1990) 39 UNBLJ 185. See e.g. *Lenoir v Ritchie* (1879), 3 SCR 575; *Canada (AG) v Ontario (AG)*, [1898] AC 247 (PC); *Maritime Bank of Canada (Liquidators of) v New Brunswick (Receiver General of)*, [1892] AC 437 (PC); *Russell v R* (1882), 7 AC 829 (PC); *Hodge v R* (1883), 9 AC 117 (PC); *Ontario (AG) v Canada (AG)*, [1896] AC 348 (PC) [*Local Prohibition Reference*]; *Ontario (AG) v Mercer* (1883), 8 AC 767 (PC).

6 John A. Macdonald to W.J. Patterson, Montreal Board of Trade (24 February 1882) in Macdonald Papers (vol 21, reel C-33, nos 664–6); Commons Debates, 6 March 1883, 119 (John A. Macdonald, Prime Minister).

7 See a report of the meeting in "Insolvency Legislation," *Journal of Commerce* 19:9 (29 August 1884) 308; "Sir John A. Macdonald on Canadian Commercial Relations," *Times* (London, UK) [nd] in Macdonald Papers (file dated 28 November 1884), (vol 165, reel 1569, nos 67380–1).

8 Under the *BNA Act*, disallowance is, in the words of Vipond, "a sweeping veto power which gives the federal government the unqualified right to strike down or nullify any act of a provincial legislature within one year of its passage." Robert C. Vipond, *Liberty & Community: Canadian Federalism and the Failure of the Constitution* (Albany: State University of New York Press, 1991) p. 114. See e.g. "Report of the Honourable the Minister of Justice, approved by His Excellency the Governor General in Council on the 24th March, 1881" in W.E. Hodgins, *Dominion and Provincial Legislation: 1867–1895* (Ottawa: Government Printing Bureau, 1896) 170.

9 "Report of the Honourable the Minister of Justice, approved by His Excellency the Governor General in Council on the 6th March, 1886" in Hodgins, *Dominion and Provincial Legislation* 198, p. 199.

10 "Report of the Honourable the Minister of Justice, approved by His Excel-

lency the Governor General in Council on the 25th April, 1887" in Hodgins, *Dominion and Provincial Legislation* 853, p. 854. See "Report of the Minister of Justice, 6th March, 1886"; "Report of the Honourable the Minister of Justice approved by His Excellency the Governor General in Council on the 4th April, 1885" in Hodgins, *Dominion and Provincial Legislation* 522.

11 The 1887 conference adopted a series of resolutions on provincial grievances against Ottawa, including resolutions on the provincial view of sovereignty and disallowance. See Cook, *Provincial Autonomy*, pp. 41–4. See also Romney, *Mr Attorney*, p. 257.

12 Resolution 14, Premiers Conference Quebec as reported in Montreal Board of Trade Council Annual Reports, 45th Annual Report, Montreal Board of Trade Papers (reel M-2804, p. 13).

13 *Crombie v Jackson*; *Kinney, Assignee v Dudman*; *Rumsey v Hare*; *Ex Parte Ellis* (1878), 17 NBR 593 (CA); *Re Killam* (1878) 14 Can LJ (NS) 242 (Yarmouth County Court).

14 *Cushing v Dupuy*, pp. 415–16.

15 See e.g. *Clarkson v Ontario Bank* (1887), 13 OR 666 (Ch).

16 A.H.F. Lefroy, "The Privy Council on Bankruptcy" (1894) 30:6 Can LJ (NS) 182, p. 186.

17 See Commons Debates, 4 May 1887, 272–3 (Thompson; Edgar).

18 *Clarkson v Ontario Bank* (CA); *Edgar v Central Bank of Canada* (1888), 15 OAR 193; *Kennedy v Freeman* (1888), 15 OAR 216; *Hunter v Drummond* (1888), 15 OAR 232. For a discussion of these cases, see "Is the Act Respecting Assignments for Creditors Constitutional?," *Monetary Times* 21:40 (30 March 1888) 1221.

19 *Edgar v Central Bank of Canada*, p. 204.

20 See Duncan, *Law and Practice of Bankruptcy*, pp. 21–2; and an eloquent description of the statute by Master Dalton in *Union Bank v Neville*, p. 154.

21 "Is the Act Respecting Assignments for Creditors Constitutional?," *Monetary Times* 21:40 (30 March 1888) 1221.

22 *Clarkson v Ontario Bank*, p. 193 (CA).

23 "The Creditors' Relief Act," *Monetary Times* 21:45 (4 May 1888) 1365; "A General Insolvency Act," *Journal of Commerce* 33:1 (3 July 1891) 17, p. 18; E.D. Armour, "The Constitution of Canada: III," Note, (1891) 11:10 Can LT 233, p. 244. See also "The Creditors' Relief Act: Is it Constitutional?," *Monetary Times* 13:46 (7 May 1880) 1321.

24 "Report of the Honourable the Minister of Justice, approved by His Excellency the Governor General in Council on the 7th June, 1888" in Hodgins, *Dominion and Provincial Legislation* 204, p. 205. The constitutionality of provincial legislation was also being tested in Manitoba, where the Manitoba

Court of Appeal upheld the validity of the Manitoba assignments legislation: *Stephens v McArthur* (1890), 6 Man LR 496 (CA); Bohémier, *La faillite*, p. 111.

25 "A General Insolvency Act," *Journal of Commerce* 33:1 (3 July 1891) 17; " Assignments for the Benefit of Creditors," *Monetary Times* 27:8 (25 August 1893). Bohémier, *La faillite*, p. 113.

26 *Re Assignments and Preferences Act, Section 9*, pp. 489, 498.

27 Editorial, "The Assignments Act" (1893) 13:5 Can LT 125.

28 Letter (12 May 1893) in Department of Justice Files (vol 2374, file 198/1893).

29 Attorney-General of Ontario to Mr Christopher Robinson (3 November 1893) in Department of Justice Files (vol 2374, file 198/1893).

30 See John T. Saywell, *The Lawmakers: Judicial Power and the Shaping of Canadian Federalism* (Toronto: University of Toronto Press, 2002) p. 130.

31 Lefroy, "Privy Council on Bankruptcy."

32 For constitutional scholars, the stakes may have been limited to the issue of federalism. See R.C.B. Risk, "Constitutional Scholarship in the Late Nineteenth Century: Making Federalism Work" (1996) 46:3 UTLJ 427, p. 449.

33 G. Blaine Baker, "The Province of Post-Confederation Rights" (1995) 45:1 UTLJ 77, p. 86.

34 Vipond, *Liberty and Community*, p. 51. Blake argued some of the major constitutional cases of the late nineteenth century.

35 *The Insolvency Case in the Privy Council, Argument of Mr Blake for the Appellant* (Toronto: Bryant Press, 1894) in Blake Papers, AO (MV 266-C-2) [hereafter Blake Papers] (box 128, env 35).

36 *Cushing v Dupuy*, pp. 415–16.

37 *The Insolvency Case in the Privy Council, Argument of Mr Blake for the Appellant* (Toronto: Bryant Press, 1894) in Blake Papers (box 128, env 35) pp. 20–1.

38 *Ibid.*, pp. 8, 20.

39 *Ibid.*, pp. 4, 5. Blake did not mention the numerous federal private Member's bills that had been debated throughout the 1880s and early 1890s. Nor did Blake note that a year earlier, Prime Minister Abbott had announced a new government initiative.

40 *Ibid.*, p. 11.

41 *Ibid.*, p. 16.

42 *Ontario (AG) v Canada (AG)*, pp. 200–1.

43 Hogg argues that the Privy Council was "explicitly influenced by the absence of any federal legislation." Peter W Hogg, *Constitutional Law of Canada*, loose-leaf (consulted on 5 July 2013), 5th ed (Toronto: Carswell,

2007) vol 1, p. 25-14. See also Saywell, *Lawmakers*, p. 130: Privy Council "was undoubtedly influenced by the absence of federal legislation."

44 *Ontario (AG) v Canada (AG)*, p. 201.

45 Lefroy, "The Privy Council on Bankruptcy," pp. 190, 193.

46 Bill S-C, *An Act respecting Insolvency*, 4th Sess, 7th Parl, 1894.

47 Senate Debates, 3 April 1894, 97 (Bowell in response to Gowan); *ibid.*, 17 April 1894, 246–7 (Scott); *ibid.*, 233 (Dickey).

48 British Empire League, *Canadian Insolvency Legislation*, p. 5.

49 Senate Debates, 3 April 1894, 239 (McClelan).

50 *Ibid.*, 29 May 1895, 151 (McClelan).

51 British Empire League, *Canadian Insolvency Legislation*, p. 5.

52 See New Brunswick: c 6 (1895); Nova Scotia: c 11 (1898).

53 Department of Justice Papers (vol 2310, file 23/1902).

54 W.S. Fielding to Charles Fitzpatrick (19 February 1902) in Department of Justice Papers (vol 2311, file 117/1902).

55 "Address of the President of the Canadian Bankers' Association: Delivered at the Eighth Annual Meeting of the Canadian Bankers' Association" (1900) 7:2 Journal of the Canadian Bankers' Association 109, p. 112.

56 Commons Debates, 17 March 1898, 2032 (Laurier). See *ibid.*, 1 April 1898, 2928 (Cartwright). In 1899, Laurier refused to move on federal reform, as progress had been made in Nova Scotia and New Brunswick. See *ibid.*, 17 May 1899, 3253 (Laurier).

57 *Ibid.*, 18 May 1903, 3248 (Laurier).

Chapter 8

1 The conflict between local and distant creditors is explored in US literature. See Freyer, *Producers versus Capitalists*, pp. 9, 11, 21, 38, 85–7 (exploring the conflict between the local "associational economy" and corporate and mercantile enterprises tied more directly into the national market).

2 For a discussion of the US experience and the problem of preferential payments to local and family creditors, see Balleisen, *Navigating Failure*, pp. 90–4; Tabb, "Century of Regress or Progress?," p. 357 (national law neutralized advantages of creditors receiving preferential payments); Skeel, *Debt's Dominion*, p. 36; Mann, *Republic of Debtors*, pp. 34, 48–9.

3 Commons Debates, 18 April 1894, 246 (Vidal).

4 *Ibid.*, 17 April 1894, 238 (Lougheed).

5 *Ibid.*, 12 June 1894, 507 (Sanford). The *Journal of Commerce* recognized in 1887 that "business transactions are carried on by creditors who trade in all the different Provinces, and who ought to be protected by the operation of a law dealing with insolvents, uniform in its operation throughout the

Dominion." "Insolvency Legislation," *Journal of Commerce* 24:19 (13 May 1887) 1060.

6 Senate Debates, 12 June 1894, 514 (Ferguson); see also Editorial, "Insolvency Legislation" (1899) 35:6 Can LJ (NS) 179, p. 180.

7 David Monod, *Store Wars: Shopkeepers and the Culture of Mass Marketing, 1890–1939* (Toronto: University of Toronto Press, 1996) pp. 103, 116, 124; Drummond, *Progress Without Planning*, p. 278.

8 Canadian Manufacturers Association to Wilfrid Laurier (10 March 1900) in Laurier Papers (reel C-774, p. 43210).

9 Taylor & Baskerville, *A Concise History of Business in Canada*, p. 314; Monod, *Store Wars*, pp. 99–101.

10 Monod, *Store Wars*, p. 99.

11 Vipond draws parallels between the desire for regional diversity and the issue of Home Rule. See Vipond, *Liberty and Community*, p. 90; Bliss, *Northern Enterprise*, pp. 286–7.

12 "Report of a Committee of the Winnipeg Board of Trade on a Draft of an Insolvent Act submitted by the Montreal Board" (1892) in Department of Justice Papers (vol 1879, file 438/1892).

13 Population of Canada, 1871–1921 (Millions)

Year	Urban	Rural
1871	0.7	3.0
1881	1.1	3.2
1891	1.5	3.3
1901	2.0	3.4
1911	3.3	3.9
1921	4.4	4.4

Pomfret, *Economic Development of Canada*, p. 53.

14 Commons Debates, 29 March 1882, 608 (Shaw).

15 "Sir John A. Macdonald on Canadian Commercial Relations," *Times* (London, UK) [nd] in Macdonald Papers (file dated 28 November 1884), (vol 165, reel 1569, nos 67380–1). It was pointed out to Macdonald in an 1885 letter that the unanimous resolution of the Tillsonburg Board of Trade against the re-enactment of a bankruptcy law corroborated Macdonald's statement to the English press that rural constituencies were against a bankruptcy law. See Sinclair to John A. Macdonald (5 March 1885) and H.J. Caulfield to John A. Macdonald (3 March 1885) in Macdonald Papers (vol 413, pt 1, reel C-1770, nos 199648–51).

16 "Sir John A. Macdonald on Canadian Commercial Relations," *Times* [nd] in Macdonald Papers (file dated 28 November 1884), (vol 165, reel 1569, nos 67380–1); "The Insolvent Bill," *Journal of Commerce* 20:15 (10 April 1885) 523. Rural opposition to the discharge also surfaced in the debates in 1887. See Commons Debates, 5 May 1887, 290 (Dupont).
17 Anonymous, "The Reason Explained: The Seeming Apathy and indifference to the Insolvent Debtor's Act, complained of by John Macdonald" (1885) in Macdonald Papers (reel C-1565, p. 61873).
18 Charles Julyan to John A. Macdonald (27 January 1884) in Macdonald Papers (reel C-1765, pp. 192552–5); Auer Incandescent Light Mfg Co, Toronto, to Wilfrid Laurier (11 September 1896) in Laurier Papers (reel C-742, pp. 6905–7).
19 "Bankruptcy Legislation," *Journal of Commerce* 36:3 (20 January 1893) 95.
20 *Ibid.*
21 *Ibid.*
22 *Ibid.*
23 "Insolvency Legislation," *Monetary Times* 31:20 (12 November 1897) 630; "Sir John A. Macdonald on Canadian Commercial Relations," *Times* [nd] in Macdonald Papers (file dated 28 November 1884), (vol 165, reel 1569, nos 67380–1).
24 Montreal Board of Trade Council Annual Reports in Montreal Board of Trade Papers (reel M-2804, p. 15).
25 "Reform in Bankruptcy Laws," *Monetary Times* 31:20 (12 November 1897) 637. See R.T. Naylor, *The History of Canadian Business, 1867–1914*, vol 1 (Toronto: James Lorimer & Co, 1975) p. 82 (Naylor argues that British wholesale houses lost large sums after the repeal of the federal legislation); "Interesting Paper on the Subject of Insolvency," *Toronto Mail* (23 April 1881) 10 in Macdonald Papers (reel 10, no 11059).
26 Petition (22 June 1881) in Macdonald Papers (reel C-1497, no 11056); "Proposed Canadian Insolvency Legislation," *Monetary Times* 36:1 (4 July 1902) 15. See also Memorial from Trade Association of Manchester to Prime Minister Macdonald (16 May 1884) in Macdonald Papers (reel C-1497, nos 11004 and 11005); Incorporated Chamber of Commerce of Liverpool to John A. Macdonald (25 June 1881) in Macdonald Papers (reel C-1497, p. 11058).
27 See e.g. European Exporters' Association of Toronto to Prime Minister Laurier (17 May 1899) in Laurier Papers (reel C-765, no 33672).
28 Resolution of British Empire League, requesting a law abolishing preferences and providing for a *pro rata* distribution. British Empire League, *Canadian Insolvency Legislation*, p. 10; "Without an Insolvency Act," *Monetary*

Times 17:47 (23 May 1884) 1314. See also Montreal Board of Trade to Prime Minister Laurier (10 March 1899) in Laurier Papers (reel C-752, no 18597); *Monetary Times* 15:2 (8 July 1881) 42. Commons Debates, 6 February 1885, 47 (Macdonald). See also "Insolvency Legislation," *Journal of Commerce* 46:7 (18 February 1898) 242 (outlining the various efforts of English merchants).

29 Commons Debates, 6 February 1885, 47 (Macdonald).

30 J. Craven of the Home Trade Association of Manchester, to John A. Macdonald (16 May 1884) [enclosure: Petition of Trade Association] in Macdonald Papers (reel C-1497, pp. 11003–6).

31 Commons Debates, 6 February 1885, 47 (Macdonald); British Empire League, *Canadian Insolvency Legislation*, p. 7.

32 Commons Debates, 1 April 1898, 2926 (Tupper); *ibid.*, 18 May 1898, 3249 (Monk).

33 "Uniform Insolvency Legislation," *Journal of Commerce* 53:21 (22 November 1901) 2134; Lord Strathcona, Canadian High Commissioner in England to Charles Fitzpatrick, Minister of Justice (10 December 1902) in Department of Justice Papers (vol 2310, file 23/1902).

34 "Uniform Insolvency Legislation," *Journal of Commerce* 53:21 (22 November 1901) 2134.

35 Russell, "Provisions of the British North America Act," p. 524.

36 Charles Tupper in British Empire League, *Canadian Insolvency Legislation*, p. 10; William Lukes to John A. Macdonald (16 April 1885) in Macdonald Papers (reel C-1565, no 61889).

37 "Insolvency Legislation," *Journal of Commerce* 45:19 (5 November 1897) 712. Provincial diversity affected the ability of Canadian merchants to obtain credit from overseas. Commons Debates, 17 March 1898, 2020–2 (Fortin; Bourassa).

38 "Insolvency Legislation," *Journal of Commerce* 45:19 (5 November 1897) 712; William Lukes to John A. Macdonald (16 April 1885) in Macdonald Papers (reel C-1565, no 61889).

39 "Insolvency Legislation," *Journal of Commerce* 45:19 (5 November 1897) 712; "Sir John A. Macdonald on Canadian Commercial Relations," *Times* (London, UK) [nd] in Macdonald Papers (file dated 28 November 1884), (vol 165, reel 1569, nos 67380–1); see S. Hurley (UK) to John A. Macdonald (22 June 1884) [enclosure: Petition of UK Merchants to John A. Macdonald [nd]] in Macdonald Papers (reel C-1497, nos 11046–51).

40 Clarkson, *Bankruptcy Legislation*, pp. 8, 14; T.G. McMaster, "A Dominion Insolvency Act" (1899–1900) 7:2 Journal of the Canadian Bankers' Association 129, p. 133; "Bankruptcy Legislation," *Journal of Commerce* 35:26 (23 December 1892) 985.

41 Commons Debates, 17 March 1898, 2029 (Beausoleil); *ibid.*, 5 May 1887, 288 (Bechard); N.D. Snetsinger, Colborne, to John A. Macdonald (17 April 1890) in Macdonald Papers (reel C-1800, pp. 241636–8); Ryan and Son, Timber, Lumber, Logs, Toronto, to Wilfrid Laurier (8 November 1895) in Laurier Papers (reel C-740, pp. 3893–9); Christie & Co to Wilfrid Laurier (17 February 1906) in Laurier Papers (vol 403, reel C-850, no 107234).

42 JLF, Letter to the Editor (14 April 1883), *Monetary Times* 16:42 (20 April 1883) 1181. See also Commons Debates, 6 March 1883, 120.

43 Bliss notes that between 1880 and 1896 several hundred thousand Canadians migrated to the United States. See Bliss, *Northern Enterprise*, p. 287. This shift in population must be re-evaluated in light of the repeal of federal bankruptcy legislation.

44 Commons Debates, 29 March 1882, 608 (Gault); *ibid.*, 5 May 1887, 283 (Edgar); "Sir John A. Macdonald on Canadian Commercial Relations," *Times* (London, UK) [nd] in Macdonald Papers (file dated 28 November 1884), (vol 165, reel 1569, nos 67380–1); Ryan and Son, Timber, Lumber, Logs, Toronto, to Wilfrid Laurier (8 November 1895) in Laurier Papers (reel C-740, pp. 3893–9); Auer Incandescent Light Mfg Co, Toronto, to Wilfrid Laurier (11 September 1896) in Laurier Papers (reel C-742, pp. 6905–7).

45 Commons Debates, 5 May 1887, 283 (Edgar); JLF, Letter to the Editor, *Monetary Times* 16:32 (9 February 1883) 885; Christie & Co to Wilfrid Laurier (17 February 1906) in Laurier Papers (vol 403, reel C-850, no 107234). See also Soclean Chemical Co to Wilfrid Laurier (9 August 1907) in Laurier Papers (vol 470, reel C-850, no 127611), referring to the fact that many people were compelled to leave Canada following the bursting of the Toronto boom.

46 Senate Debates, 17 April 1894, 236 (Gowan); *ibid.* 19 June 1894, 593 (McCallum).

47 "The lack of any legal discharge for an old debt may prove an injustice towards new creditors." JLF, Letter to the Editor, *Monetary Times* 16:32 (9 February 1883) 885.

48 Editorial, "Insolvency Legislation" (1899) 35:6 Can LJ (NS) 179, p. 180; JLF, Letter to the Editor, *Monetary Times* 16:32 (9 February 1883) 885.

49 Toronto Board of Trade, *An Act to Provide for the Equitable Distribution of Insolvent Debtors' Estates.*

50 Clarkson, *Bankruptcy Legislation*, pp. 8, 14. The insurance of a discharge ensured that businessmen would be able to re-emerge from their debts and return to the world of commerce where they would make valuable contributions. The recognition of unfortunate circumstances was also addressed by McMaster, "Dominion Insolvency Act," p. 133.

51 Clarkson, *Bankruptcy Legislation*, pp. i, 4–8.

52 "Insolvency Laws," Thomas Ritchie, President Belleville Board of Trade, to John A. Macdonald (24 April 1880) in Macdonald Papers (reel C-1565, pp. 61893–5).

53 Thomas Ritchie, *Fallacy of Insolvency Laws and their Baneful Effects* (1885) pp. 8, 18–19.

54 Commons Debates, 5 May 1887, 287 (Bechard); *ibid.*, 29 May 1895, 155 (McDonald, Cape Breton); "That Insolvent Law: An Open Letter to Parliament Against its Reenactment: What Canada's Prosperity is Due To," *Toronto World* (10 April 1882) 3. See also "Insolvency Law," *Winnipeg Daily Times* (3 July 1883) 5.

55 Commons Debates, 5 May 1887, 287 (Bechard); A. McLeod, "Insolvency Legislation," Letter to the Editor, (1899) 35:12 Can LJ (NS) 411, p. 413; A. McLeod, "Insolvency Legislation," Letter to the Editor, (1899) 35 Can LJ 411, p. 413. To grant an insolvent trader the legal means for discharging his debts was "immoral." Senate Debates, 29 May 1895, 155 (McDonald, Cape Breton).

56 Commons Debates, 6 March 1883, 121 (Cameron, North Victoria); "Getting into Business," *Canadian Druggist Magazine* 9:12 (December 1897) 275; Commons Debates, 6 March 1883, 121 (Cameron, North Victoria).

57 Senate Debates, 19 June 1894, 597 (Ferguson, Welland).

58 Commons Debates, 29 March 1882, 608 (Wallace, Norfolk); *ibid.*, 5 May 1887, 285 (Paterson, Brant).

59 Senate Debates, 29 May 1895, 150 (McClellan). For example, the Montreal Board of Trade was of the view in 1883 that the issue of a discharge be "left entirely to the option of the creditors." "Insolvency Legislation," *Journal of Commerce* 15:25 (2 February 1883) 778.

60 Thomas Ritchie, Letter to the Editor (2 April 1894), in "Fallacy of Insolvency Laws," *Monetary Times* 27:41 (13 April 1894) 1275 (emphasis in original).

61 Senate Debates, 17 April 1894, 237 (Gowan).

62 Thomas Ritchie, President Belleville Board of Trade, to John A. Macdonald (31 March 1885) in Macdonald Papers (reel 1565, p. 61876).

63 Ritchie, *Fallacy of Insolvency Laws*, p. 17; Thomas Ritchie, President Belleville Board of Trade, to John A. Macdonald (31 March 1885) in Macdonald Papers (reel 1565, p. 61876).

64 Commons Debates, 5 May 1887, 290 (Dupont).

65 *Ibid.*

66 E. Giles to John A. Macdonald (15 May 1882) in Macdonald Papers (vol 384 pt 1, reel C-1756, nos 180377–8).

67 "It is no misfortune to the country to lose men who will not do justice to their creditors." Commons Debates, 5 May 1887, 287 (Bechard).

68 "Without a Bankruptcy Law," *Monetary Times* 14:3 (16 July 1880) 67.

69 Carrie Harris, *Cyril Whyman's Mistake* (Toronto: William Bryce, 1894), pp. 70, 71.

70 Carrie Harris, *A Modern Evangeline* (Windsor, NS: JJ Anslow, 1896) pp. 93, 94.

71 Sarah Tytler, *Logie Town* (Toronto: National Publishing, 1888) pp. 272, 290.

Chapter 9

1 The next major revision of bankruptcy law occurred in 1949: *Bankruptcy Act, 1949*, SC 1949, c 7. See Ferron, "Bankruptcy Court and Administration in Ontario," p. 131; Canada, "Tassé Report," p. xiii; Jacob S. Ziegel, "Canada's Phased-in Bankruptcy Law Reform" (1996) 70:4 Am Bank LJ 383.

2 Editorial, "Bankruptcy" (1920) 40:7 Can LT 546, p. 546; F.G.T. Lucas, "The New 'Bankruptcy Act'" (1920) 40:8 Can LT 668, p. 668.

3 Thomas GW Telfer, "The Canadian Bankruptcy Act of 1919: Public Legislation or Private Interest?" (1995) 24:3 Can Bus LJ 357.

4 Larry A. Glassford, "Meighen, Arthur" in *Dictionary of Canadian Biography*, online: <http://biographi.ca/en/bio/meighen_arthur_18E.html>.

5 W.M. Crichton, Crichton, McClure & Co, Barristers and Solicitors, Winnipeg, to Arthur Meighen (29 August 1919) in Meighen Papers, LAC (MG 26-I) [hereafter Meighen Papers] (reel C-3218, p. 6612-14); Arthur Meighen to W.M. Crichton (2 September 1919) in Meighen Papers (reel C-3218, pp. 6612–14).

6 On the influence of institutions and their effect on policy development, see Ernst, "Law and American Political Development"; Robertson, "Politics and the Past"; Thelen & Steinmo, "Historical Institutionalism in Comparative Politics."

7 Broad economic change may influence policy direction over time. Yet the federal character of the state may have an autonomous influence on policy choice. Additionally, the law itself may have an independent role to play, in that law reform may depend on the innovations known to lawyers. English bankruptcy law was a significant influence. On the interplay between macroeconomic change and state structures, see Dodd & Jillson, "Conversations on the Study of American Politics," p. 10. On the influence of law, see Watson, "Legal Change," p. 1154.

8 Norrie & Owram, *History of the Canadian Economy*, p. 406. Doug Owram, *The Government Generation: Canadian Intellectuals and the State 1900–1945* (Toronto: University of Toronto Press, 1986) pp. 16–17. Bliss notes that, apart from "temporary setbacks during seasons of contraction and tight

money in 1903 and 1907," there was a "Laurier boom." Bliss, *Northern Enterprise*, p. 314.

9 Soclean Chemical Co to Wilfrid Laurier (9 August 1907) in Laurier Papers (vol 470, reel C-850, no 127611).

10 Wilfrid Laurier to Christie & Co, Wholesale Dealers in Lumber, Shingles, Laths, Cedar, Fence Posts, Piling and All Kinds of Building Material (24 February 1906) in Laurier Papers (vol 403, reel C-850).

11 Robert Craig Brown & Ramsay Cook, *Canada, 1896–1921: A Nation Transformed* (Toronto: McClelland and Stewart, 1974) p. 199. Brown and Cook attribute the decline to the tightening of credit by the London money markets, and the growing distrust by foreign financiers of Canadian securities; Owram, *Government Generation*, p. 73.

12 Brown & Cook, *Canada, 1896–1921*, p. 199; Norrie & Owram, *History of the Canadian Economy*, pp. 412–14. On the impact of the recession on western farmers, see Jeremy Adelman, "Prairie Farm Debt and the Financial Crisis of 1914" (1990) 71:4 Canadian Historical Review 491.

13 Norrie & Owram, *History of the Canadian Economy*, p. 414. Statistics on commercial failures in the following table are drawn from the *Monetary Times*, which does not define the term.

Commercial Failures in Canada, 1902–1918

Year	Number
1902	1101
1903	978
1904	1246
1905	1347
1906	1184
1907	1278
1908	1640
1909	1442
1910	1262
1911	1332
1912	1357
1913	1719
1914	2898
1915	2261
1916	1685
1917	1097
1918	873

Sources: "Commercial Failures in Canada, 1902 to 1915," *Monetary Times* 56:1 (7 January 1916) 64; "Commercial Failures in Canada, 1903–1918," *Monetary Times* 60:13 (28 March 1918) 46; see also *Monetary Times* 56:1 (7 January 1916) 156.

14 The issue regained prominence around 1912–13. The efforts of the CCMTA began in 1916. See A.C. McMaster, "The Bankruptcy Act" (Address to the Institute of Chartered Accountants of Ontario, 20 January 1913), (1912–13) 2 Canadian Chartered Accountant 236. There is evidence to suggest that the Minister of Justice considered the issue as early as 1912. See "Montreal Board of Trade Seventh Annual Report, 1912" in Montreal Board of Trade Papers (reel M-2806).

15 *Saturday Night* (10 January 1914) 1.

16 Edward H. Levi & James W.M. Moore, "Bankruptcy and Reorganization: A Survey of Changes" (1937) 5:1 U Chicago L Rev 1, p. 2.

17 Jamie Benidickson, "The Combines Problem in Canadian Legal Thought, 1867–1920" (1993) 43:4 UTLJ 799, p. 801.

18 This contrasted to the nineteenth century, where "[s]mall firms, often with a local orientation, typified most industries." R.T. Naylor, *The History of Canadian Business, 1867–1914: Industrial Development*, vol 2 (Toronto: James Lorimer & Co, 1975) p. 280. On the growth of corporations, see William L. Marr & Donald G. Patterson, *Canada: An Economic History* (Toronto: Gage, 1980) p. 239; Drummond, *Progress Without Planning*, pp. 112–13.

19 Brown & Cook, *Canada, 1896–1921*, pp. 90–2; Benidickson, "Combines Problem," p. 801. Benidickson notes that there were ninety-seven mergers involving 221 firms (p. 803). See also Robert Bothwell, Ian Drummond & John English, *Canada, 1900–1945* (Toronto: University of Toronto Press, 1987) p. 74.

20 The term *Great Boom* is used in Bothwell, Drummond & English, *Canada, 1900–1945*, pp. 55–83. The general economic changes are discussed in more detail below.

21 Pomfret, *Economic Development of Canada*, p. 53.

22 Canadian Population 1871–1921 (Millions)

Year	Urban	Rural
1871	0.7	3.0
1881	1.1	3.2
1891	1.5	3.3
1901	2.0	3.4
1911	3.3	3.9
1921	4.4	4.4

Source: Pomfret, *Economic Development of Canada*, p. 53; Brown & Cook, *Canada, 1896–1921*, p. 50.

23 Owram, *Government Generation*, p. 20.

24 See Commons Debates, 15 May 1919, 2477 (Guthrie); *Bankruptcy Act of 1919*, s 8. In the United States the exclusion preserved the "integrity, dignity and independence" of the farming community. See Papke, "Rhetoric and Retrenchment," p. 877.

25 House of Commons, Special Committee on Bill No. 25, *Respecting Bankruptcy, 1918*, LAC (RG 14 87-88/146 Wallet on Bankruptcy at 17 April 1918) [hereafter House of Commons, Bill No. 25] pp. 8–11, 24–5.

26 *Wage earner* was defined as "one who works for wages, salary or commission or hire at a rate of compensation not exceeding fifteen hundred dollars per year, and who does not on his own account carry on business." See *Bankruptcy Act of 1919*, ss (kk), 8. The wage-earner protection against involuntary proceedings is found in the *Bankruptcy and Insolvency Act*, s 48; however, the monetary limit is now $2500 a year.

27 Senate Debates, 29 May 1919, 592 (Michener).

28 See Sgard, "Do Legal Origins Matter?"

29 The best overview of the provincial system can be found in Osler Wade, "Insolvency Including Assignments and Winding-Up Proceedings under the Dominion and Ontario Winding-Up Acts" (Address to the Chartered Accountants Students' Association, 1 December 1919), (1919–20) 9 Canadian Chartered Accountant 167.

30 Canada, "Tassé Report," p. 16.

31 "Proposed Bankruptcy Act," *Monetary Times* 59:10 (7 September 1917) 14 [emphasis added].

32 Honsberger, "Bankruptcy Administration in the United States and Canada," p. 1530.

33 H.P. Grundy, "Synopsis of the Canadian Bankruptcy Act" (1920–1) 1 CBR 325, p. 326.

34 In an article published in 1917, the General Manager of the CCMTA reviewed the state of provincial law: H. Detchon, "Uniform Assignment Act Necessary: Irritating Phase of Canadian Business Should be Removed," *Monetary Times* 58:1 (5 January 1917) 154; James Aikins to R.C. Smith, Vice President of Canadian Bar Association (20 May 1915) in Canadian Bar Association Papers, LAC (MG 28 I 169) [hereafter CBA Papers]; CCMTA to Canadian Bankers' Association (14 November 1916) in Canadian Bankers' Association Papers, Toronto, Canadian Bankers' Association Archives [hereafter Canadian Bankers' Association Papers] (87-536-01, Legislative Reports from Council).

35 Henry Detchon, General Manager, CCMTA, to C.J. Doherty, Minister of

Justice (27 December 1913) in Department of Justice Papers (vol 182, file 1913-1701); Resolution of CCMTA in letter from CCMTA to Canadian Bar Association (5 July 1916) in CBA Papers.

36 *Ontario (AG) v Canada (AG)*, [1894] AC 189 (PC) p. 200. While the Privy Council never expressed a view on whether a discharge was an essential part of the federal field, Blake had made the argument that the provincial law was not a bankruptcy law, as it did not contain a compulsory provision and there was no discharge: *The Insolvency Case in the Privy Council, Argument of Mr Blake for the Appellant* (Toronto: Bryant Press, 1894) in Blake Papers (box 128, env 35) pp. 9–13.

37 Thomas GW Telfer, "The Evolution of Bankruptcy Exemption Law in Canada 1867–1919: The Triumph of the Provincial Model" [2007] Ann Rev Insol L 18, appendix.

38 *Bankruptcy Act*, 1914, (UK), 4 & 5 Geo V, c 59, s 38(2). See e.g. *Re Roberts*, [1900] 1 QBD 122 (CA).

39 The provincial model continues to this day. *Bankruptcy and Insolvency Act*, s 67(1)(b). See Thomas GW Telfer, "The Proposed Federal Exemption Regime for the Bankruptcy and Insolvency Act" (2005) 41:2–3 Can Bus LJ 279, p. 280.

40 Richard M Hynes, Anup Malani & Eric A. Posner, "The Political Economy of Property Exemption Laws" (2004), 47:1 JL & Econ 19, pp. 40–1 (existing law always provides a starting point for reform, with old law always exerting an influence over reform).

41 Editorial, "Exemptions from Execution" (1914) 50:10 Can LJ (NS) 321, pp. 322–4.

42 *Ibid*. The *Execution Act*, RSO 1914 c 80, s 3(d) provided "all necessary fuel, meat, fish, flour and vegetables, actually provided for family use, not more than sufficient for the ordinary consumption of the debtor and his family for thirty days, and not exceeding in value $40."

43 *Bankruptcy Act of 1919*, s 25. This provision was included in the bills introduced in 1918 and 1919. See Bill C-25, *An Act respecting Bankruptcy* 1st Sess, 13th Parl, 1918, cl 48; Bill C-18, *An Act respecting Bankruptcy*, 2nd Sess, 13th Parl, 1919, cl 25.

44 Senate Debates, 26 May 1919, 503 (Power). See Bill C-71, *An Act for the discharge of Insolvent Debtors whose Estates have been distributed rateably among their Creditors* 4th Sess, 5th Parl, 1886; Bill C-9, *An Act for the discharge of Insolvent Debtors whose Estates have been distributed Rateably among the Creditors* 1st Sess, 6th Parl, 1887. During the 1880s, the model of a federal discharge in combination with provincial distribution schemes had taken the form of an actual federal bill.

45 Senate Debates, 26 May 1919, 503 (Ross).

46 Commons Debates, 28 March 1919, 992 (Guthrie).
47 Senate Debates, 28 May 1919, 563 (Dandurand).
48 See Bill C-18, *An Act Respecting Bankruptcy*, 2nd Sess, 13th Parl, 1918, cl 11. Commons Debates, 1 May 1919, 1982 (Guthrie).
49 Commons Debates, 2 May 1919, 2008 (Cannon). See also *ibid.*, 1 May 1919, 1987 (Archambault).
50 The 1918 Bankruptcy Bill included a provision specifying that the Act was to "extend to all the provinces of the Dominion of Canada." Bill C-25, *An Act Respecting Bankruptcy*, 1st Sess, 13th Parl, 1918, cl 2. The Special Committee later struck the provision from the bill. See House of Commons, Bill No 25.
51 Commons Debates, 28 March 1919, 991 (Guthrie).
52 Lefroy's interpretation of *Cushing v Dupuy* was read into the record. Commons Debates, 28 March 1919, 991 (Guthrie). See also Senate Debates, 26 May 1919, 501 (Lougheed).
53 Commons Debates, 1 May 1919, 1987 (Guthrie). See e.g. Grundy, "Synopsis of the Canadian Bankruptcy Act"; Bicknell, "Advisability of Establishing a Bankruptcy Court in Canada," p. 36; Jacobs, "Canadian Bankruptcy Act." See also Cameron, "Annotation," pp. 137–41.
54 Commons Debates, 2 May 1919, 2008 (Guthrie). When the debate moved to the Senate, the government was also forced to defend the constitutionality of the bill. See Senate Debates, 28 May 1919, 563 (Lougheed).
55 Commons Debates, 27 March 1918, 206 (Jacobs).
56 House of Commons, Bill No. 25, p. 24; W.H. Malkin Co, Limited Importers & Wholesale Grocers, Vancouver, to Minister of Justice (18 April 1919) in Department of Justice Papers (vol 221, file 1918-735); Fleck Bros, Ltd, Mill, Mine and Marine Supplies, Vancouver, to Minister of Justice (22 April 1918) in Department of Justice Papers (vol 221, file 1918-735).
57 Monod, *Store Wars*, p. 260. See also Carman D. Baggaley, *The Emergence of the Regulatory State in Canada 1867–1939* (Ottawa: Economic Council of Canada, 1981) p. 50. See J.A. Corry, "The Growth of Government Activities In Canada 1914–1921" [1940] Canadian Historical Association Annual Report 63; Bernard J Hibbitts, "A Bridle for Leviathan: The Supreme Court and the Board of Commerce" (1989) 21:1 Ottawa L Rev 65, p. 67.
58 *The War Measures Act 1914*, SC 1914, c 2, s 6. See Hibbitts, "Bridle for Leviathan," p. 82; Bernard J. Hibbitts, "A Change of Mind: The Supreme Court and the Board of Railway Commissioners, 1903–1929" (1991) 41:1 UTLJ 60, p. 96.
59 S.W. Jacobs to Peter Ryan (17 April 1918) in Jacobs Papers, LAC (MG 27 III C3) [hereafter Jacobs Papers] (vol 1, no 213).

60 On the general growth of federal regulation, see Corry, "Growth of Government Activities in Canada 1914–1921"; Brown & Cook, *Canada, 1896–1921*, p. 321.
61 Hibbitts, "Bridle for Leviathan," p. 68.
62 Legislation in Manitoba, for example, prevented secured creditors from foreclosing on mortgages for six months. Ontario legislation required holders of mortgages to obtain an order of the court before selling the property. John Appleton, "Ending Moratoria in Canada" (1920) 27:4 Journal of the Canadian Bankers' Association 438.
63 Norrie & Owram, *History of the Canadian Economy*, pp. 415–18. See "Commercial Failures in Canada, 1902 to 1915," *Monetary Times* 56:1 (7 January 1916) 64; "Commercial Failures in Canada, 1903–1918," *Monetary Times* 60:13 (28 March 1918) 46. See statistics summarized at figure 9.1.
64 See, for example, the following letters: National Biscuit and Confection to Department of Justice (16 April 1918) in Department of Justice Papers (vol 221, file 735); Ramsay Bros to Department of Justice (16 April 1918) in Department of Justice Papers (vol 221, file 735).
65 Brown & Cook, *Canada, 1896–1921*, p. 247.
66 *Ibid.*, p. 325. On the efforts of the federal government after the war, see Corry, "Growth of Government Activities in Canada," p. 72.
67 SC 1919, c 37.
68 SC 1919, c 45.
69 Monod, *Store Wars*, p. 253; Owram, *Government Generation*, p. 110; and see generally, Hibbitts, "Bridle for Leviathan," p. 71.
70 Urban Boards of Trade also continued to press for reform, but did not take a leading role. See correspondence of December 1912 and January 1913 from Boards of Trade demanding a new national act, Department of Justice Papers (vol 1912, file no 1912-1591).
71 See Skeel, *Debt's Dominion*, pp. 14–15; Skeel, "Public Choice and the Future of Public Choice–Influenced Legal Scholarship," p. 651.
72 Bicknell, "Advisability of Establishing a Bankruptcy Court in Canada"; Thomson, "Bankruptcy Legislation," p. 177. See also "Bankruptcy Act Will Help Business World: New Measure Wipes Out Variety of Provincial Laws," *Financial Post* (5 July 1919).
73 "Canadian Bankruptcy Law: Montreal Barrister Makes Strong Plea for Its Enactment," *Monetary Times* 60:11 (15 March 1918) 18; Senate Debates, 26 May 1919, 501 (Lougheed).
74 Wade, "Insolvency including Assignments and Winding-Up Proceedings," p. 182.
75 Commons Debates, 2 May 1919, 2004 (Guthrie).

76 "Constitution of the Canadian Bar Association, 1914" in CBA Papers (vol 1, file 2).
77 See Lee Gibson & Dale Gibson, "Sir James Aikins' Seamless Web: Finding Fortune and Fame as a Lawyer in the Adolescent Canadian West" (1992) 21:2 Man LJ 161, p. 186.
78 "Uniform Laws for Various Provinces: Inaugurated at a Banquet of Credit Men After an Address by Sir James Aikins," *Manitoba Free Press* (22 December 1914) in CBA Papers (vol 1, file 2, correspondence (1914–1917)). For a full text of the address, see James Aikins, "Uniformity in Provincial Legislation" (Address to the CCMTA, 21 December 1914) in CBA Papers (vol 1, file 2).
79 James Aikins, "The Advancement of the Science of Jurisprudence in Canada" (1915) 1 Proceedings of the Canadian Bar Association 3, p. 6.
80 Aikins, "Uniformity in Provincial Legislation."
81 James Aikins, "Commercial Law Must Be Standardized: Lack of Uniformity in Legislation here is Costly to Canadian Business," *Monetary Times* 56:1 (7 January 1916) 46.
82 S.W. Jacobs, "The Proposed Bankruptcy Act" (Address to the Canadian Bar Association, 1918), (1918) 3 Proceedings of the Canadian Bar Association 164.
83 "Canadian Credit Men's Association: Review of Purposes and Activities of Recently Organized League," *Financial Post* (18 June 1912) 18. See also H.P. Grundy to James Aikins (15 January 1917) in CBA Papers (vol 1).
84 Canada, "Tassé Report," p. 16.
85 Bram Thompson, "Canadian Bankruptcy Act: Monopoly of the Trusteeship and of the Law" (1921) 41:2 Can LT 96, pp. 102–3. See H.P. Grundy to C.J. Doherty, Minister of Justice (13 July 1917) in Department of Justice Papers (vol 213, file 1074-1092).
86 Resolution of CCMTA in letter from CCMTA to CBA (5 July 1916) in CBA Papers. "In 1917 the Canadian Bar Association drafted an Act which was not satisfactory. Mr Grundy was then asked to draft an Act." "Proposed Bankruptcy Act," *Monetary Times* 60:14 (5 April 1918) 14.
87 Canada, "Tassé Report," p. 16.
88 H.P. Grundy to James Aikins (15 January 1917) in CBA Papers (vol 1).
89 Two different forms of the memorandum are reprinted in the following sources: "Bankruptcy Legislation: Credit Men's Proposed Legislation and Recommendations," *Monetary Times* 58:10 (9 March 1917) 22; Editorial, "Federal Bankruptcy Legislation: Reasons Given Before CCMTA why there Should be a Dominion Bankruptcy Act" (1916–17) 6 Canadian Chartered Accountant 282.

90 "As requested by the Honourable Arthur Meighen, I enclose you herewith a copy of the Credit Men's Journal containing a draft Bankruptcy Act which I have prepared during the winter months at the request of the CCMTA." H.P. Grundy to C.J. Doherty, Minister of Justice (21 June 1917) in Department of Justice Papers (vol 213, file 1081).
91 H.P. Grundy to C.J. Doherty, Minister of Justice (13 July 1917) in Department of Justice Papers (vol 213, file 1074-1092).
92 "The English Act is drawn on the assumption that every estate should come before and be under the supervision of the Court, its judges and officers, whereas I have adopted the principle that the administration of insolvent estates is a matter that should be kept out of the Court so far as possible and that better results, less delay and expense could be obtained if the Trustee deals direct with the debtor and creditors without the intervention of the Court, care being taken in the appointment and bonding of trustees." H.P. Grundy to C.J. Doherty, Minister of Justice (13 July 1917) in Department of Justice Papers (vol 213, file 1074-1092).
93 The Minister of Justice personally wrote to the General Manager of the CCMTA to advise that the government would not be able to take action during that session. See C.J. Doherty, Minister of Justice, to H.P. Grundy (25 June 1917) in Department of Justice Papers (vol 1081); C.J. Doherty, Minister of Justice, to H.P. Grundy (17 July 1917) in Department of Justice Papers (vol 1081).
94 The Liberal Party appointed a subcommittee of its National Advisory Committee in 1916, to "study and report upon the question of … adopting a Federal Insolvency Law." S.W. Jacobs was appointed as chair of the subcommittee. National Liberal Advisory Committee to S.W. Jacobs (3 January 1916) in Jacobs Papers (vol 1, no 1).
95 Commons Debates, 27 March 1918, 205 (Jacobs).
96 Canadian Bankers' Association Circular No 3L (12 April 1918); Meeting of the Executive Council of the Canadian Bankers' Association (19 March 1918), Minute Book II Executive Council in Canadian Bankers' Association Papers.
97 House of Commons, Bill No. 25.
98 H.P. Grundy to S.W. Jacobs (15 May 1918) in Jacobs Papers (vol 1, no 237); S.W. Jacobs to H.P. Grundy (23 May 1918) in Jacobs Papers (vol 1, no 239).
99 Commons Debates, 6 March 1919, 229; *ibid.*, 28 March 1919, 991. The Union coalition was formed in 1917 and was confirmed in the winter election of that year. Brown & Cook, *Canada, 1896–1921*, pp. 272–3.
100 "I hear from a source somewhat high up that there is just a possibility that the Bill may not go through. Sinister influences, which I have reason

to believe are connected with the Banking Federation, are apparently at work and unless we make a determined effort the Bill may not go through this session." S.W. Jacobs to L. Garneau (11 April 1919) in Jacobs Papers (vol 2, no 395).

101 H.P. Grundy to S.W. Jacobs (8 April 1919) in Jacobs Papers (vol 1, no 387).

102 S.W. Jacobs to H.P. Grundy (17 April 1919) in Jacobs Papers (vol 2, no 388).

103 H.P. Grundy to Secretary of the Toronto Board of Trade (25 April 1919) in Toronto Board of Trade Papers, LAC (MG 28 III 56) [hereafter Toronto Board of Trade Papers] (vol 235, file bankruptcy 1918–36). See enclosure in letter from Montreal Board of Trade to S.W. Jacobs (14 May 1919) [enclosure: Resolution of Montreal Board of Trade (14 May 1919)] in Jacobs Papers (vol 2, no 514).

104 In accordance with s 98, the Bankruptcy Act was to "come into operation at a date to be named by proclamation of the Governor in Council." *Bankruptcy Act of 1919*, s 98. The proclamation (31 December 1919) stated that the Act was to come into force on 1 July 1920. "A Proclamation," 31 December 1919 reproduced in *The Bankruptcy Act with Amendments, 1920: Together with Rules and Forms Thereunder* (Ottawa: Thomas Mulvey King's Printer, 1920).

105 Jacob Ziegel, "What Can the United States Learn from the Canadian Means Testing System?" [2007] U Ill L Rev 195, p. 197.

106 *Bankruptcy Act of 1919*, s 14(1)(3).

107 H.P. Grundy to C.J. Doherty, Minister of Justice (13 July 1917) in Department of Justice Papers (vol 213, file 1074-1092).

108 *Bankruptcy Act of 1919*, s 9. For powers of the trustee, see ss 17 to 24. Creditors were able to exercise an influence over the conduct of the trustee through the position of inspectors. Creditors could appoint up to five inspectors who had to approve certain acts of the trustee. See s 20.

109 H.P. Grundy, "The Bankruptcy Act" in Canadian Legal History Project Archives, Manitoba (AWCLH A-41) p. 1; H.P. Grundy, "The Bankruptcy Act" (Address to the Toronto Bankers' Educational Association, 11 May 1920), (1920) 27:4 Journal of the Canadian Bankers' Association 426, p. 428.

110 "Proposed Bankruptcy Act," *Monetary Times* 59:10 (7 September 1917) 14.

111 See Dunlop, *Creditor-Debtor Law in Canada*, p. 99; *An Act respecting the Imperial Debtors Act of 1869*, SA 1908, c 6, s 1; *An Act to amend the Statute Law (Pt 1)*, SA 1909, c 4, s 20; *An Act respecting the Imperial Debtors Act of 1869*, SS 1918–1919, c 83.

112 *A Protest against the Bankruptcy Act Now before the Dominion Parliament:*

Bankruptcy Laws Have in the Past Proved to the Chief Occasion of Bankruptcy in Department of Justice Papers (vol 221, p. 4).

113 See also Letter to Editor, *Globe* (9 July 1918) 4.

114 *Saturday Night* (10 January 1914) 1.

115 McMaster, "Bankruptcy Act," p. 241.

116 Lucas, "New 'Bankruptcy Act,'" p. 669.

117 *An Act Against Such Persons as do Make Bankrupts*, 1542–3, c 4.

118 *An Act to Prevent Frauds Frequently Committed by Bankrupts*, 1705 (UK), 4 Ann, c 17.

119 Jay Cohen, "The History of Imprisonment for Debt and Its Relation to the Development of Discharge in Bankruptcy" (1982) 3:2 J Legal Hist 153, p. 156.

120 The 1705 statute provided for the death penalty for bankrupts who did not cooperate. Kadens, "Last Bankrupt Hanged," p. 1231; Tabb, "Historical Evolution of the Bankruptcy Discharge," p. 337.

121 Tabb, "Historical Evolution of the Bankruptcy Discharge," p. 334.

122 Lester, *Victorian Insolvency*, p. 17; Weisberg, "Commercial Morality," p. 30. See also Ian PH Duffy, "English Bankrupts, 1571–1861" (1980) 24:4 Am J Legal Hist 283, p. 287.

123 Tabb, "Historical Evolution of the Bankruptcy Discharge," p. 332. W.R. Cornish & G. de N. Clark, *Law and Society in England, 1750–1950* (London: Sweet & Maxwell, 1989) p. 231, argue that bankruptcy was a deterrent aimed at those who failed to submit to ordinary processes.

124 Kadens, "Last Bankrupt Hanged," p. 1234.

125 Christie & Co, Wholesale Dealers in Lumber, Shingles, Lath, Cedar, Fence Posts, Piling, Winnipeg, to Wilfrid Laurier (17 February 1906) in Laurier Papers (vol 403, reel C-850, no 107231); R.J. White & Co, Ltd, Wholesale Dry Goods, to Department of Justice (17 April 1918) in Department of Justice Papers (vol 221, file 735).

126 McMaster, "Bankruptcy Act," p. 241; *Saturday Night* (10 January 1914) 1.

127 A resolution was introduced by C.W. Cross providing for a discharge of a debtor. This quotation is taken from a news clipping enclosed in a letter from Henry Detchon to Minister of Justice (17 September 1917) in Department of Justice Papers (vol 213, file 1081). See also Soclean Chemical Co to Laurier (9 August 1907). See also Commons Debates, 18 May 1903, 3249.

128 *Saturday Night* (10 January 1914) 1. The same article further claimed that exiled Canadian debtors were to be found in "every leading city of the American Union." This point was also made at a Liberal Party convention in Winnipeg. See Henry Detchon to Minister of Justice (17 September 1917) in Department of Justice Papers (vol 213, file 1081). See also Soclean

Chemical to Laurier (9 August 1907); Commons Debates, 18 May 1903, 3249.

129 J.A. Christie, Christie & Co to Laurier (17 February 1906).

130 *Saturday Night* (10 January 1914) 1. This included transferring property to a wife to evade legitimate debts. In Ontario the enactment of the *Married Women's Property Act, 1884* abolished the role of the husband as trustee over the wife's property. Under the Act, women were entitled to hold and convey property. This created opportunities for spousal transfers to avoid debts. Chambers found more than 130 cases of attempted fraud in unreported court documents: Chambers, *Married Women and Property Law*, pp. 148–65.

131 Angus Lyell, "Bankruptcy Act Means Better Business Methods," *Monetary Times* 65:4 (23 July 1920) 34; Lucas, "New 'Bankruptcy Act,'" p. 669.

132 H.G. Smith Ltd, Regina, to Department of Justice (16 April 1918) in Department of Justice Papers (vol 221, file 735); Grundy, "The Bankruptcy Act" (1920), p. 427; Kilgour Rimer Co, Wholesale Boots and Shoes, Winnipeg, to Minister of Justice (15 April 1918) in Department of Justice Papers (vol 221, file 1918-735); Quebec Board of Trade to Robert Borden (13 January 1913) in Borden Papers, LAC (MG 26-H, reel 4422, p. 143644).

133 McMaster, "Bankruptcy Act," p. 239.

134 E.R.C. Clarkson, "The Bankruptcy Act" (1920–1) 10 Canadian Chartered Accountant 154, p. 155.

135 "[T]he door is left open to abuses produced through the desire by certain creditors to obtain advantages over others. The debtor could be harassed by his creditors, with the threat that failure to pay an increased dividend on the side would bring about organized opposition of those who have it in their power to prevent the victim's rehabilitation." "Canadian Bankruptcy Law," *Monetary Times* 60:11 (15 March 1918) 18 (reprints portions of Address to Canadian Bar Association by S.W. Jacobs).

136 Wade, "Insolvency including Assignments and Winding-Up Proceedings," p. 186.

137 Jacobs, "Proposed Bankruptcy Act."

138 McMaster, "Bankruptcy Act," p. 240; S.W. Jacobs, "Canadian Bankruptcy Law," *Monetary Times* 60:11 (15 March 1918) 18 (reprint of Jacobs's speech to Canadian Bar Association).

139 For a discussion of why creditors in the United States found a discharge acceptable, see Coleman, *Debtors and Creditors in America*, pp. 273–86.

140 "Proposed Bankruptcy Act: Draft Prepared by Mr H.P. Grundy, Winnipeg Is Explained," *Monetary Times* 59:10 (1 September 1917) 14.

141 Ramsay Bros and Company Limited, Manufacturers of Confectionary

Macaroni and Syrup, Vancouver, to Department of Justice (16 April 1918) in Department of Justice Papers (vol 221, file 735).

142 *Saturday Night* (10 January 1914) 1; Bicknell, "Advisability of Establishing a Bankruptcy Court in Canada," p. 51; Jacobs, "Proposed Bankruptcy Act"; Lucas, "New 'Bankruptcy Act,'" p. 671.

143 Owram, *Government Generation*, pp. 76–7.

144 Grundy, "Bankruptcy Act" in Canadian Legal History Project Archives, Manitoba (AWCLH A-41) p. 13; Lucas, "New 'Bankruptcy Act,'" p. 671.

145 Editorial, "Federal Bankruptcy Act: Reasons Given Before Canadian Men's Trust Association Why There Should be a Dominion Bankruptcy Act" (1916–17) 6 Canadian Chartered Accountant 282; Grundy, "Synopsis of the Canadian Bankruptcy Act"; Grundy, "Bankruptcy Act" (Address to the Toronto Bankers' Educational Association).

146 Jacobs, "Canadian Bankruptcy Act," p. 608. Commons Debates, 27 March 1918, 206 (Jacobs); Commons Debates, 2 May 1919, 2004 (Guthrie). See also "Proposed Bankruptcy Act," *Monetary Times* 59:10 (7 September 1917) 14.

147 H.P. Grundy to C.J. Doherty, Minister of Justice (13 July 1917) in Department of Justice Papers (vol 213, file 1074-1092, 1917).

148 Grundy, "Bankruptcy Act" (Address to the Toronto Bankers' Educational Association), p. 435.

149 Grundy, "The Bankruptcy Act," Canadian Legal History Project Archives, pp. 13, 14; H.P. Grundy to C.J. Doherty, Minister of Justice (21 June 1917) in Department of Justice Papers (vol 213, file 1081, p. 10).

150 G. Blaine Baker, "The Reconstitution of Upper Canadian Legal Thought in the Late-Victorian Empire" (1985) 3:2 LHR 219, p. 274. See also Hibbitts, "Bridle for Leviathan," p. 105; Hibbitts, "Change of Mind," p. 89.

151 Ziegel, "What Can the United States Learn," p. 197.

152 Edouard Martel, "The Debtor's Discharge from Bankruptcy" (1971) 17:4 McGill LJ 718, p. 724; N.L. Martin, "A New Bankruptcy Act" (1918–19) 8 Canadian Chartered Accountant 24, p. 29.

153 *Bankruptcy Act of 1919*, ss 58, 59.

154 Bicknell, "Advisability of Establishing a Bankruptcy Court in Canada," p. 43.

155 Ziegel, "What Can the United States Learn," p. 197.

156 *Bankruptcy Act of 1919*, s 58(5). See also Lucas, "New 'Bankruptcy Act,'" p. 672.

157 *Bankruptcy Act of 1919*, s 59.

158 S.W. Jacobs, "Canadian Bankruptcy Law," *Monetary Times* 60:11 (15 March 1918) 18 (reprint of Jacobs's speech to Ontario Bar Association).
159 Jacobs, "Proposed Bankruptcy Act."
160 Bicknell, "Advisability of Establishing a Bankruptcy Court in Canada," p. 43.
161 Jacob Ziegel, "The Modernization of Canada's Bankruptcy Law in a Comparative Context" (1998) 33:1 Tex Int'l LJ 1, p. 4. (Ziegel claims that the "1919 Act did not adopt an unconditional fresh start policy for discharge from bankruptcy for consumers.")
162 John L. Campbell, "Ideas, Politics, and Public Policy" (2002) 28:1 Annual Review of Sociology 21, p. 33.
163 Hall, "Policy Paradigms, Social Learning, and the State," p. 280.
164 Several sources describe the *Bankruptcy Act of 1919* in great detail. See Duncan, *Law and Practice of Bankruptcy*; Grundy, "Synopsis of the Canadian Bankruptcy Act"; Cameron, "Annotation: Bankruptcy Act of Canada, 1920"; Lucas, "New 'Bankruptcy Act.'"
165 Commons Debates, 9 May 1919, 2272, 2274, 2276; House of Commons, Bill No. 25, p. 2; S.W. Jacobs, "The New Bankruptcy Act" in Jacobs Papers (vol 11, no 3943, file bankruptcy bill and other legislation).
166 "Proposed Bankruptcy Act," *Monetary Times* 59:10 (7 September 1917) 14.
167 Commons Debates, 1 May 1919, 1990 (Guthrie). The primacy of liquidation would later be confirmed with the amendments to the Act in 1923, which effectively nullified the ability to make compositions. The 1923 amendment required that before a composition proceeding could be invoked, first one had to be in a state of bankruptcy. Canada, "Tassé Report," p. 19.

Chapter 10

1 Patrick Fridenson, "Business Failure and the Agenda of Business History" (2004) 5:4 Enterprise & Society 562.
2 "Insolvency Laws," Thomas Ritchie, President Belleville Board of Trade, to John A. Macdonald (24 April 1880) in Macdonald Papers (reel C-1565, pp. 61893–5).
3 Fridenson, "Business Failure," p. 569.
4 Although arguably Parliament did step in and regulate one aspect of bankruptcy and insolvency when it enacted *An Act Respecting Insolvent Banks, Insurance Companies, Loan Companies, Building Societies and Trading Corporations*, SC 1882, c 23. The statute was later renamed the *Winding-Up Act*, RSC 1886, c 129. Neither statute applied to insolvent individuals.

5 See list of reform bills 1880–1903 in the bibliography.
6 "Bankruptcy Legislation," *Journal of Commerce* 36:3 (20 January 1893) 95.
7 See Hansen, "Commercial Associations."
8 Jacobs, "Canadian Bankruptcy Act."
9 E.g. James Aikins, "Commercial Law must be Standardized: Lack of Uniformity in Legislation here is Costly to Canadian Business," *Monetary Times* 56:1 (7 January 1916).
10 See e.g. Ritchie, *Fallacy of Insolvency Laws.*
11 Hall, "Policy Paradigms, Social Learning, and the State," p. 280.
12 On the growing acceptability of bankruptcy law in a modernizing American economy, see Coleman, *Debtors and Creditors in America.* In England, see Weiss, *Hell of the English.*
13 Lester, *Victorian Insolvency.*
14 *Broddy v Stuart* (1886), 7 Can LT 6 (Ont QB); *Clarkson v Ontario Bank* (Ch); *Clarkson v Ontario Bank* (CA); *Edgar v Central Bank; Hunter v Drummond* (1888), 15 OAR 232; *Union Bank v Neville; Re Assignments and Preferences Act, Section 9.*
15 Commons Debates, 6 March 1883, 119; "Insolvency Legislation," *Journal of Commerce* 19:9 (29 August 1884) 308.
16 Skeel, *Debt's Dominion*, pp. 24–5.
17 *Ibid.*, p. 2.
18 *Ibid.*, p. 17.
19 *Ibid.*, p. 38. See Lester, *Victorian Insolvency*, p. 289.
20 *Bankruptcy Act, 1914* (UK). The 1914 UK Act was only a consolidation of the landmark reforms of 1883. See *Bankruptcy Act, 1883* (UK) 46 & 47 Vict, c 52.
21 See e.g., Rafael La Porta, Florencio Lopez-de-Silanes & Andrei Shleifer, "Law and Finance" (1998) 106:6 Journal of Political Economy 1113.
22 Rafael La Porta, Florencio Lopez-de-Silanes & Andrei Shleifer, "The Economic Consequences of Legal Origins" (2008) 46:2 Journal of Economic Literature 285, p. 326. See also Lisa Fairfax, "The Legal Origins Theory in Crisis" [2009] BYUL Rev 1571, pp. 1572–4.
23 Sgard, "Do Legal Origins Matter?," pp. 390–1.
24 *Ibid.*, p. 410.
25 On the importance of economic development, see *ibid.*
26 John Bell, "Path Dependence and Legal Development" (2013) 87:4 Tul L Rev 787, p. 791.
27 Prado & Trebilcock, "Path Dependence," pp. 350, 355.
28 Pierson & Skocpol, "Historical Institutionalism," p. 703.
29 Baker, "Reconstitution of Upper Canadian Legal Thought," p. 286.

30 Jacob Ziegel, "Canada's Dysfunctional Insolvency Reform Process and the Search for Solutions" (2010) 26:1 BFLR 63, p. 67. See also Ziegel, "What Can the United States Learn," p. 197.
31 Ziegel, "Canada's Phased-In Bankruptcy Law Reform," p. 386. See also Jacob Ziegel, *Comparative Consumer Insolvency Regimes: A Canadian Perspective* (Oxford: Hart Publishing, 2003) p. 14.
32 See Telfer, "Evolution of Bankruptcy Exemption Law in Canada"; Telfer, "Proposed Federal Exemption Regime."
33 *Bankruptcy and Insolvency Act*, ss 173, 172(2). The basic list of factors in s 173 remains the same, with some additional amendments.
34 *Bankruptcy Act of 1919*, s 59.
35 For a discussion of more recent reforms, see Anthony Duggan & Thomas GW Telfer, "Canadian Preference Law Reform" (2007), 42:3 Tex Int'l LJ 661.
36 *Bankruptcy and Insolvency Act*, s 95(2). See *St Anne-Nackawic Pulp Co (Trustee of) v Logistec Stevedoring (Atlantic) Inc* (2005), 255 DLR (4th) 137, para 6 (NBCA).
37 *An Act to Amend the Bankruptcy Act*, SC 1920, c 34.
38 Duggan & Telfer, "Canadian Preference Law Reform," pp. 674–5. See *Bankruptcy and Insolvency Act*, s 95(2).
39 Duggan & Telfer, "Canadian Preference Law Reform."
40 Ziegel, "Modernization of Canada's Bankruptcy Law," p. 5.
41 *Assignments and Preferences Act*, RSO 1990, c A.33. Current Creditors' Relief legislation can be traced back to the nineteenth century and continues to operate today. See e.g. *Creditors' Relief Act, 2010*, SO 2010, c 16, Sch 4.
42 *Robinson v Countrywide Factors Ltd*, [1978] 1 SCR 753.
43 The *Insolvent Act of 1875* applied to companies, but the provisions were rarely relied upon.

Bibliography

Archival Collections

Library and Archives Canada (Ottawa)

Robert Borden Papers
Alexander Campbell Papers
Canadian Bar Association Papers
Department of Agriculture Papers
Department of Finance Papers
Department of Justice Papers
Department of Trade and Commerce Papers
Dominion Board of Trade, Annual Meetings
Government Records Papers
S.W. Jacobs Papers
Wilfrid Laurier Papers
Liberal Party of Canada Papers
John A. Macdonald Papers
Arthur Meighen Papers
Montreal Board of Trade Council Annual Reports
Montreal Board of Trade Papers
Secretary of State Papers
Toronto Board of Trade Papers

Archives of Ontario (Toronto)

Edward Blake Papers
Alexander Campbell Fonds
Haldimand County Court Insolvency Files, 1879–80
Huron County Court Insolvency Procedure Book, 1864–85
Kent County Court Insolvency Files, 1874–81
Lambton County Court Insolvency Procedure Book, 1865–80
Lanark County Court Insolvency Minute Books
James Langton Fonds, 1875–9
Lennox and Addington County Court Insolvency Case Files, 1871–2
Oxford County Court Official Assignee's Insolvency Docket Books, 1865–9
Peel County Court Insolvency Minute Book 1867–80
Perth County Insolvency Docket Books, 1871–9
Wentworth County Court Insolvency Files, 1864–80

Canadian Bankers' Association Archives (Toronto)

Canadian Bankers' Association Papers

Cases

Adams v McCall (1866), 25 UCQB 219.
Agnew v Ross (1879), 8 PR 67 (UC Pract Ct).
Allan v Clarkson (1870), 17 Gr 570 (UC Ch).
Archibald v Haldan (1871), 31 UCQB 295.
Austin v Gordon (1872), 32 UCQB 621.
Bank of Montreal v Munro (1864), 23 UCQB 414.
Bank of Toronto v McDougall (1865), 15 UCCP 475.
Beekman v Jarvis (1847), 3 UCQB 280.
Bell v Rickaby (1877), 3 QLR 243 (QB, Appeal Side), aff'd on other grounds (1878), 2 SCR 560.
Bleasdell v Townsend (1883), 3 Can LT 509 (Man QB).
Brayley v Ellis (1882), 1 OR 119 (Ch), aff'd (1884), 9 OAR 565.
Broddy v Stuart (1886), 7 Can LT 6 (Ont QB).
Brown v Wright (1874), 35 UCQB 378.
Buchanan v Smith (1870), 17 Gr 208 (UC Ch).
Bullen v Harding (1871), 13 NBR 499 (SC).
Burland v Larocque (1867), 12 LC Jur 292 (QB).
Cameron v Holland (1870), 29 UCQB 506.

Campbell v Barrie (1871), 31 UCQB 279.
Canada (AG) v Ontario (AG), [1898] AC 247 (PC).
The Case of the Bankrupts (1584), 2 Co Rep 25, (*sub nom Smith v Mills*) 76 ER 441 (KB).
Churcher v Johnston (1874), 34 UCQB 528.
Clarkson v Ontario Bank (1887), 13 OR 666 (Ch).
Clarkson v Ontario Bank (1888), 15 OAR 166.
Clarkson v White (1882), 4 OR 663 (HCJ (Ch Div)).
Clemmow v Converse (1869), 16 Gr 547 (UC Ch).
Cochran v Chipman (1876–7), 11 NSR 254 (SC).
Colwell v Robertson (1877), 17 NBR 481 (CA).
Cook v Rogers (1879), 26 Gr 599 (UC Ch).
Creighton v Merchants' Bank (1882), 15 NSR 139 (SC).
Crombie v Jackson (1874), 34 UCQB 575.
Cushing v Dupuy (1880), 5 AC 409 (PC).
Davidson v McInnes (1876), 24 Gr 414 (UC Ch).
Davidson v Ross (1876), Gr 22 (UC Err App).
Dever v Morris (1873), 14 NBR 270 (SC).
Duncan v Smart (1874), 35 UCQB 532 (CA).
Dupont v La Cie de Moulin (1888), 11 LN 225 (Qc Sup Ct).
Edgar v Central Bank (1888), 15 OAR 193.
Ex parte Bejeau (1874), 15 NBR 200 (SC).
Ex parte Ellis (1878), 17 NBR 593 (CA).
Ex parte Jones (1878), 18 NBR 136 (SC).
Forrester v Thrasher (1882), 2 OR 38 (QB).
Fowler v Perrin (1866), 16 UCCP 258.
Gilbert v Girouard (1878), 18 NBR 148 (SC).
Godkin v Beech (1876), 10 NSR 261 (SC).
Gordon v Young (1866), 12 Gr 318 (UC Ch).
Gottwalls v Mullholland (1864), 15 UCCP 62 aff'd (1866), 3 E & A 194 (UC Err App).
Green v Swan (1872), 22 UCCP 307.
Griffiths v Perry (1881), 6 OAR 672.
Harman v Clarkson (1872), 22 UCCP 291.
Harvey v Cotter (1873), 9 NSR 161 (CA).
Hersee v White (1869), 29 UCQB 232.
Hodge v R (1883), 9 AC 117 (PC).
Hunter v Drummond (1888), 15 OAR 232.
Jones v Kinney (1884), 11 SCR 708.
Joseph v Haffner (1881), 29 Gr 421 (UC Ch).

Kalus v Hergert (1876), 1 OAR 75.
Keays v Brown (1875), 22 Gr 10 (UC Ch).
Kennedy v Freeman (1888), 15 OAR 216.
Kinney, Assignee v Dudman (1876), 11 NSR 19 (CA).
Lenoir v Ritchie (1879), 3 SCR 575.
Lewis v Brown (1884), 10 OAR 639.
Long v Hancock (1885), 12 SCR 532.
Maritime Bank of Canada (Liquidators of) v New Brunswick (Receiver General of), [1892] AC 437 (PC).
Martin v McAlpine (1883), 8 OAR 675.
Mason v Hamilton (1872), 22 UCCP 411.
Mathers v Lynch (1868), 27 UCQB 244.
McCrae v White (1883), 9 SCR 22.
McEdwards v Palmer (1878), 2 OAR 439 (CA).
McFarlane v McDonald (1874), 21 Gr 319 (UC Ch).
McGregor v Hume (1869), 28 UCQB 380.
McLean v Garland (1885), 13 SCR 366.
McLean v McLellan (1870), 29 UCQB 548.
McLeod v Wright (1877), 17 NBR 68 (SC (Eq App)).
McPherson v Reynolds (1857), 6 UCCP 491.
McWhirter v Royal Canadian Bank (1870), 17 Gr 480 (UC Ch).
McWhirter v Thorne (1869), 19 UCCP 302.
Milloy v Kerr (1879), 8 SCR 474.
Molson Bank v Halter (1890), 18 SCR 88.
Morton v Nihan (1880), 5 OAR 20.
Murphy v Stadacona Bank (1879), 5 QLR 321 (Sup Ct).
Nelles v Bank of Montreal (1881), 28 Gr 449 (UC Ch) aff'd (1882), 7 OAR 743.
Nelles v Paul (1879), 4 OAR 1.
Newton v Ontario Bank (1868), 15 Gr 283 (UC Err App).
Ogden v Saunders 25 US (12 Wheat) 213 (1827).
Ontario (AG) v Canada (AG), [1894] AC 189 (PC).
Ontario (AG) v Canada (AG), [1896] AC 348 (PC) [*Local Prohibition Reference*].
Ontario (AG) v Mercer (1883), 8 AC 767 (PC).
Parke v Day (1875), 24 UCCP 619.
Patterson v Kingsley (1878), 25 Gr 425 (UC Ch).
Payne v Hendry (1873), 20 Gr 142 (UC Ch).
Pineo v Gavaza (1887), 20 NSR 249 (SC).
Re Andrews, An Insolvent (1877), 2 OAR 24.
Re Assignments and Preferences Act, Section 9 (1893), 20 OAR 489.
Re Barrett (1880), 5 OAR 206.

Re Botsford (1871), 22 UCCP 65.
Re Bullivant (1880), 5 OAR 638.
R v Chandler (1869), 12 NBR 556 (CA).
Re Cobourg & Peterborough Railway (1869), 16 Gr 571 (UC Ch).
Re Donald Matheson, An Insolvent (1872–5), 9 NSR 538 (SC).
Re Frederick BK Marter (1882), 15 NSR 412 (CA).
Re Garratt & Co (1869), 28 UCQB 266.
Re Gearing (1879), 4 OAR 173.
Re Gooding (1880), 5 OAR 643.
Re Hill (1882), 7 OAR 694.
Re Hurst, an Insolvent (1876), 6 PR 329 (UC Pract Ct).
Re Hutchinson, Insolvent (1877), 12 NSR 40.
Re Jones (1868), 4 PR 317 (UC Pract Ct).
Re Killam (1878) 14 Can LJ (NS) 242 (Yarmouth County Ct).
Re Lamb, An Insolvent (1866), 4 PR 16 (UC Pract Ct).
Re Martin and English (1880), 5 OAR 647.
Re Mooney, Insolvent (1876–7), 11 NSR 563 (CA).
Re Perks (1870), 13 NBR 120 (SC).
Re Robert Holt and John Gray (1867), 13 Gr 568 (UC Ch).
Re Roberts, [1900] 1 QBD 122 (CA).
Re Smith, an Insolvent (1867), 4 PR 89 (UC Pract Ct).
Robinson v Countrywide Factors Ltd, [1978] 1 SCR 753.
Robinson v Ellis and Carter (1879), 19 NBR 6 (SC).
Roe v Smith (1868), 15 Gr 344 (UC Ch).
Rowe v Jarvis (1863), 13 UCCP 495.
Royal Canadian Bank v Kerr (1870), 17 Gr 47 (UC Ch).
Rumsey v Hare (1877), 12 NSR 4 (CA).
Russell v R (1882), 7 AC 829 (PC).
Shaw v Massie (1871), 21 UCCP 266.
Shields v Peak (1883), 8 SCR 579.
Slater v Oliver (1884), 7 OR 158 (HCJ (Ch Div)).
Smith v Hutchinson (1878), 2 OAR 405.
Smith v McLean (1878), 25 Gr 567 (UC Ch).
St Anne-Nackawic Pulp Co (Trustee of) v Logistec Stevedoring (Atlantic) Inc (2005), 255 DLR (4th) 137 (NBCA).
Standard Bank of Canada v Johnson (1877), 42 UCQB 16 (HCJ (QB)).
Stephens v McArthur (1890), 6 Man LR 496 (CA).
Stephens v McArthur (1891), 19 SCR 446.
Sturges v Crowninshield 17 US (4 Wheat) 122 (1819).
Suter v Merchants Bank (1877), 24 Gr 365 (UC Ch).

Thomas v Hall (1874), 6 PR 172 (UC Pract Ct).
Topping v Joseph (1859), 1 E & A 292 (UC Err App).
Totten v Bowen (1882), 8 OAR 602.
Tucker v Young, [1877] Man R temp Wood 186 (QB).
Union Bank v Neville (1891), 21 OR 152 (CA).
Wallace v Bossom (1876–7), 11 NSR 419 (SC).
Vanwart v Shepherd (1878), 18 NBR 225 (SC).
Vassie v Vassie (1882), 22 NBR 76 (SC (Eq App)).

Printed Sources

Primary Sources

STATUTES

An Act against Such Persons as do Make Bankrupts, 1542–43 (UK), 34 & 35 Hen VIII, c 4.
An Act respecting Insolvent Banks, Insurance Companies, Loan Companies, Building Societies, and Trading Corporations, SC 1882, c 23.
An Act respecting Assignments for the Benefit of Creditors, SO 1885, c 26.
An Act Respecting the Fraudulent Preferences of Creditors by Persons in Insolvent Circumstances, RSO 1877, c 118.
An Act respecting the Imperial Debtors Act of 1869, SA 1908, c 6, s 1.
An Act respecting the Imperial Debtors Act of 1869, SS 1918–1919, c 83.
Act to amend the Act respecting Assignments for the Benefit of Creditors, SO 1886, c 25.
An Act to amend the Bankruptcy Act, SC 1920, c 34.
An Act to amend "The Insolvent Act of 1875," SC 1876, c 30.
An Act to amend "The Insolvent Act of 1875, and the Act amending the Same," SC 1877, c 41.
An Act to amend the Statute Law (Pt 1), SA 1909, c 4, s 20.
An Act to authorize and provide for the winding up of the Consolidated Bank of Canada, SC 1880, c 46.
An Act to authorize and provide for the winding up of the Stadacona Bank, SC 1880, c 48.
An Act to confirm and give effect to a certain agreement between the Government of Canada, and the Great Western Railway Company, SC 1869, c 61.
An Act to grant relief to the Canada Agricultural Insurance Company, SC 1878, c 38.
Act to make further provisions respecting Assignments for the Benefit of Creditors, SO 1887, c 19.

An Act to make provision for the winding up of insolvent incorporated Fire or Marine Insurance Companies, SC 1878, c 21.
An Act to Prevent Frauds Frequently Committed by Bankrupts, 1705 (UK), 4 Ann, c 17.
An Act to repeal the Acts respecting Insolvency now in force in Canada, SC 1880, c 1.
Assignments and Preferences Act, RSO 1887, c 124.
Assignments and Preferences Act, RSO 1990, c A33.
Bankruptcy Act, 1883 (UK), 46 & 47 Vict, c 52.
Bankruptcy Act, 1914 (UK), 4 & 5 Geo V, c 59.
Bankruptcy Act of 1919, SC 1919, c 36.
Bankruptcy and Insolvency Act, RSC 1985, c B-3.
Board of Commerce Act, 1919, SC 1919, c 37.
British North America Act, 1867 (UK), 30 & 31 Vict, c 3.
Combines and Fair Prices Act, 1919, SC 1919, c 45.
Constitution Act, 1867 (UK), 30 & 31 Vict, c 3.
Creditors' Relief Act, RSO 1880, c 78.
Creditors' Relief Act, 2010, SO 2010, c 16.
Creditors' Relief Act, SA 1910(2), c 4.
Creditors' Relief Act, 1902, SBC 1902, c 17.
Creditors' Relief Act, SNB 1902, c 3.
Creditors' Relief Act, SNS 1903, c 14.
The Creditors' Relief Ordinance, Ord No 25 1893 (NWT).
Execution Act, RSO 1914, c 80.
Insolvent Act of 1864, S Prov C 1864 (27 & 28 Vict), c 17.
Insolvent Act of 1869, SC 1869, c 16, as amended by SC 1873, c 2; SC 1874, c 46.
Insolvent Act of 1875, SC 1875, c 16.
The Queen's Bench Act, SM 1895.
War Measures Act 1914, SC 1914, c 2.
Winding-Up Act, RSC 1886, c 129.

FEDERAL BILLS

1869 (2nd Sess 1st Parl)
Bill, *An Act to repeal the Act respecting Insolvency*.
1871 (4th Sess 1st Parl)
Bill, *An Act to repeal the Insolvency Laws now existing in the Dominion*.
1872 (5th Sess 1st Parl)
Bill C-3, *An Act to repeal the Insolvency Laws*.

1877 (4th Sess 3rd Parl)
Bill C-2, *An Act to repeal the Insolvency Laws now in force in the Dominion of Canada.*
Bill C-39, *An Act to repeal the Insolvent Act of 1875 and all Acts passed in amendment thereof.*
1878 (5th Sess 3rd Parl)
Bill C-2, *An Act to repeal the Insolvency Laws now in force in the Dominion of Canada.*
1879 (1st Sess 4th Parl)
Bill C-15, *An Act to repeal the Acts respecting Insolvency now in force in the Dominion.*
Bill C-22, *An Act to repeal the Insolvent Act of 1875 and to make provision in lieu thereof.*
Bill C-85, *An Act to repeal the Insolvent Act of 1875 and the Acts amending It, and to make provision for the liquidations of the estates of Insolvent Debtors.*
1880 (2nd Sess 4th Parl)
Bill C-2, *An Act to repeal the Acts respecting Insolvency now in force in Canada.*
Bill C-101, *An Act to provide for the distribution of the assets of Insolvent Debtors.*
1882 (4th Sess 4th Parl)
Bill C-136, *An Act for the equitable distribution of Insolvents' Estates.*
Bill C-137, *An Act for the Discharge of Past Insolvents.*
1883 (1st Sess 5th Parl)
Bill C-8, *An Act to provide for the Discharge of Past Insolvents.*
Bill C-9, *An Act for the equitable distribution of Insolvents' Estates.*
Bill C-99, *An Act to provide for the distribution of the assets of Insolvent Traders.*
1884 (2nd Sess 5th Parl)
Bill C-71, *An Act to provide for the distribution of the assets of Insolvent Debtors.*
Bill C-79, *An Act for the equitable distribution of Insolvents' Estates.*
1885 (3rd Sess 5th Parl)
Bill C-4, *An Act to provide for the distribution of assets of Insolvent Debtors.*
Bill C-32, *An Act respecting Insolvency.*
Bill C-33, *An Act for the equitable distribution of Insolvent Estates.*
Bill C-34, *An Act for the Discharge of Past Insolvents.*
1886 (4th Sess 5th Parl)
Bill C-71, *An Act for the discharge of Insolvent Debtors whose Estates have been distributed rateably among their Creditors.*

Bill C-93, *An Act to provide for the distribution of the assets of Insolvent Debtors.*

1887 (1st Sess 6th Parl)
Bill C-9, *An Act for the discharge of Insolvent Debtors whose Estates have been distributed rateably among the Creditors.*

1894 (4th Sess 7th Parl)
Bill C-152, *An Act respecting Insolvency.*
Bill S-C, *An Act respecting Insolvency.*

1895 (5th Sess 7th Parl)
Bill S-A, *An Act respecting Insolvency.*

1898 (3rd Sess 8th Parl)
Bill C-84, *An Act respecting Insolvency.*

1903 (3rd Sess 9th Parl)
Bill C-53, *An Act respecting Insolvency.*

1918 (1st Sess 13th Parl)
Bill C-25, *An Act respecting Bankruptcy.*

1919 (2nd Sess 13th Parl)
Bill C-18, *An Act respecting Bankruptcy.*

GOVERNMENT SOURCES AND DOCUMENTS

Debates of the Senate 1867–1919.

House of Commons Debates 1867–1919.

House of Commons, Select Committee. "Third Report of the Select Committee on Bankruptcy and Insolvency" in House of Commons, *Journals*, 1st Parl, 1st Sess, vol 1 (17 April 1868) A5. Also reported in (1868) 4:2 LCLJ 47 & 62.

House of Commons. Special Committee on Bill No. 25, *An Act Respecting Bankruptcy, 1918*, Ottawa, Library and Archives Canada (RG 14 87–8 / 146 Wallet on Bankruptcy at 17 April 1918).

Journals of the House of Commons and Senate, 1867–1919.

"Report of the Honourable the Minister of Justice approved by His Excellency the Governor General in Council on the 24th March, 1881" in W.E. Hodgins, *Dominion and Provincial Legislation: 1867–1895* (Ottawa: Government Printing Bureau, 1896) 170.

"Report of the Honourable the Minister of Justice approved by His Excellency the Governor General in Council on the 4th April, 1885" in W.E. Hodgins, *Dominion and Provincial Legislation: 1867–1895* (Ottawa: Government Printing Bureau, 1896) 522.

"Report of the Honourable the Minister of Justice, approved by His Excellency the Governor General in Council on the 6th March, 1886" in W.E. Hodgins,

Dominion and Provincial Legislation: 1867–1895 (Ottawa: Government Printing Bureau, 1896) 198.
"Report of the Honourable the Minister of Justice, approved by His Excellency the Governor General in Council on the 25th April, 1887" in W.E. Hodgins, *Dominion and Provincial Legislation: 1867–1895* (Ottawa: Government Printing Bureau, 1896) 853.
"Report of the Honourable the Minister of Justice, approved by His Excellency the Governor General in Council on the 7th June, 1888" in W.E. Hodgins, *Dominion and Provincial Legislation: 1867–1895* (Ottawa: Government Printing Bureau, 1896) 204.
Thayer, Robert H. "Report on Bankruptcy Administration in Canada" in *Administration of Bankruptcy Estates*, Committee Print (71st Cong, 3rd Sess, 1931).

PERIODICALS AND NEWSPAPERS

Broad-Axe [Charlottetown]
Canada Law Journal
Canada Law Times
Canadian Chartered Accountant
Canadian Druggist [Toronto]
The Canadian Dry Goods Review [Toronto]
Canadian Illustrated News
Canadian Law Review
The Canadian Monthly and National Review [Toronto]
The Daily Globe [Toronto]
Diogenes [Montreal]
Financial Post
The Globe
Grinchuckle [Montreal]
Halifax Citizen
Journal of Commerce: Finance and Insurance Review [Montreal]
Journal of the Canadian Bankers' Association
Local Courts & Municipal Gazette [Toronto]
Mainland Guardian [New Westminster]
The Monetary Times and Trade Review, Insurance Chronicle [Toronto]
Morning Freeman [Saint John]
The Nation
The Nineteenth Century [New York]
Saturday Night [Toronto]
Saturday Reader [Montreal]

Toronto World
Trade Review and Intercolonial Journal of Commerce [Montreal]
Upper Canada Law Journal
Winnipeg Daily Times

OTHER PRINTED PRIMARY SOURCES

Books and Pamphlets

Abbott, The Hon JJC. *The Insolvent Act of 1864 with Notes together with the Rules of Practice* (Quebec: George Desbarats and Malcolm Cameron, 1864).

The Bankruptcy Act with Amendments, 1920: Together with Rules and Forms Thereunder (Ottawa: Thomas Mulvey King's Printer, 1920).

Beausoleil, C. *La loi de faillite* (Montreal: Plinguet, 1877).

Bengough, J.W. *A Caricature of Canadian Politics: Events from the Union of 1841, As Illustrated by Cartoons from "Grip," and Various Other Sources*, vol 2 (Toronto: Grip, 1886).

Bradford, S.H. & J.H. Greenberg. *Bankruptcy Law of Canada* (Toronto: Burroughs & Co, 1926).

British Empire League. *Canadian Insolvency Legislation: Report of Meeting of the League held on Wednesday, December 4th, 1895, including a statement by the Hon Sir Charles Tupper* (London, UK: Commerce Print, 1895).

Bromfield, E.T. *Practical Hints to the Retail Merchant, or How to Make a Business Successful: With an Appendix Containing Advice to Embarrassed Debtors and Remarks on the Present Law of Bankruptcy in Canada* (Toronto: E.T. Bromfield, 1869).

Cameron, J.A.C. *The Law of Bankruptcy in Canada* (Toronto: Canada Law Book, 1920).

Clarke, Katherine A. "My Ship," in Katherine A. Clarke, *Lyrical Echoes* (Toronto: W. Briggs, 1899).

Clarke, Samuel Robinson. *The Insolvent Act of 1875, and Amending Acts* (Toronto: R. Carswell, 1877).

Clarkson, E.R.C. *Bankruptcy Legislation* (Toronto: 1885).

Commentaries on the Present Bankrupt Act in a Series of Letters Addressed to the Editor of the Morning Courier (Montreal: Lovell and Gibson, 1848).

Duncan, Lewis. *The Law and Practice of Bankruptcy in Canada* (Toronto: Carswell, 1922).

Edgar, James D. *The Insolvent Act of 1864, with Tariff, Notes, Forms, and a Full Index* (Toronto: Rollo & Adam, Law Publishers, 1864).

– *The Insolvent Act of 1869; with Tariff, Notes, Forms, and a Full Index* (Toronto: Copp, Clark & Co, 1869).

Edgar, James D. & F.H. Chrysler. *The Insolvent Act of 1875, with an Introductory Chapter; Notes Forms, Tariffs of Ontario, Quebec, and New Brunswick; and a Full Index* (Toronto: Copp, Clark & Co, 1875).

Grundy, H.P. "The Bankruptcy Act" in Canadian Legal History Project Archives, Manitoba (AWCLH A-41).

Harris, Carrie J. *Cyril Whyman's Mistake* (Toronto: William Bryce, 1894).

– *A Modern Evangeline* (Windsor, NS: JJ Anslow, 1896).

Heaton, E., ed. *The Commercial Handbook of Canada of Interest to Traders Investors and Intending Settlers* (Toronto: 1905).

The Insolvency Case in the Privy Council, Argument of Mr Blake for the Appellant (Toronto: Bryant Press, 1894).

Johnson, William Wickliffe. *Sketches of the Late Depression; Its Cause, Effect and Lessons* (Montreal: J Theo Robinson, 1882).

Leavitt, Lydia & Thad W.H. Leavitt. *Wise or Otherwise* (Toronto: Wells Publishing, 1898).

Mackintosh, C.H., ed. *The Canadian Parliamentary Companion and Annual Register, 1879* (Ottawa: Citizen, 1879).

MacMahon, Hugh. *The Insolvent Act of 1875, including Full Notes to Each Section, Tariff of Costs, Index, and List of Cases* (Toronto: Willing & Williamson, 1875).

Oliphant, Mrs. *At His Gates* (Toronto: Hunter, Rose, 1872).

Popham, John. *The Insolvent Act of 1869; with Notes and Decisions of the Courts of Ontario and Quebec; Together with the Rules of Practice and the Tariff of Fees for the Provinces of Ontario, Quebec, Nova Scotia, and New Brunswick* (Montreal: Dawson Brothers, 1870).

Ritchie, Thomas. *Fallacy of Insolvency Laws and their Baneful Effects* (1885).

Shakespeare, William. *"Othello, the Moor of Venice"* in Michael Neill, ed, *Othello: The Oxford Shakespeare* (New York: Oxford University Press, 2006).

Tytler, Sarah. *Logie Town* (Toronto: National Publishing, 1888).

Weir, Robert Stanley. *An Insolvency Manual* (Montreal: A. Periard, 1890).

Wilson, William. *Analyse et index de l'Acte de faillite de 1875* (Ottawa: Maclean Roger, 1875).

Wotherspoon, Ivan. *The Insolvent Act of 1875: with the Rules of Practice and Tariffs of Fees in Force in the Different Provinces of the Dominion* (Montreal: Dawson Brothers, 1875).

Articles

Aikins, James. "The Advancement of the Science of Jurisprudence in Canada" (1915) 1 Proceedings of the Canadian Bar Association 3.

Appleton, John. "Ending Moratoria in Canada" (1920) 27:4 Journal of the Canadian Bankers' Association 438.
Armour, E.D. "The Constitution of Canada: III," Note, (1891) 11:10 Can LT 233.
Bicknell, James. "The Advisability of Establishing a Bankruptcy Court in Canada" (1913) 33:1 Can LT 35.
– "The Advisability of Establishing a Bankruptcy Court in Canada" (Address delivered before the Ontario Bar Association, [nd]), (1913) 49:4 Can LJ (NS) 81.
Book Review of *The Insolvent Act of 1869; with Tariff, Notes, Forms, and a Full Index* by James D. Edgar, (1870) 6 Local Ct Gaz 31.
Cameron, J.A.C. "Annotation: Bankruptcy Act of Canada, 1920" (1920) 53 DLR 135.
Canadian Bankers' Association. "Address of the President of the Canadian Bankers' Association: Delivered at the Eighth Annual Meeting of the Association" (1900) 7:2 Journal of the Canadian Bankers' Association 109.
– "Proceedings of the Fourth Annual Meeting of the Canadian Bankers' Association (11, 12 September 1895)" (1895) 3:1 Journal of the Canadian Bankers' Association 15.
– "Proceedings of the Seventh Annual Meeting of the Canadian Bankers' Association (26, 27 October 1898)" (1899) 6:2 Journal of the Canadian Bankers' Association 103.
– "Proceedings of the Third Annual Meeting of the Association (26, 27 July 1894)" (1894) 2:1 Journal of the Canadian Bankers' Association 5.
– "Report of the Proceedings of the First Annual Meeting (19 May 1892)" (1892) 1 Journal of the Canadian Bankers' Association 309.
Cassels, R.S. "Mercantile Preferences," Note, (1891) 11:3 Can LT 61.
Clarkson, G.T. "The Bankruptcy Act" (1920–1) 10 Canadian Chartered Accountant 154.
Duncan, Lewis. "The Operation and Effect of the Bankruptcy Act" (Address delivered before the Toronto Bankers' Educational Association, 22 February 1922), (1922) 29:4 Journal of the Canadian Bankers' Association 502.
Editorial. (1879) 15 Can LJ (NS) 119.
– (1879) 15 Can LJ (NS) 146.
– (1880) 16 Can LJ (NS) 69.
– "The Act Respecting Insolvency" (1864) 10 UCLJ 225.
– "The Assignments Act" (1893) 13:5 Can LT 125.
– "Bankruptcy" (1920) 40:7 Can LT 546.
– "Bankruptcy Act" (1922) 42:3 Can LT 141.
– "Bankruptcy and Insolvency" (1861) 7 UCLJ 10.
– "A Bankruptcy Law Required" (1863) 9 UCLJ 141.

– "Colonial Bankruptcy Law" (1861) 7 UCLJ 165.
– "Exemptions from Execution" (1914) 50:10 Can LJ (NS) 321.
– "Federal Bankruptcy Act: Reasons Given Before Canadian Men's Trust Association Why There Should be a Dominion Bankruptcy Act" (1916–17) 6 Canadian Chartered Accountant 282.
– "The Insolvency Acts" (1872) 8 Local Ct Gaz 65.
– "Insolvency Legislation" (1899) 35:6 Can LJ (NS) 179.
– "The Proposed Bankruptcy Bill" (1884) 4:2 Can LT 62.
– "Repeal of Bankruptcy Law in United States" (1878) 14 Can LJ (NS) 189.
– "Shall We Have a Bankruptcy Law?" (1858) 4 UCLJ 2.
– "Uncle Wordly's Letters To His Nephews," *Grinchuckle* 1:5 (4 November 1869) 41.
Fisher, The Honourable Mr Justice. "The Bankruptcy Law of Canada" [1924] 3 DLR 217.
Girouard, D. "Can a Person Who Ceased to be a Trader Before Passing of the *Insolvent Act of 1869*, Take Benefit of the Act" (1872) 2:1 RCLJ 65.
– "Can a Trader without Assets Make an Assignment?" (1872) 2:1 RCLJ 63.
– "Le droit constitutionnel du Canada" (1871) 1:2 RCLJ 189.
Grundy, H.P. "Bankruptcy Act" (1920) 27 Beaver 426.
– "The Bankruptcy Act" (Address delivered before the Toronto Bankers' Educational Association, 11 May 1920), (1920) 27:4 Journal of the Canadian Bankers' Association 426.
– "Synopsis of the Canadian Bankruptcy Act" (1920–1) 1 CBR 325.
Jacobs, S.W. "A Canadian Bankruptcy Act: Is it A Necessity?" (1917) 37:8 Can LT 604.
– "The Proposed Bankruptcy Act" (Address delivered before the Canadian Bar Association, 1918), (1918) 3 Proceedings of the Canadian Bar Association 164.
Kerr, William H. "Deeds of Composition and Discharge Between Co-Partners and their Creditors under the *Insolvent Act of 1869*" (1871) 1:2 RCLJ 171.
Labatt, C.B. "The Doctrine of Pressure" (1899) 35:10 Can LJ (NS) 322.
Lefroy, A.H.F. "The Privy Council on Bankruptcy" (1894) 30:6 Can LJ (NS) 182.
Lucas, F.G.T. "The New 'Bankruptcy Act'" (1920) 40:8 Can LT 668.
Martin, N.L. "A New Bankruptcy Act" (1918–19) 8 Canadian Chartered Accountant 24.
McMaster, A.C. "The Bankruptcy Act" (Address delivered before the Institute of Chartered Accountants of Ontario, 20 January 1913), (1912–13) 2 Canadian Chartered Accountant 236.
McMaster, T.G. "A Dominion Insolvency Act" (1900) 7:2 Journal of the Canadian Bankers' Association 129.

Proudfoot, W.M. "An Insolvent Law," Note, (1894) 14:12 Can LT 305.
Quinte. "Insolvent Acts: Assignees," Letter to the Editor, (1868) 4 Can LJ (NS) 101.
"Report of the Committee on Bankruptcy and Insolvency" (1868) 4:2 LCLJ 47.
R.M.F. "Legislation Upon Insolvency" (1873) 2:5 Canadian Monthly and National Review 419.
Russell, B. "Provisions of the British North America Act for Uniformity of Provincial Laws" (1898) 34:14 Can LJ (NS) 513.
Scarboro. "Assignees in Bankruptcy Matters – The Operation of the Act," Letter to the Editor, (1868) 4 Can LJ (NS) 83.
– "Insolvent Acts – Assignees," Letter to the Editor, (1868) 4 Can LJ (NS) 159.
– "A Question under the Bankrupt Law" (1867) 3 Can LJ 193.
Thompson, Bram. "Canadian Bankruptcy Act: Monopoly of the Trusteeship and of the Law" (1921) 41:2 Can LT 96.
Thomson, D.E. "Assignment for Creditors' Benefit," Note, (1881) 1:17 Can LT 669.
– "Bankruptcy Law in Canada" (1894) 1:1 Barrister 39.
– "Bankruptcy Legislation in Canada" (1902) 1:4 Can L Rev 173.
– "The Proposed Bankruptcy Bill," Note, (1883) 3:14 Can LT 559.
Union. "The Insolvent Law of 1864 – Assignees," Letter to the Editor, (1868) 4 Can LJ (NS) 131.
Wade, Osler. "The Dominion Bankruptcy Act" (1920–1) 10 Canadian Chartered Accountant 234.
– "Insolvency Including Assignments and Winding-Up Proceedings under the Dominion and Ontario Winding-Up Acts" (Address delivered before the Chartered Accountants Students' Association, 1 December 1919), (1919–20) 9 Canadian Chartered Accountant 167.

Secondary Sources

BOOKS AND ARTICLES

Adelman, Jeremy. "Prairie Farm Debt and the Financial Crisis of 1914" (1990) 71:4 Canadian Historical Review 491.
Baggaley, Carman D. *The Emergence of the Regulatory State in Canada 1867–1939* (Ottawa: Economic Council of Canada, 1981).
Baker, G. Blaine. "The Province of Post-Confederation Rights" (1995) 45:1 UTLJ 77.
– "The Reconstruction of Upper Canadian Legal Thought in the Late Victorian Empire" (1985) 3:2 LHR 219.
Balleisen, Edward J. *Navigating Failure: Bankruptcy and Commercial Society in Antebellum America* (Chapel Hill: University of North Carolina Press, 2001).

– "Vulture Capitalism in Antebellum America: The 1841 Federal Bankruptcy Act and the Exploitation of Financial Distress" (1996) 70:4 Bus Hist Rev 473.

Baskerville, Peter. *A Silent Revolution: Gender and Wealth in English Canada, 1860–1930* (Montreal and Kingston: McGill-Queen's University Press, 2008).

Batzel, Victor. "Parliament, Businessmen and Bankruptcy, 1825–1883: A Study in Middle Class Alienation" (1983) 18:2 Can J Hist 171.

Béland, Daniel. "Ideas, Interests and Institutions: Historical Institutionalism Revisited" in André Lecours, ed, *New Institutionalism: Theory and Analysis* (Toronto: University of Toronto Press, 2005).

Beck, J. Murray. *Pendulums of Power: Canada's Federal Elections* (Toronto: Prentice Hall, 1968).

Bell, John. "Path Dependence and Legal Development" (2013) 87:4 Tul L Rev 787.

Benidickson, Jamie. "The Combines Problem in Canadian Legal Thought, 1867–1920" (1993) 43:4 UTLJ 799.

Ben-Ishai, Stephanie & Virginia Torrie. "Farm Insolvency in Canada" (2013) 2 Journal of the Insolvency Institute of Canada 33.

Bliss, Michael. "Another Anti-Trust Tradition: Canadian Anti-Combines Policy, 1899–1910" (1973) 47:2 Bus Hist Rev 177.

– *A Living Profit: Studies in the Social History of Canadian Business 1883–1911* (Toronto: McClelland and Stewart, 1974).

– *Northern Enterprise: Five Centuries of Canadian Business* (Toronto: McClelland and Stewart, 1987).

Bohémier, Albert. *La faillite en droit constitutionnel canadien* (Montreal: Les Presses de l'Université de Montréal, 1972).

– *Faillite et insolvabilité*, t 1 (Montreal: Éditions Themis, 1992).

Boshkoff, Douglass G. "The Bankrupt's Moral Obligation to Pay His Discharged Debts: A Conflict between Contract Theory and Bankruptcy Policy" (1971) 47:1 Ind LJ 36.

– "Fresh Start, False Start or Head Start" (1995) 70:2 Ind LJ 549.

– "Limited, Conditional, and Suspended Discharges in Anglo-American Bankruptcy Proceedings" (1982) 131:1 U Pa L Rev 69.

Bothwell, Robert, Ian Drummond & John English. *Canada, 1900–1945* (Toronto: University of Toronto Press, 1987).

Bradshaw, Mark. "The Role of Politics and Economics in Early American Bankruptcy Law" (1997) 18:3 Whittier L Rev 739.

Brown, Robert Craig & Ramsay Cook. *Canada, 1896–1921: A Nation Transformed* (Toronto: McClelland and Stewart, 1974).

Burley, David G. *A Particular Condition in Life: Self-Employment and Social Mobility in Mid-Victorian Brantford* (Montreal and Kingston: McGill-Queen's University Press, 1994).

– "Good for All He Would Ask: Credit and Debt in the Transition to Industrial Capitalism – The Case of Mid-Nineteenth-Century Brantford, Ontario" (1987) 20:39 Social History 79.

Cairns, Alan C. "The Judicial Committee and Its Critics" (1971) 4:3 Canadian Journal of Political Science 301.

Caminker, Evan H. "Why Must Inferior Courts Obey Superior Court Precedents?" (1994) 46:4 Stan L Rev 817.

Campbell, John L. "Ideas, Politics and Public Policy" (2002) 28:1 Annual Review of Sociology 21.

Carignan, Pierre. "La compétence législative en matière de faillite et d'insolvabilité" (1979) 57:1 Can Bar Rev 47.

Carlson, David Gray. "Debt Collecting as Rent Seeking" (1995) 79:3–4 Minn L Rev 817.

Chabot, Marc. *Faillite et insolvabilité* (Quebec: Presses de l'Université du Québec, 1991).

Chambers, Lori. *Married Women and Property Law in Victorian Ontario* (Toronto: University of Toronto Press, 1997).

Cohen, Jay. "The History of Imprisonment for Debt and Its Relation to the Development of Discharge in Bankruptcy" (1983) 3:2 J Legal Hist 153.

Coleman, Peter. *Debtors and Creditors in America: Insolvency, Imprisonment for Debt, and Bankruptcy, 1607–1900* (Madison: State Historical Society of Wisconsin, 1974).

Cook, Ramsay. *Provincial Autonomy, Minority Rights and the Compact Theory, 1867–1921* (Ottawa: Queen's Printer, 1969).

Cornish W.R. & G. de N. Clark. *Law and Society in England, 1750–1950* (London: Sweet & Maxwell, 1989).

Corry, J.A. "The Growth of Government Activities in Canada 1914–1921" [1940] Canadian Historical Association Annual Report 63.

– *The Growth of Government Activities Since Confederation, Study Prepared for the Royal Commission on Dominion-Provincial Relations* (Ottawa: King's Printer, 1939).

Countryman, Vern. "Bankruptcy and the Individual Debtor: A Modest Proposal to Return to the Seventeenth Century" (1983) 32:4 Cath U L Rev 809.

– "A History of American Bankruptcy Law" (1976) 81:6 Com LJ 226.

Dalhuisen, Jan H. "Development of Bankruptcy Remedies in Western Europe and United States in the Ninetieth and Twentieth Centuries" in David A. Botwinik & Kenneth W. Weinrib, eds, *European Bankruptcy Laws*, 2nd ed

(Washington, DC: Section of International Law and Practice, American Bar Association, 1986).

Dal Pont, Gino & Lynden Griggs. "The Journey from Ear-Cropping and Capital Punishment to the Bankruptcy Legislation Amendment Bill 1995" (1995) 8 Corp & Bus LJ 155.

de la Durantaye, Louis-Joseph. *Traité de la faillite en la province de Québec à l'usage des praticiens et des commerçants* (Montreal: Chez l'auteur, 1934).

Di Martino, Paolo. "The Historical Evolution of Bankruptcy Law in England, the US and Italy up to 1939: Determinants of Institutional Change and Structural Differences" in Karl Gratzer & Dieter Stiefel, eds, *History of Insolvency and Bankruptcy from an International Perspective* (Huddinge: Södertörns högskola, 2008) 263.

Dodd, Lawrence C. & Calvin Jillson. "Conversations on the Study of American Politics: An Introduction" in Lawrence C. Dodd & Calvin Jillson, eds, *The Dynamics of American Politics: Approaches & Interpretations* (Boulder: Westview, 1994) 1.

Drummond, Ian M. *Progress Without Planning: The Economic History of Ontario From Confederation to the Second World War* (Toronto: University of Toronto Press, 1987).

Duffy, Ian P.H. *Bankruptcy and Insolvency in London During the Industrial Revolution* (New York: Garland, 1985).

– "English Bankrupts, 1571–1861" (1980) 24:4 Am J Legal Hist 283.

Duggan, Anthony & Thomas Telfer. "Canadian Preference Law Reform" (2007) 42:3 Tex Int'l LJ 661.

– "Voidable Preferences" in Stephanie Ben-Ishai & Anthony Duggan, eds, *Canadian Bankruptcy and Insolvency Law: Bill C-55, Statute c.47 and Beyond* (Toronto: LexisNexis, 2007) 145.

Duncan, Andrew J. "From Dismemberment to Discharge: The Origins of Modern American Bankruptcy Law" (1995) 100:2 Com LJ 191.

Dunlop, Bruce, David McQueen & M.J. Trebilcock. *Canadian Competition Policy: A Legal and Economic Analysis* (Toronto: Canada Law Book, 1987).

Dunlop, C.R.B. *Creditor-Debtor Law in Canada*, 2nd ed (Toronto: Carswell, 1995).

Ernst, Daniel R. "Law and American Political Development, 1877–1938" (1998) 26:1 Reviews in American History 205.

Fairfax, Lisa. "The Legal Origins Theory in Crisis" [2009] BYUL Rev 1571.

Ferron, J. Murray. "The Bankruptcy Court and Administration in Ontario" (1990) 24:2 L Soc'y Gaz 130.

Finn, Margot C. *The Character of Credit: Personal Debt in English Culture, 1740–1914* (Cambridge, UK: Cambridge University Press, 2003).

Forster, Ben. "Finding the Right Size: Markets and Competition in Mid- and Late Nineteenth-Century Ontario" in Roger Hall, William Westfall & Laurel Sefton MacDowell, eds, *Patterns of the Past: Interpreting Ontario's History* (Toronto: Dundurn Press, 1988) 150.

Freyer, Tony A. *Forums of Order: The Federal Courts and Business in American History* (Greenwich, Conn: JAI Press, 1979).

– *Producers versus Capitalists: Constitutional Conflict in Antebellum America* (Charlottesville: University of Virginia Press, 1994).

Fridenson, Patrick. "Business Failure and the Agenda of Business History" (2004) 5:4 Enterprise & Society 562.

Friedman, Lawrence M. & Thadeus F. Niemira. "The Concept of the 'Trader' in Early Bankruptcy Law" (1958) 5:2 St Louis ULJ 223.

Frimet, Rhett. "The Birth of Bankruptcy in the United States" (1991) 96:2 Com LJ 160.

Gervais, Gaétan. "Le commerce de détail au Canada: 1870–1880" (1980) 33:4 Revue d'histoire de l'Amérique française 521.

Gibson, Dale. "Development of Federal Legal and Judicial Institutions in Canada" (1996) 23:3 Man LJ 450.

Gibson, Lee & Dale Gibson. "Sir James Aikins' Seamless Web: Finding Fortune and Fame as a Lawyer in the Adolescent Canadian West" (1992) 21:2 Man LJ 161.

Girard, Philip. "The Making of a Colonial Lawyer: Beamish Murdoch of Halifax, 1822–1842" in Carol Wilton, ed, *Essays in the History of Canadian Law: Inside the Law: Canadian Law Firms in Historical Perspective*, vol 7 (Toronto: University of Toronto Press, 1996) 57.

– "The Maritime Provinces, 1850–1939: Lawyers and Legal Institutions" (1996) 23:3 Man LJ 379.

– "Married Women's Property, Chancery Abolition and Insolvency Law: Law Reform in Nova Scotia, 1820–1867" in Philip Girard & Jim Phillips, eds, *Essays in the History of Canadian Law: Nova Scotia*, vol 3 (Toronto: University of Toronto Press, 1990) 80.

Glassford, Larry A. "Meighen, Arthur" in *Dictionary of Canadian Biography*, online: <http://biographi.ca/en/bio/meighen_arthur_18E.html>.

Gleixner, Micheline & Michael J. Bray. "La gestion des risques des créanciers et la réhabilitation des débiteurs surendettés: objectifs contradictories ou complémentaires?" (March 2013), online: Office of the Superintendent of Bankruptcy Canada <http://www.ic.gc.ca/eic/site/bsf-osb.nsf/eng/home>.

Gross, Karen. *Failure and Forgiveness: Rebalancing the Bankruptcy System* (New Haven: Yale University Press, 1997).

Gross, Karen, Marie Stefanini Newman & Denise Campbell. "Ladies in Red: Learning from America's First Female Bankrupts" (1996) 40:1 Am J Legal Hist 1.

Haagen, Paul. "Eighteenth Century Society and the Debt Law" in Stanley Cohen & Andrew Scull, eds, *Social Control and the State* (Oxford: Blackwell, 1983) 229.

Hall, Peter A. "Policy Paradigms, Social Learning, and the State: The Case of Economic Policymaking in Britain" (1993) 25:3 Comparative Politics 275.

Hall, Peter A. & Rosemary C.R. Taylor. "Political Science and the Three New Institutionalisms" (1996) 44:5 Political Studies 936.

Hallinan, Charles. "The 'Fresh Start' Policy in Consumer Bankruptcy: A Historical Inventory and an Interpretative Theory" (1986) 21:1 U Rich L Rev 49.

Hansen, Bradley. "Commercial Associations and the Creation of a National Economy: The Demand for Federal Bankruptcy Law" (1998) 72:1 Business History Review 86.

– *The Origins of Bankruptcy Law in the United States, 1789–1898* (PhD thesis, Washington University, 1995) [unpublished].

Hansen, Ivan A. *Bankruptcy in the Beginning: A Historical Survey of the Laws of Bankruptcy* (Wellington: New Zealand Institute of Credit and Financial Management, 1980).

Hay, Colin. "Ideas, Interests and Institutions in the Comparative Political Economy of Great Transformations" (2004) 11:1 Review of International Political Economy 204.

Hibbitts, Bernard J. "A Bridle for Leviathan: The Supreme Court and the Board of Commerce" (1989) 21:1 Ottawa L Rev 65.

– "A Change of Mind: The Supreme Court and the Board of Railway Commissioners, 1903–1929" (1991) 41:1 UTLJ 60.

Hogg, Peter W. *Constitutional Law of Canada*, loose-leaf, vol 1 (consulted on 5 July 2013), 5th ed (Toronto: Carswell, 2007).

Holdsworth, W.S. *A History of English Law*, vol 8 (London, UK: Methuen, 1925).

Honsberger, John. "Bankruptcy: A Comparison of the Systems of the United States and Canada" (1971) 45:2 Am Bank LJ 129.

– "Bankruptcy Administration in the United States and Canada" (1975) 63:6 Cal L Rev 1515.

– "The Nature and Purpose of Bankruptcy" (1973) 16 CBR (NS) 209.

– "The Nature of Bankruptcy and Insolvency in a Constitutional Perspective" (1972) 10:1 Osgoode Hall LJ 199.

– "The Need for a Rapprochement of the Bankruptcy Systems of Canada and the United States" (1972) 18:2 McGill LJ 147.

– "Philosophy and Design of Modern Fresh Start Policies: The Evolution of Canada's Legislative Policy" (1999) 37:1–2 Osgoode Hall LJ 171.

Hoppit, Julian. "Attitudes to Credit in Britain, 1680–1790" (1990) 33:2 Historical Journal 305.

– "Financial Crises in Eighteenth-Century England" (1986) 39:1 The Economic History Review 39.

– *Risk and Failure in English Business, 1700–1800* (New York: Cambridge University Press, 1987).

– "The Use and Abuse of Credit in Eighteenth-Century England" in Neil McKendrick & R.B .Outhwaite, eds, *Business Life and Public Policy: Essays in Honour of D.C. Coleman* (Cambridge, UK: Cambridge University Press, 1986) 64.

Houlden, Lloyd W. "Bankruptcy" in *Special Lectures of the Law Society of Upper Canada 1956* (Toronto: Richard de Boo, 1956).

Howard, Margaret. "A Theory of Discharge in Consumer Bankruptcy" (1987) 48:4 Ohio St LJ 1047.

Hutchison, Paul P. "Sir John J.C. Abbott: Barrister and Solicitor" (1948) 26:6 Can Bar Rev 934.

Hyman, Louis. *Debtor Nation: The History of America in Red Ink* (Princeton: Princeton University Press, 2011).

Hynes, Richard M., Anup Malani & Eric A. Posner. "The Political Economy of Property Exemption Laws" (2004) 47:1 JL & Econ 19.

Immergut, Ellen M. "The Theoretical Core of the New Institutionalism" (1998) 26:1 Politics & Society 5.

Jackson, Thomas H. *The Logic and Limits of Bankruptcy Law* (Cambridge, Mass: Harvard University Press, 1986).

Johnson, J.K. & Carole B. Stelmack, eds. *The Letters of Sir John A. Macdonald, 1858–1861* (Ottawa: Public Archives of Canada, 1969).

Jones, W.J. *The Foundations of English Bankruptcy: Statutes and Commissions in the Early Modern Period* (Philadelphia: American Philosophical Society, 1979).

Joslin, G. Stanley. "Bankruptcy: Anglo American Contrasts" (1966) 29:2 Mod L Rev 149.

– "The Philosophy of Bankruptcy – A Re-examination" (1964) 17:2 U Fla L Rev 189.

Kadens, Emily. "The Last Bankrupt Hanged: Balancing Incentives in the Development of Bankruptcy Law" (2010) 59:7 Duke LJ 1229.

Kagan, Robert A. "The Routinization of Debt Collection: An Essay on Social Change and Conflict in the Courts" (1984) 18:3 L & Soc'y Rev 323.

Kelley, Ninette & Michael Trebilcock. *The Making of the Mosaic: A History of Canadian Immigration Policy* (Toronto: University of Toronto Press, 1998).

Khemani, R.S. & W.T. Stanbury, eds. *Historical Perspectives on Canadian Competition Policy* (Halifax: Institute for Research on Public Policy, 1991).

Kim, Pauline T. "Lower Court Discretion" (2007) 82:2 NYUL Rev 383.

Kolish, Evelyn. "Imprisonment for Debt in Lower Canada, 1791–1840" (1987) 32:3 McGill LJ 602.

– "L'introduction de la faillite au Bas-Canada: conflit social ou national?" (1986) 40:2 Revue d'histoire de l'Amérique française 215.

– *Nationalismes et conflits de droits: le débat du droit privé au Québec 1760–1840* (Quebec: Hurtubise HMH, 1994).

– "Some Aspects of Civil Litigation in Lower Canada 1785–1825: Towards the Use of Court Records for Canadian Social History" (1989) 70:3 Canadian Historical Review 337.

Lahey, William. "Constitutional Adjudication, Provincial Rights and the Structure of Legal Thought in Late Nineteenth-Century New Brunswick" (1990) 39 UNBLJ 185.

La Porta, Rafael, Florencio Lopez-de-Silanes & Andrei Shleifer. "Law and Finance" (1998) 106:6 Journal of Political Economy 1113.

– "The Economic Consequences of Legal Origins" (2008) 46:2 Journal of Economic Literature 285.

Lecours, André. "New Institutionalism: Issues and Questions" in André Lecours, ed, *New Institutionalism: Theory and Analysis* (Toronto: University of Toronto Press, 2005) 3.

Lester, V. Markham. *Victorian Insolvency: Bankruptcy, Imprisonment for Debt and Company Winding-Up in Nineteenth-Century England* (Oxford: Clarendon Press, 1995).

Levi, Edward H. & James W.M. Moore. "Bankruptcy and Reorganization: A Survey of Changes" (1937) 5:1 U Chicago L Rev 1.

Levinthal, Louis Edward. "The Early History of Bankruptcy Law" (1918) 66:5–6 U Pa L Rev 223.

– "The Early History of English Bankruptcy Law" (1919) 67:1 U Pa L Rev 1.

Mann, Bruce H. *Republic of Debtors: Bankruptcy in the Age of American Independence* (London, UK: Harvard University Press, 2002).

Marr, William L. & Donald G. Patterson. *Canada: An Economic History* (Toronto: Gage, 1980).

Martel, Edouard. "The Debtor's Discharge From Bankruptcy" (1971) 17:4 McGill LJ 718.

McBride, Stephen. "The Political Economy Tradition and Canadian Policy Studies" in Laurent Dobuzinskis, Michael Howlett & David Laycock, eds, *Policy Studies in Canada: The State of the Art* (Toronto: University of Toronto Press, 1996) 49.

McCalla, Douglas. "An Introduction to the Nineteenth-Century Business World" in Tom Traves, ed, *Essays in Canadian Business History* (Toronto: McClelland and Stewart, 1984) 13.
– *Planting the Province: The Economic History of Upper Canada, 1784–1870* (Toronto: University of Toronto Press, 1993).
– *The Upper Canada Trade, 1834–1872: A Study of the Buchanans' Business* (Toronto: University of Toronto Press, 1979).
McCoid, John C., II. "The Discharge: The Most Important Development in Bankruptcy History" (1996) 70:2 Am Bank LJ 163.
– "The Occasion for Involuntary Bankruptcy" (1987) 61:3 Am Bank LJ 195.
– "The Origins of Voluntary Bankruptcy" (1988) 5:2 Bankr Dev J 361.
McLaren, John. "The Legal Historian, Masochist or Missionary? A Canadian's Reflections" (1994) 5:1 Legal Education Review 67.
Miller, Carman. "Mowat, Laurier and the Federal Liberal Party, 1887–1897" in Donald Swainson, ed, *Oliver Mowat's Ontario* (Toronto: Macmillan, 1972) 69.
– "Sir John Joseph Caldwell Abbott" in *Dictionary of Canadian Biography* online: <http://www.biographi.ca/en/bio/abbott_john_joseph_caldwell_12E.html>.
Monod, David. *Store Wars: Shopkeepers and the Culture of Mass Marketing, 1890–1939* (Toronto: University of Toronto Press, 1996).
Mueller, Dennis C. *Public Choice III* (Cambridge: Cambridge University Press, 2003).
Muldrew, Craig. *The Economy of Obligation: The Culture of Credit and Social Relations in Early Modern England* (Hampshire, UK: Macmillan, 1998).
Naylor, R.T. *The History of Canadian Business, 1867–1914*, vols 1 & 2 (Toronto: James Lorimer & Co, 1975).
Noel, F. Regis. *A History of the Bankruptcy Clause of the Constitution of the United States of America* (Gettysburg: Gettysburg Compiler Print, 1918).
Norrie, Kenneth & Douglas Owram. *A History of the Canadian Economy* (Toronto: Harcourt Brace, 1991).
North, Douglass. *Institutions, Institutional Change and Economic Performance* (New York: Cambridge University Press, 1990).
Oliver, Peter. *Terror to Evil Doers: Prisons and Punishments in Nineteenth-Century Ontario* (Toronto: University of Toronto Press, 1998).
Owram, Doug. *The Government Generation: Canadian Intellectuals and the State, 1900–1945* (Toronto: University of Toronto Press, 1986).
Pal, Leslie A. "Missed Opportunities or Comparative Advantage? Canadian Contributions to the Study of Public Policy" in Laurent Dobuzinskis, Michael Howlett & David Laycock, eds, *Policy Studies in Canada: The State of the Art* (Toronto: University of Toronto Press, 1996) 359.

Papke, David Ray. "Rhetoric and Retrenchment: Agrarian Ideology and American Bankruptcy Law" (1989) 54:4 Mo L Rev 871.

Pearlston, Karen. "Married Women Bankrupts in the Age of Coverture" (2009) 34:2 Law & Soc Inquiry 265.

Pierson, Paul & Theda Skocpol. "Historical Institutionalism in Contemporary Political Science" in Ira Katznelson & Helen V. Milner, eds, *Political Science: The State of the Discipline* (New York: Norton, 2002) 693.

Plank, Thomas E. "The Constitutional Limits of Bankruptcy" (1996) 63:3 Tenn L Rev 487.

Pomfret, Richard. *The Economic Development of Canada* (Toronto: Methuen, 1981).

Prado, Mariana & Michael Trebilcock. "Path Dependence, Development, and The Dynamics of Institutional Reform" (2009) 59:3 UTLJ 341.

Priest, Margot & Aron Wohl. "The Growth of Federal and Provincial Regulation of Economic Activity, 1867–1978" in W.T. Stanbury, ed, *Government Regulation: Scope, Growth, Process* (Montreal: The Institute for Research on Public Policy, 1980) 69.

Radin, Max. "The Nature of Bankruptcy" (1940) 89:1 U Pa L Rev 1.

Richardson, Lynne E. "Young, James" in *Dictionary of Canadian Biography*, online: <http://biographi.ca/en/bio/young_james_1835_1913_14E.html>.

Risk, R.C.B. "A.H.F. Lefroy: Common Law Thought in Late Nineteenth-Century Canada: on Burying One's Grandfather" (1991) 41:3 UTLJ 307.

– "The Beginnings of Regulation" in EG Baldwin, ed, *The Cambridge Lectures: Selected Papers Based upon Lectures Delivered at the Conference of the Canadian Institute for Advanced Legal Studies* (Toronto: Butterworths, 1984) 252.

– "Blake and Liberty" in Janet Ajzenstat, ed, *Canadian Constitutionalism: 1791–1991* (Ottawa: Canadian Study of Parliament Group, 1992) 195.

– "Canadian Courts Under the Influence" (1990) 40:4 UTLJ 687.

– "Constitutional Scholarship in Late Nineteenth Century: Making Federalism Work" (1996) 46:3 UTLJ 427.

– "Constitutional Thought in the Late Nineteenth Century" in Dale Gibson & W. Wesley Pue, eds, *Glimpses of Canadian Legal History* (Winnipeg: University of Manitoba Legal Research Institute, 1991) 205.

– "The Golden Age: The Law about the Market in Nineteenth-Century Ontario" (1976) 26:3 UTLJ 307.

– "Last Golden Age: Property and the Allocation of Losses in Ontario in the Nineteenth Century" (1977) 27:2 UTLJ 199.

– "Law and the Economy in Mid-Nineteenth-Century Ontario: A Perspective" (1977) 27:4 UTLJ 403.

– "Lawyers, Courts and the Rise of the Regulatory State" (1984) 9:1 Dal LJ 31.

– "The Nineteenth-Century Foundations of the Business Corporation in Ontario" (1973) 23:3 UTLJ 270.
– "A Prospectus for Canadian Legal History" (1973) 1:2 Dal LJ 227.
– "The Scholars and the Constitution: P.O.G.G. and the Privy Council" (1996) 23:3 Man LJ 496.
Risk, Richard & Robert C. Vipond. "Rights Talk in Canada in the Late Nineteenth Century: 'The Good Sense and Right Feeling of the People'" (1996) 14:1 LHR 1.
Robertson, David Brian. "Politics and the Past: History, Behaviouralism, and the Return to Institutionalism in American Political Science" in Eric H. Monkkonen, ed, *Engaging the Past: The Uses of History Across the Social Sciences* (Durham: Duke University Press, 1994) 113.
Roe, Mark. *Strong Managers, Weak Owners: The Political Roots of American Corporate Finance* (Princeton: Princeton University Press, 1996).
Rubin, G.R. & David Sugarman, eds. *Law, Economy and Society, 1750–1914: Essays in the History of English Law* (Abingdon: Professional Books, 1984).
Sandage, Scott A. *Born Losers: A History of Failure in America* (Cambridge, Mass: Harvard University Press, 2005).
Sauer, Richard C. "Bankruptcy Law and the Maturing of American Capitalism" (1994) 55:2 Ohio St LJ 291.
Saywell, John T. *The Lawmakers: Judicial Power and the Shaping of Canadian Federalism* (Toronto: University of Toronto Press, 2002).
Scheiber, Harry N. "Federalism and the American Economic Order, 1789–1910" (1975) 10:1 Law & Soc'y Rev 57.
Schneiderman, David. "Constitutional Interpretation in an Age of Anxiety: A Reconsideration of the *Local Prohibition Case*" (1996) 41:2 McGill LJ 411.
Sgard, Jérôme. "Do Legal Origins Matter? The Case of Bankruptcy Laws in Europe 1808–1914" (2006) 10:3 European Review of Economic History 389.
Skeel, David A., Jr. *Debt's Dominion: A History of Bankruptcy Law in America* (Princeton: Princeton University Press, 2001).
– "Public Choice and the Future of Public Choice–Influenced Legal Scholarship" (1998) 50:3 V and L Rev 647.
Skocpol, Theda. *Protecting Soldiers and Mothers: The Political Origins of Social Policy in the United States* (Cambridge, Mass: Belknap Press of Harvard University Press, 1992).
– "Reply: Against Evolutionism: Social Policies and American Political Development" (1994) 8:1 Studies in American Political Development 140.
Skowronek, Stephen. *Building a New American State: The Expansion of National Administrative Capacities, 1877–1920* (New York: Cambridge University Press, 1982).

Smith, Allan. "The Myth of the Self-made Man in English Canada, 1850–1914" (1978) 59:2 Canadian Historical Review 189.

Smith, Julianne. "Private Practice: Thomas De Quincey, Margaret Oliphant, and the Construction of Women's Rhetoric in the Victorian Periodical Press" (2004) 23:1 Rhetoric Review 40.

Springman, Melvin A. et al. *Frauds on Creditors: Fraudulent Conveyances and Preferences* (Toronto: Carswell, 1994).

Stanford, G.H. *To Serve the Community: The Story of Toronto's Board of Trade* (Toronto: University of Toronto Press, 1975).

Steinmo, Sven H. "American Exceptionalism Reconsidered: Culture of Institutions" in Lawrence C. Dodd & Calvin Jillson, eds, *The Dynamics of American Politics* (Boulder: Westview Press, 1994) 106.

Stewart, Walter. *Belly Up: The Spoils of Bankruptcy* (Toronto: McClelland & Stewart, 1995).

Sullivan, Teresa A., Elizabeth Warren & Jay Lawrence Westbrook. "The Persistence of Local Legal Culture: Twenty Years of Evidence from the Federal Bankruptcy Courts" (1994) 17:3 Harv JL & Pub Pol'y 801.

Tabb, Charles Jordan. "A Century of Regress or Progress? A Political History of Bankruptcy Legislation in 1898 and 1998" (1999) 15:2 Bankr Dev J 343.

– "The Historical Evolution of the Bankruptcy Discharge" (1991) 65:3 Am Bank LJ 325.

– "The History of the Bankruptcy Laws in the United States" (1995) 3:1 Am Bankr Inst L Rev 5.

– "Rethinking Preferences" (1992) 43:4 SCL Rev 981.

Taylor, Graham D. & Peter A. Baskerville. *A Concise History of Business in Canada* (Toronto: Oxford University Press, 1994).

Telfer, Thomas G.W. "The Canadian Bankruptcy Act of 1919: Public Legislation or Private Interest?" (1995) 24:3 Can Bus LJ 357.

– "A Canadian 'World without Bankruptcy Law': the Failure of Bankruptcy Reform at the End of the Nineteenth Century" (2004) 8:1 Austl J Legal Hist 83.

– "The Evolution of Bankruptcy Exemption Law in Canada 1867–1919: The Triumph of the Provincial Model" [2007] Ann Rev Insol L 18.

– "Ideas, Interests, Institutions and the History of Canadian Bankruptcy Law, 1867–1880" (2010) 60:2 UTLJ 603.

– "The Proposed Federal Exemption Regime for the Bankruptcy and Insolvency Act" (2005) 41:2–3 Can Bus LJ 279.

– "Voidable Preference Reform: Shifting Rules, Standards and Goal Posts: A New Zealand Perspective" (2003) 12:2 Int'l Insol Rev 55.

Thelen, Kathleen & Sven Steinmo. "Historical Institutionalism in Comparative

Politics" in Sven Steinmo, Kathleen Thelen & Frank Longstreth, eds, *Structuring Politics: Historical Institutionalism in Comparative Analysis* (Cambridge, UK: Cambridge University Press, 1992) 1.

Thompson, Elizabeth Lee. *The Reconstruction of Southern Debtors: Bankruptcy After the Civil War* (Athens, Ga: University of Georgia Press, 2004).

Traves, Tom, ed. *Essays in Canadian Business History* (Toronto: McClelland and Stewart, 1984).

Trebilcock, Michael et al. *The Law and Economics of Canadian Competition Policy* (Toronto: University of Toronto Press, 2003).

Treiman, Israel. "Acts of Bankruptcy: A Medieval Concept in Modern Bankruptcy Law" (1938) 52:2 Harv L Rev 189.

Tucker, Eric. "The Recurring Dilemma of Wage Priority in Bankruptcy" in Eric Tucker, *Labour Law's Recurring Regulatory Dilemmas* (2012) [unpublished, archived at Western University Faculty of Law].

Tuohy, Caroline Hughes. "National Policy Studies in Comparative Perspective: An Organizing Framework Applied to the Canadian Case" in Laurent Dobuzinskis, Michael Howlett & David Laycock, eds, *Policy Studies in Canada: The State of the Art* (Toronto: University of Toronto Press, 1996) 317.

Underhill, Frank. "The Development of National Political Parties in Canada" in Dan Azoulay, ed, *Canadian Political Parties* (Toronto: Irwin, 1999) 65.

Vaughan, Frederick. "Critics of the Judicial Committee of the Privy Council: The New Orthodoxy and an Alternative Explanation" (1986) 19:3 Canadian Journal of Political Science 495.

Vipond, Robert C. *Liberty and Community: Canadian Federalism and the Failure of the Constitution* (Albany: State University of New York Press, 1991).

Warren, Charles. *Bankruptcy in United States History* (Cambridge, Mass: Harvard University Press, 1935).

Watkins, Beverly. "To Surrender All His Estate: The 1867 Bankruptcy Act" (1989) 21:3 Prologue (Quarterly of the National Archives) 207.

Watson, Alan. "Legal Change: Sources of Law and Legal Culture" (1983) 131:5 U Pa L Rev 1121.

Weaver, R. Kent & Bert A. Rockman. "Assessing the Effects of Institutions" in R. Kent Weaver & Bert A. Rockman, eds, *Do Institutions Matter? Government Capabilities in the United States and Abroad* (Washington, DC: Brookings Institution Press, 1993) 1.

Wehberg, Hans. "Pacta Sunt Servanda" (1959) 53:4 AJIL 775.

Weir, Margaret. "Ideas and the Politics of Bounded Innovation" in Sven Steinmo, Kathleen Thelen & Frank Lonstreth, eds, *Structuring Politics: Historical Institutionalism in Comparative Analysis* (Cambridge, UK: Cambridge University Press, 1992) 188.

Weisberg, Robert. "Commercial Morality, the Merchant Character and the History of the Voidable Preference" (1986) 39:1 Stan L Rev 3.
Weiss, Barbara. *The Hell of the English: Bankruptcy and the Victorian Novel* (Lewisburg: Bucknell University Press, 1986).
Welbourne, E. "Bankruptcy Before the Era of Victorian Reform" (1932) 4:1 Cambridge Historical Journal 51.
Ziegel, Jacob. "Canada's Dysfunctional Insolvency Reform Process and the Search for Solutions" (2010) 26:1 BFLR 63.
– "Canada's Phased-in Bankruptcy Law Reform" (1996) 70:4 Am Bank LJ 383.
– *Comparative Consumer Insolvency Regimes: A Canadian Perspective* (Oxford: Hart, 2003).
– "The Modernization of Canada's Bankruptcy Law in a Comparative Context" (1998) 33:1 Tex Int'l LJ 1.
– "What Can the United States Learn from the Canadian Means Testing System?" [2007] U Ill L Rev 195.
Zuber, T.G. *Report of the Ontario Courts Inquiry* (Toronto: Queen's Printer, 1987).

OTHER GOVERNMENT SOURCES

Alberta Law Reform Institute. *Enforcement of Money Judgments*, vol 1, report no 61 (Edmonton: Alberta Law Reform Institute, 1991).
British Columbia Law Reform Commission. *Report on Creditors' Relief Legislation: A New Approach* (Vancouver: BC Law Reform Commission, 1979).
– *Working Paper No. 21: The Enforcement of Judgments: The Creditors' Relief Act* (Vancouver: BC Law Reform Commission, [nd]).
Canada. *Report of the Study Committee on Bankruptcy and Insolvency Legislation* (Ottawa: Queen's Printer, 1970) ["Tassé Report"].
Cuming, R.C.C. *Research Paper on the British Columbia Creditors' Relief Act* (Prepared for the British Columbia Law Reform Commission, June 1974).
Ontario Law Reform Commission. *Report on the Enforcement of Judgment Debts and Related Matters*, part 5 (Toronto: Ministry of the Attorney General, 1983).

Index

Abbott, John, 36, 64, 110, 203n18, 232n68; and repeal debate, 30*illus;* role in drafting bankruptcy legislation, 27, 110
abscondence of debtors. *See* debtor abscondence
Act Respecting Assignments and Preferences Act by Insolvent Persons (Ontario), 119, 120
Act Respecting Assignments for the Benefit of Creditors, An, 105, 119
Act to Abolish Priorities Among Execution Creditors, 97
Act to Abolish Priorities Of and Amongst Execution Creditors, An. See Creditors' Relief Act
Adams v McCall, 37, 204n29
Agnew v Ross, 224n52
Allan v Clarkson, 208n82, 208n86
American Bankruptcy Act, 95–6
Archibald v Haldan, 209n101
assets, distribution of, 7; across regional boundaries, 8; under common law, 7, 8
Assignees, Official: appointment of, 11; case examples, 33, 39–40, 41, 44–5, 46, 47–8, 49–50; corruption of, 11, 81, 85, 86–92, 175, 180; income of, 90–2, 93*illus*, 105; insufficiencies of, 23, 89, 98; James D. Edgar on, 85–7; and preferences, 44–5, 48, 57; role under *Insolvent Acts*, 37, 42, 43, 47, 48, 51, 85, 89; undermining of, 33–4, 43, 44, 46–7, 48, 57
Assignments and Preferences Act (Ontario), 12, 121, 185
Attorney General of Ontario v Attorney General for the Dominion of Canada, 11, 17, 117, 123–4
Austin v Gordon, 212n10

Bank of Monteal v Munro, 189n21, 202n5
Bank of Toronto v McDougall, 208n93
bankruptcy, attitudes towards, 9–10, 134–40, 146–7, 178–9
bankruptcy, defined, 24

Bankruptcy Act of 1800 (US), 77
Bankruptcy Act of 1898 (US), 182
Bankruptcy Act of 1919, 145–6, 152; as commercial necessity, 9; creditor acceptance of, 170–1; debate preceding passing of, 102; discharge under, 163–8; economic context of, 147–50, 171; English precedent for, 14; exemptions under, 151–3; and federalism, 11, 151; impact of war on, 155–6; impact of First World War on passing of, 155–6; institutional factors in passing of, 179–81; legacy of, 184–6; role of interest groups in passing of, 146–7, 157–62; section 59 (debtor conduct), 169
bankruptcy law: American, 4, 14, 77, 95–6, 182; compared with common law, 7, 34–6; English (*see* English bankruptcy law); fundamental policies of, 6–7; list of federal bills, 267–9; list of statutes, 266–7; summarized (1869–1919), 4–6, 21. *See also Bankruptcy Act of 1919;* federal bankruptcy legislation; *Insolvent Acts of 1869* and *1875;* provincial bankruptcy legislation
bankruptcy proceedings, voluntary, 28–9, 29*t*, 200–1n46; abolition of, 73
Beekman v Jarvis, 189n21, 202n5
Belleville Board of Trade, 137
Bell v Rickaby, 207n69, 208n81
Bill 15 (repeal bill), 31
Bill 85 (proposed reform bill), 31, 63
Blake, Edward: on bankruptcy law, 36–7; on discharge, 64; on *Insolvent Act of 1875*, 82–3; and Ontario Act, 121–3
BNA Act. See British North America Act
Board of Commerce Act, 1919, 156
Boards of Trade, 52, 57; American, 96; lack of consensus, 114, 126; legislative proposals of, 102, 107–8, 109–10, 111–12, 114, 126, 132; lobbying activities of, 8, 54–6, 102, 105, 127, 128, 130, 140, 160–1, 177
Borden, Robert, 160, 165
Brayley v Ellis, 209n108
British Empire League, 132
British North America Act (BNA Act): calls for amendment of, 119; on jurisdiction over bankruptcy, 22, 92–4, 113, 117, 154–5, 175, 188n12, 226n92; Privy Council decision on, 122, 123–4
Broddy v Stuart, 259n14
Brown v Wright, 37, 204n30
Buchanan v Smith, 215n59
Bullen v Harding, 202n7, 203n17
Burland v Larocque, 203n16

Cameron v Holland, 59–60, 74, 211n6, 218n108
Campbell, Alexander, 96–7
Campbell v Barrie, 49–50, 208n88, 208n89, 208n94
Canada (AG) v Ontario (AG), 236n5
Canadian Bankers' Association, 111
Canadian Bar Association (CBA) and CCMTA, 146, 151, 159, 171
Canadian Credit Men's Trust Association (CCMTA), 8–9; and bankruptcy reform debates, 171; lobbying efforts, 146, 150–1, 157–2; support for discharge, 166, 168
Canadian Manufacturing Association, 129

Cartier, George-Étienne: on *Insolvent Act of 1869*, 82
cartoons, political, 24*illus*, 25*illus*, 30*illus*, 88*illus*, 93*illus*
Case of the Bankrupts, The, 35, 189n20, 202n11
cases, list of, 262–6
CBA. *See* Canadian Bar Association
CCMTA. *See* Canadian Credit Men's Trust Association (CCMTA)
Churcher v Johnston, 208n78
Clarkson v Ontario Bank (1887), 237n15
Clarkson v Ontario Bank (1888), 237n18, 237n22, 259n14
Clarkson v White, 227n2
Clemmow v Converse, 208n95
Cochran v Chipman, 206n57
Colby, Thomas, 97
collusion, 11, 35, 73, 77–8, 80, 85, 175, 180, 219n127
Colwell v Robertson, 215n64
Combines and Fair Prices Act, 1919, 156
commercial failures in Canada, 23; 1873–85, 23*f*, 197n12; 1902–18, 149*f*, 246n13
commercial interests. *See* Boards of Trade
common law: compared with bankruptcy law, 7, 34–6; doctrine of pressure, 33; effects of, on foreign creditors, 177; and English bankruptcy law, 35; James Young on, 36; John A. Macdonald on, 36; Justice Wilson on, 34; in provinces, 96, 102–6; common law race, 7, 8, 35, 177, 202n4, 211n132; and Boards of Trade, 54, 210n131
Cook v Rogers, 209n106
court rulings. *See* cases, list of
courts, 11, 33–4; and collusion, 77–8, 180; Ontario Court of Chancery, 51; pro-debtor interpretation of legislation, 73–80, 218n105; on provincial legislation, 117; role in granting discharges, 60–2, 76–7, 169–70, 174, 219n114; role in undermining equality principle, 42–53; Supreme Court of Canada, 52. *See also* Ontario Court of Appeal decisions; Privy Council
creditors: *An Act Respecting Assignments for the Benefit of Creditors* (Ontario), 119; benefits of bankruptcy law for, 9, 22; family and preferred, 33; legal recourse regarding discharge, 61; local vs distant, 6, 8, 17, 36–42, 52, 53–4, 57, 102, 105, 131, 189n23. *See also* equality principle; preferential transactions
Creditors' Relief Act (Ontario), 11, 98, 104, 106, 113, 121, 180, 181, 226n85, 226n92
Creighton v Merchants' Bank, 206n55, 207n63
Crichton, W.M., 146
Crombie v Jackson, 94, 224n67, 225n69, 237n13
Crowe, James, 3–4, 113
Cushing v Dupuy, 94, 122, 225n71, 237n14, 238n36, 250n52

Davidson v McInnes, 209n102
Davidson v Ross, 50–2, 53, 204n28, 206n55, 208n96, 209n99, 209n108, 209n109
debt and debtors, moral judgment of, 16, 26–7, 60–1, 64, 69–71, 79, 139–40, 179, 213n42

debt forgiveness. *See* discharge
debtor abscondence, 39, 58–9, 65–7, 80, 95, 127–8, 135, 140–1, 164, 202n2, 243n43
demographics, shifting, 149–50
Department of Justice, 84–5, 87–9, 179–80. *See also under* institutions
Dever v Morris, 204n28
discharge, 7, 64–7, 178–9, 243n50; changing attitudes towards, 9–10; classes of, 60–1; opposition to, 67–71; second-class, 73, 76–7, 80, 178; support for, 134–40; transformation of, 9–10, 146–7, 162–8, 173
Dominion Board of Trade, 8, 55–6, 57, 177
Duncan v Smart, 199n35, 211n9
Dupont v La Cie de Moulin, 196n8

economy, Canadian, 38, 128–9, 134, 147–50, 155–6, 171, 172; effect of absconding debtors on, 135; recession of 1913, 148, 188–9n16; structural changes, 148–9
Edgar, James D.: on discharges, 61; on Official Assignees, 85–7
Edgar v Central Bank of Canada, 237n18, 237n19, 259n14
English Bankruptcy Act of 1914, 182, 183
English bankruptcy law, 6, 35, 168–9, 182, 188n13; of 1543, 163–4; of 1705, 163–4, 255n120; 1883 *Bankruptcy Act*, 14, 26, 106, 170–1, 180; discharges under, 61, 163–4, 189n18; exemption law, 151–2, 153; as template for *Bankruptcy Act of 1919*, 159, 253n92; voluntary assignments under, 161–2
equality principle, 7, 33–8, 189n18, 204n27; undermining of, 48–53, 175, 180
equitable distribution. *See* equality principle
exemption law, provincial, 153
Ex parte Bejeau, 224n67
Ex parte Ellis, 237n13
Ex parte Jones, 207n74
Ex parte Topham, 208n83

farmers: in Canadian economy 1875 to 1910, 128, 129; exclusion from *Insolvent Act*, 6, 16, 28, 60, 71–3, 80, 111; and Fortin bill proposal, 112–13; position of, in 1898 proposal, 71–3
federal bankruptcy legislation: reform bills, 106–13; summarized history of, 21–31. *See also Insolvent Acts of 1869* and *1875*
federal bills, list of, 267–9
federalism, 81–2, 92–8, 116–26, 130, 146, 150–5, 180–1
First World War, 5, 8, 12, 107, 113, 117, 130, 146, 155–6, 178, 181, 182
Forrester v Thrasher, 218n105
Fortin, Thomas, 112, 113
Fowler v Perrin, 204n28

Gilbert v Girouard, 219n121, 219n124
Godkin v Beech, 207n64
Gordon v Young, 208n85
Gottwalls v Mulholland, 34, 202n6
Green v Swan, 188n14
Griffiths v Perry, 207n64
Grundy, H.P., 145, 146, 152, 153, 159, 160–2; on discharge, 167, 168

Halifax Board of Trade, 55
Hamilton Board of Trade, 56, 109

Harman v Clarkson, 60, 199n35, 211n7, 211n9
Harvey v Cotter, 85, 204n28, 222n26
Herschell, Lord, 123
Hersee v White, 208n83
historical institutionalism, 10, 12, 183
Hodge v R, 236n5
Home Trade Association of Manchester, 132
Hunter v Drummond, 237n18, 259n14

ideas: urban vs rural, 130. *See also* bankruptcy, attitudes towards; debt and debtors, moral judgment of; discharge, transformation of
insolvency, defined, 24
Insolvent Act of 1864, 27, 36
Insolvent Act of 1869, 21, 27; Assignee appointments under, 87; attempts to repeal, 27–8; discharge provisions under, 60, 76, 175; Dominion Board of Trade support for, 54, 55; George-Étienne Cartier on, 82; party politics and, 82, 221n5; scope of, 28, 175, 212n11; voluntary proceedings under, 28–9, 29*t*. *See also* *Insolvent Acts of 1869* and *1875*
Insolvent Act of 1875, 21; 1879 cartoon regarding, 30*illus;* Assignee appointments under, 11, 87; attempts to reform, 31; attempts to repeal, 21, 29–31; collusion under, 77–8; discharge provisions under, 61–2, 73–4, 75–6; opposition to in British Columbia, 77–8; party politics and, 82–3, 221n5; passage of, 29; press reaction to, 77–80; scope of, 12; section 58, 61–2; and voluntary proceedings, 11, 13, 28, 29. *See also* *Insolvent Acts of 1869* and *1875*
Insolvent Act of 1875, repeal of, 31, 174; Dominion Board of Trade on, 56; effect on court decisions, 51–2; equality vs preference, 31; House of Commons vote on, 84*t*; Select Committee on Bankruptcy and, 63
Insolvent Acts of 1869 and *1875*, 6–7, 175; on absconding debtors, 65; and discharges, 76–7, 178; and equality principle, 7, 35, 202–3n13; party politics and, 82–4, 221n5; scope of, 6, 12, 60, 111, 185–6
institutions, 113–14, 179–81; bankruptcy administration, 84–92; political parties, 82–4; role of, 10–13. *See also* regulatory state, emergence of
interest groups, 8–9, 157–62. *See also* Boards of Trade; Canadian Credit Men's Trust Association (CCMTA); farmers
interest group theory, 8

Jones v Kinney, 204n32, 224n67

Kalus v Hergert, 205n39, 207n66
Keays v Brown, 204n28, 208n90, 209n101
Kennedy v Freeman, 237n18
Kinney, Assignee v Dudman, 94, 224n67, 225n70, 237n13

Laurier, Wilfrid: government of, 111–12, 124–5; letters to, 3–4, 112, 129, 132, 134, 135, 147–8, 164, 177; support for provincial law, 4, 12, 113, 114–15, 125, 147, 181
legal change, theories of: legal origins, 182–3; path dependence, 183–4

legal origins theory, 182, 183
legislation: provincial, 11. *See* federal bills, list of; statutes, list of
Lenoir v Ritchie, 236n5
Levis Board of Trade, 55
Lewis v Brown, 207n74
lobbying. *See* interest groups
Long v Hancock, 209n110
Lower Canadian Bankruptcy Act of 1839, 26

Macdonald, John A., 110; government of, 29–31, 109, 110; letters to, 31, 54, 55, 89, 92, 132, 228n16, 240n15; on provincial jurisdiction, 94, 95; support for national bankruptcy law, 27, 36
Maritime Bank of Canada (Liquidators of) v New Brunswick (Receiver General of), 236n5
Martin v McAlpine, 209n108
Mason v Hamilton, 204n28
Mathers v Lynch, 207n68
McCrae v White, 46–7, 52, 207n75, 209n109
McDonald, James (Minister of Justice), 37
McEdwards v Palmer, 207n74, 209n104
McFarlane v McDonald, 208n83, 209n101
McGregor v Hume, 207n67
McLean v Garland, 209n110
McLean v McLellan, 219n117
McLeod v Wright, 37, 42, 204n31, 206n53, 206n55, 209n102, 225n73
McPherson v Reynolds, 202n6
McWhirter v Royal Canadian Bank, 208n87
McWhirter v Thorne, 188n14, 204n28, 206n55, 208n89
Meighen, Arthur, 146
Milloy v Kerr, 38, 204n32
Molson Bank v Halter, 209n110
Montreal Board of Trade, 8, 131–2, 160–1, 231n55, 244n59; on discharge, 109; and proposed legislation, 111–13, 129; support for insolvency law, 54, 55
Morton v Nihan, 58
Mowat, Oliver (premier of Ontario), 116, 117–18; and Ontario Act, 96–7, 121, 181
Murphy v Stadacona Bank, 207n63

Nelles v Bank of Montreal, 209n107
Nelles v Paul, 48, 208n80
Newton v Ontario Bank, 206n55, 207n72, 208n87

Ogden v Saunders, 196n7
Ontario Act, 97–8, 120; Charles Tupper on, 97
Ontario Commission on Unemployment, 167
Ontario Court of Appeal decisions, 40–1, 45, 47–8, 51–2, 74–6, 94, 117, 119–21, 181, 209n108
Ontario Court of Chancery, 51
Ontario (AG) v Canada (AG), 122, 192n54, 229n27, 238n42, 239n44, 249n36
Ontario (AG) v Canada (AG) [1898], 236n5
Ontario (AG) v Mercer, 236n5
Ottawa Board of Trade, 55

pacta sunt servanda, 9
Parke v Day, 205n43, 219n133
Parliamentary Special Committee, 132, 155, 159–60

path dependence theory, 183–4
Patterson v Kingsley, 207n74
Payne v Hendry, 204n31, 206n55
Pineo v Gavaza, 44–5, 207n65
Popham, John, 61
preferential transactions, 42–53; thirty-day payments, 47–8; unjust preferences, 42–7
press, the: on *Insolvent Act* implementation, 78–80
pressure, doctrine of, 48–53, 184–5, 208n81, 209n101, 209n108; in Quebec, 208n81. *See also* preferential transactions
private interest groups. *See* interest groups
Privy Council, 11–12, 119, 249n36; ruling in *Cushing v Dupuy*, 94, 122; ruling on provincial legislation, 17, 117, 120–4
property rights of women, 41–2
pro rata. *See* equality principle
Protest Against the Bankruptcy Act Now before the Dominion Parliament, A, 162–3
Province of Canada Acts of 1843 and 1864, 26
provincial legislation, 11–12, 81–2, 101–2; BC support for, 11–12; vs federal legislation, 94–5; insufficiencies of, 102–6; moves towards, 96–8; Ontario Act, 97–8, 120; overlap with federal legislation, 22, 92, 185; pre-Confederation, 26; Privy Council ruling on, 17, 94; provincial court rulings on, 94; reforms, 104, 105; repeal of statutes, 21; Supreme Court of Canada ruling on, 95; Wilfrid Laurier on, 4
public choice theory, 8

Quebec, 125, 154; bankruptcies 1872–1880, 23; civil code, 94, 96, 225n79, 229n22; doctrine of pressure in, 208n81; *Insolvent Act of 1864*, 26
Quebec Board of Trade, 56, 165

Re Andrews, An Insolvent, 222n24
Re Assignments and Preferences Act, Section 9, 192n54, 228n18, 238n26, 259n14
Re Barrett, 94, 196n8, 204n28, 204n31, 224n67, 225n69
Re Botsford, 224n50
Re Boughner, 222n30
Re Bullivant, 75, 219n114
Re Cobourg & Peterborough Railway, 192n49
Re Donald Matheson, 219n121, 219n123
Re Frederick B.K. Marter, 224n67
Re Garratt & Co., 75, 218n110, 218n112
Re Gearing, 40–1, 205n47
Re Gooding, 218n113, 219n120
regulatory state, emergence of, 106–7, 146, 155–7, 172–3, 179–80
Re Hill, 218n105, 219n114
Re Hurst, an Insolvent, 188n14, 204n29, 208n82, 208n87, 208n88, 208n89, 208n95
Re Hutchinson, Insolvent, 219n119
Re Jones, 39, 205n42, 219n116
Re Killam, 237n13
Re Lamb, An Insolvent, 74
Re Martin and English, 74, 218n109
Re Mooney, Insolvent, 219n121, 219n122
repeal (of *Insolvent Act*): effect on assignees, 93*illus*, 227n2; House of Commons debates on, 21, 31, 198n18; movement, 28, 83, 175;

role of Senate in, 28, 31, 56, 82, 97; vote on, 84*t*
Re Perks, 224n68
Re Robert Holt and John Gray, 212n17
Re Roberts, 249n38
Re Smith, an Insolvent, 215n60
Retail Merchants' Association, 149–50, 155
Robinson v Coutrywide Factors Ltd, 260n42
Robinson v Ellis and Carter, 225n73
Roe v Smith, 33, 202n1
Rowe v Jarvis, 189n21, 202n5
Royal Canadian Bank v Kerr, 207n71, 208n85, 208n87
Rumsey v Hare, 204n28, 237n13
Russell v R, 236n5
R v Chandler, 188n12, 196n7

Select Committee on Bankruptcy (1879), 31, 63, 189n18
Senate: and bankruptcy law reform, 110–11; role in repeal of *Insolvent Act*, 28, 31, 54, 56, 82, 97
Shaw v Massie, 204n28
Shields v Peak, 189n17, 225n72
Slater v Oliver, 209n108
Smith v Hutchinson, 47–8, 51, 208n79, 209n105
Smith v McLean, 46, 207n70, 209n107
Standard Bank of Canada v Johnson, 211n6, 218n111
St Anne-Nackawic Pulp Co (Trustee of) v Logstec Stevedoring (Atlantic) Inc, 260n36
statutes, list of, 266–7
Stephens v McArthur (1890), 238n24
Stephens v McArthur (1891), 209n110
Sturges v Crowninshield, 196n7
Supreme Court of Canada: and *Davidson v Ross*, 52; and doctrine of pressure, 52
Suter v Merchants' Bank, 209n106

thirty-day payments, 43, 45, 47–8, 206n56, 206n58
thirty-three-cent test, 61, 62, 73
Thomas v Hall, 87, 199n35, 212n9, 219n118, 222n31
Tillsonburg Board of Trade, 108, 240n15
Topping v Joseph, 189n21, 202n5
Toronto Board of Trade, 8, 54, 56, 109, 110, 160–1, 231n55, 231n57
Totten v Bowen, 209n108
traders, 199n35; application of laws to, 6, 16, 28, 60, 71–3, 111, 112–13, 124, 188n13; defined, 199n35, 199–200n36, 211–12n9
Tucker v Young, 208n85, 208n87, 208n91
Tupper, Charles, 97, 124, 133

Union Bank v Neville, 120, 192n54, 237n20, 259n14
United States bankruptcy law, 4, 14–15, 23–6, 54, 56, 77, 95–6, 188n10; *American Bankruptcy Act*, 95–6; *Bankruptcy Act of 1800*, 77; *Bankruptcy Act of 1867*, 56; *Bankruptcy Act of 1898*, 182

Vanwart v Shepherd, 224n67
Vassie v Vassie, 225n70
voluntary bankruptcy proceedings. *See* bankruptcy proceedings, voluntary

wage earners, 202–3n13, 248n26; exclusion of, 6, 16, 149–50, 186

Wallace v Bossom, 203n16
War Measures Act, 156
William Irvine v William Thompson, 205n44
Winding-Up Act, 12
Winnipeg Board of Trade, 109, 129
women: involvement in bankruptcy proceedings, 40–2, 164; property rights of, 41–2, 206n51, 206n52, 256n130

Young, James, 36

PUBLICATIONS OF THE OSGOODE SOCIETY FOR CANADIAN LEGAL HISTORY

2014 Christopher Moore, *The Court of Appeal for Ontario: Defining the Right of Appeal, 1792–2013*
Paul Craven, *Petty Justice: Low Law and the Sessions System in Charlotte County, New Brunswick, 1785–1867*
Thomas GW Telfer, *Ruin and Redemption: The Struggle for a Canadian Bankruptcy Law, 1867–1919*
Dominique Clément, *Equality Deferred: Sex Discrimination and British Columbia's Human Rights State, 1953–1984*

2013 Roy McMurtry, *Memoirs and Reflections*
Charlotte Gray, *The Massey Murder: A Maid, Her Master, and the Trial that Shocked a Nation*
C. Ian Kyer, *Lawyers, Families, and Businesses: The Shaping of a Bay Street Law Firm, Faskens 1863–1963*
G. Blaine Baker and Donald Fyson, eds., *Essays in the History of Canadian Law, Volume XI: Quebec and the Canadas*

2012 R. Blake Brown, *Arming and Disarming: A History of Gun Control in Canada*
Eric Tucker, James Muir, and Bruce Ziff, eds., *Property on Trial: Canadian Cases in Context*
Shelley Gavigan, *Hunger, Horses, and Government Men: Criminal Law on the Aboriginal Plains, 1870–1905*
Barrington Walker, ed., *The African Canadian Legal Odyssey: Historical Essays*

2011 Robert J. Sharpe, *The Lazier Murder: Prince Edward County, 1884*
Philip Girard, *Lawyers and Legal Culture in British North America: Beamish Murdoch of Halifax*
John McLaren, *Dewigged, Bothered, and Bewildered: British Colonial Judges on Trial, 1800–1900*
Lesley Erickson, *Westward Bound: Sex, Violence, the Law, and the Making of a Settler Society*

2010 Judy Fudge and Eric Tucker, eds., *Work on Trial: Canadian Labour Law Struggles*
Christopher Moore, *The British Columbia Court of Appeal: The First Hundred Years*
Frederick Vaughan, *Viscount Haldane: 'The Wicked Step-father of the Canadian Constitution'*
Barrington Walker, *Race on Trial: Black Defendants in Ontario's Criminal Courts, 1858–1958*

2009 William Kaplan, *Canadian Maverick: The Life and Times of Ivan C. Rand*
R. Blake Brown, *A Trying Question: The Jury in Nineteenth-Century Canada*
Barry Wright and Susan Binnie, eds., *Canadian State Trials, Volume III: Political Trials and Security Measures, 1840–1914*
Robert J. Sharpe, *The Last Day, the Last Hour: The Currie Libel Trial* (paperback edition with a new preface)

2008 Constance Backhouse, *Carnal Crimes: Sexual Assault Law in Canada, 1900–1975*
Jim Phillips, R. Roy McMurtry, and John T. Saywell, eds., *Essays in the History of Canadian Law, Volume X: A Tribute to Peter N. Oliver*
Greg Taylor, *The Law of the Land: The Advent of the Torrens System in Canada*
Hamar Foster, Benjamin Berger, and A.R. Buck, eds., *The Grand Experiment: Law and Legal Culture in British Settler Societies*

2007 Robert Sharpe and Patricia McMahon, *The Persons Case: The Origins and Legacy of the Fight for Legal Personhood*
Lori Chambers, *Misconceptions: Unmarried Motherhood and the Ontario Children of Unmarried Parents Act, 1921–1969*
Jonathan Swainger, ed., *A History of the Supreme Court of Alberta*
Martin Friedland, *My Life in Crime and Other Academic Adventures*

2006 Donald Fyson, *Magistrates, Police, and People: Everyday Criminal Justice in Quebec and Lower Canada, 1764–1837*
Dale Brawn, *The Court of Queen's Bench of Manitoba, 1870–1950: A Biographical History*
R.C.B. Risk, *A History of Canadian Legal Thought: Collected Essays*, edited and introduced by G. Blaine Baker and Jim Phillips

2005 Philip Girard, *Bora Laskin: Bringing Law to Life*
Christopher English, ed., *Essays in the History of Canadian Law: Volume IX – Two Islands: Newfoundland and Prince Edward Island*
Fred Kaufman, *Searching for Justice: An Autobiography*

2004 Philip Girard, Jim Phillips, and Barry Cahill, eds., *The Supreme Court of Nova Scotia, 1754–2004: From Imperial Bastion to Provincial Oracle*
Frederick Vaughan, *Aggressive in Pursuit: The Life of Justice Emmett Hall*
John D. Honsberger, *Osgoode Hall: An Illustrated History*
Constance Backhouse and Nancy Backhouse, *The Heiress versus the Establishment: Mrs Campbell's Campaign for Legal Justice*

2003 Robert Sharpe and Kent Roach, *Brian Dickson: A Judge's Journey*
Jerry Bannister, *The Rule of the Admirals: Law, Custom, and Naval Government in Newfoundland, 1699–1832*

George Finlayson, *John J. Robinette, Peerless Mentor: An Appreciation*
Peter Oliver, *The Conventional Man: The Diaries of Ontario Chief Justice Robert A. Harrison, 1856–1878*

2002 John T. Saywell, *The Lawmakers: Judicial Power and the Shaping of Canadian Federalism*
Patrick Brode, *Courted and Abandoned: Seduction in Canadian Law*
David Murray, *Colonial Justice: Justice, Morality, and Crime in the Niagara District, 1791–1849*
F. Murray Greenwood and Barry Wright, eds., *Canadian State Trials, Volume II: Rebellion and Invasion in the Canadas, 1837–1839*

2001 Ellen Anderson, *Judging Bertha Wilson: Law as Large as Life*
Judy Fudge and Eric Tucker, *Labour before the Law: The Regulation of Workers' Collective Action in Canada, 1900–1948*
Laurel Sefton MacDowell, *Renegade Lawyer: The Life of J.L. Cohen*

2000 Barry Cahill, *'The Thousandth Man': A Biography of James McGregor Stewart*
A.B. McKillop, *The Spinster and the Prophet: Florence Deeks, H.G. Wells, and the Mystery of the Purloined Past*
Beverley Boissery and F. Murray Greenwood, *Uncertain Justice: Canadian Women and Capital Punishment*
Bruce Ziff, *Unforeseen Legacies: Reuben Wells Leonard and the Leonard Foundation Trust*

1999 Constance Backhouse, *Colour-Coded: A Legal History of Racism in Canada, 1900–1950*
G. Blaine Baker and Jim Phillips, eds., *Essays in the History of Canadian Law: Volume VIII – In Honour of R.C.B. Risk*
Richard W. Pound, *Chief Justice W.R. Jackett: By the Law of the Land*
David Vanek, *Fulfilment: Memoirs of a Criminal Court Judge*

1998 Sidney Harring, *White Man's Law: Native People in Nineteenth-Century Canadian Jurisprudence*
Peter Oliver, *'Terror to Evil-Doers': Prisons and Punishments in Nineteenth-Century Ontario*

1997 James W.St.G. Walker, *'Race,' Rights and the Law in the Supreme Court of Canada: Historical Case Studies*
Lori Chambers, *Married Women and Property Law in Victorian Ontario*
Patrick Brode, *Casual Slaughters and Accidental Judgments: Canadian War Crimes and Prosecutions, 1944–1948*
Ian Bushnell, *The Federal Court of Canada: A History, 1875–1992*

1996 Carol Wilton, ed., *Essays in the History of Canadian Law: Volume VII – Inside the Law: Canadian Law Firms in Historical Perspective*
William Kaplan, *Bad Judgment: The Case of Mr Justice Leo A. Landreville*

Murray Greenwood and Barry Wright, eds., *Canadian State Trials: Volume I – Law, Politics, and Security Measures, 1608–1837*

1995 David Williams, *Just Lawyers: Seven Portraits*

Hamar Foster and John McLaren, eds., *Essays in the History of Canadian Law: Volume VI – British Columbia and the Yukon*

W.H. Morrow, ed., *Northern Justice: The Memoirs of Mr Justice William G. Morrow*

Beverley Boissery, *A Deep Sense of Wrong: The Treason, Trials, and Transportation to New South Wales of Lower Canadian Rebels after the 1838 Rebellion*

1994 Patrick Boyer, *A Passion for Justice: The Legacy of James Chalmers McRuer*

Charles Pullen, *The Life and Times of Arthur Maloney: The Last of the Tribunes*

Jim Phillips, Tina Loo, and Susan Lewthwaite, eds., *Essays in the History of Canadian Law: Volume V – Crime and Criminal Justice*

Brian Young, *The Politics of Codification: The Lower Canadian Civil Code of 1866*

1993 Greg Marquis, *Policing Canada's Century: A History of the Canadian Association of Chiefs of Police*

Murray Greenwood, *Legacies of Fear: Law and Politics in Quebec in the Era of the French Revolution*

1992 Brendan O'Brien, *Speedy Justice: The Tragic Last Voyage of His Majesty's Vessel Speedy*

Robert Fraser, ed., *Provincial Justice: Upper Canadian Legal Portraits from the Dictionary of Canadian Biography*

1991 Constance Backhouse, *Petticoats and Prejudice: Women and Law in Nineteenth-Century Canada*

1990 Philip Girard and Jim Phillips, eds., *Essays in the History of Canadian Law: Volume III – Nova Scotia*

Carol Wilton, ed., *Essays in the History of Canadian Law: Volume IV – Beyond the Law: Lawyers and Business in Canada, 1830–1930*

1989 Desmond Brown, *The Genesis of the Canadian Criminal Code of 1892*

Patrick Brode, *The Odyssey of John Anderson*

1988 Robert Sharpe, *The Last Day, the Last Hour: The Currie Libel Trial*

John D. Arnup, *Middleton: The Beloved Judge*

1987 C. Ian Kyer and Jerome Bickenbach, *The Fiercest Debate: Cecil A. Wright, the Benchers, and Legal Education in Ontario, 1923–1957*

1986 Paul Romney, *Mr Attorney: The Attorney General for Ontario in Court, Cabinet, and Legislature, 1791–1899*

Martin Friedland, *The Case of Valentine Shortis: A True Story of Crime and Politics in Canada*

1985 James Snell and Frederick Vaughan, *The Supreme Court of Canada: History of the Institution*

1984 Patrick Brode, *Sir John Beverley Robinson: Bone and Sinew of the Compact*
David Williams, *Duff: A Life in the Law*

1983 David H. Flaherty, ed., *Essays in the History of Canadian Law: Volume II*

1982 Marion MacRae and Anthony Adamson, *Cornerstones of Order: Courthouses and Town Halls of Ontario, 1784–1914*

1981 David H. Flaherty, ed., *Essays in the History of Canadian Law: Volume I*

www.ingramcontent.com/pod-product-compliance
Lightning Source LLC
LaVergne TN
LVHW090151080826
844660LV00013B/761/J

* 9 7 8 0 8 0 2 0 9 3 4 3 1 *